## DATE DUE

|  |  |  |  |
|--|--|--|--|
|  |  |  |  |
|  |  |  |  |
|  |  |  |  |
|  |  |  |  |
|  |  |  |  |
|  |  |  |  |
|  |  |  |  |
|  |  |  |  |
|  |  |  |  |
|  |  |  |  |
|  |  |  |  |
|  |  |  |  |
|  |  |  |  |
|  |  |  |  |
|  |  |  |  |
|  |  |  |  |
|  |  |  |  |
|  |  |  |  |

# Division and Discord

## The Supreme Court
## under Stone and Vinson, 1941–1953

# CHIEF JUSTICESHIPS
## OF THE UNITED STATES SUPREME COURT

*Herbert A. Johnson, General Editor*

*The Chief Justiceship of Melville W. Fuller, 1888–1910*
James W. Ely, Jr.

*The Supreme Court in the Early Republic*
*The Chief Justiceships of John Jay and Oliver Ellsworth*
William R. Casto

*The Chief Justiceship of John Marshall*
Herbert A. Johnson

*Division and Discord*
*The Supreme Court under Stone and Vinson, 1941–1953*
Melvin I. Urofsky

R

# Division and Discord

## The Supreme Court under
## Stone and Vinson, 1941–1953

Melvin I. Urofsky

University of South Carolina Press

Copyright © 1997 Melvin I. Urofsky

Published in Columbia, South Carolina, by the
University of South Carolina Press

Manufactured in the United States of America

01   00   99   98   97   5   4   3   2   1

Library of Congress Cataloging-in-Publication Data
Urofsky, Melvin I.
    Division and discord : the Supreme Court under
Stone and Vinson, 1941–1953 / Melvin I. Urofsky.
    p.   cm.—(Chief justiceships of the United States Supreme
Court)
    Includes bibliographical references and index.
    ISBN 1–57003–120–7
    1. Stone, Harlan Fiske, 1872–1946.   2. Vinson, Fred M.,
1890–1953.   3. United States. Supreme Court—History.   4. Judges—
United States—History.   5. United States—Constitutional history.
I. Title.   II. Series.
KF8742.U76   1997
347.73′2634—dc20
[347.3073534]                                          96–25392

For Melissa—
Welcome

# CONTENTS

# EDITOR'S PREFACE

This volume is something of an anomaly in a series organized around chief justiceships of the Supreme Court of the United States. Indeed, it examines two examples of chief justices who, for various reasons, did not exert the leadership of the Court that we have come to expect of all who occupy this office. As Professor Urofsky points out, it has frequently been the case that the "side justices," one or more of the associate justices on the bench, have exerted intellectual leadership of the Court. However, the chief justice has, even in those circumstances, succeeded in managing the work of the Court and in maintaining a collegial and dignified atmosphere in which the justices can conduct their work in a modicum of tranquillity.

The chief justiceships of Harlan Fiske Stone and Fred M. Vinson share the unenviable distinction of being perhaps the least collegial and most internally vindictive periods of the Court's history. As such they give rise to the supposition that leadership in the person of the chief justice is an essential ingredient of institutional cohesiveness and thus a critical element in the effective conduct of Court business. Being a "people person" may be one of the salient characteristics of a successful chief justice. The chief justiceship of Melville W. Fuller, discussed by Professor Ely in an earlier contribution to this series, can be read as a very useful foil to the events depicted in this study of the Stone-Vinson Courts. Fuller never rose to intellectual leadership over a Court dominated by fine minds and determined ideologies; but he did keep the Court on an even keel as it dealt with the difficult problems of its day. By way of contrast one wonders how the Stone and Vinson Courts conducted any business whatsoever given the animosity and personality clashes among its members.

The materials in this volume also suggest that diversity has worked changes in the way leadership is exercised in the Supreme Court during the twentieth century. Professor Casto's work on the Jay and Ellsworth Courts during the first decade of our existence under the Constitution provides a view of a Court not unlike that of the Stone-Vinson Court. This is to say that under the first two chief justices, the Court members seem to have operated as individuals, writing their seriatim opinions and having little interaction with other justices. Circuit duties kept them away from each other, it is true. However, they also shared common social backgrounds and ingrained habits of self-control and moderate behavior. The relatively mild leadership exerted by Chief Justices Jay and Ellsworth was adequate for their day but counterproductive in the first half of the twentieth century.

Despite the shortcomings of Stone and Vinson, it is also quite apparent that these two Courts promised to be a challenge to any chief justice. Professor Urofsky observes that four of the justices who were on the Court when Stone became chief justice were still on the bench when Fred Vinson died and Earl Warren succeeded him. These were Justices Black, Reed, Frankfurter, and Douglas. Among those four, Black, Frankfurter, and Douglas were destined to launch the hostile conflict of judicial philosophies and abrasive personalities that would challenge any chief justice who attempted to provide direction and moderation to the Court's deliberations. Not only did they frequently clash in conference and in their public utterances, but as the author diplomatically phrases it, they were not attractive as human beings. Pettiness and personal animosities marred the Court during this eventful period.

On the other hand, the Stone-Vinson era made a monumental contribution to the constitutional history of the nation. Professor Urofsky shows that this time was strongly influenced by the Court-packing struggle and the Court's shifting its concerns to the Bill of Rights provisions and the judicial exposition of individual liberties. From a rather checkered performance in regard to suppressed civil liberties during World War II, the Supreme Court emerged as a tribunal that began the process that dominated the Warren Court. Cautiously but deliberately it began to examine issues of individual liberty and constitutional guarantees that shaped the concept of human freedom within the Constitution. In this way the Stone-Vinson Courts laid the foundation for the more obvious advances that characterized the Warren era.

The study looks forward to the Warren Court, just as it looks back at the chief justiceships that preceded Harlan Fiske Stone's move to the presiding position on the Supreme Court bench. It provides a new viewpoint from which to analyze the leadership achievements of Chief Justice Earl Warren. These are nothing short of miraculous considering the evidence of animosity and interpersonal loathing that plagued the Court at the end of the Vinson chief justiceship.

The author's careful review of the manuscript papers of the justices, coupled with his firm grasp of the constitutional trends of this period, provides us with an intriguing view of a Court in turmoil and adrift without the stabilizing influence of a moderating chief justice. If the picture is not a happy or inspiring one, it adds much to our knowledge and appreciation for the Court's work and the creative leadership contributions of at least most of its chief justices.

Herbert A. Johnson

# PREFACE

The period between the great Constitutional crisis of 1937 and the ascension of Earl Warren to the chief justiceship in 1953 is not one that has received a great deal of attention. With the exception of a few cases such as those involving Japanese internment and Nazi saboteurs during World War II, or the *Dennis* case during the Cold War, this is not an era that grabs the observer's attention. It lacks the drama of the Roosevelt Court-packing plan and the nobility of the Warren Court's striking down racial segregation. Scholars may discuss the Black-Frankfurter debate in *Adamson,* but in terms of a story, it cannot compete with the tale of Gideon's trumpet.

Yet I believe that these dozen years were critical ones in modern American constitutional history because they bridged the era that led up to and included the Court-packing fight on the one hand and the judicial activism of the Warren Court on the other. Transitions often lack drama, but, as I think these pages show, drama existed. If Harlan Stone and Fred Vinson do not measure up as chief justices to those who preceded and succeeded them—Charles Evans Hughes and Earl Warren—nonetheless they presided over benches that included some of the most important figures in our judicial history—Hugo Black, Felix Frankfurter, William O. Douglas, and the underrated but very important Robert Jackson. These men had not only strong intellects but strong wills as well, and they generated not only jurisprudential but personal turmoil that their chiefs could not control.

The book, therefore, has a twin focus, one on the men who sat on the nation's high court and the other on the cases that I believe signal the transition from an older era concerned primarily with property rights to the modern era's focus on individual liberties and civil rights. Given the nature of the series, decisions had to be made about selection. The Court heard many cases that are not mentioned in this volume. Indeed, there are some areas such as tax law in which the Court rendered significant decisions but which I chose to bypass in order to keep attention focused on the theme of transition.

   This era also benefits from the fact that the justices for the most part preserved their papers, and these are open to scholars. William O. Douglas's conference notes, Felix Frankfurter's homilies to his brethren, and Harlan Fiske Stone's complaints to his close friends about his "wild horses" allow us a glimpse into how the Stone and Vinson Courts operated. We know more about the inner workings of the Court in these years than we do about their predecessors. That, too, is an important part of this story.

# ACKNOWLEDGMENTS

While an author may toil alone to produce a manuscript, help is needed to turn the typescript pages into a book such as you now hold in your hands. Herbert Johnson invited me to contribute this volume in the series and also gave the manuscript a careful reading, making many helpful suggestions. Professor Philippa Strum of the City University of New York read the draft with her usual sharp eye for detail and meaning and an ear for language and nuance. Both of them made this a far better book because of their suggestions.

At the University of South Carolina Press, I want to thank acquisitions editor Joyce Harrison, designer Carleton Giles, and managing editor Peggy Hill, who made it all come together. Thanks also are due the copy editor, Jean W. Ross. None of them, of course, is responsible for any deficiencies in this work; I managed those all by myself.

This book is dedicated to the newest member of our family, my daughter-in-law Melissa, as a token of love and welcome.

# INTRODUCTION

The Supreme Court during the tenures of Harlan Fiske Stone and Fred M. Vinson as chief justices can be viewed through several prisms. The years 1941 to 1953 included a major world war, a cold war, and a "police action," all of which affected the members of the Court individually and collectively just as it affected the general populace. Another way of looking at the Court in this period would be through the jurisprudential lenses of the individual justices, especially the conflicting views of Felix Frankfurter and Hugo Black. But while it is legitimate to look at the various issues raised by hot and cold wars and by the philosophies of the justices, it would be a mistake to focus on just these areas. In many ways, the Stone and Vinson Courts are transitional courts, located between the conservative, property-oriented courts of the Taft and early Hughes era and the individualistic activism of the Warren years. To look at this period as a transition, however, requires that we first examine what many scholars consider the defining moment in the Court's history in the first half of this century, the constitutional crisis of 1937.

Beginning in the late nineteenth century, a jurisprudential debate arose around the issue of how far the state could go in regulating private property and labor contracts. On one side stood the Progressive reformers, who wanted to use the police powers of the states and the federal government to meliorate the worst aspects of the industrial revolution. They proposed measures to regulate working conditions, wages, hours, and changes in employer liability laws to protect workers. Other reformers backed laws to regulate what railroads and other utilities could charge the public. From a legal point of view, the proposals rested on the police powers, the implicit powers of the state to protect the health, safety, and morals of the citizenry. Probably no broader view of the reach of these powers can be found than in Justice Holmes's comment in a 1911 case. "The police power," he declared, "may be put forth in aid of what is sanctioned by usage, or held by

1

the prevailing morality, or strong and preponderant opinion to be greatly and immediately necessary to the public welfare."[1]

Against this view stood the notions of the sanctity of private property, embodied in the concept of substantive due process, and so-called freedom of contract. As argued by two of the leading law writers of the late nineteenth century, Thomas M. Cooley and Christopher Tiedeman, the police power had very narrow applications. The state could do little more than maintain public order and safety, primarily for the purpose of protecting private property. It had no business interfering with voluntary transactions between adults, such as agreements between employers and employees.[2]

At first, reform legislation met heavy resistance in the courts, but by the time of American entry into World War I it appeared to have been accepted by both state and federal courts. A variety of measures establishing railroad and utility rates, hours and wages legislation, and other limitations upon property and contract received judicial approval.[3] But during the 1920s the justices who dominated the Taft Court reestablished both substantive due process and freedom of contract and reversed what had appeared to be judicial acceptance of protective legislation. In the 1920s these decisions affected millions of workers but evoked relatively little public controversy. The nation enjoyed what appeared to be a never-ending prosperity generated by the entrepreneurial talents of American business leaders. "The business of the nation is business," intoned President Calvin Coolidge, and no one wanted to interfere with the successful workings of private enterprise.

Then came the Great Depression, and the barriers that conservative justices had erected against reform legislation now prevented state and federal governments from responding to the emergency. The enormity of the crisis soon overwhelmed private and local relief agencies, and the national character of the Depression limited state action to a few palliative measures; only the national government had the resources or the power to respond. President Herbert Hoover refused to invoke those powers except in a very restricted manner, however, and the people turned him out of

---

1. *Noble State Bank v. Haskell,* 219 U.S. 104, 111 (1911).

2. Thomas M. Cooley, *A Treatise on Constitutional Limitations* . . . (Boston: Little, Brown, 1868); Christopher G. Tiedeman, *A Treatise on the Limitations of Police Power in the United States* . . . , 2 vols. (St. Louis: F. H. Thomas, 1886). For a further discussion of these men and their ideas, see Clyde E. Jacobs, *Law Writers and the Courts: The Influence of Thomas M. Cooley, Christopher G. Tiedeman, and John F. Dillon upon American Constitutional Law* (Berkeley: University of California Press, 1954).

3. John E. Semonche, *Charting the Future: The Supreme Court Responds to a Changing Society, 1890–1920* (Westport, Conn.: Greenwood, 1978); Melvin I. Urofsky, "State Courts and Protective Legislation during the Progressive Era: A Reevaluation," 72 *Journal of American History* 63 (1985).

office in November 1932. Franklin D. Roosevelt, who had laid out practically no specific proposals in his 1932 presidential campaign, nonetheless promised a New Deal and action to meet the crisis.

In the famous Hundred Days of 1933, Congress enacted fifteen major laws including the National Industrial Recovery Act, permitting the cartelization of industry; the Agricultural Adjustment Act, establishing crop subsidies tied to production limits; and the Tennessee Valley Authority, which used public power development (itself a radical idea) as a basis for a seven-state regional planning effort (an even more radical idea). Then in 1935 Congress approved the National Labor Relations Act, guaranteeing labor the right to organize and bargain collectively; the Guffey Coal Act, bringing wage and price controls to the coal industry; the Social Security Act, creating old-age pension and unemployment insurance programs; and the Public Utility Holding Company Act, which imposed a "death sentence" on the enormous power combinations created in the 1920s.[4]

There is ongoing debate as to whether the New Deal solved the Depression or not, but there is general agreement that many of the measures brought at least temporary relief and that in some areas the government introduced reforms that had long been overdue. Most important, though, is the sense of commitment that the Roosevelt administration gave to the American people, a sense that the government cared about their welfare and that the powers of the state would be invoked to prevent people from going hungry and without shelter. The notion that government had a responsibility to help people in need would inform American politics for the next half-century.

But even while enacting the New Deal, Roosevelt and his advisors worried about the response of the Supreme Court. In the first four years of his administration, men staunchly opposed to reform held the upper hand on the bench. The so-called Four Horsemen—James C. McReynolds, Willis Van Devanter, Pierce Butler, and George Sutherland—comprised a solid core of four votes against any and all measures that utilized an expanded notion of the power of the state. In essence, they believed that the government could do only what the Constitution expressly permitted it to do. They would be opposed by the liberal bloc of Louis D. Brandeis, Harlan Fiske Stone, and Benjamin Nathan Cardozo, whose creed of judicial restraint permitted the state to engage in a variety of activities provided that no specific constitutional prohibition stood in the way. The balance of power rested with Chief Justice Charles Evans Hughes and Owen J.

---

4. The best overview of the New Deal remains William E. Leuchtenburg, *Franklin D. Roosevelt and the New Deal, 1932–1940* (New York: Harper & Row, 1963); see especially chaps. 3 and 7.

Roberts. While Roberts was not as conservative as the Four Horsemen, his sympathies ran in that direction. Hughes, a former progressive leader in New York, frequently voted with the conservatives to avoid a 5–4 decision, although he seemed more comfortable in the jurisprudential company of Brandeis and Stone than in that of McReynolds and Butler.

After initially approving a few state measures,[5] the Court went on a sixteen-month campaign against the New Deal and in one case after another struck down its key legislative components. The National Industrial Recovery Act, the Agricultural Adjustment Act, the Guffey law, the Railroad Retirement Act and others fell before the constitutional ax. While a few of the votes were unanimous, such as the decision in *Schechter v. United States*,[6] invalidating the National Industrial Recovery Act, most of the time the Court split 5–4 with Roberts joining the conservatives and Hughes siding with Brandeis, Stone, and Cardozo. In some cases the Court seemed to go out of its way to tie up the administration, reviving doctrines that had lain dormant for years, interpreting the Constitution in an extremely narrow manner, and ignoring the stated intention of Congress. State measures fared no better than federal laws, and by the winter of 1936 it appeared that both the states and the national government would be entirely paralyzed by the Court's restrictive view of governmental powers.

Although Franklin Roosevelt made little mention of the Court in his 1936 presidential campaign, the issue of judicial obstruction brooded just beneath the surface. Unless the Court changed its mind, or could be changed, the president saw little chance for his administration to respond to the ongoing Depression. On February 5, 1937, a month after taking the oath of office for the second time, Roosevelt sent Congress a proposal for reorganizing the judiciary. Declaring that a shortage of personnel had led to serious overcrowding of federal court dockets, Roosevelt blamed part of the problem on "aged or infirm judges" who allegedly could no longer keep up with the workload. He therefore proposed that when a federal judge who had served at least ten years waited more than six months past his seventieth birthday to resign or retire, the president could add a new judge to the bench. The proposal limited the number of such additional judges to six on the Supreme Court and forty-four on the lower benches. Rather than stating the real intent of the measure—packing the Supreme

5. In *Home Building & Loan Association v. Blaisdell*, 290 U.S. 398 (1934), the Court upheld a state mortgage moratorium; and in *Nebbia V. New York*, 291 U.S. 523 (1934), a majority approved a state milk pricing scheme. In *Perry v. United States*, 294 U.S. 330 (1935) and the other Gold Clause cases, a bare majority reluctantly approved the administration's renunciation of the gold standard in both private and government contracts.
6. 295 U.S. 495 (1935).

Court to secure judicial approval of the New Deal—Roosevelt attempted to portray it as a plan to increase judicial efficiency.[7]

The Court-packing plan generated an enormous controversy, both in the country and in the Congress, and eventually Roosevelt's attempt to be clever led to its defeat. But in the middle of the uproar, the Court suddenly reversed course. With both Hughes and Roberts voting with the liberals, the Court approved a Washington State minimum wage law that did not differ in any significant degree from a New York measure struck down ten months before. That same day, March 29, 1937, the Court gave its blessing to three acts extending federal power. "What a day!" Robert Jackson later wrote. "To labor, minimum-wage laws and collective bargaining; to farmers, relief in bankruptcy; to law enforcement, firearms control. The Court was on the march!"[8] Within a few weeks the Court endorsed additional federal measures including critical labor and social security provisions; and then in August 1937, the very month in which Congress finally buried the Court-packing plan, Willis Van Devanter resigned, giving Roosevelt the first of the nine appointments he would make to the high court.

The crisis had ended, but its impact would be felt for years to come. In later years Roosevelt would claim that he had lost the battle but won the war, and in some ways that is true. Starting that March day in 1937, the Court upheld every New Deal law that came before it. The doctrine of judicial restraint, which Brandeis and Stone had preached with such intensity throughout the late 1920s and early 1930s, now stood triumphant. The Court would not attempt to second-guess the wisdom of the legislature; or, as Chief Justice Hughes wrote, "It is of the essence of the plenary power conferred that Congress may exercise its discretion in the use of the power."[9] The Court would henceforth ask only if Congress had the power; if it did, then the justices would not question whether the legislature had exercised that power wisely or foolishly. Moreover, the new court would give recognized constitutional powers a far greater scope than ever before, especially in the area of regulation of commerce.

In some areas, then, the story of the Stone and Vinson Courts is the playing out of the 1937 crisis, as the Court vindicated a wide range of federal powers. With Felix Frankfurter picking up the Brandeis-Stone mantle of judicial restraint, a majority of the justices in the new court showed no desire either to second-guess Congress or to limit its powers. Even before Chief Justice Hughes stepped down in 1941, this part of the revolution had

---

7. For a more extensive analysis of the details and origins of the plan, see William E. Leuchtenburg, *The Supreme Court Reborn* (New York: Oxford University Press, 1995), chaps. 4 and 5.

8. Robert H. Jackson, *The Struggle for Judicial Supremacy* (New York: Knopf, 1941), 213.

9. *Currin v. Wallace*, 306 U.S. 1, 14 (1939).

been essentially completed. Moreover, in expanding the scope of federal authority, the Court also enlarged state power, doing away with the so-called no-man's-land that the conservatives had created in which neither the states nor the federal government could act.

Commentators immediately started using the phrase "constitutional revolution of 1937," and for some this meant the destruction of the Court as a coequal partner in the government. "In 1937, the constitutional foundation of common-law thought collapsed," wrote historian Donald Gjerdingen. "The Court, judicial review and constitutional law have not been the same since."[10] In fact, the real legacy of the events of that year is that the Court retained its role as a major player in governmental affairs. While it has tended not to strike down federal legislation except on rare occasions, the power remains and has been used. If one tries to view the events of 1937 as a break with the larger themes of American constitutional development, one will look in vain. Like the *Dred Scott* decision of the 1850s, the Court's obstructionist tactics in the 1930s caused a problem but did not destroy the constitutional framework.

One reason is that the Court's agenda had already started to change, and that is where the real "revolution" is to be found. The cases that led to the 1937 crisis nearly all dealt with property and labor relations. But starting in the 1920s, a new type of case had begun appearing on the Supreme Court's docket, dealing with questions of individual liberties. In 1833 the Supreme Court had ruled, in *Barron v. Baltimore*,[11] that the liberties protected in the Bill of Rights applied only to the federal government and not to the states. Nearly ninety years later the Court affirmed this doctrine,[12] but the following year a new note could be heard. Justice McReynolds declared that the doctrine of substantive due process also covered certain basic individual freedoms.[13] Then in 1925 Justice Edward Sanford commented, almost in passing, "For present purposes we may and do assume that freedom of speech and of the press—which are protected by the First Amendment from abridgement by Congress—are among the fundamental rights protected by the due process clause of the Fourteenth Amendment from impairment by the States."[14]

So for the first time the Supreme Court put forward what came to

---

10. Quoted in Leuchtenburg, *Supreme Court Reborn*, 216.

11. 7 Pet. 243 (1833).

12. *Prudential Insurance Company v. Cheek*, 259 U.S. 530 (1922).

13. *Meyer v. Nebraska*, 262 U.S. 390 (1923). The idea that the Fourteenth Amendment's Due Process Clause might incorporate the liberties of the Bill of Rights had first been suggested by Louis Brandeis in his dissent in *Gilbert v. Minnesota*, 254 U.S. 325, 343 (Brandeis dissenting).

14. *Gitlow v. New York*, 268 U.S. 562, 566 (1925).

be known as the doctrine of "incorporation," by which the Fourteenth Amendment "incorporated" the liberties protected in the Bill of Rights and applied them to the states. By 1941, however, this process had not gone very far, and the criteria by which these protections would be applied had not been articulated. That process would take up much of the attention of the Stone and Vinson Courts and would set the stage for the rights explosion of the Warren era.

If it is this shift and not the events of 1937 that comprises the real judicial upheaval of this century, the crisis of that year is nonetheless important in its own right. The specter of judges interposing their biases to thwart the legislative will has cast a shadow over the Court ever since. Indeed, the very terms "conservative" and "liberal" as applied to judges changed during this era. In the years before the Court crisis, "conservative" judges imposed their views of property on the law in order to thwart economic reform, while "liberals" advocated judicial restraint, by which they meant that judges should not try to impose their personal views but should defer to the wisdom of the political branches. During the Stone and Vinson era the meanings of these words changed. The "conservatives" utilized the notion of judicial restraint to avoid clashing with the legislature and executive over issues affecting individual liberties, while "liberals" advocated judicial activism in opposing the political branches in order to protect civil rights and civil liberties. Especially in regard to the Cold War cases, the defense of individual rights often came into conflict with notions of judicial restraint. In that area, as in others, we can properly call the Stone-Vinson era one of transition.

Both academics and laypersons tend to periodicize the Court by reference to the chief justice; we talk of the "Marshall Court" or the "Taney Court" or the "Warren Court," and at least in some instances, the appellation is correct. John Marshall and William Howard Taft, for example, did lead their colleagues and put the impress of their own jurisprudential views on the decisions of their courts. But historians recognize that there is a continuity on the Court of the associate justices, whose terms are not coterminous with those of their chiefs. Hugo Black, Stanley Reed, Felix Frankfurter, and William O. Douglas all joined the Court before Harlan Fiske Stone took the center chair, and they were still on the bench after Fred Vinson died in 1953. Sometimes it is these "side judges," as Holmes called them, who really provide the intellectual and political leadership of the Court. I have heard it said on more than one occasion, for example, that the Court from 1956 until 1986 should be called the Brennan Court, since William Brennan, Jr., at least in the eyes of his admirers, dominated the tribunal in these years.

During the Stone and Vinson years neither man provided the leadership that Charles Evans Hughes had exercised in the 1930s or Earl Warren would display in the 1950s and 1960s. Stone certainly had the intellectual capacity, but he did not have the strength of will that would have allowed him to dominate such strong personalities as Black, Frankfurter, Douglas, or Robert H. Jackson. Moreover, although Stone had pointed the way of the new agenda in his famous *Carolene Products* footnote, he played little role in the debate over incorporation. Vinson had neither the intellectual nor the political skills to lead the Court, and with the exception of the communist cases, he played a relatively minor role in shaping the Court's jurisprudence.

So even though this series is organized by chief justiceships, the reader of this volume will find that the key characters are Felix Frankfurter, Hugo Black, and, to a slightly lesser extent, Black's ally and friend William O. Douglas. They, not Stone or Vinson, delineated the jurisprudential debates; they laid out the key arguments regarding incorporation, the proper role of the courts, the limits of constitutional protection, and the meaning of due process and equal rights. If at times the reader hears nothing of the chief justice, it is because the critical ideas are those of the side judges, not those of the center chair.

Frankfurter, Black, and Douglas are among the giants who have sat on this nation's high court, and even today one must deal with their ideas and opinions. But one does not find them attractive as human beings, and their frequent ill-temper (indeed, nastiness, in the cases of Frankfurter and Douglas) also played a role in the dynamics of the Court during these years. Felix Frankfurter may not have been the most disagreeable person ever to sit on the Supreme Court, but it is hard to think of anyone who has left us such an extensive record not only of his jurisprudential views but of his pettiness and disagreeable nature. That, too, is part of this story, and I hope it will lead the reader to understand that the Supreme Court of the United States is a place where individual ideas and personalities play a strong role, one that is sometimes as strong as the constitutional mandate the justices are sworn to uphold.

# 1

# THE STONE COURT

As he and his wife drove across the country in mid-June 1941, William O. Douglas often listened to the car radio, and somewhere in Arkansas he heard the news. President Franklin D. Roosevelt had named Associate Justice Harlan Fiske Stone to replace retiring Chief Justice Charles Evans Hughes. Several days later, when Douglas reached San Francisco, he wrote to congratulate his new chief. "I am delighted," he declared, and informed Stone that wherever Douglas had been, the nomination had been "hailed enthusiastically without a single dissent." To his close friend and Court ally Hugo Black, however, Douglas confided his doubts about the appointment. He detected Felix Frankfurter's hand in the event, which he saw as a sop thrown to the conservative bar. More important, unless Stone changed, he said, "it will not be a particularly happy or congenial atmosphere in which to work."[1]

Both Douglas's analysis and his prediction proved correct; Frankfurter had indeed played a hand in the president's decision. Hughes had informed Roosevelt of his decision to retire on June 2, 1941, and for a number of reasons, Roosevelt had to act quickly in filling not only the Court's center chair but also the seat vacated by James C. McReynolds a few months earlier. A number of cases hung fire in the Court, and as Stone had written to his sons in April, "a certain gentleman in California is about to be hanged because this Court, by reason of a 4 to 4 vote, was unable to disturb his judgment of conviction. I am quite sure that he will think Mr. Roosevelt owes it to him to appoint a judge who could sit in and decide his case."[2]

Speculation on Hughes's successor had quickly focused on Stone and Attorney General Robert H. Jackson. Roosevelt had in fact promised the next vacancy on the Court to Jackson, one of the most widely respected members of the administration and a member of the president's inner circle of poker friends and advisors. But he had not expected the vacancy to be that of the center chair, and in the summer of 1941 sound political

---

1. William O. Douglas to Harlan Fiske Stone, June 30, 1941, and to Hugo LaFayette Black, June 22, 1941, William O. Douglas Papers, Manuscript Division, Library of Congress.
2. Stone to Lauson and Marshall Stone, April 25, 1941, cited in Alpheus T. Mason, *Harlan Fiske Stone: Pillar of the Law* (New York: Viking, 1956), 564.

reasons supported the appointment of Stone, who had first been named to the Court by Calvin Coolidge in 1925.[3]

Stone had been born in 1872 in rural New Hampshire, and after attending Amherst College (where he first met Coolidge), he took a law degree at Columbia. Upon graduation Stone began practicing law in New York, and for a few years he also taught part-time at the Columbia Law School. Then in 1910 he gave up his practice to become professor and dean of the school, where he soon earned praise from both students and faculty. By all reports, Stone's classroom performance challenged and inspired students, while his willingness to stand up to the autocratic president of Columbia, Nicholas Murray Butler, won him the respect of the faculty. In 1923, tired of fighting Butler and worn down by what he termed "administrivia," Stone resigned the deanship and joined the prestigious Wall Street firm of Sullivan & Cromwell.

This turn in private practice proved short-lived, as his old friend, Calvin Coolidge, now President Coolidge, named Stone attorney general and gave him a mandate to clean out the corruption in the Justice Department left from the tenure of Harding's crony Harry M. Daugherty. Stone won plaudits for his work, and according to some sources, his very success led to his being "kicked upstairs" to the Supreme Court in 1925. He was the first nominee to the high court to appear in person before a Senate committee to answer questions. Liberal senators objected that Stone was too probusiness and that he had been J. P. Morgan's lawyer (Sullivan & Cromwell did count the House of Morgan among its clients). But Stone handled the questions easily, and the Senate confirmed the appointment by a vote of 71–6.

Despite the fears of progressives, Stone soon aligned himself with the liberals on the bench, Holmes and Brandeis in the 1920s and then Cardozo when he took Holmes's seat. In the '20s, Stone tended to let Holmes and Brandeis write the stinging dissents against the judicial activism of the Taft Court, but he believed just as passionately as they did in judicial restraint, the idea that courts should not try to second-guess the wisdom of the legislature and that legislation should not be struck down unless it violated a clear constitutional prohibition.

With the retirement of Holmes and the aging of Brandeis, Stone took a more vocal position in the 1930s, and by the time Hughes retired, Stone had emerged as the chief opponent of judicial conservatism. During the constitutional struggles over New Deal legislation, Stone had consistently

---

3. Biographical information on Stone can be found in Mason's *Stone*, which is a model of judicial biography. See also Noel T. Dowling, "The Methods of Mr. Justice Stone in Constitutional Cases," 41 *Columbia Law Review* 1160 (1941).

defended the administration's efforts to deal with the Depression, and his views on the proper role of the judiciary and the necessity for judges to practice self-restraint can be found in his dissenting opinion in *United States v. Butler* (1936). There he objected to the majority's striking down the Agricultural Adjustment Act, and in his dissent he claimed that "the power of courts to declare a statute unconstitutional is subject to two guiding principles of decision which ought never to be absent from judicial consciousness. One is that courts are concerned only with the power to enact statutes, not with their wisdom. The other is that while unconstitutional exercise of power by the executive and legislative branches is subject to judicial restraint, the only check upon our own exercise of power is our own sense of self-restraint. For the removal of unwise laws from the statute books appeal lies not to the courts but to the ballot and to the processes of democratic government."[4]

Following the constitutional crisis of 1937 (in which Stone opposed Roosevelt's Court-packing plan), the fight over economic legislation began to diminish, to be replaced by a concern for civil liberties. One of Stone's great contributions to American constitutional jurisprudence came in what appeared to be a minor case, *United States v. Carolene Products Co.* (1938). A federal law prohibited interstate transportation of "filled milk," skimmed milk mixed with animal fats. The Court had no trouble sustaining the legislation, but in his opinion for the majority Stone wrote what has since become the most famous footnote in the Court's history. In that note he erected the foundation for separate criteria in which to evaluate legislation embodying economic policy and laws that affected civil liberties. The latter restrictions, he declared, are to "be subjected to more exacting judicial scrutiny under the general prohibitions of the 14th Amendment than are most other types of legislation." Moreover, "statutes directed at particular religious . . . or national . . . or racial minorities" as well as "prejudice against discrete and insular minorities may be a special condition . . . which may call for a correspondingly more searching judicial inquiry."[5]

Stone's footnote, which has been cited in hundreds of cases since, ratified the change that had taken place following the Court-packing plan; economic legislation would henceforth receive a minimal level of scrutiny, with the justices relying on what came to be known as a rational basis test. So long as the legislature had the power and a reasonable justification for its use, courts would not question the wisdom of that legislation. But when statutes impinged on personal rights, there would be a much higher standard of review. With the *Carolene Products* footnote, the Court embarked on

---

4. *United States v. Butler*, 297 U.S. 1, 78–79 (1936).
5. *United States v. Carolene Products Co.*, 304 U.S. 144, 152–53 (1938).

a major sea change that would climax with the due process revolution and the civil rights decisions of the Warren Court in the 1950s and 1960s.[6] Much of what may be called the transitional nature of the Stone and Vinson era derives from the Court's efforts to work out the implications of Stone's footnote.

While his jurisprudence appealed to the Democrats, Stone's opposition to the Court-packing plan and his support of the Court's prerogatives won approval from conservatives. Newspapers across the political spectrum called for Stone's elevation to the center chair. Then over lunch at the White House, Felix Frankfurter urged his friend the president to name Stone, and to do so at once rather than waiting until the fall, when the Court convened.

Frankfurter, diminutive in frame but gigantic in persuasion, had a number of practical Court-related reasons, but his strongest argument concerned matters not of jurisprudence but of politics and international affairs. "It doesn't require prophetic powers," Frankfurter argued, "to be sure that we shall, sooner or later, be in war—I think sooner. It is most important that when war does come, the country should feel that you are a national, the Nation's President, and not a partisan President. Few things would contribute as much to confidence in you as a national and not a partisan President than for you to name a Republican, who has the profession's confidence, as Chief Justice."[7]

Confronted on all sides by this demand, Roosevelt sent Stone's name to the Senate on June 12 and was immediately rewarded with a wave of public approval. *Time* magazine caught the country's mood when it noted: "Last week the U.S. realized how much it liked the idea of a solid man as Chief Justice to follow Charles Evans Hughes. And solid is the word for Chief Justice Stone—200 lb., with heavy, good-natured features and a benign judicial air. . . . [He] is almost as impressive as a figure of justice as were Taft and Hughes before him."[8] When the nomination came before the Senate on June 27, it received unanimous approval. The redoubtable George W. Norris of Nebraska, who had led the fight against Stone in 1925,

6. According to David P. Currie, in his twenty years on the bench Stone "had done more perhaps than any other Justice to bring constitutional law into the twentieth century. We are indebted to him for one of the most effective protests against the old order [his *Butler* dissent] and for the authoritative program of the new." *The Constitution in the Supreme Court: The Second Century, 1888–1986* (Chicago: University of Chicago Press, 1990), 334.

7. Felix Frankfurter, memorandum on the chief justiceship cited in Mason, *Stone,* 566–67; see also Frankfurter to Stone, July 3, 1941, Harlan Fiske Stone Papers, Manuscript Division, Library of Congress.

8. *Time,* June 23, 1941; for a sampling of the overwhelming approval that met the nomination, see Mason, *Stone,* 568–73.

now in 1941 made the only speech prior to the Senate's confirmation of Stone as chief justice. Noting that he had opposed Stone's original appointment to the Court, Norris said, "I am now about to perform one of the most pleasant duties that has ever come to me in my official life when I cast a vote in favor of his elevation to the highest judicial office in our land. . . . It is a great satisfaction to me to rectify, in a very small degree, the wrong I did him years ago."[9]

Stone took the center chair on October 6, 1941, in a brief and low-key ceremony occasioned by the death of Louis Brandeis the day before. That day, however, in addition to Stone, two new justices also took their seats; James Byrnes replaced McReynolds, and Robert Jackson took the side chair vacated by Stone's promotion. As he looked around, Stone must have felt both anticipation and trepidation at the task before him, and both feelings would have been occasioned by what he called the group of "wild horses" he now had to lead.

Always seated immediately to the chief justice's right is the senior associate justice. For nearly all of Stone's tenure this would be Owen Josephus Roberts, who also carried impeccable Republican credentials. Roberts had grown up in a Philadelphia suburb and had built an extremely successful law practice in the city, specializing in corporate matters, especially banking and railroads. As an assistant district attorney during World War I, Roberts had earned public notice for prosecutions under the federal Espionage Act. When Calvin Coolidge succeeded Warren G. Harding, he needed a Republican with strong ties to business and a spotless reputation to investigate the Teapot Dome scandals. Roberts fit the bill perfectly, and after successfully prosecuting Harding's secretary of the interior, Albert G. Fall, for his role in Teapot Dome, Roberts returned to private practice.

In 1930 President Hoover's first nomination to the high court, federal judge John J. Parker, had run into opposition from labor and civil rights groups.[10] When the Senate refused to confirm Parker, Hoover turned to Roberts, the prosecutor of Teapot Dome, as a nominee above reproach. And Roberts, who had no judicial experience and had not sought the nomination, won unanimous Senate approval.

Although Roberts served for fifteen years, he and the Court were not a good match. His experience lay in prosecution and private practice, and while academically inclined, he did not pretend to be a scholar. He lacked a philosophical and theoretical temperament and thus had difficulty find-

---

9. *Congressional Record*, 77th Cong., 1st Sess. (June 27, 1941), 5618.
10. See Kenneth W. Goings, *"The NAACP Comes of Age": The Defeat of Judge John J. Parker* (Bloomington: University of Indiana Press, 1990).

ing a comfortable niche. He joined a bench torn by warring factions, battling over questions of economic philosophy and the proper role of the Court. While basically conservative, Roberts lacked the ideological certitude of a McReynolds or a Butler, and he opposed many New Deal measures more from instinct than because of a well-reasoned critique. Neither did he have firm beliefs in the proper role of the judiciary, and in one of his most famous opinions he claimed that judges had little more than a mechanical role to perform. "When an act of Congress is appropriately challenged in the courts as not conforming to the constitutional mandate," he declared, "the judicial branch of Government has only one duty—to lay the article of the Constitution which is invoked beside the statute which is challenged and to decide whether the latter squares with the former."[11]

Roberts tended to take his cue from Chief Justice Hughes, who for jurisprudential as well as political reasons sometimes voted with the liberal bloc and sometimes with the conservatives. When the two agreed with Brandeis, Stone, and Cardozo, the liberals could eke out a 5–4 victory; when they sided with the Four Horsemen, reform legislation could be killed by a clear 6–3 vote. Occasionally Roberts and the chief justice disagreed, and in these instances Roberts provided the critical fifth vote for the conservatives. Although he was basically a moderate, Roberts's tendency to vote with the conservatives played a major role in triggering the 1937 Court fight; then, at the height of the debate over the Court-packing plan, Roberts reversed his vote and the Court upheld a state minimum wage law in *West Coast Hotel v. Parrish* (1937).[12]

Only a year earlier Roberts had voted to strike down a minimum wage law in *Morehead v. New York ex rel. Tipaldo.*[13] Critics claimed that his vote had been purely political, and for the rest of his life Roberts had to endure the charge that "a switch in time saves nine." However, although the decision in *West Coast Hotel* was announced during the debate, the vote had actually been taken much earlier, before Roosevelt had announced his plan. The reason that Roberts changed his vote reflects the lack of judicial sophistication and the mechanical jurisprudence that marked all of his opinions. In the earlier case, counsel had not asked the Court to overrule *Adkins v. Children's Hospital* (1923),[14] which had held minimum wage regulation unconstitutional, and in the absence of a direct challenge Roberts had felt bound by precedent. In the second case, there had been a request to reverse *Adkins,* and Roberts had voted to do so. Some commentators have

11. *United States v. Butler,* 397 U.S. 1, 62 (1935).
12. 300 U.S. 379 (1937).
13. 298 U.S. 587 (1936).
14. 261 U.S. 525 (1923).

suggested that Roosevelt's overwhelming electoral victory in the 1936 election shocked Roberts into self-doubt. It is difficult to verify any particular theory about Roberts's change other than to note his almost complete lack of a consistent jurisprudential philosophy.

After *West Coast Hotel,* Roberts tended to support New Deal legislation, but he explained that he did so because the later statutes had been more carefully drafted. In what is certainly a far more striking reversal than his minimum wage votes, Roberts wrote the opinion for the Court in *Mulford v. Smith* (1939),[15] sustaining the second Agricultural Adjustment Act even though it differed in only minor details from the act he had voted to strike down four years earlier.

Roberts's votes in the emerging civil rights agenda also lacked any jurisprudential or philosophical pattern. He delivered the Court's opinion in *Grovey v. Townsend* (1935),[16] which upheld the constitutionality of an all-white primary, and he was the sole dissenter when the Court overturned that decision nine years later.[17] Yet in 1938 Roberts had voted with the Court to strike down a Missouri statute excluding African Americans from the state's law school,[18] and he wrote the strongest dissent of his tenure in one of the Japanese relocation cases.[19] Roberts's career on the court constituted an ultimately unsuccessful search for a coherent judicial philosophy.[20]

To the chief justice's left sits the second most senior associate justice, and there sat one of the century's judicial giants, Hugo Lafayette Black of Alabama. Black had joined the Court amid a cloud of controversy. At the time, many people believed Roosevelt had named Black, then a senator, to the Court for his support of the president's Court-packing plan. Moreover, since the Senate would not turn down one of its own, Roosevelt in effect humiliated those in the Senate who had not backed the plan by foisting off on them a man who apparently lacked credentials for the bench and whose populist political views irritated conservatives. Robert Jackson later recalled: "I had been rather amused at the President's maneuver, which enabled him to get even with the court and with the Senate, which had beat

---

15. 307 U.S. 38 (1939).

16. 295 U.S. 45 (1935).

17. *Smith v. Allwright,* 321 U.S. 649 (1944); see below, pp. 100–101.

18. *Missouri ex rel. Gaines v. Canada,* 305 U.S. 337 (1938).

19. *Korematsu v. United States,* 323 U.S. 214 (1944); see below, pp. 76–79.

20. There is no full biography of Roberts. The sketch by David Burner in Leon Friedman and Fred Israel, eds., *The Justices of the United States Supreme Court,* 4 vols. (New York: Chelsea House, 1969), 3:2253, is somewhat generous in its efforts to discern a pattern in his votes, as is Charles A. Leonard, *A Search for a Judicial Philosophy: Mr. Justice Roberts and the Constitutional Revolution of 1937* (Port Washington, N.Y.: Kennikat, 1971).

his plan, at the same time. He knew well enough that the Senate could not reject the nomination because of senatorial courtesy. He knew perfectly well it would go against their grain to confirm it. He knew it would not be welcomed by the court."[21] Then shortly after he had been sworn in, it turned out that Black had once belonged to the Ku Klux Klan.[22] All in all, it hardly made for an auspicious start of a judicial career.

Black grew up in rural Alabama, graduated first in his University of Alabama Law School class, and then, after practicing in his native Ashland for a few years, moved to Birmingham in 1907. To supplement his income, Black also served part-time as a municipal court judge and then for three years full-time as Jefferson County prosecuting attorney. In his most famous case, he investigated and prosecuted several police officers for beating and forcing confessions from black defendants. The experience marked him for life and gave him something no other member of the Stone Court had—litigation experience in criminal law; as a result, he brought a discernible passion to criminal cases.

In his private practice Black tried hundreds of cases and honed his already considerable talents as a debater and orator, skills that led to his election to the United States Senate in 1926. In 1932 he won a second term and immediately became a staunch defender of Franklin D. Roosevelt's New Deal policies, a position that often put him at odds with his fellow southerners. Most important, both on the Senate floor and as head of several important special committees, Black espoused a view that the federal government had sufficient authority under the Commerce Clause to enact legislation to deal with the Depression, that in fact Congress could regulate any activity that directly or indirectly affected the national economy, and that the judiciary had no power to interfere with these decisions.

Black had some difficulty adjusting to the Court, and Harlan Fiske Stone asked Felix Frankfurter, then at the Harvard Law School, if he could instruct the new member in the proper judicial protocol. "Do you know Black well?" a troubled Stone asked in early 1938. "You might be able to render him great assistance. He needs guidance from someone who is more familiar with the workings of the judicial process than he is." Black's tradition-ignoring dissents worried both Stone and Brandeis, and as Stone noted, "There are enough present-day battles to be won without wasting our efforts to remake the Constitution *ab initio,* or using the judicial opinion as a political tract." Frankfurter gladly took up the invitation and re-

---

21. Jackson Memoirs, Columbia Oral History Collection, Columbia University Library.
22. See William E. Leuchtenburg, "A Klansman Joins the Court," in his *The Supreme Court Reborn* (New York: Oxford University Press, 1995), chap. 7; Roger K. Newman, *Hugo Black: A Biography* (New York: Pantheon, 1994), chaps. 6 and 17.

ported to Brandeis that the Alabaman, while not "technically equipped," had a "good head" and was "capable of learning if . . . properly encouraged."[23] Black probably did not know that Frankfurter came to him at Stone's request, since the Harvard professor was on familiar terms with several members of the Court, most notably Brandeis. But a few years later Black no doubt did resent Stone's denigration of his abilities. Stone often took morning walks with Marquis Childs of the *St. Louis Post-Dispatch,* and complained to the reporter that Black was not very lawyer-like and was having trouble keeping up with the Court's work. The comment found its way into Childs's column, and Black probably did not have too much difficulty figuring out its source, even though Stone personally denied being responsible.[24]

In fact, despite Stone's concern, Black went onto the Court with a fairly well developed judicial philosophy that included a clear reading of the constitutional text, limited judicial discretion, the protection of individual rights, and broad powers for the government to address a wide range of economic and social problems. Someone once commented that Black's lasting influence on the Court grew out of his willingness to "reinvent the wheel." Like his friend and ally William O. Douglas, Black had little use for precedent, especially if he thought the case erroneously decided. In his first year alone, Black issued eight solo dissents including an almost unprecedented dissent to a *per curiam* decision.[25]

At the heart of Black's philosophy lay a populist belief in the Constitution as an infallible guide. He opposed judicial subjectivity; the Constitution did not empower judges to select from competing alternatives. He distrusted the so-called experts, and leaving either legislative or judicial decision making in their hands smacked too much of elitism. He offered instead the imposition of absolutes through a literal reading of the Constitution. This narrowed the scope of judicial discretion, but it also helped to make the judiciary the prime vehicle for guaranteeing the values of those absolutes.[26]

---

23. Mason, *Stone,* 469; Frankfurter to Louis Brandeis, May 28, 1938, Felix Frankfurter Papers, Manuscript Division, Library of Congress.

24. Years later Childs confirmed to Black that Stone had been the source. Newman, *Black,* 277–78.

25. *McCart v. Indianapolis Water Co.,* 302 U.S. 419 (1938). *Per curiam* opinions are short memorandum opinions "by the Court," issued primarily in cases that the Court decides do not require full-scale oral argument or opinion. Since then such dissents have become fairly common.

26. One of the best discussions of Black's judicial philosophy is Mark Silverstein, *Constitutional Faiths: Felix Frankfurter, Hugo Black, and the Process of Judicial Decision Making* (Ithaca: Cornell University Press, 1984), especially chap. 4. One should also see Black's *A Constitutional Faith* (New York: Knopf, 1968).

Throughout his career Black searched the text of the Constitution for guidance. He understood that one could not always read the document literally, but he sought the meaning he believed had been intended by its framers. Thus, despite his populist political views and his strong defense of civil liberties, in many ways Black's was an extremely conservative approach, and indeed he saw himself as a strict constructionist. During the Stone and Vinson years Black would be the jurisprudential leader of the liberal bloc on the Court, a group whose ideas would triumph in the 1960s.[27]

Part of Black's effectiveness derived from the considerable political skills he possessed and had honed in the Senate. More than any other justice of his time, Black proselytized, "working" the other justices as he had once worked his senatorial colleagues in order to gain a majority. The columnist Irving Brant, an admirer of Black, reported a story Black told that explained a good deal of his effectiveness. Black would talk about an unnamed senator who said that when he wanted to accomplish something he would introduce two bills—the one he wanted passed and another that made the first one seem conservative. Robert Jackson somewhat disdainfully noted that while these methods were appropriate in a legislative body where one deals with adversaries, he considered them unsuited to a court in which the members were supposed to be colleagues. Stone, according to Jackson, found Black's methods very unsettling, and they caused the chief justice "a great deal of discomfort and dissatisfaction."[28]

Roosevelt's second appointment to the high court had been Stanley Forman Reed of Kentucky, a genial man who lived to be ninety-five and told Potter Stewart that he would not want to live his life over again, as "it could not possibly be as good the second time."[29] After graduating from Yale Law School, Reed had built a thriving law practice in Maysville, Kentucky, dabbled in state politics, and helped manage his friend Fred Vinson's congressional campaigns. Then in 1929 he moved to Washington when Herbert Hoover named him counsel to the Federal Farm Board, a position he retained in the Roosevelt administration. Reed's geniality as

---

27. There is a great body of literature on Black. The most recent and most comprehensive study is Newman, *Black* (1994). See also Gerald T. Dunne, *Hugo Black and the Judicial Revolution* (New York: Simon & Schuster, 1977); James J. Magee, *Mr. Justice Black: Absolutist on the Court* (Charlottesville: University of Virginia Press, 1980); and the unique double biography by James F. Simon, *The Antagonists: Hugo Black, Felix Frankfurter and Civil Liberties in Modern America* (New York: Simon & Schuster, 1989). For evaluations of Black's judicial philosophy, see Tony Freyer, ed., *Justice Hugo Black and Modern America* (University: University of Alabama Press, 1990); and Tinsley E. Yarbrough, *Mr. Justice Black and His Critics* (Durham: Duke University Press, 1988).

28. Jackson Memoirs, Columbia Oral History Collection.

29. Daniel L. Breen, "Stanley Forman Reed," in Melvin I. Urofsky, ed., *The Supreme Court Justices: A Biographical Dictionary* (New York: Garland, 1994), 367.

well as his passionate belief in the desirability of the federal government's playing a major role in the nation's social and economic life soon caught the attention of the president, who named him solicitor general.[30] His performance in that role was lackluster at best, but in early 1938 Roosevelt named Reed to replace George Sutherland, the second of the Four Horseman to retire.

Once on the Court, Reed tended to defer to Congress, and a determination of what Congress had intended often proved dispositive for him, whether the issue was of constitutional, administrative, or statutory interpretation. Like the other Roosevelt appointees, Reed could be considered liberal in that he believed the Court had no right to deny Congress full use of its commerce powers. He had less faith in state and local powers, however, and seemed to have had little interest in the protection of individual liberties. The one area that did arouse his concern was the First Amendment, and during his tenure Reed voted often but not in every case to broaden First Amendment rights. On the whole, his record is marked primarily by inconsistency, a not unfamiliar characteristic of many New Dealers.[31]

Sitting next to Black on the bench and the leader of the conservative bloc was Black's erstwhile instructor Felix Frankfurter, appointed to succeed Benjamin Nathan Cardozo in 1938 amid high hopes that he would become the intellectual leader of the Court. Solicitor General Robert H. Jackson, in a sentiment echoed by Harlan Stone, claimed that only Frankfurter had the legal resources "to face Chief Justice Hughes in conference and hold his own in discussion."[32] Upon news of his nomination, New Dealers had gathered in the office of Secretary of the Interior Harold Ickes to celebrate, and all those present heartily agreed with Ickes's judgment of the nomination as "the most significant and worthwhile thing the President has done."[33] There is, unfortunately, no way one can predict whether

---

30. John Sapienza, one of Reed's first clerks, noted that the justice was "friendly with everyone. He didn't even exchange any nasty words with McReynolds, and he was on good terms with Frankfurter, with Black, with Butler. . . . He never engaged in any feuds with anybody. He never had an unkind word to say about anybody." Addendum to Reed Memoirs, Columbia Oral History Collection.

31. The only full-scale biography—John D. Fassett, *New Deal Justice: The Life of Stanley Reed of Kentucky* (New York: Vantage, 1994)—is by a former clerk and is completely uncritical. See also William O'Brien, *Justice Reed and the First Amendment: The Religion Clauses* (Washington: Georgetown University Press, 1958); and an unpublished dissertation by Mark J. Fitzgerald, "Justice Reed: A Study of a Center Judge" (University of Chicago, 1950).

32. Eugene Gerhart, *America's Advocate: Robert H. Jackson* (Indianapolis: Bobbs-Merrill, 1958), 166; Mason, *Stone*, 482.

33. Harold L. Ickes, *The Secret Diaries of Harold L. Ickes*, 3 vols. (New York: Simon & Schuster, 1954), 2:552.

an appointee will be great or mediocre once on the bench, and Frankfurter ranks as one of the great disappointments in modern times.

Born in Vienna, Frankfurter had emigrated to the United States as a child, and his innate brilliance had shone first at the City College of New York and then at the Harvard Law School. Upon graduation, he had briefly joined a Wall Street firm but had soon fled to work with U.S. Attorney Henry L. Stimson; he then followed Stimson into the Roosevelt and Taft administrations. Short, exuberant, a brilliant conversationalist and an inveterate idol worshipper, Frankfurter soon became the center of a group of young bureaucrats and writers who shared quarters on 19th Street, a place they dubbed the "House of Truth." There Gutzom Borgum sketched his proposed presidential monument, Herbert Croly and Walter Lippmann expounded on contemporary problems, and Oliver Wendell Holmes and Louis Brandeis were frequent visitors.

Frankfurter and Holmes fell under each other's spell; the younger man adored Holmes, and the sentiment was reciprocated. When Frankfurter accepted a position at the Harvard Law School after World War I, he took responsibility for choosing Holmes's clerks. Holmes appealed to Frankfurter for a number of reasons, but from a jurisprudential point of view, Holmes held high the banner of judicial restraint, a banner that Frankfurter in his own time would also carry. Frankfurter later wrote, "You must bear in mind that the great influences of my formative years were Dean Ames and Harry Stimson; later Holmes and to some, but less extent, Brandeis. . . . They all converged toward making me feel deeply that it makes all the difference in the world whether you put truth in the first place or the second."[34]

Despite this comment, in many ways the relationship with Brandeis proved more decisive. In Frankfurter Brandeis found a surrogate to carry on his reform work; he urged Frankfurter to take the professorship at Harvard, and he provided a financial subsidy to enable Frankfurter, who lacked an independent income, to devote himself to reform efforts.[35] During the 1920s Frankfurter, through his defense of Sacco and Vanzetti and his writings for the *New Republic,* became a leading reformer in his own right, a man Brandeis called "the most useful lawyer in the United States."[36] Frank-

34. Frankfurter to Learned Hand, June 27, 1946, Frankfurter Papers, Library of Congress.

35. There has been a great deal made of this relationship, especially by Bruce Murphy in *The Brandeis/Frankfurter Connection* (New York: Oxford University Press, 1982). A somewhat different picture emerges from the correspondence contained in Melvin I. Urofsky and David W. Levy, eds., *"Half Brother, Half Son": The Letters of Louis D. Brandeis to Felix Frankfurter* (Norman: University of Oklahoma Press, 1991).

36. Brandeis to Harold Laski, November 29, 1928, in Melvin I. Urofsky and David W. Levy, eds., *Letters of Louis D. Brandeis,* 5 vols. (Albany: State University of New York Press, 1971–78), 5:364.

furter's influence also was spread by his students. A brilliant teacher, he trained a whole generation of lawyers in administrative law, and when the Depression came and government burgeoned under the New Deal, Frankfurter became a one-man placement agency, staffing one federal office after another with his former students.[37] He also exerted a quiet but effective influence on several New Deal policies, not only through his many contacts with leading administration figures but with President Roosevelt as well. The two men had known each other since World War I, and during the 1930s Frankfurter was a frequent guest at the White House.[38]

Frankfurter, like Black, went onto the Court with a well-developed judicial philosophy but one far different from the Alabaman's. Both men believed in judicial restraint, but Frankfurter took what Black considered a much too subjective approach, leaving too great a power in the hands of judges to "interpret" constitutional injunctions. Most importantly, however, Black drew a sharp distinction between economic legislation and restrictions on individual liberties, with judges carrying a special obligation to protect the latter; Frankfurter considered all legislation equal and demanded that judges defer to the legislative will unless they found a clearcut constitutional prohibition. The debate between these two views would fragment the Stone Court and make it one of the most contentious in history.[39]

One week after Frankfurter took his seat, his longtime mentor, Louis D. Brandeis, retired, and to replace him Roosevelt named William Orville Douglas. A true product of the Pacific Northwest, Douglas had grown up in Yakima, Washington, where, as a child, he contracted infantile paralysis. Gradually he regained limited use of his legs, but he was still a sickly child at the time of his father's death. He later wrote that in the middle of the funeral he stopped crying only after he looked up and saw Mount Adams in the distance. "Adams stood cool and calm, unperturbed

---

37. In this regard, see G. Edward White, "Felix Frankfurter, the Old Boy Network, and the New Deal: The Placement of Elite Lawyers in Public Service in the 1930s," 39 *Arkansas Law Review* 631 (1986).

38. See Max Freedman, ed., *Roosevelt and Frankfurter: Their Correspondence, 1928–1945* (Boston: Atlantic Little, Brown, 1967).

39. For Frankfurter's pre-Court career, see Michael Parrish, *Felix Frankfurter and His Times: The Reform Years* (New York: Free Press, 1982); for the Court years, see Melvin I. Urofsky, *Felix Frankfurter: Judicial Restraint and Individual Liberties* (Boston: Twayne, 1991). Harlan Philips, ed., *Felix Frankfurter Reminisces* (New York: Reynal, 1960), is an anecdotal and often unreliable memoir drawn from Frankfurter's oral history at Columbia. For an insightful look at Frankfurter's personality and jurisprudence by a disciple and admirer, see the notes by Joseph Lash of an interview with Alexander Bickel, September 12, 1974, in Joseph Lash Papers, Franklin D. Roosevelt Library, Box 5. (I wish to thank William E. Leuchtenburg for providing me a copy of this document.)

. . . Adams suddenly seemed to be a friend. Adams subtly became a force for me to tie to, a symbol of stability of strength."[40]

Between the strong will of his mother and his own self-determination, Douglas overcame his physical disabilities. He started to hike in the mountains, an experience that not only built up his strength but led to his life-long devotion to the environment. The drive to build himself physically carried over into other areas of his life. The Yakima High School yearbook of 1916 noted that its valedictorian that year had been "born for success."

After graduation from Whitman College, Douglas headed east in the summer of 1922 with $75 in his pocket to attend Columbia Law School. He entered Columbia at a time when its faculty had just begun to explore new areas of legal research that would eventually lead to the "Legal Realism" movement. The Realists believed that in order to understand the law and the behavior of legal institutions, one had to look at individual behavior and use the social sciences to find the real causes of particular actions. Douglas became a devoted adherent to this new philosophy, and after a miserable two years working in a Wall Street law firm, he returned to Columbia as a teacher in 1927. Within a year, however, he resigned to accept a position at the Yale Law School, which under the leadership of its brilliant young dean, Robert M. Hutchins, quickly became the center of Legal Realism, and Douglas became one of its star exponents.[41]

Douglas's tenure at Yale may have been the most peaceful time in his life, but beneath a surface tranquillity he remained restless, especially when he looked to Washington and saw the dynamic activities going on under the New Deal umbrella. In 1934 Douglas secured an assignment from the newly created Securities and Exchange Commission (SEC) to study protective committees, the agencies stockholders use during bankruptcy reorganization to protect their interests. He began commuting between New Haven and Washington and soon came to the attention of the SEC chair, Joseph P. Kennedy, who arranged for Douglas, then thirty-seven years old, to be named to the Commission in 1935. Two years later, President Roosevelt named Douglas chair of the SEC.[42]

During these years in Washington, Douglas became part of Franklin D. Roosevelt's inner circle, often joining the weekly poker games at the White House. There was a great deal of speculation that the bright, handsome westerner might have a future in politics. In fact, Douglas had already tired of the game and wanted to return to Yale. When a messenger interrupted

---

40. Douglas, *Of Men and Mountains* (New York: Harper, 1950), 29.

41. See Laura Kalman, *Legal Realism at Yale, 1927–1960* (Chapel Hill: University of North Carolina Press, 1986), especially chaps. 3 and 4.

42. For Douglas's tenure at the SEC, see Michael E. Parrish, *Securities Regulation and the New Deal* (New Haven: Yale University Press, 1970).

a golf game on March 19, 1939, to tell Douglas that the president wanted
to see him at the White House, Douglas almost did not go, since he fully
expected that Roosevelt was going to ask him to take over the troubled
Federal Communications Commission. But after teasing him for a few minutes, Roosevelt offered Douglas the seat on the Supreme Court vacated by
Louis D. Brandeis a month earlier.

Although Douglas always claimed the offer came as a surprise, in fact
he had had his friends busily at work promoting his name for the opening.
Following the bruising court battle of 1937, Roosevelt wanted to make sure
that his appointees would support his program, and in Douglas he had a
confirmed New Deal liberal, someone who could mix it up with the conservatives, a quick mind, a westerner, and a loyal personal friend.

Douglas, the youngest person ever appointed to the Supreme Court,
would establish a record of longevity for service before illness forced him
to retire in late 1975. Moreover, no other justice ever engaged in so extensive and public a nonjudicial life. Douglas always claimed that the work of
the Court never took more than three or four days a week; he read petitions rapidly, rarely agonized over decisions, could get to the heart of an
issue instantly, and wrote his opinions quickly. This left him time for other
activities, such as travel, lecturing, writing, climbing mountains, and, as
some critics claimed, getting into trouble.

Douglas and Frankfurter had been friends, and friendly rivals, from
their days as law school professors, and the younger Douglas had often
looked to the more established Frankfurter for advice.[43] Jurisprudentially,
the two seemed to share the same basic values, but the shifting agenda of
the Court soon highlighted the fact that on the crucial issues to confront
the judiciary in the 1940s and 1950s they differed significantly. During the
first years of the Stone regime, Douglas allied himself with Black, but eventually he proved far more activist than his friend. Douglas, however, proved
an able second to Black in the battles shaping up over which direction the
Court should take.[44]

Roosevelt made his fifth appointment to the Court in early 1940, when
he named Frank William Murphy to replace Pierce Butler and with that

---

43. See, for example, Douglas to Frankfurter, December 8, 1933, Douglas Papers, Library
of Congress.

44. Douglas wrote what amounted to a three-volume autobiography consisting of *Of Men
and Mountains; Go East, Young Man: The Early Years* (New York: Random House, 1974); and
*The Court Years: 1939–1975* (New York: Random House, 1980). An excellent work on him
is James F. Simon, *Independent Journey: The Life of William O. Douglas* (New York: Harper &
Row, 1980). Howard Ball and Phillip J. Cooper, *Of Power and Right: Hugo Black, William O.
Douglas and America's Constitutional Revolution* (New York: Oxford University Press, 1992)
fails to do justice either to the men or to their ideas.

move sealed the constitutional revolution triggered by the New Deal. After more than two decades of conservative domination, the Court now had a majority committed to the idea that the political branches should determine economic policies and that courts had no right to pass judgment on the wisdom of those policies. Roosevelt, of course, wanted men on the bench who would endorse New Deal policies, but as the Court's agenda changed in the later 1940s, several of his appointees seemed to grow more conservative. With Frank Murphy, however, Roosevelt got a thoroughgoing liberal, one who had little use for technical questions and believed that the objectives of law should be justice and human dignity. Murphy cared even less for precedents than Douglas and Black; he openly relied on what one commentator has called "visceral jurisprudence." The law knows no finer hour, Murphy wrote, "than when it cuts through formal concepts and transitory emotions to protect unpopular citizens against discrimination and persecution."[45]

Murphy inherited his radical politics from his father, who had been jailed in his youth for Fenian sympathies, and his devout Catholicism from his mother. From the beginning, he saw law and politics as intertwined, with law the avenue to political success. In 1923 he won election as a criminal court judge in Detroit, in which position he reformed an antiquated system. Labor and minority groups propelled him into the mayor's office in 1930, and he set about creating a welfare system to help those thrown out of work by the Depression. Roosevelt named Murphy, one of his early backers, governor general of the Philippines, but while Murphy proved popular and effective in that job, he saw it as a detour on the way to the White House.

Murphy returned to the country to run for and win the Michigan gubernatorial race in 1936, and shortly after he took office the auto workers began the sit-down strikes of 1937. Company officials immediately went to court to seek injunctions against the strikers, but Murphy refused to enforce the orders. He called out the national guard to maintain peace while he worked behind the scenes to avert outright bloodshed. He succeeded, but each side accused him of favoring the other, and he lost his reelection bid in 1938. Roosevelt owed Murphy for taking the heat off Washington during the strikes and so named him attorney general in 1939. Murphy was in that office less than a year, but during his tenure he set up a civil liberties unit that for the first time employed the power of the federal government to protect individual rights. This activity did not sit well with many people, especially southerners, and to some extent Roosevelt's sending Murphy to the Court was a way of kicking him upstairs. Murphy recognized this and

---

45. Quoted in Peter Irons, "Frank Murphy," in Urofsky, *Supreme Court Justices,* 331.

did not really want to go. He still had his sights set on the presidency, and no one had ever gone from the bench to the Oval Office. Murphy also thought he would be on the sidelines, away from the real action. "I fear that my work will be mediocre up there while on the firing line where I have been trained to action I could do much better."[46]

Even Murphy's admirers make no claim that he had special talents as a jurist, and he recognized his own limitations. He felt inferior in the company of Stone and Black, Douglas and Frankfurter. He knew little constitutional law, and his prior judicial experience had been on a municipal criminal bench. But he learned, and he relied on bright clerks to draft his opinions.

Murphy, however, did develop a jurisprudence, one based on the *Carolene Products* notion that restrictions on individual liberties required strict scrutiny by the courts. He also adopted Hugo Black's notion that the liberties protected by the First Amendment held a "preferred position" in the constitutional firmament. Murphy's first opinion indicated the path he would take. New justices may pick their first opinion, and Murphy chose a case overturning a state law that banned virtually all picketing by union members. Although Brandeis had earlier suggested that picketing might be a form of protected speech, this notion did not become law until Murphy's opinion in *Thornhill v. Alabama* (1940). There the new justice extended First Amendment protection to peaceful picketing and forcefully cited the *Carolene Products* footnote to justify the judiciary's overturning of a law that invaded civil liberties. In 1969 Justice Tom Clark wrote that the opinion was "the bedrock upon which many of the Court's civil rights pronouncements rest."[47]

Although Murphy initially appeared willing to follow Frankfurter's lead and joined him in the first flag salute case,[48] he soon gravitated to his natural moorings on the liberal side of the Court and, along with Black and Douglas, consistently fought for greater protection of the individual.[49]

On the same day that Roosevelt sent Stone's nomination to the Senate, he named two other men to the high court, Robert Houghwout Jackson to

---

46. Frank Murphy to Bishop William Murphy, January 8, 1940, in Sidney Fine, *Frank Murphy: The Washington Years* (Ann Arbor: University of Michigan Press, 1984), 133.

47. *Thornhill v. Alabama*, 310 U.S. 88 (1940); the Brandeis suggestion is in *Senn v. Tile Layers Protective Union*, 301 U.S. 468, 478 (1937). The *Thornhill* opinion proved to be both influential and enduring; it has been cited in more than three hundred subsequent opinions.

48. *Minersville School District v. Gobitis*, 310 U.S. 586 (1940); see below, pp. 106–9.

49. Sidney Fine has written a definitive three-volume biography of Murphy, of which *The Washington Years* covers his tenure at the Justice Department and on the Court. An earlier work, J. Woodford Howard, Jr., *Mr. Justice Murphy: A Political Biography* (Princeton: Princeton University Press, 1968), is more critical.

replace Stone as an associate justice and James Francis Byrnes to take the seat vacated by the last of the Four Horsemen, James C. McReynolds. Jackson is in some ways one of the least known members of the Court despite the fact that he had a notable career and a facile pen and helped create the modern doctrinal rules for judicial review of economic regulation. Although Jackson did not share the First Amendment views of Black and Douglas, he wrote one of the outstanding defenses of the First Amendment right to free exercise of religion.[50]

Jackson was, in fact, one of the better stylists on the Court in this century. Following one of his early opinions, Judge Jerome Frank, himself a brilliant writer, told Jackson, "I've never admired you as much as now. . . . And I am tickled silly that you spoke in good plain American, just as you did before you became a judge. Ordinary folks like me can understand you."[51] A good example of Jackson's style can be found in his concurrence in a case explaining why he now supported a position at odds with one he had taken ten years earlier while still attorney general:

> Precedent . . . is not lacking for ways by which a judge may recede from a prior opinion that has proven untenable and perhaps misled others. Baron Bramwell extracted himself from a somewhat similar embarrassment by saying, "The matter does not appear to me now as it appears to have appeared to me then." . . . And Mr. Justice Story, accounting for his contradiction of his own former opinion, quite properly put the matter: "My own error, however, can furnish no ground for its being adopted by the Court." . . . Perhaps Dr. Johnson really went to the heart of the matter when he explained a blunder in his dictionary— "Ignorance, sir, ignorance." But an escape less self-deprecating was taken by Lord Westbury, who it is said rebuffed a barrister's reliance on an earlier opinion of his Lordship: "I can only say that I am amazed that a man of my intelligence should have been guilty of giving such an opinion." If there are other ways of gracefully and good-naturedly surrendering former views to a better considered position, I invoke them all.[52]

Born on a western Pennsylvania farm, Robert Jackson was self-educated; he briefly attended Albany Law School but then qualified for the

---

50. *West Virginia State Board of Education v. Barnette*, 319 U.S. 624 (1943); see below, pp. 111–12.

51. Frank to Jackson, November 27, 1941, Robert H. Jackson Papers, Manuscript Division, Library of Congress. See also the appraisal by Arthur Krock in his column in the *New York Times*, June 15, 1943.

52. *McGrath v. Kristensen*, 340 U.S. 162, 177–78 (1950).

bar by reading law as an apprentice in a lawyer's office (he was the last Supreme Court justice to do so). He set up a thriving and varied practice in western New York and, as a fourth-generation Democrat, became active in state politics and an advisor to Governor Franklin Roosevelt. After Roosevelt entered the White House in 1933, he brought Jackson to Washington, where the New York lawyer advanced from general counsel at the Bureau of Internal Revenue to solicitor general and then attorney general. Jackson later described his tenure as solicitor general as the happiest part of his life, and he won high marks for his role as the government's chief litigator; Louis Brandeis once commented that Jackson should have been named solicitor general for life.

Many people considered Jackson a possible presidential candidate, and his name was frequently mentioned for the 1940 Democratic nomination until Roosevelt decided to run for a third term. The president had promised Jackson a seat on the Supreme Court when he asked him to head the Justice Department; the next vacancy, however, arose with the resignation of Charles Evans Hughes, and Roosevelt felt he had to name Stone to the center chair. A loyal supporter of the president, Jackson agreed, but it appears that Roosevelt may have also assured Jackson that he would elevate him to be chief upon Stone's departure from the Court. Both men assumed that Stone, who was sixty-nine when he was appointed chief, would probably not stay on the Court more than five or six years, and that would leave Jackson, then only fifty, a fair amount of time to lead the high court.

Had Jackson been chief justice, he might have been happier on the Court, but his activist nature chafed at the restrictions of judicial propriety. During the war he felt cut off from the great events going on around him; he remarked that the Monday after Pearl Harbor the Court heard arguments about the taxability of greens fees. While he, like Frankfurter and Douglas, continued secretly to advise Roosevelt, he wanted to do more. Thus he leaped at the opportunity when President Harry S. Truman asked him to head the American prosecutorial team at the Nuremberg trial of Nazi war criminals.

Although Jackson tended to join Frankfurter on many issues, he could not be considered a predictable vote for the conservatives. He parted from Frankfurter, for example, in the second flag salute case; his decision in *Wickard v. Filburn* (1942) is a ringing endorsement of an all-encompassing congressional power over commerce,[53] yet he took a far more restricted view of presidential power during the Korean conflict.[54] Some of his opinions seemed quirky—for example, his dissent in *Beauharnais v. Illinois*

---

53. 317 U.S. 111 (1942); see below, pp. 118–19.
54. *Youngstown Sheet & Tube Co. et al. v. Sawyer*, 343 U.S. 579 (1952); see below, pp. 206–11.

(1952),[55] in which he endorsed the idea of treating racist speech as group libel yet argued that the defendant had a right to a jury trial to prove the truth of the libel.[56]

James Byrnes sat on the Court for only one term and then resigned to become the so-called assistant president, Roosevelt's special aide during the war. Born in Charleston, South Carolina, Byrnes had little formal schooling and, like Jackson, had learned his law by reading as an apprentice. Byrnes's first and foremost love, however, was politics; he served in the House of Representatives from 1910 to 1925 and then in the Senate from 1931 to 1941. During that decade he became a trusted ally and adviser of the president and was one of the few southern senators besides Black fully committed to the New Deal. He also earned Roosevelt's gratitude for working out a face-saving compromise in the aftermath of the Court-packing debacle. He urged Roosevelt not to push the bill, especially after Willis Van Devanter resigned. "Why run for a train after you caught it?" he asked.

Byrnes's main contribution to the Court appears to have been social; he regularly had the justices over to his house for dinner and then led them in postprandial songs. He wrote only one major opinion, *Edwards v. California* (1941),[57] and fifteen other minor rulings, with no dissents or concurrences, thus leaving a virtually uncharted jurisprudence. Byrnes, like other members of the Stone Court, felt isolated from the great events happening around him. The Court's slow and deliberate pace frustrated him, and he declared, "I don't think I can stand the abstractions of jurisprudence at a time like this." When Roosevelt intimated that he needed Byrnes off the bench, the South Carolinian jumped at the chance.[58]

To replace Byrnes, Roosevelt named his ninth and last appointment to the Court, Wiley Blount Rutledge, Jr. Although he was born in Kentucky,

---

55. 343 U.S. 250 (1952); see below, pp. 168–69.

56. There is, unfortunately, no good biography of Jackson. Eugene Gerhart, *America's Advocate: Robert H. Jackson* (Indianapolis: Bobbs-Merrill, 1958) is sympathetic and uncritical; Glendon Schubert, *Dispassionate Justice: A Synthesis of the Judicial Opinions of Robert H. Jackson* (Indianapolis: Bobbs-Merrill, 1969) focuses primarily on his written Court record. A highly perceptive analysis of Jackson is in G. Edward White, *The American Judicial Tradition,* expanded ed. (New York: Oxford University Press, 1988), chap. 11.

57. 314 U.S. 160 (1941); see below, pp. 88–89.

58. Byrnes wrote an autobiography, *All in One Lifetime* (New York: Harper, 1958), which devotes only eleven pages to his Court career. The several biographies that have been written about him also ignore his tenure oy the bench and concentrate on his political career. Two biographical sketches that do look at his Court record are by Walter F. Murphy in Friedman and Israel, *Justices of the Supreme Court,* 4:2517–33, and Victoria Saker Woeste in Urofsky, *Supreme Court Justices,* 87; there is also a brief evaluation by William Petit, "Justice Byrnes and the U.S. Supreme Court," 6 *South Carolina Law Quarterly* 423 (1954).

Rutledge made his home in the Midwest. He taught law and served as dean first at Washington University in St. Louis and then at the University of Iowa. While at Washington in the early 1930s, he solved a tense racial situation at a conference of white and black lawyers. Because Missouri enforced segregation, the African American lawyers could not sit at the same tables as the white participants; Rutledge invited all the minority members to join him at the dean's table. A few years later he gained national attention as one of the few law school deans to support Roosevelt's Court-packing plan, a position that won him more than a little notoriety in conservative Iowa.

Rutledge's name figured prominently in 1938 and 1939 when vacancies opened on the Supreme Court, but Roosevelt used those opportunities to name Frankfurter and Douglas. However, the president did name Rutledge to the prestigious Court of Appeals for the District of Columbia, which heard many of the cases arising under the National Labor Relations Act. There Rutledge consistently voted on the prolabor side and also endorsed other New Deal measures. When Byrnes stepped down, Rutledge was a natural choice as his successor.

Unfortunately, Rutledge died of a cerebral hemorrhage at fifty-five, after serving on the Court for only six years. During that time he carved out a consistently liberal position, one that took its cue from the double standard enunciated in Stone's *Carolene Products* footnote. Joining Stone, Black, Douglas, and Murphy, Rutledge provided the fifth vote necessary to begin the expansion of protected freedoms under the First Amendment. Moreover, he was willing to go beyond Black's position regarding the meaning of the Fourteenth Amendment's Due Process Clause. Where Black believed the clause included just the protections enunciated in the Bill of Rights and no more, Rutledge tended to agree with Murphy and Douglas in arguing that it included at least those protections and possibly more. The area in which he had the most impact involved the religion clauses of the First Amendment, and Rutledge played a key role in the several Jehovah's Witnesses cases the Court heard during the early 1940s.

At Rutledge's death in 1949, just a few months after that of Frank Murphy, articles appeared in the law reviews in a quantity one would associate with a justice with far longer service on the bench. Part of this resulted from Rutledge's friendly and open character; he treated his law clerks well and debated with them as democratic equals. He also invited a friend, a Republican who owned a small Jewish delicatessen, to sit with the justices at Harry Truman's inauguration. But as A. E. Keir Nash points out, at least part of it grew out of the belief that had Rutledge lived longer, he would have been a great justice; as two of his former clerks put it, "Death met him . . . after he had completed his apprenticeship but before he had proceeded far in a master's work."[59] Certainly Rutledge and the other Roosevelt appointees strike one as of a higher level of competence and craftsmanship than those appointed by Harry Truman to take their place.

In his letter to Black, Douglas had also predicted that Stone, so universally respected, would have a difficult time as chief, a sentiment that Stone himself recognized. As he told his predecessor, he would have to bear "some burdens which John Marshall did not know."[60] Roosevelt named nine men to the bench, more than any other president except George Washington, and all of them possessed sharp intellects and strong wills. That they agreed on the government's extensive commerce powers actually mattered very little; that battle had been won before Stone became chief justice. Stone presided over one of the most fractious courts in American history, and his "wild horses," as he called them, proved beyond his capacity for control. Even though for the sake of simplicity we call a Court by the name of its chief justice, the Stone Court did not take on the imprint of its chief as had the Taft Court and the Hughes Court. This resulted in part from differences in temperament among the justices, in part from the personalities and abilities of the chiefs, and in no small measure from the nature of the cases coming before the bench. The Court's agenda had begun a massive shift away from the questions of property rights and government regulations that had been so central in the 1920s and 1930s to issues of individual liberties, and the Roosevelt appointees were far from united in their views on these matters. That agenda and the justices' differences form much of the story that follows.

Taft had presided in a time when the entire government—the executive, the legislative, and the judiciary—had been dominated by conservatives devoted to property rights. On the bench Taft could always count on at least five other votes on nearly every issue; during his ten years he found himself in the minority only a handful of times. He could, as he noted, "mass" the Court because on the main issues his voice did in fact represent majority opinion. Although we note the famous dissents of Holmes and Brandeis, later joined by Stone, we tend to forget that in most cases these three men voted *with* the majority.

---

59. A. E. Keir Nash, "Wiley Blount Rutledge," in Melvin I. Urofsky, *Supreme Court Justices* 391, quoting Victor Brudney and Richard F. Wolfson, "Mr. Justice Rutledge: Law Clerks' Reflections," 25 *Indiana Law Journal* 455 (1950). The only full-scale study is Fowler V. Harper, *Justice Rutledge and the Bright Constellation* (Indianapolis: Bobbs-Merrill, 1965), which is unfortunately nonanalytic and almost gushing in praise of its subject. A useful look at one part of the record is Landon G. Rockwell, "Justice Rutledge on Civil Liberties," 59 *Yale Law Journal* 27 (1949).

60. Mason, *Stone*, 574.

During the 1930s, the Court split down the middle over the New Deal, and Charles Evans Hughes not only exercised a strong hand but also utilized his formidable intellectual and political skills. Of all the chiefs in this century, he came closest to dominating the Court through his force of personality. Yet even he found it difficult to keep the new Roosevelt appointees in line, and in the last two years of his tenure he saw his control of the brethren eroding.[61] In part, at least, the reaction to Stone resembled that of unruly schoolboys who were kept in line by a strict master and who now faced a nicer, but less forceful, teacher.

Shortly before his elevation to the center chair, Harlan Stone had been asked by the American Bar Association for an article on his conception of the chief justiceship; as fortune would have it, the piece appeared soon after the nomination and was closely studied to see what ideas the new chief had about his role. Much of it dealt with the business of running the nation's highest tribunal, of getting cases heard and decided promptly and ensuring that all questions received due consideration. He believed the Court should continue the "historic shift of emphasis in constitutional interpretation" begun under Charles Evans Hughes. As for "massing the Court," as Taft had done to present a near-unanimous front on many issues, Stone confessed that he did not believe that either desirable or possible. If unanimity rested upon fully considered judgments, all well and good; but unanimity secured at the cost of "strongly held convictions" would be disastrous. A chief justice should recognize the value of dissenting opinions and thus seek a fine line that would permit dissent without anarchy. He could never force unanimity because he was little more than the "titular leader among equals."[62]

Charles Evans Hughes had kept a tight rein on the brethren and ran the weekly conferences strictly and efficiently, much to William Douglas's delight.[63] One of Douglas's colleagues, however, did not appreciate the chief justice's efficiency. Stone, according to Douglas "first, last and always a professor," wanted to "search out every point and unravel every skein." So Stone started having rump conferences in which he, Frankfurter, Roberts, Douglas, and occasionally Murphy would spend hours debating the fine points of cases before the Court.[64]

When he became chief, Stone immediately abandoned the tight control Hughes had exercised over the conference; even had he wanted to continue, it is unlikely that he had the temperament to do so. Stone liked

---

61. See Philip E. Urofsky, "The Douglas Diary, 1939–1940," 1995 *Journal of Supreme Court History* 78.

62. Stone, "The Chief Justice," 27 *American Bar Association Journal* 407 (July 1941).

63. Douglas, *Court Years*, 215, 222.

64. *Ibid.*

discussion, but unfortunately this gave way to endless debates. Often the justices had to meet at least once during the week for several hours to finish up business left over from lengthy Saturday conferences. Stone, like Frankfurter, could never quite abandon the habits of the classroom, and he tried, although without Frankfurter's nastiness, to instruct his colleagues. He carefully read every draft of every opinion, often marking them up as if they were term papers. In returning an opinion to Stanley Reed, he wrote, "I have gone over with some care your opinion in this case. While in general I agree with the results you reach it seems to me that the opinion requires some revision in the interests of clarity and brevity." He then listed his suggestions on two single-spaced typed pages.[65]

Stone, however, was also quite generous both in his own praise and in passing on praise he had heard from others. He remained ever sensitive to the comments of legal scholars. "It is worth while for us all," he told James Byrnes, "to remember that there are men who are 'in the know,' who observe and appraise carefully what we decide and write." Thus it was in the best interests of the Court when Noel Dowling of Columbia Law had commented favorably on one of Byrnes's opinions.[66]

Perhaps Stone's style might have yielded better results had he not had Felix Frankfurter as a colleague. Much of the blame for the interpersonal bickering on the Stone Court must be attributed to Frankfurter. The chief's willingness to entertain discussion led the former Harvard professor into seemingly endless lectures, and he poisoned the well of collegiality with his frustration at being unable to exercise the leadership over the Court that he thought belonged to him.[67] If at times in this volume it appears that one should refer to a "Frankfurter Court," that is not an inapt expression. Frankfurter's ideas, even when he did not prevail, formed the basis of discussion. He had specific views on almost every subject and could, in most instances, back those up with forceful arguments. Had he been more accommodating to his fellow justices instead of trying to dominate them, he would have had a great impact on the course of our judicial history. In part, as we shall see, the force of Frankfurter's views led Black and Douglas to develop an opposing jurisprudence, and in the clash of

---

65. Stone to Reed, February 23, 1943, Stone Papers, Library of Congress.

66. Stone to Byrnes, December 7, 1941, *ibid.*

67. Even had Frankfurter not been on the bench at the time, Stone would still have had to deal with other strong-willed men like Black, Douglas, and Jackson, none of whom considered Stone an effective administrator. Even the genial Stanley Reed had to admit that Stone "may not have been as good an administrator as Chief Justice Hughes." Reed Memoirs, Columbia Oral History Collection. Jackson also noted that "there was a strong feeling about Stone among some of the New Dealers," which may have contributed to the tensions. Jackson Memoirs, Columbia Oral History Collection.

those ideas, first Harlan Stone and then Fred Vinson could do little more than try to keep the conferences from exploding.

Before he even went onto the bench, Frankfurter believed that he knew just about everything about the Court's inner workings, and he took his seat more with the confidence of an insider than as a junior side judge. Frankfurter believed that his career as an academic gave him a greater understanding of the Court and its processes than even some of its members could have. He noted that "not even as powerful and agile a mind as that of Charles Evans Hughes could, with the pressures which produced adjudication and opinion writing, gain that thorough and disinterested grasp of the problem [of judicial review] which twenty-five years of academic preoccupation with the problem should have left in one."[68] For the previous twenty-five years he had studied the Court intensely, indeed obsessively, watching it, as he once said, "as closely as a mother would a sick child." His student Alexander Bickel later pointed out that Frankfurter had studied not only the written opinions but "the judges and their impact on one another," as well as the wider range of administrative and procedural concerns that affected the Court and its work.[69] Moreover, there is no question that the book Frankfurter wrote with his student James Landis, *The Business of the Supreme Court* (1927), was and remains one of the most perceptive and influential books on the Court.[70]

Just as he had taught a generation of Harvard law students to see the proper role of the Court and the limits of its jurisdiction, so Frankfurter now proposed to instruct his fellows. The teacher-student relationship, however, could not work with men who saw themselves as his equals and were not beholden to him for their positions on the nation's highest Court. Frankfurter took their refusal to follow his lead as a personal affront and unfortunately allowed full play to his considerable talent for invective.

Frankfurter loved to argue and stood ever ready to dispute almost anything for the sake of intellectual sport. At oral argument, he treated lawyers before the bar as students, heckling them as he had done in class. He also carried the professorial air into the Conference, where he tended to treat his colleagues in an abrasive manner, constantly quoting Holmes and Brandeis at them to build up his position. "We would have been inclined to

---

68. Frankfurter to Stanley Reed, December 2, 1941, Frankfurter Papers, Library of Congress.

69. Dennis J. Hutchinson, "Felix Frankfurter and the Business of the Supreme Court, O.T. 1946—O.T. 1961," 1980 *Supreme Court Review* 143; Alexander Bickel, "Applied Policies and the Science of Law: Writings of the Harvard Period," in Wallace Mendelson, ed., *Felix Frankfurter: A Tribute* (New York: Reynal, 1964), 197.

70. See John Paul Jones, "*The Business of the Supreme Court* Revisited," 1995 *Journal of Supreme Court History* 131.

agree with Felix more often in conference," Justice William Brennan said, "if he quoted Holmes less frequently to us."[71] Frankfurter's keen political insights were often lost on his brethren, who refused to be treated as inferiors. Seeking to gain Stanley Reed's vote in one case, Frankfurter took a condescending approach and told Reed: "It is the lot of professors to be often misunderstood by pupils. . . . So let me begin again." In another case he told Reed that he had taught students at Harvard that in order to construe a statute correctly, they should read it not once but thrice; he advised Reed to do the same.[72] If Frankfurter were really interested in a case, Potter Stewart recalled, he "would speak for fifty minutes, no more or less, because that was the length of the lecture at the Harvard Law School."[73]

Frankfurter's rage at the failure of the other justices to follow his lead often turned splenetic. Although he considered Frank Murphy a man of principle, he did not see him as qualified to sit on the high court, and he constantly attacked Murphy's desire to do justice and to write compassion into the law. He compared this results-oriented philosophy to what had happened in Germany and charged Murphy with being "too subservient" to his "idea of doing 'the right thing.' " Frankfurter sometimes addressed Murphy as "Dear God," and in a note regarding one case he said that even a god ought to read the record before deciding. In another note he passed to Murphy during the 1944 term, he listed as among Murphy's clients "reds, whores, crooks, Indians and all other colored people, long shoremen, mortgagors and other debtors, pacifists, traitors, Japs, women, children and most men. . . . Must I become a Negro rapist before you give me due process?"[74] He called Black "violent, vehement, indifferent to the use he was making of cases, utterly disregardful of what they stood for, and quite reckless." Hugo, he told Judge Learned Hand, "is a self-righteous, self-deluded part fanatic, part demagogue, who really disbelieves in law, thinks it essentially manipulative of language."[75] Black and Douglas, in his view, were not men of principle.

Why did Frankfurter so fail to understand what he needed to do? Some have suggested that as a Jew he was the quintessential outsider,[76] but I find

71. Hutchinson, "Frankfurter and Business of the Supreme Court," 205.

72. Fine, *Murphy,* 159. After Frankfurter came on the Court, Chief Justice Hughes continued to call him Professor Frankfurter.

73. Bernard Schwartz with Stephan Leshar, *Inside the Warren Court* (Garden City, N.Y.: Doubleday, 1983), 24.

74. Fine, *Murphy,* 258–59.

75. Frankfurter to Learned Hand, November 5, 1954, Frankfurter Papers, Library of Congress.

76. See, e.g., Robert A. Burt, *Two Jewish Justices: Outcasts in the Promised Land* (Berkeley: University of California Press, 1988).

this argument unpersuasive. There have been other Jews on the Court, and none of them has been so at odds with his or her colleagues as Frankfurter. Brandeis quickly learned how to husband his resources, when to dissent, and how to play the subtle politics of the Court.[77] There is an arrogance about Frankfurter that is absent from the others, and this trait had been present well before he went on the bench.[78] In his career at Harvard, in his reform work, and especially on the Court, he thought that he knew best and, like Woodrow Wilson, tended to personalize differences. It is an unattractive characteristic in any person, but it is disastrous in a small community of nine people.

Frankfurter's inability to manage the Court did not become apparent immediately, and neither did the growing animosity with the man he could reasonably have expected to be his most loyal supporter, William O. Douglas.[79] No one had been happier than Frankfurter at Douglas's appointment, and during the 1938 and 1939 Terms, Douglas often sent warm endorsements of Frankfurter's draft opinions. "Superb!" he scribbled on one draft, and "You have done a magnificent job" on another.[80] Even when they disagreed on cases, as was bound to happen, the early exchanges were polite, even bantering. After a minor disagreement, Frankfurter wrote feelingly that "what is really important is the warm consideration that we weave in our relationship in the daily work on the Court."[81] That "warm consideration" soon deteriorated.

Although Douglas and Frankfurter would soon part company on philosophical grounds, that development did not appear imminent in early 1939. But even before doctrinal differences separated them, Douglas's short temper reacted angrily to Frankfurter's patronizing efforts to show him what road to follow. Douglas, Potter Stewart noted, could be "absolutely devastating" after one of Frankfurter's lectures in conference. On one occasion Douglas announced that "when I came into this conference . . . I agreed with the conclusion Felix has just announced. But he's just talked me out of it." When particularly bored by Frankfurter's disquisitions, Douglas resorted to James McReynold's infuriating habit of leaving the conference table, stretching out on the couch and ignoring the conver-

---

77. See Melvin I. Urofsky, "The Brandeis-Frankfurter Conversations," 1985 *Supreme Court Review* 299 *passim.*

78. See Michael E. Parrish, *Felix Frankfurter and His Times: The Reform Years* (New York: Free Press, 1982).

79. This relationship is more fully explored in Melvin I. Urofsky, "Conflict Among the Brethren: Felix Frankfurter, William O. Douglas, and the Clash of Personalities and Philosophies on the United States Supreme Court," 1988 *Duke Law Journal* 71.

80. H. N. Hirsch, *The Enigma of Felix Frankfurter* (New York: Basic Books, 1981), 145.

81. Frankfurter to Douglas, January 3, 1941, Black Papers, Library of Congress.

sation.[82] Douglas took every opportunity to puncture Frankfurter's pretensions. He claimed that whenever some incompetent attorney was making a mess of oral argument, he would send a note over saying he understood "this chap led your class at Harvard Law School," and "Felix would be ignited, just like a match."[83] Once when Douglas suspected Frankfurter of using a clerk to draft an opinion—a practice Douglas never followed since he wrote so quickly—he said, "Felix, this opinion doesn't have your footprints," and Frankfurter turned livid.[84]

If Douglas provided the temperamental spark that ignited Frankfurter, Hugo Black's constitutional views absolutely infuriated him. It took Black the better part of a decade to reach the position that he articulated in his dissent in *Adamson v. California* in 1946.[85] By the time Black took his seat on the bench, a majority of the Court had agreed that the Due Process Clause of the Fourteenth Amendment "incorporated" at least some of the guarantees in the Bill of Rights and applied them to the states. In *Palko v. Connecticut,*[86] Justice Cardozo had articulated a philosophy of limited or "selective" incorporation, in which only those rights most important to a scheme of "ordered liberty" would be enforced against the states. Black originally accepted the *Palko* doctrine but gradually came to believe that all of the rights enumerated in the first eight amendments should be incorporated; moreover, he believed that the First Amendment, protecting freedom of expression, held a "preferred" position.

Black objected to the Cardozo position, which Frankfurter championed, because it smacked of natural law and relied too much on the justices' sense of fairness and decency. In criminal cases Frankfurter would ask whether the police conduct "shocked the conscience." Black wanted to know "whose conscience" and charged that Frankfurter's approach left too much discretion in the hands of the courts to expand or contract rights belonging to the people. Frankfurter, on the other hand, objected to Black's position as historically as well as logically flawed. Much of the language in the Bill of Rights could not be interpreted in a strictly objective manner. What, for example, constituted an "unreasonable" search? Judges had to interpret these words, and such interpretation was a proper judicial function.[87]

---

82. Schwartz and Leshar, *Inside the Warren Court,* 24; Joseph Lash, *From the Diaries of Felix Frankfurter* (New York: Norton, 1975), 241.

83. Douglas, *Court Years,* 178.

84. Simon, *Independent Journey,* 12.

85. 332 U.S. 46 (1946); see below, pp. 214–19.

86. 302 U.S. 319 (1937).

87. See Frankfurter's concurrence in *Adamson,* 332 U.S. at 59. See also Melvin I. Urofsky, *Frankfurter,* especially chap. 6; and Simon, *The Antagonists, passim.*

Black and Douglas also began developing a new jurisprudence that put First Amendment rights in a "preferred" position, and they argued for an "absolutist" interpretation of the prohibition against the abridgment of speech. The First Amendment, in their view, barred all forms of governmental restriction on speech; any other interpretation, they claimed, could "be used to justify the punishment of advocacy." Frankfurter believed that individual liberty and social order had to be balanced in First Amendment cases, and the yardstick would be the Holmes rule of "clear and present danger." Black, on the other hand, saw that doctrine as "the most dangerous of the tests developed by the justices of the Court."[88]

For Frankfurter, the evaluation and balancing implicit in the clear and present danger test fit perfectly with his conception of the judicial function. By rigorously applying the tools of logical analysis, judges would be able to determine when such a danger existed and thus justified state intervention and when it did not. In this view, explicating First Amendment issues differed not at all from any other constitutional question. In a letter to Stanley Reed, Frankfurter asked, "When onc talks about 'preferred,' or 'preferred position,' one means preference of one thing over another. Please tell me what kind of sense it makes that one provision of the Constitution is to be 'preferred' over another. . . . The correlative of 'preference' is 'subordination,' and I know of no calculus to determine when one provision of the Constitution must yield to another, nor do I know of any reason for doing so."[89]

These debates, between selective and total incorporation and between a preferred and nonpreferred reading of the First Amendment, would split the bench throughout the 1940s and 1950s. It was an important debate and worthy of being discussed in the nation's highest court. Unfortunately, the personalities of the discussants complicated the matter greatly. We can see the disastrous effects wrought by Frankfurter's personalizing issues in the disintegration of the Court during the war years. Frankfurter, of course, does not bear the full blame, and even had he been a saint, the strong personalities and philosophic factionalization of the Court and the failure of Chief Justice Stone to exercise leadership would have led to deep divisions.

An early example of the fractionalization of the Court can be seen in a set of companion cases in the 1941 Term that brought together two unlikely allies, the radical West Coast labor leader Harry Bridges and the ultra-

---

88. Black, *Constitutional Faith*, 50, 52.
89. Frankfurter to Reed, February 7, 1956, Frankfurter Papers, Library of Congress.

conservative *Los Angeles Times.*[90] California state courts had found both in contempt, the newspaper for editorially urging a judge, while sentence was pending, to send two convicted members of a labor "goon squad" to prison, and Bridges for threatening a longshoreman's strike if a state court enforced what he labeled an "outrageous" decision in a labor dispute. The two cases presented a direct confrontation between First Amendment rights of free speech and press and Sixth Amendment protection of a fair trial.

The cases had first come up in the 1940 Term, when Frankfurter apparently had a 6–3 majority to uphold the state courts; but his preparation, which he claimed included reading nearly all the relevant cases in English-speaking jurisdictions, delayed the opinion. Thus he lost McReynolds to retirement and Murphy to Black, Douglas, and Reed, creating a 4–4 tie, so the case was put over for reargument in the fall of 1941. That summer Charles Evans Hughes retired, James Byrnes took McReynolds's place, and Robert H. Jackson filled the seat vacated by Stone's elevation to chief justice. Jackson (later to be a close ally of Frankfurter) joined Black's opinion, and for the first time the Supreme Court reversed a state court finding of fact in a case of contempt by publication, and extended First Amendment freedom of the press to published comments regarding pending court decisions.

Black's opinion, which eventually won over all the bench save Frankfurter, applied the traditional speech test of clear and present danger, and ruled that the "substantive evil" must have a "degree of imminence extremely high" before courts could punish allegedly contemptuous speech or writings.[91] States would have to show that comments posed a real threat to a fair trial, and neither the *Times* editorial nor the Bridges telegram met that test. Judges might find such criticism disrespectful, but "the assumption that respect for the judiciary can be won by shielding judges from published criticism wrongly appraises the character of American public opinion. For it is a prized American privilege to speak one's mind, although not always with perfect good taste, on all public institutions."[92]

The decision infuriated Frankfurter, not only because he had lost the majority by his own pedantic delay, but also because the opposition had invoked Holmes, whom he believed that he—and only he—really understood. Black, who had not yet arrived at his absolutist position on the First Amendment, had in fact applied the same balancing test between state

---

90. *Bridges v. California* and *Times-Mirror Co. v. Superior Court of California,* decided together at 314 U.S. 252 (1941).
91. 314 U.S. at 263.
92. *Ibid.* at 270.

authority and individual liberty that Frankfurter had earlier endorsed. Frankfurter recognized that Black gave far more weight to the First Amendment and thus far less deference to governmental authority; this could in time lead courts to ignore the legislature if liberal judges determined to expand civil liberties as the old conservatives had expanded property rights. In his dissent he charged the majority with mischievous use of the clear and present danger test, which had deprived the state of the proper "means of securing to its citizens justice according to law."[93]

There is a fascinating letter in the Frankfurter files that Frankfurter wrote to an old friend, the great Harvard historian Samuel Eliot Morison, who had questioned the extent to which the First Amendment protected speech. Frankfurter argued that the Court should have ignored the question of whether the *Los Angeles Times* editorial had been contemptuous and asked only whether the Constitution prohibited California from punishing that speech.[94]

> Whether the Commonwealth of Massachusetts, through its appropriate organ, should have put Sedgwick and me in durance vile for The Atlantic article on the Sacco-Vanzetti case is one thing; whether Massachusetts would have been forbidden to do so by the Constitution of the United States quite another.
>
> The main function of law is drawing lines. Should an American state really be denied those standards and practices of judicial administration which are the commonplaces of an England which is more alert to civil liberty even during time of war than we are as a matter of national habit in times of peace?

That Frankfurter showed consistency is admirable; that he showed absolutely no sensitivity to the need to protect unpopular speech is deplorable. One wonders whether he and so many others would have labored so hard to save Sacco and Vanzetti if they could have been sent to jail for suggesting that a judge had been biased.

The situation deteriorated further in the October 1942 Term as philosophical differences within the Court widened. Stone's disinclination to keep a tight rein on the Saturday conference often allowed the discussions to degenerate into lengthy and inconclusive debates. Frankfurter, whose fifty-minute lectures contributed greatly to the problem, began complain-

---

93. *Ibid.* at 279.
94. Frankfurter to Samuel Eliot Morison, January 6, 1942 (misdated 1941), Frankfurter Papers, Harvard Law School Library.

ing about the "easy-going, almost heedless way in which views on Constitutional issues touching the whole future direction of this country were
floated" at the conferences, and he circulated memoranda urging the
brethren to limit the meetings to no more than four hours.[95] Douglas complained that "we have [conferences] all the time these days and they seem
eternally long—and often dull."[96]

The divisiveness in the conference could be seen in the rising rate of
nonunanimous opinions. In the 1941 Term nonunanimous opinions had
constituted 36 percent of the total, the highest in Court history to that
time, but the number jumped to 44 percent in the 1942 Term.[97] "I have
had much difficulty herding my collection of fleas," the chief justice confided to a friend, and he complained that he himself had had to write an
excessive number of opinions since the brethren were "so busy disagreeing
with each other."[98]

By now even outsiders could see the split in the Court. The *Wall Street
Journal* remarked that the justices tended "to fall into clamorous argument
even on the rare occasions when they agreed on the end result."[99] Within
the Court, Frankfurter's temper grew shorter and his invective more vitri-
olic. He began to talk about "enemies" on the bench, especially Douglas,
and once yelled at his clerk, "Don't you get the idea that this is a *war* we
are fighting?"[100] He referred derisively to Black, Douglas, and Murphy as
"the Axis."

Whatever Frankfurter's private feelings, public discourse within the
Court remained fairly civil. One can, in fact, question whether his colleagues even recognized the extent of his antipathy toward them at this
time. Frankfurter's diaries, however, show that often after a seemingly calm
discussion of a case, he returned to his chamber to vent his spleen in writing. The *Johnson* case is a good example.[101]

---

95. Frankfurter to Stone, October 21, 1942, and Frankfurter to Brethren, October 22,
1942, Stone Papers, Library of Congress. A few months later Frankfurter noted in his
diary: "We were . . . in Conference for almost eight hours, a perfectly indefensible way of
deliberating on the kind of stiff issues with which we are concerned (Lash, *Diaries*, 217,
entry for March 15, 1943). Frankfurter later claimed that Stone's personal defects greatly
exacerbated the problems. "He was fundamentally a petty character, self-aggrandizing and
ungenerous. . . . Hardly anybody was any good, hardly any lawyer was any good, hardly any
argument was adequate, hardly anybody ever saw the real point of a case, etc., etc." Frankfurter to T. R. Powell, December 21, 1953, Powell Papers, Harvard Law School Library.
96. Douglas to Fred Rodell, October 25, 1943, quoted in Fine, *Murphy*, 243.
97. C. Herman Pritchett, *The Roosevelt Court: A Study in Judicial Values and Politics* (New
York: Macmillan, 1948), 39–41.
98. Stone to Sterling Carr, June 13, 1943, Stone Papers, Library of Congress.
99. November 25, 1941.
100. Murphy, *Brandeis/Frankfurter Connection*, 266–67.
101. *Johnson v. United States*, 318 U.S. 189 (1943).

Enoch "Nucky" Johnson, a Republican party chieftain, had been convicted of tax evasion for concealing funds received from gambling rakeoffs and had appealed his sentence. On February 2, 1943, Douglas dropped in to Frankfurter's chambers to discuss the case, and said that after studying the record and checking authorities, he could dismiss all of the claims for error save one, and he thought that one "a very close and fine point."[102] (The "fine point" involved the presiding judge's allowing Johnson to claim the privilege of self-incrimination in order not to testify about receipt of alleged gambling income but then allowing the jury to consider the refusal to testify as bearing upon his overall credibility as a witness.) Frankfurter disagreed, explained why, and said that, in any event, "if error it was, it was not an error involving deprivation of a Constitutional right, it was an error pertaining to the ruling on evidence."[103]

Frankfurter continued to speak "stiffly on the function of appellate review in criminal cases" and lectured Douglas on the role of the Court. For more than fifty years, as far as Frankfurter knew, no criminal conviction had been reversed by the Court for so minor an error. Douglas, according to the diary entry, "feebly" said there might be such cases, although he could not remember them, but in any event it boiled down to a fine point. Frankfurter replied that "a conviction has no business to be upset on a point so fine . . . [and] . . . one who has as strong views as I have against any kind of unfairness in the conduct of criminal cases in the federal courts can't even see the point." The talk had been carried on "in the best of temper," but when the two men met the next day, Frankfurter noted in exasperation, Douglas said that the conversation had been "very valuable because it showed that the case got down to a very fine point."[104]

The situation got even stickier and Frankfurter even angrier when Douglas involved Owen Roberts, normally a strong supporter of Frankfurter. In discussing the "fine point" with Roberts, Douglas asked him if he knew how Black felt about it, and Roberts dutifully went off to see Black. The Alabaman explained why he agreed with Douglas and then almost offhandedly raised a matter of fairness. Earlier in the year Douglas had written the Court's opinion reversing a contempt conviction of Democratic

---

102. Lash, *Diaries,* 177, entry for February 2, 1943.

103. Earlier in the term, however, Frankfurter had not considered the case so simple. He had, he told the chief justice, meant to read the entire record over the summer since "from such whiffs of it as I had when it was first here, it disturbed me. . . . Additional glimpses . . . have not erased my doubts." He questioned whether the conviction could be sustained, but he was prepared to study the entire case "as though I were writing an article for a law review." Frankfurter to Stone, October 21, 1942, Stone Papers, Library of Congress.

104. Lash, *Diaries,* 178.

boss Thomas J. Pendergast,[105] and Black had been glad when Chief Justice Stone had assigned the *Johnson* opinion to the same New Deal justice, since it would show impartiality. But if the Johnson conviction were upheld, Black explained, it would look as if Douglas had let a Democratic boss out of jail and kept a Republican one in, and this would not be fair to Douglas. Roberts asked Black to speak to Stone about this, but Black declined, saying the chief justice usually knew about such considerations when making assignments. So Roberts offered to speak to Frankfurter.

An astounded Frankfurter could not bring himself to "shock" the naive Roberts by telling him how "outraged I was—the very notion of thinking about men after they were on this Court in terms of New Deal or Old Deal; the shocking irrelevance of whether any Justice would or would not be criticized for doing his duty, reaching the conclusion in a case that conscience required." Over the next few days Frankfurter continued to fume and told the story to Reed and Jackson, both of whom, he claimed, expressed shock at Roberts's naïveté and Douglas's duplicity.[106] Shortly afterward, Frankfurter wrote bitterly about the Axis and how Black, Douglas, and Murphy were speaking about what "we" would do.[107]

The divisions in the Court widened perceptibly in the October 1943 Term, when, for the first time in history, a majority of the Court's decisions—58 percent—came down with divided opinions.[108] "The justices," as Sidney Fine noted, "not only continued to disagree but to be disagreeable on occasion in doing so."[109] Court watchers had been aware of the growing divisiveness; now even those who did not follow the Court closely could hardly fail to see that internal strife burdened the nation's highest tribunal. On January 3, 1944, the Court handed down decisions in fourteen cases, but the justices agreed unanimously only in three. The other eleven elicited twenty-eight full majority or dissenting opinions and four shorter notations of partial disagreement or concurrence. In one case Douglas wrote the majority opinion; Roberts and Reed concurred; Jackson and Frankfurter dissented in separate opinions; and Black, joined by Murphy, en-

---

105. *Pendergast v. United States*, 317 U.S. 412 (1943).

106. Lash, *Diaries*, 177–86, entries for February 2–8, 1943. In the end, the Court, speaking through Douglas, affirmed the conviction; Frankfurter filed a concurrence, 318 U.S. at 202.

107. Lash, *Diaries*, at 197–98, entry for February 26, 1943. In his oral history memoirs, Jackson noted that "there came to be a bloc of Black, Douglas, Murphy, and later, Rutledge. . . . They had a sort of understanding." Jackson Memoirs, Columbia Oral History Collection.

108. Pritchett, *Roosevelt Court*, 42.

109. Fine, *Murphy*, 244.

tered a concurrence that was in effect a "dissent from the dissent," in which he lambasted Jackson and Frankfurter.[110]

As the justices presented their opinions, Black and Murphy admonished Frankfurter that "for judges to rest their interpretation of statutes on nothing but their own conceptions of 'morals' and 'ethics' is, to say the least, dangerous business."[111] In another case they commented on "what is patently a wholly gratuitous assertion as to constitutional law in the dissent of Mr. Justice Frankfurter."[112] Then Justice Jackson weighed in with a claim that the minority judges would apparently enforce the Full Faith and Credit Clause "only if the outcome pleases" them.[113] Murphy charged the majority with "rewriting" a criminal statute;[114] Jackson labeled as "reckless" a decision to bring insurance within the reach of the Sherman Antitrust Act;[115] while Roberts fumed about the Court's tendency to override precedent and assume "that knowledge and wisdom reside in us which was denied to our predecessors."[116]

This chaotic decision day brought forth a chorus of protest. Charles C. Burlingham, a pillar of the New York bar, lashed out at the "unhappy state of the Court" in a letter to the *New York Herald-Tribune*. While one could not expect total agreement on all issues, he wrote, "there seems to be a growing tendency to disagree, and if this is not checked the effect on the public will be unfortunate, making for doubt and uncertainty and a lack of respect and a loss of confidence in the Court." The multitude of opinions left the law uncertain, and in particular he condemned the "turnabout" of Douglas and others in the flag salute cases. "One would think that in cases involving the Bill of Rights a judge would know his own mind in 1940 as well as in 1943." Burlingham also chastised the justices for airing their personal differences, which "should be confined within the council chamber and not proclaimed from the bench." On the same page the newspaper editorially reminded the Court of its obligation "to provide a coherent doctrine" and, in the interests of the people who must know the law to abide by it, prayed the justices would stop their fighting and resume their work in a clear manner.[117]

---

110. *Mercoid Corp. v. Mid-Continent Investment Co.*, 320 U.S. 661 (1944).

111. *Ibid.* at 674.

112. *Federal Power Commission v. Hope Natural Gas Co.*, 320 U.S. 591, 619–20 (1944).

113. *Magnolia Petroleum Co. v. Hunt*, 320 U.S. 430, 477 (1943).

114. *United States v. Gaskin*, 320 U.S. 527, 530 (1944).

115. *United States v. South-Eastern Underwriters Association*, 322 U.S. 533 (1944).

116. *Smith v. Allwright*, 321 U.S. 649, 666 (1944) (Roberts dissenting).

117. *New York. Herald Tribune*, January 10, 1944. For the flag salute cases, see below, pp. 106–12. Thomas Reed Powell, then a friend of William O. Douglas as well as Frankfurter, gently chided him that "it is a very nerve-racking enterprise to run a class [on constitutional law] Monday afternoon . . . without knowing whether what I was saying is still so." Powell to Douglas, May 23, 1944, Powell Papers, Harvard Law School Library.

One might as well have tried to whistle up the wind. Frankfurter continued to seethe over real or imaginary slights and to gripe endlessly about them. In the *Mercoid* patent case,[118] he complained to the chief justice about Douglas's "perfectly gratuitous treatment" of contributory negligence in patent matters. Douglas, he claimed, treated patentees as "such enemies of the Republic that all sorts of hallowed principles must be twisted out of shape to block their nefarious iniquities." He conceded that for the law to be a living force in society it had to adapt to the times, "but there is such a thing as throwing the baby out with the bath. . . . Past decisions ought not be needlessly overruled." With obvious reference to Black and Douglas, he asked Stone if he were wrong "in finding at present a too eager tendency not merely to bring the law in conformity to our present needs but gloatingly to show up the unwisdom, if not injustice of our predecessors?"[119]

Yet shortly after this, Stone, joined by Douglas and Black, did exactly the same thing. In an otherwise obscure admiralty case,[120] Stone employed what his biographer called "his favorite technique of trimming authority to meet his own needs."[121] Roberts dissented, joined by Frankfurter, and with the latter's encouragement entered a dissent extraordinarily bitter not only in light of his own previous writing but in terms of decisional decorum up to that time. Roberts also conceded the necessity for change, but he protested against abandoning precedent in a manner that undermined the authority of law. Taking aim directly against Black, Douglas, and Murphy, Roberts charged: "The tendency to disregard precedents . . . has become so strong in this court of late as, in my view, to shake confidence in the consistency of decision and leave the courts below on an uncharted sea of doubt and difficulty without any confidence that what was said yesterday will hold good tomorrow."[122] Whether or not one agreed with the rulings in these cases, the multiplicity of opinions did introduce an element of instability.[123] "Those bozos," complained the eminent circuit court judge Learned Hand, referring to the high court, "don't seem to comprehend the very basic characteristic of the job, which is to keep some kind of coherence and simplicity in the body of rules which must be applied by a vastly

---

118. *Mercoid Corp. v. Mid-Continental Investment Co.*, 320 U.S. 661 (1944).

119. Frankfurter to Stone, December 28, 1943, Stone Papers, Library of Congress.

120. *Mahnich v. Southern Steamship Co.*, 321 U.S. 96 (1944).

121. Mason, *Stone*, 610.

122. 321 U.S. at 113. Roberts also charged that the consequence of the majority strategy would be that "the administration of justice will fall into disrepute."

123. In just four terms, the percentage of nonunanimous opinions went from 28 to 58, and the number of dissenting opinions rose from 117 to 194 (Pritchett, "Dissent on the Supreme Court, 1943–44," 39 *American Political Science Review* 42, 43 [1945]).

complicated society."[124] Hand, who shared much of Frankfurter's frustration and anger at the Axis, protested that "they are sowing the wind, those reforming colleagues of yours. As soon as they convince the people that they can do what they want, the people will demand of them that they do what the people want. I wonder whether in times of bland reaction—[and] they are coming—Hillbilly Hugo, Good Old Bill and Jesus lover of my Soul [Murphy] will like that."[125]

The 1944 Term saw more of the same, with three out of every five decisions eliciting multiple opinions. Frankfurter complained to Rutledge near the end of the term about "an increasing tendency on the part of members of the Court to behave like little schoolboys and throw spitballs at one another."[126] It is unclear whether he included himself in that description. When the Southern Conference for Human Welfare gave Hugo Black its Jefferson Award in April 1945, Douglas, Murphy, Rutledge, and Reed attended the ceremony; Frankfurter, Roberts, Jackson, and the chief justice did not—a clear example of the demarcation within the Court.

The most shameful dispute came when Owen J. Roberts, weary of the continuous infighting on the bench, resigned at the end of the 1944 Term. Although he and Frankfurter disagreed on certain issues of law, they had found themselves united in their dislike of Douglas and Black and what they viewed as the disastrous tendency of the Axis to overthrow the law.[127] In his last full term, Roberts dissented fifty-three times, or in almost one-third of the nonunanimous cases.

Following Court custom, Chief Justice Stone drafted a farewell letter that, in light of the Court's rancorous division, sounded a relatively neutral tone. Stone sent the letter to the senior justice, now Black, asking him to sign it and pass it on to the next most senior member of the Court. But Black objected to two phrases, one of which expressed the regret that the remaining brethren supposedly felt at Roberts's departure, and the other of which read, "You have made fidelity to principle your guide to decision." Black wanted to delete both phrases. Stone reluctantly agreed to the deletions, but Frankfurter did not, and he protested. In the end, only Douglas agreed fully with Black's draft.[128] Murphy, Reed, and Rutledge

---

124. Hand to Frankfurter, March 11, 1942, Frankfurter Papers, Library of Congress.

125. Hand to Frankfurter, February 6, 1944, *ibid.*

126. Fine, *Murphy*, 245.

127. Lash, *Diaries*, 227, 229, entries for April 20 and 23, 1943.

128. A draft of the original letter, dated August 20, 1945, shows Black's deletions; Douglas's comments, dated September 5, 1945, show that the changes were "wholly agreeable" to him. This as well as other correspondence among the justices on this subject is in the Black Papers, Library of Congress.

were willing to sign either version in order to secure agreement, while
Frankfurter and Jackson took an uncompromising stand and insisted on
retaining the sentence on "fidelity to principle."[129] Neither side would
budge, and as Alpheus Mason noted, "Emily Post would have disposed of
the Justices' problem in a paragraph, . . . but etiquette was not the real
issue." This "Lilliputian campaign, fought in dead earnest," mirrored the
pettiness and personal animosities that marred the Court under Stone's
stewardship.[130]

---

129. Frankfurter to Brethren, August 30, 1945, Rutledge Papers, Library of Congress. As
usual, Frankfurter had to quote authority: "I *know* that that was Justice Brandeis' view of
Roberts, whose character he held in the highest esteem."
130. Mason, *Stone,* 768.

# 2

# THE COURT AT WAR

The day after Pearl Harbor, Felix Frankfurter told his law clerk, Philip Elman, "Everything has changed, and I am going to war."[1] It was a sentiment the other justices shared; some wanted to resign from the Court in order to provide greater service to their country. Robert Jackson later recalled that while there were "occasional cases of importance involving the war power," such cases were "peaks of interest in a rather dreary sea of briefs and arguments, many of which seemed to have little relationship to the realities of what was going on about us."[2] In the end, however, only James Byrnes stepped down to assume a key role in the Roosevelt administration. William O. Douglas, Frank Murphy, and Robert Jackson also yearned to go back to the executive branch, but Roosevelt, although sorely tempted at times to take them, had gone through too much effort to get them on the Court.[3] Moreover, if any wartime measures actually came before the judiciary, the president wanted to have men in sympathy with his programs hearing those cases.

This did not, of course, mean that the Court and the justices played no role in wartime affairs. The Court as a whole had to deal with occasional war-related requests from the administration, such as a change in the rules of admiralty to allow admiralty courts to impound documents that might be of aid to the enemy and to conduct hearings in secret.[4] Even before Pearl Harbor, Douglas, Murphy, Jackson, and Frankfurter helped out in many ways, from drafting speeches and legislation to suggesting people for key roles. When the president had to replace the isolationist Harry Woodring as secretary of war in 1940, it was Frankfurter who arranged matters to bring Henry L. Stimson back to the War Department. The justice

---

1. James F. Simon, *The Antagonists: Hugo Black, Felix Frankfurter and Civil Liberties in Modern America* (New York: Simon & Schuster, 1989), 133.

2. Jackson Memoirs, Columbia Oral History Collection.

3. Roosevelt evidently asked Douglas to head what would become the War Production Board but then changed his mind. Douglas to Hugo Black, September 8, 1941, Black Papers, Library of Congress.

4. Charles Fahy (the Solicitor General) to Stone, April 30, 1942; Stone, Memorandum to Court, May 20, 1942; Jackson, comments on proposed rule, May 20, 1942. All in Jackson Papers, Library of Congress.

also helped draft the Lend-Lease Act and made key recommendations on industrial policy.[5]

Frank Murphy especially wanted to leave the bench, and in the year after he took his seat he made it quite clear to Roosevelt that he would gladly resign to take up a more active wartime role. Frankfurter wanted Murphy off the Court and, evidently with Roosevelt's blessing, offered Murphy other positions including the ambassadorship to Mexico. Murphy would not bite; he said he would resign only for the War Department. But Henry Stimson had that position, and the president was not about to get rid of the highly respected Republican. Roosevelt did offer Murphy his old post as governor general of the Philippines, with the hint that he would eventually be Stimson's successor, but the justice showed no interest.[6] When the president wanted to extend aid to the Soviet Union and feared that American Catholics would react negatively, the administration asked the Catholic Murphy if he would present the case for aid at the annual convention of the Knights of Columbus. Murphy did so, and according to historian George Herring, he made "the most effective presentation" of the case to that time.[7]

Following Pearl Harbor, Murphy grew even more restless and tried unsuccessfully to secure a commission in the army. But legislation prohibited him from going on active status unless he resigned from the Court. Army Chief of Staff George C. Marshall, probably to get Murphy off his back, suggested that the justice be commissioned a lieutenant colonel in the infantry and placed on duty in an inactive status during Court recess. Moreover, Marshall advised Murphy he could begin his training by attending officers' training school at Fort Benning, Georgia. Two days after Court recessed on June 8, 1942, Frank Murphy accepted a commission as a lieutenant colonel.

Popular approval greeted Murphy's histrionic gesture, but Chief Justice Stone was furious. When Congressman Emanuel Celler of New York wrote to Stone questioning whether Murphy could be both a justice and a member of the armed forces, the chief had to admit that Murphy had not discussed the matter with him, and in fact his first knowledge of what Murphy had done came to him in the newspapers.[8]

---

5. Melvin I. Urofsky, *Felix Frankfurter: Judicial Restraint and Individual Liberties* (Boston: Twayne, 1991), 65–67.

6. Sidney Fine, *Frank Murphy: The Washington Years* (Ann Arbor: University of Michigan Press, 1984), 206–12.

7. George C. Herring, Jr., *Aid to Russia, 1941–1946* (New York: Columbia University Press, 1973), 7.

8. Celler to Stone, August 13, 1942; Stone to Celler, August 15, 1942. Jackson Papers, Library of Congress.

Stone could not very well stop his wild horses from yearning for a more active role; after all, with a nation at war and patriotism running so high, he could hardly tell them they were wrong. But he firmly believed that the justices had a job to do on the bench, and that the doctrine of separation of powers ought to be as rigidly enforced in wartime as in peace. He fumed quietly when Owen Roberts accepted a presidential commission to head the investigation into what had gone wrong at Pearl Harbor,[9] but when Roosevelt asked Stone himself to head an investigation of rubber supply problems, the chief justice firmly declined.[10] When Congress proposed a War Ballot Commission to be chaired by the chief justice, Stone objected that it was an improper role for a justice to administer the law, an executive function; in deference to his wishes, Congress altered the statute to lodge the responsibility elsewhere.[11] The wisdom of Stone's decision would become clearer a few years later when Robert Jackson accepted Harry Truman's invitation to be chief American prosecutor at the Nuremberg war crimes trial, and a generation after that many people believed Earl Warren and the Court would have been better off if Warren had not headed the commission investigating John F. Kennedy's assassination.

Franklin D. Roosevelt assumed a great deal of authority during the war and took the broadest possible interpretation of the president's role as commander in chief; in addition, Congress granted him even further statutory powers.[12] Not everyone welcomed this expansion of executive government, especially when such agencies as the Office of Price Administration (OPA) began to restrict property rights. As a result, the Court heard a number of challenges to wartime policies regulating the economy, but considering the sea change that had taken place after 1937, it is not surprising that the wartime Court validated every federal economic measure brought

---

9. The so-called Roberts Commission was the first of eight groups to investigate what had happened at Pearl Harbor. It met from December 18, 1941 to January 23, 1942 and, among other things, found no evidence of espionage either in Hawaii or on the American West Coast. Compared to Robert Jackson's later role in the War Crimes trials of 1945 and 1946, which involved a lengthy absence from the Court, most of the Roberts Commission's work took place while the Court was in recess.

10. Roosevelt to Stone, July 17, 1942; Stone to Roosevelt, July 20, 1942; Stone to John Bassett Moore, December 31, 1942. Stone Papers, Library of Congress.

11. Alpheus T. Mason, *Harlan Fiske Stone: Pillar of the Law* (New York: Viking, 1956), 713–14. Stone also managed, a few years later, to prevent having the chief justice named a member of the Atomic Energy Commission.

12. Paul L. Murphy, *The Constitution in Crisis Times, 1918–1969* (New York: Harper & Row, 1972), 220–22.

before it, including price controls,[13] rent controls,[14] and restrictions on profiteering.[15] As the Court noted in *Bowles v. Willingham,* "A nation which can demand the lives of its men and women in the waging of a war is under no constitutional necessity of providing a system of price controls on the domestic front which will assure each landlord a 'fair return' on his property."[16] Justices who had sustained strong governmental powers over the economy in peacetime could hardly have been expected to rein in strong governmental policies in wartime.

The key case involving price controls did not reach the high court until 1944, over two years after Congress had enacted the 1941 Emergency Price Control Act establishing an Office of Price Administration with powers to fix maximum prices and rents. In some ways, the Emergency Price Control Act bore a striking resemblance to the grant of legislative authority that an earlier Court had struck down in *Schechter v. United States* (1935),[17] when the justices had unanimously declared the National Industrial Recovery Act unconstitutional on grounds that Congress had exceeded both its Commerce Clause powers and its authority in delegating power to the executive without clear guidelines. But by 1944 only two of the justices from the *Schechter* Court, Stone and Roberts, still remained, and Roberts stood alone in objecting to the price controls measure, lamenting that *Schechter* "is now overruled."[18]

Stone, however, spoke for the rest of the Court in upholding the act and declared that, unlike what had happened in *Schechter,* here Congress had "laid down standards to guide the administrative determination of both the occasions for the exercise of the price-fixing power, and the particular prices to be established." This was only partially true. While the act gave the OPA administrator some guidelines, such as using the base period of October 1 to 15, 1941, as a standard by which to measure reasonableness in prices, in general it left to executive discretion the implementation of price controls and the criteria to be used to achieve "generally fair and equitable" prices. But the two cases came to the Court in different eras.

---

13. *Yakus v. United States,* 321 U.S. 414 (1944); *Steuart and Co. v. Bowles,* 322 U.S. 398 (1944). See Note, "The Constitutionality of the Emergency Price Control Act (O.P.A.)," 18 *Temple University Law Quarterly* 518 (1944); and Symposium, "Some Aspects of O.P.A. in the Courts," 12 *George Washington Law Review* 414 (1944).

14. *Bowles v. Willingham,* 321 U.S. 503 (1944).

15. *Lichter v. United States,* 334 U.S. 742 (1948).

16. 321 U.S. at 518. See also Robert A. Sprecher, "Price Control in the Courts," 44 *Columbia Law Review* 34 (1944).

17. 295 U.S. 495 (1935).

18. *Yakus v. United States,* 321 U.S. at 451–52 (Roberts dissenting). Roberts's dissent, however, dealt solely with the issue of delegation; he joined the majority in the second issue in the case, jurisdiction, which is discussed below.

*Schechter* had been decided when a majority of the justices opposed the philosophy behind the New Deal's recovery program; *Yakus* found a far more hospitable bench willing, indeed at times eager, to defer to executive and legislative judgment.

The latter case, however, also involved a thornier issue—the limits of judicial review. In the Emergency Price Control Act, Congress had provided that appeals from price regulations could be filed with the OPA administrator and, if denied there, could be taken to an Emergency Court of Appeals. But no court would have "jurisdiction or power to consider the validity of such regulation, order, or price schedule, or to stay, restrain, enjoin or set aside" any parts of the act. The first challenge to this provision had come in a suit in federal district court, where the plaintiffs had claimed that the OPA-established maximum wholesale beef prices were so low as to deprive them of their property without due process of law. The district court had dismissed the case on the grounds that it lacked jurisdiction, and the Supreme Court had then unanimously affirmed the ruling.[19] Chief Justice Stone noted that Article III permitted but did not require Congress to create lower federal courts and that in doing so it could choose to withhold granting equity jurisdiction to all courts. Moreover, the Emergency Court of Appeals, whose members were drawn from the regular federal courts, had jurisdiction to enjoin unconstitutional regulations.

In *Yakus* there had been a criminal prosecution for violating the OPA regulations, and two members of the Court, Rutledge and Murphy, argued that by denying courts authority to review the constitutionality of the regulations, Congress was in effect requiring the courts themselves to act unconstitutionally. The dissenters could not accept the majority's argument, as expressed by the chief justice, that Congress had the power to limit appeals as to both timeliness and venue; while the provisions may have been harsh, they did not exceed congressional power, and under the new dispensation the Court would defer to legislative judgment, especially in wartime.[20]

That the Court would defer to the political branches regarding wartime economic policies should hardly be surprising. Civil liberties, however, raised different problems. The members of the wartime Court all remembered quite vividly the excesses of the Wilson administration during

---

19. *Lockerty v. Phillips*, 319 U.S. 182 (1943); in this case the plaintiffs had not violated the regulations by selling meat above the set price but were attempting to challenge the validity of the regulation itself.

20. *Yakus v. United States*, 321 U.S. at 444. Shortly after the decision, Congress determined that perhaps the time and venue restrictions were too severe and repealed them in the Stabilization Extension Act of 1944.

World War I; and some, such as Frank Murphy and Robert Jackson, had, in their terms as attorney general, taken steps to make sure that such excesses would not be repeated should the United States enter this conflict.[21] Nonetheless, the justices still recognized the government's need to protect itself.

Under this rationale, the Justice Department sought to revoke the citizenship of naturalized citizens of German and Italian origin who either displayed disloyal behavior or had secured their citizenship illegally or under false pretenses. Within a year after America's entry into the war, the government had initiated over two thousand investigations and had secured the denaturalization of forty-two people. The case testing this campaign, however, involved not a Nazi or fascist sympathizer but a communist, William Schneiderman.

Born in Russia in 1905, Schneiderman had come with his parents to the United States in 1908; he applied for citizenship in 1927 and by then had already joined several communist groups. In 1932 he ran for governor of Minnesota as the Communist Party candidate. In 1939 the government moved to strip Schneiderman of his citizenship on the grounds that his communist activities in the five years prior to the naturalization process showed that had not been truly "attached" to the principles of the United States Constitution. Schneiderman, in turn, argued that he did not believe in using force or violence and that, in fact, he had been a good citizen; he had never been arrested and had used his rights as a citizen to advocate change and greater social justice.

Schneiderman's case came before the Court in early 1942, by which time the United States had entered the war and had publicly acknowledged the Soviet Union as an ally. Wendell Willkie, the Republican candidate for president in 1940, represented Schneiderman and eloquently pleaded with the Court not to establish a legal rule that a person could be punished for alleged adherence to abstract principles. The government, recognizing how embarrassing a victory might be, privately suggested to Chief Justice Stone that the Court delay its decision. Although Stone understood the Justice Department's quandary, he believed more important issues were at stake, namely that the political branches should not interfere in the business of the Court. Moreover, Stone believed that people like Schneiderman, who did not support American institutions, ought not to avail themselves of American citizenship. At the conference on December 5, 1942, Stone led off discussion of the case with a forceful statement that the government ought to have the power to rid the nation of agitators who not

---

21. Murphy, *Constitution in Crisis Times*, 176–78; Frank Murphy's tenure as attorney general is detailed in Fine, *Murphy*, chaps. 1–7.

only did not believe in the Constitution but worked actively to overthrow the government.[22]

Given his idolization of Holmes and Brandeis, Frankfurter might have been expected to speak in defense of Schneiderman, as Holmes had done so eloquently in defense of Rosika Schwimmer, another immigrant who held unpopular views. Schwimmer, a Quaker, had been denied citizenship because in the application form she had resolutely responded no to the question "If Necessary, are you willing to take up arms in defense of this country?" even though women normally were excused from answering that item. "If there is any principle of the Constitution that more imperatively calls for attachment than any other," Holmes had written in a dissent joined by Brandeis, "it is the principle of free thought—not free thought for those who agree with us but freedom for the thought we hate."[23]

But Frankfurter supported Stone's view, and he explained his position in conference at length and with great emotion. This case, he began, "arouses in me feelings that could not be entertained by anyone else around this table. It is well-known that a convert is more zealous than one born to the faith. None of you has had the experience that I have had with reference to American citizenship." He had been in college when his father received his naturalization papers, "and I can assure you that for months preceding, it was a matter of moment in our family life." For Frankfurter, "American citizenship implies entering upon a fellowship which binds people together by devotion to certain feelings and ideas and ideals summarized as a requirement that they be attached to the principles of the Constitution." While mere membership in the Communist Party did not constitute grounds for either denying or revoking citizenship, Frankfurter believed that Schneiderman's actions went far beyond paying dues. Schneiderman had committed himself to the "holy cause," and "no man can serve two masters when two masters represent not only different, but in this case, mutually exclusive ideas."[24] Frankfurter voted to affirm the conviction, but only he, Roberts, and Stone did so.[25]

After several delays, the Court finally handed down its decision in the spring of 1943. Frank Murphy's opinion for the majority conceded that naturalization constituted a privilege granted by Congress, but once that

22. "Summary of discussion at Conference on Saturday, December 5, 1942," Frankfurter Papers, Harvard Law School Library.

23. *United States v. Schwimmer*, 279 U.S. 644, 653, 654–55 (1929) (Holmes dissenting).

24. "Summary of discussion . . . ," Frankfurter Papers, Harvard Law School Library.

25. Douglas evidently believed at first that Schneiderman's petition ought to be dismissed on the grounds that there was sufficient evidence he had sworn allegiance falsely at the time of naturalization. During the conference, however, he changed his mind. Conference notes re: *Schneiderman* [n.d.], Douglas Papers, Library of Congress.

privilege had been granted, a person became a citizen and enjoyed all the rights guaranteed by the Constitution, including freedom of thought and expression. Membership in the Communist Party had not been illegal at the time Schneiderman had taken out his papers, and the government had not proven current membership "absolutely incompatible" with loyalty to the Constitution.[26]

Frankfurter gave Murphy a hard time during the circulations of the majority opinion. One day he suggested that Murphy might want to add to his opinion the statement that "Uncle Joe Stalin was at least a spiritual co-author with Jefferson of the Virginia Statute for Religious Freedom." A few days later Frankfurter sent a note, signed "F. F. Knaebel," offering Murphy the following as a headnote for the decision: "The American Constitution ain't got no principles. The Communist Party don't stand for nuthin'. The Soopreme Court don't mean nuthin,' and ter Hell with the U.S.A. so long as a guy is attached to the principles of the U.S.S.R." Murphy wrote back in the same vein, "My dear F. F.: Many thanks for your original and revised headnotes in the *Schneiderman* case. Not only do they reveal long and arduous preparation, but best of all, they are done with commendable English understatement and characteristic New England reserve."[27]

Stone, joined by Frankfurter and Roberts, entered a vigorous dissent that seemed strange coming from the man who had stood alone in the first flag salute case. "My brethren of the majority," he said, "do not deny that there are principles of the Constitution . . . civil rights and . . . life, liberty and property, the principle of representative government, and the principle that constitutional laws are not to be broken down by planned disobedience. I assume also that all the principles of the Constitution are hostile to dictatorship and minority rule."[28]

Shortly after Murphy circulated his draft opinion, he stopped to talk with Frankfurter and confessed that while everybody should have freedom of opinion, Congress did have the right to set conditions for citizenship. He conceded that the opinion "skates on the thinnest possible ice—awfully thin," but Murphy did not like the idea of cancelling a person's citizenship ten years after it had been conferred. Frankfurter casually dismissed the issue as none of the Court's business. If Congress had set conditions, "then it is our business to enforce what Congress has commanded and not over-rule the legislative power."[29]

---

26. *Schneiderman v. United States*, 320 U.S. 119 (1943).

27. Frankfurter to Murphy, May 31, 1943, Stone Papers, Library of Congress; Frankfurter to Murphy, June 2, 1943, Jackson Papers, Library of Congress; Murphy to Frankfurter, June 2, 1943, Frankfurter Papers, Harvard Law School Library.

28. 320 U.S. at 181.

29. "Notes on the Schneiderman case," June 1, 1943, Frankfurter Papers, Harvard Law School Library.

But if citizenship could be canceled because of strong—or weak—beliefs held by an individual, then no naturalized citizen could be secure in his or her rights. As a naturalized citizen himself, Frankfurter believed he owed full and complete loyalty to the United States, and so did every other naturalized citizen—and with no less passion. Communists could not share that love of country that true patriots had and therefore could be stripped of their citizenship. The notion of full freedom of belief, it would seem, did not apply in this case. Conservative critics attacked the decision on just this ground. N. S. Timahseff charged that the Court had ruled one could be a loyal communist and a loyal American simultaneously, and he believed that was not possible.[30] As if in response to such comments, Douglas scribbled a memorandum in May 1944 in which he said that *Schneiderman* "was not merely a decision of an isolated case. It was a formulation by a majority of the Court as a rule of law governing de-naturalization proceedings. That rule of law is equally applicable whether the citizen against whom the proceeding is brought is a communist or nazi or a follower of any other political faith."[31]

In a letter to the chief justice offering suggestions for the dissent, Frankfurter said that it was "plain as a pikestaff" that political considerations—the need not to antagonize Russia—had been the "driving force behind the result in this case." Had the record come up with reference to a Bundist rather than a communist, the opposite result would have been reached.[32] Robert Jackson also believed that because the United States and Russia had become allies, cases like *Schneiderman* and *Bridges* were in fact decided differently than they otherwise would have been.[33]

In fact, such a situation came up a year later when the Court unanimously reversed the denaturalization order of a German American citizen the Justice Department had accused of endorsing Nazi racial doctrines. Frankfurter voted to reverse because he believed the government had failed to carry the necessary burden of proof, but in his draft opinion he did not mention the earlier decision in *Schneiderman*. At Stone's suggestion, Frankfurter added a sentence distinguishing *Baumgartner* from *Schneiderman*, but the original omission led Murphy, joined by Black, Douglas, and Rutledge, to file a concurrence that ringingly endorsed freedom of expres-

30. "The Schneiderman Case: Its Political Aspects," 12 *Fordham Law Review* 209 (1943).

31. Memorandum, May 17, 1944, Douglas Papers, Library of Congress.

32. Frankfurter to Stone, May 31, 1943, Stone Papers, Library of Congress; see also Frankfurter to Stanley Reed, June 2, 1943, Jackson Papers, Library of Congress.

33. Jackson Memoirs, Columbia Oral History Collection. For contemporary criticism of the case as decided upon political grounds, see Robert Emmet Heffernan, "Communism, Constitutionalism and the Principle of Contradiction," 32 *Georgetown Law Journal* 405 (1944).

sion for all citizens, native-born as well as naturalized, that included the right to criticize their country.[34] Not until 1946 did the Court uphold a denaturalization order. In that case, *Knauer v. United States,* the government presented conclusive evidence that at the time Knauer had sought American citizenship, he had been seeking to promote Nazism in the United States.[35]

Deference to Congress in terms of naturalization led the three *Schneiderman* dissenters to acquiesce in what even Frankfurter saw as a legislative vendetta, the government's lengthy effort to deport Harry Bridges, the controversial maritime union leader, for alleged affiliation with the Communist Party. When the Justice Department reported that it did not have the necessary authority under the law, Congress had changed the law, and the sponsor had announced that the amendment would now permit the deportation of Bridges and "all others of similar ilk."[36]

Five members of the Court—Black, Douglas, Rutledge, Murphy, and Reed—believed that while there might be constitutional problems with the law, it would be easier to thwart the deportation on procedural grounds; and Douglas's opinion, couched in a deliberately noncondemnatory tone, did just that.[37] Stone agreed that Congress had attempted "a rotten thing," but along with Frankfurter and Roberts, he dissented, claiming that it had long been settled law that Congress had plenary power in controlling resident aliens. Because the law dealt with a civil matter rather than criminal law, it did not fall under the constitutional prohibition against *ex post facto* laws or bills of attainder. The Court in the dissenters' view stood powerless to respond to a manifest injustice.

One final denaturalization decision dealt with conscientious objectors, those men who for reasons of conscience or religion refused to bear arms. The Selective Service Act of 1940 dealt with the issue in a straightforward and enlightened manner; it exempted those who could not bear arms from combat training and service but required that they serve in a noncombatant position. The law left interpretation of the phrase "religious training and belief" up to local draft boards, some of which read the clause very narrowly and in a prejudicial manner. For the most part, however, local boards dealt with conscientious objectors fairly.[38]

The Nationality Act of 1940, on the other hand, apparently included

---

34. *Baumgartner v. United States,* 322 U.S. 665 (1944); the Murphy concurrence is at 678. See also conference notes, Douglas Papers, Library of Congress.

35. 328 U.S. 654 (1946).

36. The effort to deport Bridges is told in Stanley I. Kutler, *The American Inquisition: Justice and Injustice in the Cold War* (New York: Hill & Wang, 1982), chap. 5.

37. *Bridges v. Wixon,* 326 U.S. 135 (1945).

38. Murphy, *Constitution in Crisis Times,* 230.

the principle that a pacifist who would not bear arms in defense of the United States was ineligible for citizenship. This, of course, followed earlier Supreme Court decisions, most notably the *Schwimmer* case. Holmes's dissent had questioned whether people were undesirable citizens "who believe more than some of us do in the teachings of the Sermon on the Mount."[39] The 1940 legislation did not, however, specifically rule that pacifists could not be naturalized; rather, by not directly indicating that they could, the rules of statutory construction would lead courts to assume that Congress had not intended to overrule the existing interpretation. Stone, Frankfurter, and Reed chose to follow this path despite the fact that Stone had dissented in each of the earlier decisions and Frankfurter had applauded Holmes's dissent in *Schwimmer*. But a majority of the Court believed otherwise. Speaking through Douglas, the Court ruled that a pacifist who would not bear arms but would serve in the armed forces as a noncombatant could be admitted to citizenship. A man's religious scruples, Douglas noted, would not disbar him from becoming a member of Congress or holding any other elected office, and Congress could not set a stricter standard for citizenship than it did for those who made the nation's laws.[40]

The case, decided just one day before Stone's death, is indicative of the old liberalism versus the new. For Stone and Frankfurter, judicial liberalism meant judicial restraint, and it was not up to the courts to legislate; even if the Court had been wrong in the previous cases, Congress by not specifically overruling those precedents had validated them. To the dissenters, adherence to judicial restraint meant support of a principle more important than any particular decision, a point Stone emphasized in his dissent.[41] For the majority, a wrong decision in the past did not carry any obligation for future courts to adhere to it as precedent; if an earlier Court had been wrong and Congress had failed to rectify the error, there was no reason why the Court should not correct its own mistake. Adherence to process without any regard for the substantive issues involved could, in their opinion, lead only to a sterile, mechanistic jurisprudence.

One question that many civil libertarians asked at the start of the war was whether the Roosevelt administration would launch attacks on free speech similar to those promulgated by the Wilson government during

---

39. *United States v. Schwimmer*, 279 U.S. 644, 655 (1929) (Holmes dissenting). The two other cases in which the Court followed this interpretation were *United States v. Macintosh*, 283 U.S. 605 (1931), and *United States v. Bland*, 283 U.S. 636 (1931).

40. *Girouard v. United States*, 328 U.S. 61, 65 (1946).

41. *Ibid.* at 76 (Stone dissenting); see also Frankfurter to Stone, March 30 and April 19, 1946, Stone Papers, Library of Congress; and the discussion of the case in Mason, *Stone*, 804–6.

World War I. The fact that war required some limits on individual rights could not be denied, but opinion varied on where to draw the line. One major difference between the two wars, however, is that the example of the European dictatorships in the 1930s provided a salutary warning of what should not be allowed. Although there were some efforts to ferret out dissidents, Roosevelt's public promise to sustain free speech and press, Attorney General Francis Biddle's commitment to civil liberties, and the absence (except on the West Coast) of the antialien hysteria of 1917–18 added up to a relatively healthy civil liberties climate during this time. According to Robert Cushman, during the war civil liberties enjoyed "a vitality which even the optimists had hardly dared hope for."[42]

Even before the war broke out, the Court had sent signals that it would not contemplate state disregard of personal liberties. In *DeJonge v. Oregon* (1937), the Court had unanimously struck down the state's criminal syndicalism law after police, at the instigation of conservative local politicians, had broken up a peaceful meeting sponsored by the communists.[43] That same term a divided Court reversed the conviction of a Communist Party organizer charged with incitement to riot. The evidence, according to Justice Roberts, showed no clear and present danger, nor did it even show any tendency toward violence. The statute merely served as a "dragnet which may enmesh anyone who agitates for a change of government."[44]

Since many of the abuses during World War I had resulted from state prosecutions of alleged subversives, the Roosevelt administration moved quickly to assert sole federal control over internal security, mainly through the Alien Registration Act of 1940.[45] A few months later the Supreme Court affirmed federal supremacy in *Hines v. Davidowitz* (1941), overturning a Pennsylvania alien registration law on the grounds that the federal statute had preempted the field.[46]

The Court also proved cool to prosecutions arising under the old Espionage Act of 1917, with its laundry list of subversive activities aimed as much at punishing deviant behavior as at catching spies or traitors. In *Hartzel v. United States* (1944), a split Court overturned the conviction of a man who had distributed racist literature vilifying Jews, Englishmen, and President Roosevelt and calling on the United States to form an alliance with Nazi Germany.[47] When the justices discussed the case in conference on

---

42. Quoted in Edward S. Corwin, *Total War and the Constitution* (New York: Knopf, 1947), 106.
43. 299 U.S. 353 (1937).
44. *Herndon v. Lowry*, 301 U.S. 242, 263 (1937).
45. 54 Stat. 670 (1940).
46. 312 U.S. 52 (1941). See Lewis R. Donelson III, "Federal Supremacy and the Davidowitz Case," 29 *Georgetown Law Journal* 755 (1941).
47. 322 U.S. 680 (1944).

April 29, 1944, they split 5–4, with Reed, Frankfurter, Douglas, Murphy, and Jackson in favor of affirming the conviction and Stone, Roberts, Black, and Rutledge for reversal. Reed, as the senior justice in the majority, assigned the case to Murphy, who agreed to take it on condition that he might yet come out for reversal. One month later, Murphy did just that, circulating a draft opinion with the note that "research and reflection have convinced me that I can only cast my vote to reverse."[48] In his opinion Murphy declared that "an American citizen has a right to discuss these matters by temperate reasoning, or by immoderate and vicious invective without running afoul of the Espionage Act."[49] Frankfurter angrily noted in the files that Murphy had told him during the course of oral argument that Hartzel "was doing Hitler's work in our midst" and then later said that the defendant was "subtly endeavoring to undermine the war effort." But in the end, Murphy said, "I come up to this free speech thing and my strong instinct for protecting free speech and I have to come out the other way."[50]

In two other cases, the Court reversed convictions of alleged Nazi sympathizers. Over the dissents of Black and Douglas, the Court reversed the conviction of George Sylvester Viereck for violating the Foreign Agents Registration Act. Applying a strict and narrow construction of the statute, the majority held that the act required propaganda activities undertaken by someone acting as an agent for a foreign country to be reported to the secretary of state but that similar activities, undertaken on one's own initiative, did not have to be reported. Viereck had freely admitted acting on behalf of the German government and had listed those activities; but he had not reported work done on his own account, and it was that work for which the government had prosecuted him.

Chief Justice Stone, who announced the Court's 5–2 decision, took particular exception to the demagogic tenor of the government's prosecuting attorney, who at the trial had demanded a conviction in order to protect men then fighting at Bataan. According to Stone, the prosecutor's emotionalism was "wholly irrelevant to any facts or issues in the case, the purpose and effect of which could only have been to arouse passion and prejudice." Such remarks "were offensive to the dignity and good order with which all proceedings in court should be conducted."[51]

---

48. Conference notes, May 1, 1944, Douglas Papers, Library of Congress; Frankfurter, Memorandum on *Hartzel v. United States,* June 19, 1944; Murphy, Memorandum to the Court, May 31, 1944, Frankfurter Papers, Harvard Law School Library.

49. 322 U.S. at 689.

50. Memorandum on Hartzel, Frankfurter Papers, Harvard Law School Library.

51. *Viereck v. United States,* 318 U.S. 236, 247–48 (1943). Only a few weeks earlier Stone had lectured a gathering of federal judges on the need to ensure that the emotions of war

In still another case involving prosecutions under the Espionage Act, the Court reversed the convictions of twenty-four leaders of the German-American Bund on grounds that the evidence did not support the charges that the men had conspired to counsel draft evasion. Murphy, who voted for reversal, explained his decision in terms reminiscent of his *Hartzel* opinion: American citizens had "a right . . . to agitate to prevent discrimination."[52]

When it came to real spies and traitors, the justices still insisted on maintaining the spirit and letter of the law; but they also realized that such cases might properly belong in military courts, which utilized different criteria of evidence, procedure, and guilt. The first case arose out of the arrest of eight Nazis put ashore in June 1942 from submarines on Long Island and Florida with orders to sabotage bridges, industrial plants, and military installations. The scheme failed completely, and authorities quickly apprehended the saboteurs and their few American confederates. Roosevelt immediately named a special military tribunal of seven generals to try the saboteurs, with orders to transmit the record of the trial directly to him. In the same proclamation, he closed the civilian courts to "all persons who are subjects, citizens, or residents of any nation at war with the United States . . . and are charged with committing or attempting . . . to commit sabotage."[53]

Secretary of War Stimson, while pondering how to constitute the tribunal to try the saboteurs, turned for advice to his old protégé, Felix Frankfurter, now Mr. Justice Frankfurter. The justice recommended that the panel be composed solely of regular military officers and not include any civilians, even high-ranking civilians in the War Department. Frankfurter also backed Stimson when the secretary and Attorney General Francis Biddle clashed over whether to permit press coverage, with the War Department calling for secret trials.[54] Frankfurter, it should be noted, was the only member of the Court with any experience in military justice, having served

---

were kept out of their courtrooms. Mason, *Stone*, 684. Stone evidently wanted to make his comments on the prosecutor even stronger. Memorandum, Stone to Conference, [n.d.] 1943, Rutledge Papers, Library of Congress.

52. *Keegan v. United States*, 325 U.S. 478 (1945); Fine, *Murphy*, 430.

53. Presidential proclamation No. 2561, 7 *Federal Register* 5101 (July 2, 1942). The historical chain of events is well drawn in Cyrus Bernstein, "The Saboteur Trial," 11 *George Washington Law Review* 131 (1943).

54. Henry Stimson Diary, entries for June 29 and July 6, 1942, quoted in Michael E. Parrish, "Justice Frankfurter and the Supreme Court," in Jennifer Lowe, ed., *The Jewish Justices of the Supreme Court Revisited: From Brandeis to Fortas* (special issue of *Journal of Supreme Court History* [1994] ), 65.

THE COURT AT WAR

briefly with the army judge advocate general's office at the end of World War I.[55]

According to Michael Parrish, the Stimson diary entries probably "reveal only a fraction" of Frankfurter's extrajudicial involvement in the saboteurs' case. Frankfurter most likely discussed the issues on a regular basis with John McCloy, his confidant in the War Department, who lived near the justice in Georgetown and often walked with him in the evenings. Given this participation in developing the government's framework for trying the saboteurs, it is not surprising that Frankfurter became one of the most ardent supporters of the administration during the Court's discussion of the issues.[56]

The military panel commenced the trial in secret, but two army colonels appointed to defend the Germans, Kenneth C. Royall and Cassius M. Dowell, tried to get their clients a civilian trial on the basis of the Civil War case *Ex parte Milligan*.[57] In that decision, the Court had held that in areas apart from battle zones in which the civilian courts remained open, the government could not preempt the civil judiciary through military tribunals. This came to be known as the "open court" doctrine, which would play an important role in the martial law cases coming from Hawaii.[58]

Colonel Royall went to see Justice Roberts, who immediately acknowledged that a constitutional question existed. The two men made arrangements for a conference a few days later at Roberts's farm in Pennsylvania, to include Justice Black, Royall and Dowell, Attorney General Francis Biddle, and Judge Advocate General Myron C. Cramer. Prior to the meeting, Roberts had conferred with the chief justice, and he and Black had been authorized to bring the matter to the entire court if they believed it appropriate. Before the meeting broke up, both justices agreed that the whole court should convene to hear the appeal the following week.[59]

For the first time in over two decades, the Court interrupted its summer recess to hear a case. When the Court convened on July 29, 1942, Douglas had not yet arrived from the West Coast, and Murphy, attired in his army uniform, decided to recuse himself. When oral argument began,

55. Jonathan Lurie, *Arming Military Justice*, vol. 1, *The Origins of the United States Court of Military Appeals, 1775–1950* (Princeton: Princeton University Press, 1992), 46.

56. See Frankfurter to Stone, August 3, 1942, Stone Papers, Library of Congress; and Stone to Frankfurter, August 29, 1942, Frankfurter Papers, Harvard Law School Library.

57. 4 Wall. 2 (1866). Ironically, Stone's son Lauson, then an army major, had been assigned to help with the defense and came up with this case; when it appeared as if the appeal to the Supreme Court might be heard, the army took Lauson Stone off the case. The chief justice thought briefly about recusing himself, but both the government and defense counsel urged him to remain on the bench.

58. See below, pp. 80–82.

59. Mason, *Stone*, 654.

Frankfurter immediately began to pepper Colonel Royall, his former student, as to why the defendants had appealed directly to the Supreme Court and not gone the traditional route through a court of appeals. After several minutes of debate on questions of civil procedure, Royall got to the heart of the matter. The presidential order establishing the military commission did not provide for "review in the ordinary sense." Moreover, since the tribunal reported its findings directly to the president, he was not even sure the defendants and their lawyers would be informed of the findings; execution might be carried out before counsel could appeal. Royall's sense that only Supreme Court review of the process could ensure justice prevailed; the Court accepted the case and began to hear arguments on the legitimacy of the panel.

The Court's decision to hear the case should be seen as highly unusual since the existing rules of military justice, adopted in the so-called Chamberlain reforms of 1920, did not mention appeal to civilian courts. Not until the 1984 revision of the Uniform Code of Military Justice did Congress provide for direct appeal to the high court from the United States Court of Military Appeals, and then under very limited circumstances.[60] Although criticism of military justice procedures continued throughout this period, the issue itself did not concern the Supreme Court or its members. *Quirin,* then, is a unique case.

In conference, despite Frankfurter's alleged worries that procedures had not been strictly observed,[61] the justices agreed that they had to hand down a decision and to do so promptly. Stone, moreover, believed it would have to be a unanimous opinion to demonstrate that the Court had absolutely no reservations about the government's conduct. To effect this, Stone managed to limit the issues to whether or not the Court had jurisdiction to hear the petition for *habeas corpus* and whether the president had the authority to order the saboteurs tried by a military panel. Even deciding these questions required extensive debate in the conference over whether the saboteurs were spies or prisoners of war, since treatment of the latter was specifically provided for by Congress in the Articles of War, a body of law that rarely came before the Court. Still another issue involved the extent of the presidential war powers. Hugo Black's notes summed up the consensus: "Constitution makes President Supreme Commander and Congress can carry on war. Time out of mind it is within the power of the

---

60. Jonathan Lurie reports that in the six years following this change in the Uniform Code, the Supreme Court accepted only two cases from the military tribunal, and one of these resulted in a *per curiam* decision. *Arming Military Justice,* 184, n.44.

61. There is no indication that Frankfurter told either the chief justice or any of his colleagues about his advisory role in the case. Had any other justice acted in such a way, Frankfurter would have castigated him for overstepping the bounds of judicial propriety.

Commander-in-Chief to hang a spy. Articles of War recognize that there is a law of war. He would say the whole history of army shows there is a law (common) of war—waging war—by all usages they were not prisoners of war. Bound to give some play to Executive as to an administrative agency."[62] On July 31, 1942, less than forty-eight hours after they heard the case, the Court issued a brief *per curiam* opinion upholding the power of the military commission to try the saboteurs and announcing that a formal opinion would be filed later.[63]

The reason for the unusual procedure was simple. While all eight of the justices who sat on the case agreed that the president had the authority, they disagreed on the jurisprudential reasons to support that finding. Stone, for judicial as well as political reasons, believed it would be bad if the Court divided over this issue, so he wanted to craft as narrow an opinion as possible, one that would command the support of all the brethren. By the time the Court convened in October, the chief justice had succeeded.[64]

The rather elaborate opinion said, in essence, that under the executive war powers the president could establish military commissions to try such cases. However, Stone went beyond merely restating a truism; he took pains to rebut all the points raised by the defense counsel, pointing to thirteen separate clauses in the Constitution supporting the presidential war powers. In addition, the chief justice also ruled that the constitutional guarantee of grand jury indictment and petit jury trial did not apply to defendants appearing before a military tribunal on charges of offenses under the laws of war. Moreover, not only was the president's order valid, but the military commission had followed lawful procedures.[65]

Stone as well as some other members of the Court were concerned about that part of the presidential proclamation closing the civilian courts to this type of case, either to hear the trial or in review. As the chief justice told his friend John Bassett Moore, the case "presented a great many legal

---

62. Black, memorandum on *Ex parte Quirin*, July 29, 1942, Douglas Papers, Library of Congress.

63. *Ex parte Quirin*, 317 U.S. 1 (1942); the *per curiam* can be found at 18. Within a few days the eight men had been found guilty; six of them were executed, a seventh was sentenced to life imprisonment, and the eighth was given thirty years at hard labor. As defense counsel had feared, they learned of the execution of their clients through the press. Military law, as then constituted, did not require review by higher authority such as the president or the secretary of war (both of whom approved of the sentence), and Congress did not establish a court for military appeals until 1951.

64. For Stone's composition of the case, see Mason, *Stone*, 658–64. For different views within the Court, see two memoranda by Stone dated September 25, 1942, Douglas Papers, Library of Congress.

65. See the discussion by Robert E. Cushman, "The Case of the Nazi Saboteurs," 36 *American Political Science Review* 1082 (1942).

puzzles which had never been ironed out or considered by the courts." He pointed out that the opinion did not mention the validity of the presidential proclamation or a number of other questions regarding interpretation of the Articles of War.[66]

The press and the public greeted the decision with overwhelming approval, claiming that even in the middle of war the American tradition of liberty had been preserved. While a few law review journals noted the procedural irregularities, the writers dismissed these concerns on the ground that "in wartime quick justice and absence of delay are essential."[67] As George Schilling wrote: "The most significant feature of *Ex parte Quirin* is its actual existence. The picture of the highest court in the land convening specially to hear and pass upon the lawfulness of the trial of avowed enemies of the nation presents a strong contrast to the practices prevalent in the land whence they came."[68] The noted constitutional scholar Robert E. Cushman wrote: "The Supreme Court stopped the military authorities and required them, as it were, to show their credentials. When this had been done to the Court's satisfaction, they were allowed to proceed."[69] David Currie put it another way: *Quirin,* he declared, "is a salutary reminder that it is not the courts alone that have a responsibility to see that those charged with offenses are afforded appropriate procedural protections."[70]

Much of this acclaim, as Stone realized, was self-serving. His biographer notes that "public acclamation could not, however, hide the fact that the Court had been somewhat in the position of a private on sentry duty accosting a commanding general without his pass."[71] Had the Court voted the other way and held the president without authority, it is questionable whether or not Roosevelt would have obeyed the Court or the public would have supported the justices. Stone's elaborate opinion attempted to make the most of the situation by writing into it various safeguards for individual protection. He implied, for example, that even spies and prisoners of war had some rights under the Constitution,[72] although no basis existed for such an assertion; nowhere in American or English legal history can one

---

66. Stone to Moore, December 31, 1942, Stone Papers, Library of Congress; see also Stone to Roger Nelson, November 30, 1942, *ibid.*

67. Note, "Federal Military Commission," 56 *Harvard Law Review* 631, 642 (1943).

68. George T. Schilling, "Saboteurs and the Jurisdiction of Military Commissions," 41 *Michigan Law Review* 481, 495 (1942).

69. Cushman, "Nazi Saboteurs," 1091.

70. David P. Currie, *The Constitution in the Supreme Court: The Second Century, 1888–1986* (Chicago: University of Chicago Press, 1990), 281.

71. Mason, *Stone,* 665.

72. 317 U.S. at 25.

find evidence for the proposition that enemy military personnel have any of the rights belonging to citizens. Ever since the American Revolution, the United States had always tried enemy personnel in wartime by summary military procedures, a fact known and accepted by the framers of the Constitution. Perhaps the most the Court could hope for was to remind the nation that even in the midst of a war against totalitarianism, Americans could not ignore the Constitution and its safeguards.

The Court never developed the implications of the *Quirin* decision, such as the claim that the Constitution would follow the flag and extend its protections into captured Axis territory. In 1946 the Court backed away from this possibility in the case of the "Tiger of Malaya," Japanese general Tomoyuki Yamashita. Shortly after the Japanese surrender, General Douglas MacArthur had established a special military commission to try Yamashita for crimes committed during the Japanese occupation of the Philippines. At the trial the prosecution accused Yamashita of violating the rules of war by permitting his troops to commit brutal atrocities; no charge was made that he personally participated in these activities or that he had even ordered them. The military court nonetheless found him guilty and sentenced him to death; his army lawyers sought review first from the Supreme Court of the Philippines and then from the United States Supreme Court on the ground that his summary trial did not meet the requirements of the Fifth Amendment.[73]

With hostilities over, the justices felt no compulsion for haste as they had in the Nazi saboteur case. The Court issued a stay of execution until it could hear the appeal. The justices heard oral argument on January 7 and 8, 1946, and then settled down for the usual discussion and opinion drafting. Six of the justices quickly agreed with Stone's position upholding the conviction, and Stanley Reed, after raising a number of questions, also joined.[74] Frankfurter, aware of the differences of opinion among his colleagues, urged Stone to base the opinion on as narrow grounds as possible and to ignore questions raised regarding the Geneva convention and the Articles of War. While the military must be subordinate to the rule of law, Frankfurter noted, so must the other branches of government, and that included the Court's recognizing the boundaries of its authority. He urged Stone to take a limited view of the Court's *habeas* authority.[75] In his opinion

---

73. For a detailed critique of this case by one of the defense lawyers, see A. Frank Reel, *The Case of General Yamashita* (Chicago: University of Chicago Press, 1949). See also Richard Lael, *The Yamashita Precedent* (Wilmington, Del.: Scholarly Resources, 1982); and Philip R. Piccigallo, *The Japanese on Trial: Allied War Crimes Operations in the East, 1945–1951* (Austin: University of Texas Press, 1979).

74. For development of the case, see Mason, *Stone,* 666–71, and Fine, *Murphy,* 452–59.

75. Frankfurter to Stone, January 15 and 22, 1946, Stone Papers, Library of Congress.

the chief backed away from his assertions in *Quirin* regarding the extension of constitutional rights, but it was exactly on this point that Rutledge and Murphy objected.

"The Court does not declare expressly," Rutledge wrote, "that petitioner as an enemy belligerent has no constitutional rights, a ruling I could understand but not accept. Neither does it affirm that he has some, if but little constitutional protection. Nor does the Court defend what was done. I think the effect of what it does is in substance to deny him all such safeguards. And this is the great issue in the cause."[76] Rutledge attacked the majority for claiming that it had the power to review but then conceding that "there is no law restrictive upon these proceedings other than whatever rules and regulations may be prescribed . . . by the executive authority or the military."[77] Justice Murphy also dissented, and he declared "that the grave issue raised by this case is whether a military commission . . . may disregard the procedural rights of an accused person as guaranteed by the Constitution." For Murphy, "The answer is plain. The Fifth Amendment guarantee of due process of law applies to 'any person' who is accused of a crime by the Federal Government or any of its agencies."[78] In essence, Murphy adopted the view that the Constitution follows the flag and that in any territory under American control, federal officials must obey constitutional strictures when treating the local population, even those tried for wartime actions.

The two decisions, *Quirin* and *Yamashita,* raise a number of questions that Stone's opinions do not answer clearly, perhaps because there is no clear line of authority and precedent in this area. The constitutional wording does not delineate military from civilian courts, yet historically there have always been sharp distinctions between the two. Justice Black's view that decisions of military courts could, in normal circumstances, be reviewed only by other military courts is not idiosyncratic. The military, he wrote in a draft concurrence in *Yamashita,* had no power "to supersede the civil laws in [U.S.] territory, and to set up military tribunals there to try, convict, and punish civilians for all sorts of civil offenses." But he found nothing in the Constitution that gave civil courts authority to annul or review military trials of enemy soldiers.[79] Had Stone taken this view, he

---

76. *In re Yamashita,* 327 U.S. 1, 41, 79 (1946) (Rutledge dissenting).

77. *Ibid.* at 81.

78. 327 U.S. at 26. Murphy also claimed that federal courts had *habeas* jurisdiction in any case in which American officials allegedly imprisoned any person illegally. In *Johnson v. Eisentrager,* 339 U.S. 763 (1950), Justices Black, Douglas, and Burton, all of whom had joined Stone's opinion, argued in dissent that American courts could issue *habeas* writs whenever an American official acted illegally in any land governed by the United States—in this instance, occupied Germany.

79. Uncirculated draft opinion, Black Papers, Library of Congress.

would have had an intellectually defensible position, but he might not have been able to muster a majority. By toning down his assertions, he put together what one critic has called "a patchwork of ideas and statements, pieced together to satisfy the divergent views of men who were seeking to find 'good' reasons for a politically expedient result."[80] Stone tried to do too much, although, as Alpheus Mason points out, in both the *Quirin* and *Yamashita* opinions he was repeating the same lesson he had tried to teach a decade earlier in his fight with the Four Horsemen: "Courts are not the only agency of government that must be assumed to have capacity to govern."[81]

The Court also had to deal with a handful of treason cases. No case involving treason had previously come before the high court, although ever since the trial of Aaron Burr it had been an accepted principle of American law that only the relatively narrow definition in Article III, Section 3—"levying War against [the United States], or in adhering to their Enemies, giving them Aid and Comfort"—could be applied, and, as constitutionally mandated, confirmation by two witnesses or confession in open court was required for conviction.

The first two cases grew out of the saboteurs incident. Two of the eight Nazis had managed before their arrest to make contact with Americans who they hoped would assist in their plans. The FBI arrested two men, one a friend and the other the father of one of the Germans, and charged them with treason. At the trial of Anthony Cramer, two FBI agents testified that they had witnessed Cramer meeting with saboteur Werner Thiel in public places and that he had accepted Thiel's money for safekeeping. The government claimed that these acts constituted giving aid and comfort to the enemy and that the testimony of the two agents met the constitutional test for confirmation. The trial judge agreed and so interpreted the law to the jury, which returned a guilty verdict.

Unlike the saboteurs case, this one presented the Court no problem of jurisdiction. Cramer had filed an appropriate appeal from the verdict of a civilian court. When the justices first considered the case in March 1944, all but Stanley Reed wanted to avoid the substantive issue of whether treason had actually been committed and reverse the lower court because of trial error. The chief justice, however, wanted the Court to address the constitutional issue of what constituted treason so that the jury could be properly instructed in a retrial. The question, as Stone saw it, was "whether

---

80. Reel, *Case of General Yamashita*, 216.

81. Mason, *Stone*, 671, quoting Stone's dissent in *United States v. Butler*, 297 U.S. 1, 87 (1936).

the overt acts charged must, by themselves, standing alone, manifest a treasonable purpose."[82] Frankfurter, however, believed it to be a sound rule of
jurisprudence, as he explained to Jackson, to avoid constitutional issues
whenever possible. "The single greatest source of mischief attributable to
the work of this Court during its entire history is the disregard of its own
constantly avowed principle that a constitutional issue should not be decided unless a case unavoidably turns on that issue."[83] With the nation
in the midst of war, however, most of the justices preferred to avoid the
controversial issue if, as some of them expected, by the time the results of
a second trial returned to be heard on appeal, the war might be over and
the question could be decided in a calmer public environment.

Stone assigned the case to Black, but about a week later Black reported
that after a careful reading of the record, he believed that Cramer had
received a fair trial and that what errors there might have been had been
minor. "If a conviction is not to be sustained on evidence such as the government produced here," Black wrote, "I doubt if there could be many
convictions for treason unless American citizens were actually found in the
Army of the enemy."[84] The debate over what constituted treason continued
in a rancorous conference, where Stone argued for a more flexible definition and Frankfurter held to a strict and narrow view.[85] The Court ordered
reargument on the constitutional question, and when the justices reached
their decision about a year later, a 5–4 majority ruled the government had
not met the evidentiary standard of the Constitution.[86]

Writing for the majority, Justice Jackson ruled that the overt act had to
be traitorous in intent by itself and not merely appear to be so because of
surrounding circumstances; merely meeting the saboteurs did not, by itself,
manifest treason. The government had to prove, on the testimony of two

---

82. Stone to Douglas, March 15, 1944, and Memorandum for the Court, March 22, 1944,
Douglas Papers, Library of Congress.

83. Frankfurter to Jackson, April 27, 1944, *ibid.*

84. Black to Stone, March 1944, *ibid.*

85. At one point Stone challenged Frankfurter's view, and Frankfurter responded, "I sup-
pose we know more than those who drafted the Constitution." Stone said that there were
some things he believed he knew and understood better than the Framers, to which Frankfurter jibed that it was certainly true of Stone's knowledge of wine and cheese. According
to Murphy's notes, this nasty remark led to an uproar in the conference. Fine, *Murphy*,
407. See also Frankfurter to Roberts, March 22, 1944, Frankfurter Papers, Harvard Law
School Library; and Frankfurter to Stone, March 24, 1944, Stone Papers, Library of Congress.

86. *Cramer v. United States*, 325 U.S. 1 (1945). For treason see the classic work by J. Willard
Hurst, *The Law of Treason in the United States* (Westport, Conn.: Greenwood, 1971), which
reprints articles Hurst wrote during and immediately after the war.

witnesses, that the overt act showed "sufficient action by the accused, in its setting, to sustain a finding that the accused actually gave aid and comfort to the enemy."[87] The ruling, reaffirming John Marshall's view, placed imposing barriers against efforts to prosecute treason. Stone, Black, Reed, and Douglas dissented, and the latter complained that the opinion made "the way easy for the traitor." Between Marshall's opinion in the Burr trial and Jackson's in *Cramer,* Douglas said, treason had been practically eliminated as a crime. Douglas appears to have been most incensed at the majority reading of the constitutional requirement of an overt act, and he claimed that the framers had intended to distinguish overt treason from mere conspiracy. The requirement, as he read it, served to distinguish acts that had indeed taken place as opposed to plans and conjectures that did not.[88]

Two years later, after Stone's death, the Court reviewed the case of the other American, Hans Max Haupt, the father of one of the saboteurs, and upheld his conviction by an 8–1 vote. The government showed that Haupt had sheltered his son, gotten a car for him, and arranged for a job in a factory that manufactured the Norden bombsight. Haupt's counsel argued that under the *Cramer* criteria, none of these acts was traitorous in itself but merely manifested the natural tendencies of a father to help his son. But Justice Jackson disagreed and described Haupt's activities as "steps essential to his design for treason," which "forward[ed] the saboteur in his mission."[89] Only Justice Murphy dissented, claiming correctly that the Court had moved away from the strict tests it had enunciated in *Cramer.*

In many ways the *Haupt* decision is somewhat of a puzzle. In wartime, when the justices might have been expected to take a broader view of what constituted treason, they had adopted a strict and narrow standard. Even at the conference, Murphy's criticism of the case and the evidence presented, as well as his call to follow *Cramer,* found some receptivity. In the initial conference only Chief Justice Vinson, Black, Jackson, and Burton voted to affirm, and Black declared he could be convinced otherwise. Murphy, Reed, and Rutledge were for reversal, and Douglas and Frankfurter had not yet made up their minds. One can only conjecture, but perhaps by 1947, with the Cold War already begun, the justices concluded that what would later be called "a totality of the circumstances" test might better serve the nation's interest than the strict standard of *Cramer.* As Justice Douglas noted in his concurrence, the harboring charge could be deemed

---

87. 325 U.S. at 34.
88. *Ibid.* at 48, 67; see the discussion in Currie, *Constitution in the Supreme Court,* 296–99.
89. *Haupt v. United States,* 330 U.S. 631, 635 (1947).

treasonable not because two witnesses had seen the saboteur enter his father's house, an act seemingly innocent by itself, but because of the "circumstances surrounding the overt act."[90]

The *Haupt* case, the first in which the Supreme Court sustained a treason conviction, permitted the government to prosecute other Americans who had aided the enemy during the war, such as Douglas Chandler, who had broadcast English-language programs from Berlin. The Chandler case raised the issue of whether treason could take place only within the territorial limits of the United States; in *Kawakita v. United States* (1952), the Court ruled that treason encompassed activities by American citizens anywhere.[91]

Executive authority confronted the Court in several situations, and the resulting decisions left few people comfortable. Shortly after Pearl Harbor the Court heard a case involving an executive agreement that had wide-ranging impact. The facts of the *Pink* case are as follows. In 1918 and 1919, the new Soviet government nationalized the properties of various Russian insurance companies, including properties located outside the Soviet Union. The First Russian Insurance Company had offices and assets in New York, and that state, acting through its superintendent of insurance, seized the assets of the company and paid off its New York policyholders and creditors. In 1931, the New York Court of Appeals directed the superintendent to dispose of the remaining assets to foreign creditors. In 1933, however, the United States recognized the Soviet Union, and as part of the Litvinov agreement, the United States agreed to become the assignee of Soviet claims in the United States, which included the remaining assets of the insurance company. The United States government thereupon sued the superintendent of insurance to recover the balance of the assets. The government lost in the state court and appealed the decision to the Supreme Court.[92]

The results in the case can be seen as almost predictable, considering decisions that the Court had handed down in the preceding years concerning executive authority in foreign affairs. In 1936 the Court, speaking through Justice George Sutherland, had given its imprimatur to the "plenary and exclusive power of the President as the sole organ of the federal government in foreign relations." This power, according to Sutherland, "does not require as a basis for its exercise an act of Congress."[93] Coming

---

90. Conference notes, December 14, 1946, Douglas Papers, Library of Congress; 330 U.S. at 644–45.
91. 343 U.S. 717 (1952).
92. *United States v. Pink*, 315 U.S. 203 (1942).
93. *United States v. Curtis-Wright Export Corp.*, 299 U.S. 304 (1936); see Robert A. Divine, "The Case of the Smuggled Bombers," in John A. Garraty, ed., *Quarrels That Have Shaped the Constitution* (New York: Harper & Row, 1964), 210–21.

from someone who had consistently opposed the power of the state when it was used for internal economic regulation, the opinion adumbrated federal/executive power in foreign affairs apparently not at all limited by the constitution. Presidents from Roosevelt to the present have used this doctrine to justify a long line of executive actions, claiming that their authority in this area derived from a sovereign power that preceded the Constitution and that is inherent in the government. The following year, in *United States v. Belmont,* the Court held that recognition of the Soviet Union and the accompanying executive agreements constituted an international compact that, following the president's signature, did not require Senate approval.[94] Moreover, such agreements had the same force as treaties that, under an earlier decision, superseded any conflicting state laws.[95]

When the justices considered the case in conference, a clear majority voted to reverse in favor of the government, and only the chief justice objected. Stone objected to what he considered the Court's aiding and abetting the growth of autocratic executive power, and despite the earlier decisions, he believed the Court could still be called upon to protect property rights.[96] Douglas, writing for the majority, held simply that the Litvinov agreement made the Soviet decrees binding upon Russian assets in New York. Stone, joined by Roberts, entered a vigorous dissent, in which he departed from the Court's earlier approval of executive action and the extent of presidential power in foreign affairs and demanded that the Court review such actions as it reviewed domestic policies.[97] Stone then sent his opinion to Professor John Bassett Moore of Columbia, the noted expert on international law, who endorsed Stone's views. "Absolutely correct," he declared. In time of war, "private rights, including those in property, are always subject to violations or abridgement, but the courts are not supposed to cooperate in it. They are useless, or perhaps worse than useless when they do."[98]

Despite the disapproval of Moore and others,[99] it is difficult to see how the Court could have decided otherwise. The line of decisions set up a

94. 301 U.S. 324 (1937).

95. *Missouri v. Holland,* 252 U.S. 416 (1920).

96. Cert memorandum and Conference notes, December 20, 1941, Douglas Papers, Library of Congress.

97. 315 U.S. at 242 (Stone dissenting).

98. Stone to John Bassett Moore, February 11, 1942; Moore to Stone, February 13, 1942. Stone Papers, Library of Congress.

99. See Edwin Borchard, "Extraterritorial Confiscation," 36 *American Journal of International Law* 275 (1942); and Philip Jessup, "The Litvinov Assignment and the Pink Case," *ibid.* at 282. Both men, incidentally, sent copies of their articles to Douglas, who responded graciously that they had every right to criticize the opinion. Douglas to Borchard, March 26, 1942, and to Jessup, May 27, 1942, Douglas Papers, Library of Congress.

clear precedent: the president is the constitutionally authorized voice of the nation in foreign affairs, and executive agreements, like treaties, have the full force of law. If Congress did not agree with the terms of the executive agreement, it had its own powers by which to alter or to negate them. As it turned out, the issues involved in *Pink* affected very few people; that cannot be said for the series of cases testing the authority of the president during wartime to intern thousands of American citizens.

With the exception of slavery, the worst example of racist invasion of civil liberties in American history is the forcible transfer of 110,000 persons of Japanese ancestry—70,000 of them American citizens—away from their homes, jobs, and property to detention centers, ostensibly because they posed a security threat to the West Coast.[100] Although the military had no evidence of a single case of sabotage or even attempted sabotage, government leaders quickly gave in to the public hysteria demanding that something be done. The respected columnist Walter Lippmann informed his readers that "nobody's constitutional rights include the right to reside and do business on a battlefield. There is plenty of room elsewhere for him to exercise his rights." A few days later the less restrained columnist Westbrook Pegler called for every Japanese man and woman to be put under armed guard, "and to hell with habeas corpus until the danger is over."[101] In fairness to government officials, one should note that responsible military analysts in early 1942 viewed the Pacific as a Japanese lake, and until the Battle of Midway later in June, it appeared that nothing could stop the Imperial Fleet or prevent an invasion of the West Coast.[102]

On February 19, 1942, President Roosevelt signed Executive Order 9066, authorizing the secretary of war to designate certain parts of the country as military zones, from which any and all persons could be excluded and in which travel restrictions, including daily curfews, might be imposed. In March, Congress enacted the major provisions of 9066 into law and added stringent penalties for those who resisted relocation.

General John L. DeWitt had already begun to act under 9066; on March 2, 1942, he designated the entire Pacific Coast a military area. Three weeks later he imposed a curfew along the coastal plain between 8:00 P.M.

---

100. For the story of the internment and the resulting legal battles, see Peter Irons, *Justice at War* (New York: Oxford University Press, 1983), and U.S. Commission on Wartime Relocation, *Personal Justice Denied* (Washington: Government Printing Office, 1983). A recent book that takes a less hostile approach and tries to put the internment into the larger context of the nation at war is Page Smith, *Democracy on Trial: The Japanese-American Evacuation and Relocation in World War II* (New York: Simon & Schuster, 1995).

101. Quoted in Irons, *Justice at War*, 60–61.

102. Smith, *Democracy on Trial*, chap. 8.

and 6:00 A.M. for German and Italian nationals and for all persons of Japanese origin, both Issei (Japanese nationals) and Nisei (American citizens of Japanese ancestry). On March 27 the army prohibited these groups from leaving the coastal area, and then on May 9 it excluded them from the same area. Issei and Nisei could comply with these contradictory orders only by reporting to designated locations, from which they would be bussed to relocation centers in the interior. Amazingly, the 110,000 men, women, and children affected responded cooperatively for the most part. A number of younger Nisei volunteered to serve in the army, and their units turned out to be among the most highly decorated in the European theater of operations.

The entire relocation program proceeded on racist assumptions and brought forth such astounding statements as that of Congressman Leland Ford of California that a patriotic native-born Japanese, if he wants to make his contribution, will "permit himself to be placed in a concentration camp." Without a shred of evidence, the entire Japanese American population, including native-born American citizens, stood condemned because, as General DeWitt so eloquently put it, "A Jap is a Jap."[103]

The constitutional issue could not have been clearer. Those affected by the relocation plan had never been charged with any crimes; they had never been accused of anything other than their racial ancestry; they had never had any hearings to see if, on an individual basis, they posed a threat to security. In any circumstances, this comprised a clear violation of the Fifth Amendment's Due Process Clause. Opposed to that stood the war powers of the president and Congress and the question of how much deference the Court should pay to the other branches. The internment cases caused several of the brethren much anguish, but the majority stood solidly behind the administration's plan.

The first case to reach the Court involved Gordon Hirabayashi, a native-born American citizen and a senior at the University of Washington, who had been arrested for failing to report to a control center and for violating the curfew. He had been convicted and sentenced to two three-month prison terms and then had appealed his conviction on the grounds that the military had exceeded its constitutional authority. Both the federal district and appeals courts upheld the conviction, and the case came to the Supreme Court in the spring of 1943.[104]

Chief Justice Stone strongly supported the army's actions and used all his persuasive powers to mass the Court in back of the government. On May 30 he circulated the first draft of his opinion, which centered around

---

103. Irons, *Justice at War*, 38.
104. *Hirabayashi v. United States*, 320 U.S. 81 (1943).

a truly awesome reading of the war powers. Such authority went far beyond purely military matters on the battlefield and could be directed at any and all "evils that attend the rise and progress of the war." Black and Douglas immediately endorsed Stone's views but made significant suggestions to emphasize what they considered a key element in the Court's decision, judicial deference. Black urged Stone to include a statement making explicit that the Court had no business second-guessing the military, and Stone obliged: "It is not for any court to sit in review of the wisdom of their [the military commanders'] action or substitute its judgment for theirs."[105]

In fact, judicial deference is the key to understanding the internment cases, and it is not solely a matter of the judiciary's refusing to second-guess the commander in chief in wartime. The whole focus of the Revolution of 1937 had been judicial restraint, the right of the elected branches of government to enact policies without the courts' questioning the wisdom of those policies. In some ways, as David Currie suggests, the pendulum had swung too far. "One would not need to revert to the judicial arrogance of *Lochner* . . . to doubt whether a curfew at once so overinclusive and so underinclusive was a reasonably appropriate means of achieving the legislative goal."[106] A Court less deferential, he concluded, might well have found this exercise of congressional war powers "so arbitrary as to deprive those within its reach of their liberty without due process of law."[107]

Frankfurter, working as Black's ally, picked up on a second theme of judicial deference and urged Stone to amend the opinion in a manner to make clear to the country that "we decide nothing that is not before us." The *Hirabayashi* case dealt only with the curfew, and so should the Court's opinion; it should not address the more controversial aspects of the relocation plan. In his memo, Frankfurter wrote: "We decide the issue only as we have defined it—we decide that the curfew order as applied, and at the time it was applied, was within the boundaries of the war power." Stone recirculated the opinion with Frankfurter's language added, word for word.[108]

The chief wanted a united Court on this issue, but at least two members

---

105. *Ibid.* at 93.

106. The curfew was overinclusive since it restricted the liberty of all Japanese-Americans on the Pacific coast on the grounds that some indeterminate number of them might be dangerous; on the other hand, it was underinclusive since it did not apply in Hawaii, which was much closer to the actual war zone, nor did it apply to Americans of German or Italian ancestry even though the United States was then at war with those two countries. Military officials did not attempt to apply a curfew against people of Japanese descent in Hawaii for practical reasons; because of the large number of residents of Asian origin on the islands, it would have been impossible to isolate just the Japanese.

107. Currie, *Constitution in the Supreme Court*, 286–87.

108. 320 U.S. at 102.

had grave doubts. William O. Douglas had grown up in the Pacific Northwest with Japanese American friends, and he knew that not all of them, as Stone had insisted in his draft, had strong racial attachments to Japan. The lack of due process also troubled Douglas, but he would be willing to concur in an opinion that approved the military orders as a temporary expedient, and he urged Stone to limit the Court's decision to that holding. Moreover, he wanted the Court to issue a requirement that individuals had to have an opportunity to be classified as loyal citizens.[109]

Douglas circulated a concurring opinion incorporating his views, and Frankfurter exploded. He urged the chief to send at once "for Brother Douglas and talk him out of his opinion by making him see the dangers that he is inviting." The Douglas view would unleash thousands of *habeas corpus* proceedings, and "it would be for me deplorable beyond words to hold out hopes by any language that we use . . . hopes, which to put it very mildly, are not likely to be fulfilled." Douglas ought to be pulling along with everyone else instead of acting as if he were "in a rival grocery business." Trying to get Douglas to change his mind would probably be useless, Frankfurter concluded, because Douglas "will want to make the spread eagle speech."[110]

Frank Murphy alone on the Court seemed willing to face the issue of racism head-on. He termed the discrimination "so utterly inconsistent with our ideals and traditions, and in my judgment so contrary to constitutional requirements, that I cannot lend my assent." Frankfurter pleaded with Murphy not to dissent, for the sake of the Court. As opinion day approached, Frankfurter wrote:

Do you think it is conducive to the things you care about, including the great reputation of this court, to suggest that everybody is out of step except Johnny, and more particularly that the Chief Justice and seven other Justices of this Court are behaving like the enemy and thereby playing into the hands of the enemy. Compassion is, I believe, a virtue enjoined by Christ. Well, tolerance is a long, long way from compassion—and can't you write your views with such expressed tolerance that you won't make people think that when eight others disagree with you, you think their view means that they want to destroy the liberties of the United States and "lose the war" at home?[111]

---

109. Douglas to Stone, May 31, 1943, Douglas Papers, Library of Congress; and June 7, 1943, Stone Papers, Library of Congress. See also the discussion of Douglas's conflicting views in Irons, *Justice at War*, 237–39.

110. Frankfurter to Stone, June 4, 1943, Stone Papers, Library of Congress. That same day, Frankfurter sent another memorandum to Stone, suggesting a revision in the chief's draft that would close off the *habeas corpus* option Douglas had suggested.

111. Frankfurter to Murphy, June 10, 1943, Frankfurter Papers, Harvard Law School Library.

The appeal succeeded, and on June 21 Chief Justice Stone was able to announce an opinion upholding the curfew, in which all the members of the Court supported the result. He had labored on it through four drafts and had spent endless hours trying to assuage the doubts of at least five members of the Court about the legality of the detention program. The final opinion evaded all of the hard issues that the doubters had raised, and when Stone circulated his final draft, Frankfurter gave it his blessing: "You have labored with great forbearance and with concentration to produce something worthy of the Torah."[112]

But not all of the brethren agreed with Stone's broad enunciation of the war powers or his cavalier attitude toward labeling all Japanese Americans potentially disloyal. Douglas, Murphy, and Wiley Rutledge entered concurring opinions that came close to dissents; all indicated that they had agreed to what they considered an unconstitutional program because of the allegedly critical military situation. The tone of their opinions indicated that it would be far more difficult to get unanimity if another challenge reached the Court.[113]

Sixteen months later that challenge came, and this time the Court would not be able to evade the larger constitutional issues. Fred Korematsu had been charged with failing to report to an assembly center for relocation. His attorneys claimed that the entire exclusion order violated the Constitution by depriving citizens of their freedom without trial or other guarantees of due process. Moreover, the mass expulsion of an entire group based solely on a racial classification constituted a cruel and unusual punishment forbidden by the Eighth Amendment.[114]

At the conference on October 16, 1944, Stone tried to limit the discussion to a narrow technical question. Korematsu had been convicted of violating the exclusion order, which was designed to keep Japanese out of certain militarily designated areas. The only question the Court had to answer, according to the chief justice, was the constitutionality of that exclusion order. Framed this way, the case could be decided on narrow grounds similar to those in *Hirabayashi*.[115]

Stone turned to the senior justice, Owen J. Roberts, who had endorsed the earlier opinion, only to find Roberts dead set against the chief's plan. The combination of exclusion and prohibition orders gave Japanese

---

112. Frankfurter to Stone [n.d.], Stone Papers, Library of Congress.

113. The concurrences are at 320 U.S. at 105, 109, and 114 respectively. Rutledge wrote to the chief justice, "I have had more anguish over this case than any I have decided, save possibly one death case in the Ct. of Appeals." Rutledge to Stone, August 12, 1943, Stone Papers, Library of Congress.

114. *Korematsu v. United States*, 323 U.S. 214 (1944).

115. Conference notes, October 16, 1944, Jackson Papers, Library of Congress.

Americans a cruel choice—defy the order and be imprisoned or report to an assembly point and be relocated to a concentration camp. Black and Frankfurter supported the chief, as did Rutledge and Reed. But four justices—Roberts, Murphy, Jackson, and Douglas—planned to dissent on grounds that the military had overstepped its constitutional bounds of authority. Jackson, normally a supporter of strong government, declared, "I stop at *Hirabayashi*."[116]

Stone assigned the opinion to Black, who tried to follow the chief's lead in describing the case in the narrowest possible terms. When Black circulated his draft, Frankfurter responded the same day: "I am ready to join in your opinion without the change of a word." However, Frankfurter suggested, the elimination of one sentence would make even stronger the deference shown by the Court to congressional authority to prosecute the war. Black deleted the sentence.[117] But he concluded his opinion in a semi-apologetic manner: "We cannot—by availing ourselves of the calm perspective of hindsight—now say that at that time these actions were unjustified."[118]

This, however, struck Frankfurter as irrelevant; the Court owed deference not to the military but to the Congress. He dashed off a brief concurrence declaring that he found "nothing in the Constitution which denies to Congress the power to enforce a military order by making its violation an offense triable in civil courts." Then he saw the draft of Jackson's dissent, which included the phrase "Our forefathers were practical men, and they had no delusions about war being a lawless business." As Peter Irons notes, Frankfurter wasted no time responding to this "sacrilege." He called in the wife of his law clerk, Harry Mansfield, who was completing a graduate degree in history, and put her to work tracking down the Revolutionary War records of each member of the Constitutional Convention. Although Jackson deleted the offending sentence in his final draft, Frankfurter kept in his sentence lauding the framers and their actual knowledge of what war meant, since "a majority had had actual participation in war." Frankfurter concluded his brief concurrence declaring that DeWitt's exclusion orders could not "be stigmatized as lawless because like actions in times of peace would be lawless." As for Congress's endorsing those orders, "That is their business, not ours."[119]

Given the criticism that he had received from civil libertarians for his

116. Murphy, Minutes of Conference, October 16, 1944, in Irons, *Justice at War*, 322.
117. Frankfurter to Black, November 9, 1944, Frankfurter Papers, Harvard Law School Library; Stone to Black, November 9, 1944, Stone Papers, Library of Congress, also approving the draft but suggesting minor changes.
118. 323 U.S. at 230.
119. *Ibid.* at 224–25; Irons, *Justice at War*, 340–41.

earlier opinions, Frankfurter must have welcomed the letter that the noted philosopher and advocate of free speech Alexander Meiklejohn wrote him following this decision. Although Meiklejohn had been asked by the American Civil Liberties Union (ACLU) to keep a watching brief in Washington during the war, he wanted Frankfurter and Black to know that he disagreed with the ACLU's condemnation of the *Korematsu* holding. A grateful Frankfurter responded that "even a judge gets comfort in finding agreement in those very few whose judgment one really values."[120]

In the end, only three justices dissented—Roberts, Murphy, and Jackson. Murphy had always been unhappy about the relocation, and Roberts, from his work heading the first Pearl Harbor commission, knew that there had been absolutely no evidence of Japanese sabotage on the West Coast. Jackson, whatever his personal feelings about the relocation, took the most lawyerly approach, worrying what the decision would mean in the future if the Court approved a policy based entirely on racial classification. Whatever the military necessity might be, Jackson warned, once the Court approved that action, it would become a precedent ready to be used—and abused—in the future:

> The principle then lies about like a loaded weapon ready for the hand of any authority that can bring forward a plausible claim of an urgent need. . . . All who observe the work of the courts are familiar with what Judge Cardozo described as "the tendency of a principle to expand itself to the limit of its logic." A military commander may overstep the bound of constitutionality, and it is an incident. But if we review and approve, that passing incident has become the doctrine of the Constitution.[121]

Douglas swallowed his dissent when Black agreed to add a paragraph noting that the minority viewed the issues of evacuation and detention as inseparable, and therefore raising additional constitutional issues.[122] *Korematsu,* according to one of Black's biographers,

> was the worst judicial opinion that Justice Hugo Black wrote in his thirty-four years on the Court. It was devoid of meaningful analysis of the

---

120. Alexander Meiklejohn to Frankfurter, January 3, 1945; Frankfurter to Meiklejohn, January 8, 1945. Frankfurter Papers, Harvard Law School Library.

121. 323 U.S. at 246 (Jackson dissenting).

122. Douglas wrote in his memoirs that he always regretted not dissenting in the relocation cases, which were "ever on my conscience." *The Court Years: 1939–1975* (New York: Random House, 1980), 279–80. For a scathing critique of the constitutional analysis of the cases, see the "Leviticus" section by Jacobus ten Broek in Broek, Edward N. Barnhart, and Floyd W. Matsun, *Prejudice, War and the Constitution* (Berkeley: California University Press, 1968, orig. pub. in 1954).

underpinnings of military policy. It was deceptive in its strained narrowing of the constitutional issues that had been presented by Korematsu's attorneys. And it was a philosophically incoherent defense of broad government power by one of the most influential civil libertarians in the Court's history. . . . Although Black did not say so, he had given the military a license to trample on individual rights at will during wartime.[123]

And Frankfurter, who had opposed just this sort of trammeling in his days as a reformer, not only went along but encouraged Black and Stone in their views and denigrated the dissenters as unpatriotic. Black never regretted these decisions; years later he said that if he had been president, he would have done exactly the same thing, and he continued to justify it on grounds of military necessity.[124]

Frankfurter, however, should have known better, if for no other reason than from his frequent meetings with the officials he had helped place in the War Department, including John J. McCloy, one of the officials responsible for implementation of the internment program. By the time the cases came to the Court, the threat of a Japanese invasion of the Pacific Coast had evaporated, and the only questions the War Relocation Authority had to answer involved political risks, not military ones. But Frankfurter said nothing. He condemned Douglas for the "spread eagle speech" in opposition to the internment; he, in turn, willingly abdicated judicial responsibility in the name of patriotism.[125]

The divisions in the *Korematsu* case indicated that several of the justices felt it no longer appropriate to defer to government claims of military expediency. On December 18, 1944, the same day the Court handed down its decision in *Korematsu*, the justices unanimously authorized a writ of *habeas corpus* for Mitsuye Endo, a citizen whose loyalty had been clearly established.[126] Although the ACLU had hoped to use *Endo* to challenge the

---

123. Simon, *Antagonists*, 155. Commentators have condemned the decisions right from the beginning. Two early and still powerful critiques are Eugene V. Rostow, "The Japanese-American Cases—A Disaster," 54 *Yale Law Journal* 489 (1945); and Nanette Dembitz, "Racial Discrimination and the Military Judgment: The Supreme Court's Korematsu and Endo Decisions," 45 *Columbia Law Review* 175 (1945).

124. Gerald T. Dunne, *Hugo Black and the Judicial Revolution* (New York: Simon & Schuster, 1977), 213; see also Tinsley E. Yarbrough, *Mr. Justice Black and His Critics* (Durham: Duke University Press, 1988), 232–36.

125. In addition, recent evidence indicates that the solicitor general knew that there was no military necessity and deliberately misled the Court in this area. See Peter Irons, "Fancy Dancing in the Marble Palace," 3 *Constitutional Commentary* 35 (1986).

126. *Ex parte Endo*, 323 U.S. 283 (1944); for details, see Irons, *Justice at War*, 99–103, 307ff.

entire detention program, Justice Douglas carefully skirted that issue and confined his ruling to the single question of whether the War Relocation Authority could detain persons whose loyalty had been confirmed. He held that it could not, but he had difficulty with his opinion, since this case came perilously close to the larger issue raised in the *Korematsu* dissents—whether a person accused of no crime could be detained by military officials outside a combat zone.

In the *Milligan* case, decided *after* the Civil War had ended, the Supreme Court had said no, but Douglas now tried to distinguish between the two situations. Milligan had been held by the army, whereas Endo had been detained by a civilian agency. Douglas ignored the fact that the War Relocation Authority had been created for no other purpose than to assist the military in carrying out the evacuations. In their concurrences with the result, Justices Murphy and Roberts attacked the Court's refusal to resolve an important constitutional issue that had properly come before it—whether a loyal citizen who had committed no crime could be deprived of her liberty.[127] Ironically, Chief Justice Stone, who always emphasized the independence of the judiciary from political affairs, held up announcement of the decision until after the 1944 presidential election, eliciting a threat from Douglas to make the results known on his own.[128]

The issue of military courts' supplanting civilian courts, the same issue that the Court had addressed in the Civil War case, came before the justices in World War II as well, and once again the judiciary reached the same result. Shortly after the attack on Pearl Harbor, the government imposed martial law on the Hawaiian islands, and a comprehensive suspension of constitutional protections lasted until October 1944. Unlike the American West Coast, where the detention scheme applied only to those of Japanese ancestry, in Hawaii martial law affected the entire population of 465,000, of whom slightly more than a third were of Japanese origin.

In February 1944 a civilian shipyard worker in Honolulu, Lloyd Duncan (a Caucasian), got into a fight with two military sentries, who promptly arrested him; a military court tried and convicted him a few days later and sentenced him to six months in prison. Duncan's civilian counsel then sought *habeas corpus* in the federal district court, claiming that since the civilian courts had remained open, the provost's court had no jurisdiction over him. In response the government put General Robert C. Richardson, Jr., and Admiral Chester Nimitz on the stand to testify that although the Japanese military menace had waned, it still existed and therefore justified

---

127. Murphy's concurrence is at 323 U.S. 307, and that of Roberts is at 308.
128. Douglas to Stone, November 23, 1944, Douglas Papers, Library of Congress.

martial law.[129] Judge Delbert Metzger issued the writ ordering Duncan released from army custody; he went on to rule that despite the military testimony, the danger of an invasion by enemy troops now seemed "practically impossible" and that martial law, at least since March 1943, was illegal.

The army immediately appealed the *Duncan* decision along with another ruling freeing Harry E. White, a stockbroker tried and convicted in provost court for embezzlement. The Ninth Circuit reversed, and Judge William Healy's opinion implied that so long as the military considered it necessary, it could impose martial rule.[130] The Supreme Court accepted the petition for review and heard oral argument on December 7, 1945, four years to the day after the Japanese had attacked at Pearl Harbor and nearly four months after the war in the Pacific had ended. The government defended suspension of the civilian courts because of the danger that Hawaii might have been invaded during that time. Civil trials required jurors and took too long, so there would have been a constant shortage of civilian workers.[131] Moreover, the government pointed to the presence of a "heterogeneous population with all sorts of affinities and loyalties which are alien in many ways to the philosophy of life of the American Government."[132]

In conference, Chief Justice Stone tried to focus the question on what constituted martial law rather than on the power of the government to declare martial law. Even if martial law were justified because of the threat of invasion, this did not mean that the civilian courts could be suspended. He would reverse, therefore, solely on the grounds that the limits of martial law had been exceeded; so long as the civilian courts could operate, then proper cases must be tried there. Only Frankfurter and Burton disagreed, and Frankfurter charged his brethren with arrogance. "We sit as historians," he claimed, with knowledge of what actually happened; but in 1942 the outcome of the war remained in doubt, and he would defer to the military's judgment regarding necessity in curtailing the civilian courts.[133]

---

129. For the background of military rule in Hawaii and the origins of the case, see Harry N. Scheiber and Jane L. Scheiber, "Constitutional Liberty in World War II: Army Rule and Martial Law in Hawaii, 1941–1946," 3 *Western Legal History* 341 (1990). For contemporary critiques, see J. Garner Anthony, "Martial Law in Hawaii," 30 *California Law Review* 379 (1942), and "Recent Developments of Martial Law in the Pacific Area," 29 *Iowa Law Review* 481 (1944).

130. *Ex parte Duncan*, 146 F.2d 576 (9th Cir. 1944).

131. John P. Frank has argued that the real purpose of military rule was to keep Hawaii's labor movement under tight control. "Ex Parte Milligan v. The Five Companies: Martial Law in Hawaii," 44 *Columbia Law Review* 639 (1944).

132. The government arguments are summed up in Justice Murphy's concurrence, *Duncan v. Kahanamoku*, 327 U.S. 304, 329–34 (1946).

133. Conference notes, December 8 and 18, 1945, Douglas Papers, Library of Congress.

Black received the assignment, and his first task was to distinguish the Hawaiian situation from the West Coast internment cases. He did this by referring to the statutory authorization for the internment procedures, whereas there had been no statement by Congress authorizing or confirming the establishment of martial law in the islands. Second, Black looked to the Organic Act of 1900, which established the basic governmental structure of Hawaii, and found it lacked the sweeping authority to legitimate the army's actions. In a long section on the history of *habeas corpus* in Anglo-American history, Black eloquently portrayed army rule as the very kind of tyranny that made the writ essential to liberty.[134]

Black had been the author of *Hirabayashi*, in which he had accepted military necessity as a justification for the exclusion policy. Yet in the Hawaiian cases, where the actual danger of military invasion was far higher than on the West Coast, where a higher percentage of Japanese inhabitants lived, and where the violation of individual liberties had been less serious, Black voted to reverse. The only explanation would appear to be time; in 1943 Black took the army's word on what the generals considered necessary; in 1946, with the war over, he sat "as an historian" and found the army version unconvincing.

At one stage in writing his opinion, Black had attempted to deal with the constitutional implications of martial law, the very question Stone had originally raised in conference. But Stone now suggested that Black delete the constitutional discussion since it would be unnecessary if the opinion relied primarily on statutory interpretation.[135] Murphy, however, did want to reach the constitutional questions; as he explained, "constitutional rights were flaunted without necessity and I feel obliged to comment on it."[136] In his concurrence he not only attacked the army's arguments in justification of martial rule but, harking back to *Milligan*, reiterated the view that resort to military courts when the regular courts were open and able to function violated the Constitution. "The Bill of Rights," he charged, "disappeared by military fiat rather than military necessity."[137]

The Court during the war had, in fact, been caught up in the patriotic fervor, and a majority of its members proved more than willing to follow

---

134. 327 U.S. at 319–23.

135. Stone to Black, January 17, 1946, Stone Papers, Library of Congress. See also Black to Stone, January 18, 1946, *ibid.*, and Reed to Black, January 21, 1946, Black Papers, Library of Congress.

136. Murphy to Black, n.d., Black Papers, Library of Congress.

137. 327 U.S. at 324, 328. Stone also concurred, focusing on his view that even when military rule was justified by circumstances, it contained limits. *Ibid.* at 336. Justice Burton dissented, joined by Frankfurter; the two men found sufficient justification for the military to act, and Burton's opinion echoed much of the Ninth Circuit decsion. *Ibid.* at 337.

the lead of the civilian and military authorities. Some scholars have charged the justices with being racist; if so, they were no worse than the country itself, a point that does not excuse the internment nor the fact that the Court that most Americans see as their greatest bulwark of liberty stood by passively in the face of injustice. With the war over, the Court resumed its progress toward a jurisprudence of equal rights not only for African Americans (see chapter 9) but for Asians as well. In 1948 the Court struck down two California statutes aimed primarily at Japanese aliens and Japanese American citizens. In *Takahashi v. United States,* speaking through Justice Black, it invalidated a state statute making persons ineligible for citizenship equally ineligible for a commercial fishing license; the Court found this law violated a number of federal statutes as well as the Constitution, which pledged equal treatment of all persons.[138] In the other case, *Oyama v. California,* Chief Justice Vinson prevented California from escheating land that had been purchased by an alien resident father and titled in the name of his native-born son, an American citizen.[139] Both measures had arisen from the wartime animus against the Japanese; now, in more peaceful times, cooler heads could prevail.

Opinions on the Court and its protection of civil liberties during wartime vary. Alpheus Mason, in his biography of Chief Justice Stone, concedes that war often abridges individual liberty but concludes that "the amazing thing is not that so much freedom was sacrificed on the altar of military necessity . . . but that more was not. Even in the time of greatest stress, the Justices upheld the citizen's liberty to think, speak, and act to an extent that the nation at peace has sometimes felt it could ill afford to maintain. In this realm Stone's Court almost brought a miracle to pass."[140] Paul Murphy also notes that the "Court's favorable civil liberties record was in some ways one of the most remarkable aspects of the war period, particularly when one compares it with the black picture of World War I."[141] Other scholars have been less charitable. John Frank claimed that "the dominant lesson of our history in the relation of the judiciary to repression is that the courts love liberty most when it is under pressure least."[142]

---

138. 334 U.S. 410 (1948).

139. 332 U.S. 633 (1948).

140. Mason, *Stone,* 698.

141. Murphy, *Constitution in Crisis Times,* 247. Murphy does add, however, that this was the most popular war in the nation's history, and thus the type of civil liberties challenges present in the Civil War, World War I, and Vietnam were absent.

142. John P. Frank, "Review and Basic Liberties," in Edmond Cahn, ed., *Supreme Court and Supreme Law* (Bloomington: Indiana University Press, 1954), 114. For an immediate postwar view, see Osmond K. Fraenkel, "War, Civil Liberties and the Supreme Court, 1941–1946," 55 *Yale Law Journal* 717 (1946).

The truth is somewhere between Mason's near miracle and condemnations of the Court as repressive. Certainly some of the justices who later—and rightly—earned reputations as ardent defenders of individual liberty seemed all too willing to look the other way when the government claimed military necessity. One wonders if Black and Douglas would have voted as they did if the war had come later in their judicial careers, after they had reached their mature views on the extensive reach of the Bill of Rights. Frank Murphy and Robert Jackson intuitively opposed many of the measures undertaken in the name of the common defense, yet they too recognized that in a nation at war there would have to be sacrifices, and at times these might entail restrictions on individual liberties. If the Stone Court's decisions on Japanese internment have been condemned by history, its views on defining treason, denaturalization, the precedence of civilian courts, and freedom from an imposed flag salute have become staples in American constitutional law.

# 3

# THE EXPANSION OF INDIVIDUAL
# RIGHTS

The great expansion of civil rights and liberties that is often identified with the Warren Court (1953–1969) actually began much earlier, and part of the groundwork for that expansion can be found during the war years. Litigation involving individual rights had been coming to the Supreme Court with greater frequency ever since the World War I speech cases in 1919. During the supposedly reactionary 1920s, the Taft Court had begun the process of incorporation, by which the protections of the first eight amendments had been applied to the states through the Due Process Clause of the Fourteenth Amendment.

In 1925 the Court, almost in passing, noted that the First Amendment's protection of free speech applied to the states as well as to the federal government;[1] a few years later, it also held the Press Clause to apply.[2] The question then arose whether incorporation meant that all of the guarantees in the first eight amendments applied to the states or only some. Benjamin Nathan Cardozo, the shy, retiring successor to the flamboyant Holmes, held the same commitment to freedom that Holmes did but also believed in the necessity of drawing boundaries. A blanket application of the Bill of Rights would undermine an important aspect of federalism and deprive the nation of diversity and the states of their opportunity to experiment. In late 1937, Cardozo delivered the majority opinion in *Palko v. Connecticut* and in doing so defined much of the judicial debate for the next generation.[3]

*Palko* involved a relatively limited question: did the Fourteenth Amendment incorporate the guarantee against double jeopardy in the Fifth Amendment and apply it to the states? Cardozo said that it did not, for the Fourteenth Amendment did not automatically subsume the entire Bill of Rights. This meant that it incorporated some rights, but which ones? Cardozo included all the protections of the First Amendment, for freedom of

---

1. *Gitlow v. New York*, 268 U.S. 562 (1925).
2. *Near v. Minnesota*, 283 U.S. 697 (1931).
3. 302 U.S. 319 (1937).

thought and speech "is the matrix, the indispensable condition, for nearly every other form of [freedom]." But as for the Second through Eighth Amendments, the Court should apply only those that are "of the very essence of a scheme of ordered liberty" and "so rooted in the traditions and conscience of our people as to be ranked as fundamental." One test would be whether a violation of such a right would be "so acute and so shocking that our polity will not bear it."[4]

This doctrine of "selective incorporation" lodged enormous power and discretion in the courts. Nothing in the Constitution provided guidance; rather judges had to modernize the Bill of Rights and decide which parts applied to the states based on their views (guided at least in part by history and precedent) of what constituted a "fundamental" right. *Palko* made it possible to expand constitutional safeguards without amendment, but it required the justices to develop some hierarchy of values. Frankfurter, a friend of Cardozo, supported this approach since it coincided nicely with his own views of judicial caution.

Black had just gone onto the Court when the *Palko* decision came down, and at first he subscribed to it. But he grew increasingly uncomfortable with the philosophy and method of selective incorporation and the great power it lodged in the courts. Black's intuitive commitment to civil liberties derived from his populist background, which often led him to ignore precedent and listen to his own instincts for fair play and justice, instincts that shone through in a 1938 opinion extending the rights of counsel and *habeas corpus*.[5] Over the next decade he mulled over this problem, attempting to find a solution other than Cardozo's selective approach.

During these years Black and Frankfurter engaged in an ongoing debate over the meaning of the Fourteenth Amendment. Black's reading of history led him to believe that the framers of the amendment, especially Senator John A. Bingham, had intended to apply all of the Bill of Rights protections to the states. Frankfurter's equally detailed reading of history led him to the opposite conclusion, and he doubted whether the states would have ratified the Fourteenth Amendment if in fact it did subject them to such restrictions. Due process required no more, Frankfurter believed, than that the Court impose standards of procedural fairness on state criminal procedures.[6]

As early as 1939, Frankfurter had responded to comments Black made in conference about the applicability of the Fourteenth Amendment to

---

4. *Ibid.* at 325, 327, 328.

5. *Johnson v. Zerbst,* 304 U.S. 458 (1938).

6. Gerald T. Dunne, *Hugo Black and the Judicial Revolution* (New York: Simon & Schuster, 1977), 257–61; James F. Simon, *The Antagonists: Hugo Black, Felix Frankfurter and Civil Liberties in Modern America* (New York: Simon & Schuster, 1989), 172–76.

state action. Black had evidently said that he thought the Bill of Rights had been intended to apply to the states from the start and that the Marshall Court had been wrong in ruling that it did not.[7] Frankfurter said he could understand that position but disagreed with it. "What I am unable to appreciate is what are the criteria of selection," he said, "which applies and which does not apply."[8] This, of course, was exactly the question Black would wrestle with for almost a decade.

The debate almost came to a head in 1942 in *Betts v. Brady,* in which a majority of the Court held that the Sixth Amendment right to counsel did not apply to the states.[9] In conference Black argued passionately that Betts was "entitled to a lawyer from the history of the Fourteenth Amendment," which had been "intended to make applicable to the States the Bill of Rights." He brought up his own experience as a trial lawyer, and asked his colleagues how many of them thought that a layman could adequately plan a defense, summon witnesses, and conduct a trial against a trained prosecutor. "If I am to pass on what is fair and right," he declared, "I will say it makes me vomit to think men go to prison for a long time" because they had no benefit of counsel.[10]

Frankfurter responded just as heatedly and claimed that if the Court interpreted the Fourteenth Amendment to apply all of the Bill of Rights to the states, it would destroy the federal system and "uproot all the structure of the states."[11] About a year later, Frankfurter sent Black a lengthy letter trying to get him to be more explicit in his evidence for interpreting the Fourteenth Amendment to mean total incorporation. "Believe me," Frankfurter wrote, "nothing is farther from my purpose than contention. I am merely trying to get light on a subject which has absorbed as much thought and energy of my mature life as anything that has concerned me."[12] One can, I think, take Frankfurter seriously here despite the hyperbole. He had given much thought to the meaning of the Due Process Clause, and he did believe that, at a minimum, it required the states to provide procedural fairness in criminal trials.

But here Frankfurter and the other members of the Court ran into a

---

7. *Barron v. Baltimore,* 7 Pet. 243 (1833).

8. Frankfurter to Black, October 31, 1939, Frankfurter Papers, Library of Congress.

9. 316 U.S. 455 (1942).

10. Tinsley E. Yarbrough, *Mr. Justice Black and His Critics* (Durham: Duke University Press, 1988), 87. The reference here is to Holmes's alleged comment that his test for whether a state had violated procedural fairness is whether the action made him want to puke.

11. Frankfurter's commitment to federalism and the influence he had on that doctrine are explored in Mary Brigid McManamon, "Felix Frankfurter: The Architect of 'Our Federalism,' " 27 *Georgia Law Review* 697 (1993).

12. Frankfurter to Black, November 13, 1943, Frankfurter Papers, Harvard Law School Library.

jurisprudential conundrum. As Mark Silverstein has pointed out, Frankfurter boxed himself into a jurisprudential contradiction almost from the time he went onto the Court. On the one hand, he continued to oppose judicial subjectivity, by which judges could interpret statute or constitution to meet their own prejudices. He also opposed absolute standards as a means of controlling subjectivity because he believed judges needed some flexibility in interpreting the law. Frankfurter had as a paradigm the scientific expert, who would be able to reach a proper conclusion through correct reasoning. Theoretically, such an enlightened judge would be free from overt subjectivity as well as rigid dogma. Judges could enforce principles, but they would reach those principles in a disinterested, scientific manner. Although nominally not a Realist, Frankfurter had shared the Realists' perception that individual traits predisposed judges toward particular, subjective ends. He knew that could not be changed, yet he resisted imposing external standards to limit judicial discretion. Judges had to choose, Frankfurter believed, but they had to choose in an enlightened manner.[13]

Black not only opposed judicial subjectivity but also condemned leaving judges free to choose from among competing alternatives. He distrusted so-called experts and believed that reposing constitutional choices in their hands smacked too much of an elitism—the few choosing the right course for the many—that offended his populist sensibilities. He proposed instead the imposition of absolutes through a literal reading of the Constitution. But in narrowing the scope of judicial discretion, Black made the Court the prime vehicle for guaranteeing the values of those absolutes, thus increasing the power of judges.[14]

But what about rights that are not mentioned specifically in the first eight amendments or that can easily be subsumed under the rubrics of due process or equal protection? Are there additional rights, for example, that might be subsumed under the Privileges and Immunities Clauses of Article IV and the Fourteenth Amendment, and if so, how are they to be determined? Such an instance came up in a carryover case from the 1940 Term involving a California "anti-Okie" law, which made it a misdemeanor to bring an "indigent person" into the state.[15] After its first argument, the Conference had agreed that the law was unconstitutional; Chief Justice Hughes had said that the "right to go around these United States is a right

---

13. Mark Silverstein, *Constitutional Faiths: Felix Frankfurter, Hugo Black, and the Process of Judicial Decision Making* (Ithaca: Cornell University Press, 1984), 128–29.

14. *Ibid.*, 129–30; see also Black to Conference, March 23, 1945, Black Papers, Library of Congress.

15. For the background of the law and of the case, see Edward W. Adams, "State Control of Interstate Migration of Indigents," 40 *Michigan Law Review* 711 (1942).

of citizenship," indeed "one of the few" such rights directly protected by the Constitution.[16] The justices disagreed, however, on just which part of the Constitution protected that right, and they assigned the case for reargument the following term, by which time Stone had become chief and James Byrnes had joined the Court.

At Conference that fall, Stone urged that the law be struck down on the basis of the Commerce Clause, a position joined by Reed and Frankfurter; but a majority of Black, Douglas, Murphy, Byrnes, and Jackson wanted to base the decision on the Privileges and Immunities Clause, although Jackson said he could go with the commerce grounds. Only Roberts was willing to uphold the law.[17] Stone assigned the opinion to Byrnes and then began pressuring him to change his grounds to the Commerce Clause. Eventually Byrnes agreed and secured a majority for invalidating the California law as an unconstitutional barrier to interstate commerce.[18] Justice Douglas entered a concurring opinion, joined by Black and Murphy, contending that the right to travel from state to state comprised "an incident of *national* citizenship" and occupied "a more protected position in our constitutional system than does the movement of cattle, fruit, steel and coal across state lines."[19]

Douglas, much to Frankfurter's chagrin, was perhaps the most open-minded and creative member of the Court when it came to finding justification for the protection of individual liberties, and this is apparent in a case that was little noticed at the time but would have major ramifications afterward. *Skinner v. Oklahoma* (1942) involved a statute mandating sterilization for "compulsory criminals."[20] One might have expected challenges to this law on the basis of either the Equal Protection Clause or the Due Process Clause of the Fourteenth Amendment. But the Equal Protection Clause had been so narrowly interpreted by the Court that it had become practically moribund. Holmes, in his opinion in *Buck v. Bell* (1927) supporting a Virginia sterilization law for persons with hereditary imbecility or insanity,

---

16. Conference notes, May 3, 1941, Douglas Papers, Library of Congress.

17. Conference notes, October 25, 1941, *ibid.*

18. *Edwards v. California*, 314 U.S. 160 (1941). Stone to Byrnes, November 1, 1941, Stone Papers, Library of Congress; Memorandum, Byrnes to Conference [n.d.], *ibid.*, "Inasmuch as the enclosed opinion embodies a theory other than that which I approved in Conference." The case was Byrnes's only major opinion for the Court; see William Pettit, "Justice Byrnes and the United States Supreme Court," 6 *South Carolina Law Quarterly* 423 (1954).

19. 314 U.S. at 170 (Douglas concurring). Jackson entered a separate concurrence, arguing that both the Privileges and Immunities Clause of the Fourteenth Amendment and the Commerce Clause invalidated the California statute. 314 U.S. at 181 (Jackson concurring).

20. 316 U.S. 535 (1942). For an analysis of the case, see Note, "Constitutionality of State Laws Providing Sterilization for Habitual Criminals," 51 *Yale Law Journal* 1380 (1942).

had dismissed equal protection as "the usual last resort of constitutional arguments."[21] Moreover, the use by conservative jurists of so-called substantive due process to protect property rights and strike down reform legislation had, after the constitutional crisis of 1937, left courts reluctant to use the Due Process Clause for evaluating state legislation.

Douglas cut through the Gordian knot by noting that the law did not apply equally to all felons since it made an exception for embezzlers. This opened the door to an equal protection analysis, and Douglas charged through. He identified the right to procreate as a "fundamental right," and any legislation restricting that right would be subject to "strict scrutiny" by the courts. Oklahoma's law did not apply equally to all and therefore failed the constitutional test.[22]

At this time the Equal Protection Clause indeed lay dormant if not moribund; moreover, the Court had never identified procreation as a "fundamental right"—that is, a basic right essential for individual freedom—and Douglas did not offer a single citation to justify this assertion. Beyond that, he connected fundamental rights to a "strict scrutiny" standard even though the Court had only just begun to differentiate different criteria for reviewing constitutional claims. More than any other case of this time, *Skinner* animated the new jurisprudence suggested by Stone in his *Carolene Products* footnote. By pronouncing the "invidious discrimination" in the law's enforcement its chief evil, Douglas opened a whole new avenue for courts to review state legislation that treated some people differently than others.

Douglas breathed life back into the Equal Protection Clause, and in the years following *Skinner* the Court began to make more and more substantive judgments on equal protection claims. The justices adopted the same analytic model that Douglas had proposed. Is there a fundamental right involved? If so, does it meet the standard of strict scrutiny? Is there any evidence of invidious discrimination?[23]

The question of due process, the core of the debate between Black and Frankfurter, is crucial in criminal procedure because if the police are not restrained by procedural safeguards, then persons suspected or accused of crimes are totally at the mercy of the state. Frankfurter once pointed out that "ours is the accusatorial as opposed to the inquisitorial system. Society

---

21. 274 U.S. 200, 208 (1927).

22. For a contemporary analysis of the opinion, see Note, "Constitutionality of State Laws."

23. There has been a lively debate about Douglas's opinion in this case. For opposing views, see G. Edward White, "The Anti-Judge: William O. Douglas and the Ambiguities of Individuality," 74 *Virginia Law Review* 17 (1988); and Melvin I. Urofsky, "William O. Douglas as Common Law Judge," 41 *Duke Law Journal* 133 (1991).

carries the burden of proving its charge against the accused . . . by evidence independently secured through skillful investigation."[24] To protect against police abuse, the Bill of Rights spelled out restrictions on the national police; one did not have to incorporate those protections because the Due Process Clause by itself governed state police practices.

Frankfurter, unlike Black, did not believe in a static and absolute interpretation of due process, and he attempted to develop guidelines for lower court judges. Relying on Cardozo's *Palko* opinion, he spoke often of "those canons of decency and fairness which express the notions of justice of English-speaking peoples even toward those charged with the most heinous offenses."[25] The courts should not tolerate police tactics that "offend the community's sense of fair play and decency" or conduct that "shocks the conscience."[26] Due process, then, equated with fundamental fairness, but one can argue that fairness, like beauty, may be in the eye of the beholder. That upset Hugo Black. If judges had the discretion to determine fairness on the basis of what shocked them, then due process would vary from judge to judge and court to court. The guarantees of the Constitution had to be absolute, not dependent upon any one jurist's notions of fairness.

At first Black seemed to take a fairly flexible approach to due process, but by 1942 his view had solidified. "Due Process for me," Frankfurter recorded Black as saying, "means the first nine amendments and nothing else."[27] Frankfurter could not accept so rigid a view. He believed judges had to have flexibility in interpreting the Due Process Clause; judges, he believed, "knew" what was fundamentally fair and what was not, and they had the power and the duty to pronounce what is fair and what offends that fairness.[28]

But not everyone, not even all judges, defined "fairness" in precisely the same way, and so within rather broad parameters, Frankfurter stood ready to defer to state legislatures in their determination of proper procedure. The Fourteenth Amendment, he argued, should not be applied "so as to turn this Court into a tribunal for revision of criminal convictions in the State courts." Due process did not restrict the states "beyond the narrow limits of imposing upon them standards of decency deeply felt and widely recognized in Anglo-American jurisdictions."[29]

---

24. *Watts v. Indiana,* 338 U.S. 49, 54 (1949).
25. *Adamson v. California,* 332 U.S. 46, 67–68 (1948).
26. *Rochin v. California,* 342 U.S. 165, 172, 173 (1952).
27. Silverstein, *Constitutional Faiths,* 151, n.60.
28. See, for example, Frankfurter's comments on the case of *Buchalter v. New York,* 312 U.S. 780 (1943), in Joseph Lash, *From the Diaries of Felix Frankfurter* (New York: Norton, 1975), 241–42.
29. *Stein v. New York,* 346 U.S. 156, 199 (1953) (Frankfurter dissenting).

The problem with this approach is that it had few if any objective standards; for Frankfurter, those practices that shocked his conscience violated due process. It did not shock his conscience, for example, if states chose not to provide counsel to defendants in noncapital felony cases. Although in the famous *Scottsboro* case Justice Sutherland had come close to holding a right to counsel in capital cases as an essential of due process, the Court had grounded its opinion in that case on fundamental fairness.[30] The Court did not even recognize a right to counsel for federal defendants until 1938,[31] so a majority of the Court did not see any necessity to extend this right to the states in *Betts v. Brady* (1942).[32] Justice Roberts's opinion for the Court held that denial of counsel did not violate standards of fundamental fairness in every instance; the courts should therefore evaluate the circumstances on a case-by-case basis.

Black, however, did find the *Betts* situation offensive, and he told the Conference why. From his practice he had learned that few nonlawyers understood the law, and they could hardly know how to plan and carry out an adequate defense.[33] Frankfurter responded that the states had to be left some flexibility in a federal system; to impose the Bill of Rights on them "would uproot all the structure of the states."[34] The Court continued to hear one case after another in which defendants had been denied counsel, and in each one a majority found that "special circumstances" had existed so that "fundamental fairness" required a new trial with the assistance of counsel.[35] Not until a year after Frankfurter had retired from the bench did the Court reverse *Betts* and, with Justice Black speaking for a unanimous Court, extend the Sixth Amendment right to counsel to the states.[36]

When federal (as opposed to state) agents played fast and loose with due process, either in the Bill of Rights or in statute, the Court had no

---

30. *Powell v. Alabama,* 287 U.S. 45 (1932).

31. *Johnson v. Zerbst,* 304 U.S. 458 (1938); Justice Black wrote for the Court in this case, his first great criminal procedure opinion.

32. 316 U.S. 455 (1942).

33. Yarbrough, *Justice Black and His Critics,* 87; see also Conference notes, April 14, 1942, Douglas Papers, Library of Congress.

34. Shortly afterward Frankfurter penned a long letter to Black attempting to secure Black's justification for construing the Due Process Clause to mean total incorporation of the first nine amendments. Frankfurter to Black, November 13, 1943, Frankfurter Papers, Harvard Law School Library.

35. The Court, as Jerold Israel pointed out, "consistently whittled away at the *Betts* rule until . . . it was almost completely eroded." "Gideon v. Wainwright: The 'Art' of Overruling," 1963 *Supreme Court Review* 211, 260.

36. *Gideon v. Wainwright,* 372 U.S. 335 (1963). The story of that case, as well as the road the Court took to it from *Betts,* is magnificently told in Anthony Lewis, *Gideon's Trumpet* (New York: Random House, 1964).

problem in strictly enforcing procedural protections. In 1942 five members of the McNabb family in rural Tennessee had been arrested for killing an alcohol tax agent, and the men had been held for three days of questioning without being able to see either friends or attorneys. Finally, after three of the men had confessed, they had been brought before a magistrate for arraignment, although a federal statute required prompt arraignment. At oral argument Chief Justice Stone pressed the government lawyer to explain why there had been such a long delay, but the attorney could not give the Court an acceptable answer.[37]

Frankfurter, who ultimately wrote the opinion for the Court, charged that civilized standards of criminal procedure had not been met in this case; in short, it lacked fundamental fairness. Although Frankfurter tried to keep the opinion as narrow as possible, in effect it created a new exclusionary rule, one that prohibited the use of confessions obtained during any unnecessary delay in arraignment.[38] Black originally wanted to write a much stronger opinion striking down the confession and to base it on constitutional grounds. The McNabbs, he claimed, were "hill-billy mountaineers" and "ignorant," and the confession had been coerced, violating their Fifth Amendment rights. In the end, only Reed favored upholding the conviction, and in his dissent he noted his alarm about "broadening the possibilities of defendants escaping punishment by these more rigorous technical requirements."[39]

The Court declined to strike a major blow for civil liberties in two eavesdropping cases during the 1941 Term. During the 1920s, federal agents had adapted the new technology of the telephone in their efforts to enforce prohibition. They wiretapped the phones of suspected bootleggers, and on the basis of the conversations they overheard through this means, they secured convictions for violation of the Volstead Act. The defendants had appealed, claiming that the wiretaps had violated the Fourth Amendment ban on warrantless searches. Chief Justice William Howard Taft considered the claim irrelevant, and speaking for a bare majority of five, he had written a narrow, formalistic interpretation of the constitutional guarantee. There had been no actual entry, but only the use of an enhanced sense of hearing, he claimed, and to pay too much attention to "nice ethical conduct by government officials would make society suffer and give criminals greater immunity than has been known heretofore."[40]

---

37. Stone to Frankfurter, June 3, 1943, Frankfurter Papers, Harvard Law School Library.
38. *McNabb v. United States*, 318 U.S. 332 (1943).
39. *Ibid.* at 347, 349 (Reed dissenting). See Frankfurter's efforts to dissuade Reed in two letters, February 24 and 26, 1943, Frankfurter Papers, Harvard Law School Library. Douglas apparently was originally willing to affirm based on the record but changed his mind. Notes for conference [n.d. 1943], Douglas Papers, Library of Congress.
40. *Olmstead v. United States*, 277 U.S. 438, 468 (1928).

The Taft opinion elicited dissents from Butler, Holmes, and Brandeis. In a well-reasoned historical analysis, the generally conservative Butler repudiated Taft's interpretation of what the Fourth Amendment meant and argued for a broad view of the protections the framers had intended to place around the home.[41] Holmes, in a comment that soon caught the liberal imagination, condemned wiretapping as "a dirty business."[42] But the most impressive opinion came from Brandeis, who in response to Taft's cavalier view of government ethics declared that he considered it "less evil that some criminals should escape than that the government should play an ignoble part. . . . If government becomes a lawbreaker, it breeds contempt for law."[43]

The Brandeis dissent had enormous impact, and in the Federal Communications Act of 1934 Congress had prohibited anyone not authorized by the sender from intercepting wire and radio communications and divulging or using information so obtained. The Court had interpreted Section 605 to mean that evidence secured by wiretapping could not be used in federal trials and then had broadened that ruling to include evidence "derived" from the wiretap. Justice Frankfurter, in one of his early opinions, had denounced such evidence as the "fruit of a poisoned tree."[44]

In the first case to reach the Stone Court, the justices had to decide whether evidence secured by a wiretap could be admitted in federal court if the defendants, while convicted on the basis of that evidence, had not been parties to the intercepted material, a situation not covered by the wording of Section 605. The lower courts had ruled in favor of the government, and in what many civil libertarians took as a retreat from the *Nardone* rulings, a majority of the high court, speaking through Roberts, held the defendants, since they had not participated in the intercepted communications, to have no standing to challenge their use. The statute obviously had been violated, Roberts admitted, but that fact by itself did not taint the testimony.[45]

In a companion case, the Court upheld the use of a "detectaphone," a device similar to a stethoscope that, when placed against a wall, picked up

---

41. *Ibid.* at 485 (Butler dissenting).

42. *Ibid.* at 469, 470 (Holmes dissenting).

43. *Ibid.* at 471 (Brandeis dissenting).

44. *Nardone v. United States,* 302 U.S. 379 (1937); the case was ordered retried, and the appeal from the second conviction was overturned, 308 U.S. 338 (1939). The ruling applied only to federal trials, but in another case, *Weiss v. United States,* 308 U.S. 321 (1939), the Court extended the ban to intrastate communications. See Grover C. Young, "The Legal Status of Wire Tapping under the Federal Constitution," 6 *University of Detroit Law Journal* 69 (1943).

45. *Goldstein v. United States,* 316 U.S. 114 (1942).

and amplified sound vibrations from the adjoining room. The government argued that the device did not come within the reach of the Communications Act and was necessary so federal agents could "overhear or intercept the communication of suspected spies or saboteurs." Roberts, again writing for the majority, took an extremely narrow view of Section 605 and held that it applied only to "the means of communication," not "the secrecy of the conversation."[46]

Stone, Murphy, and Frankfurter dissented in both cases. The chief justice would have liked to overrule *Olmstead* and declare that wiretapping without a warrant violated the Fourth Amendment, but he would do that only if he had unanimous support. Unable to secure such consent, Stone, joined by Frankfurter, issued a brief dissent to the effect that they would have been "happy to join" in overruling *Olmstead;* moreover, since the majority had held the two wiretap cases indistinguishable, they saw no need to repeat the eloquent dissents in the earlier case.[47] Frank Murphy, on the other hand, wanted to attack the "dirty business" head-on and began preparing a strong dissent based on a right to privacy in one's home, the same argument Brandeis had elaborated on in his *Olmstead* dissent. He also attacked the conduct of "overzealous public officials." When Frankfurter learned of Murphy's dissent, he tried to talk him out of it. Murphy had heard his views on wiretapping, Frankfurter wrote, "and you must, therefore, know that I am as uncompromising on that subject as you are, feeling that the issue goes to the very essence of a civilized society." Would it not be better then, if the dissenters all spoke in the same language so as not to "attenuate the moral strength of our position." The best way would be to agree with the chief justice and refer to what Brandeis and Holmes had said in *Olmstead*.[48] The note merely annoyed Murphy, and he went on to write one of the most powerful dissents of his career.[49]

Ironically, the so-called Axis failed to unite on this topic; and given the views later held by Black and Douglas, one wonders why they did not join with the dissenters. Douglas, in fact, afterward admitted he had been wrong and in 1967 voted with the majority to overturn *Olmstead* and *Goldman,* following the lines laid down first by Brandeis and then by Murphy.[50] At the time Murphy thought his two colleagues did not want to hinder "going

---

46. *Goldman v. United States,* 316 U.S. 129, 133 (1942). See Nahum A. Bernstein, "The Fruit of the Poisonous Tree . . . ," 37 *Illinois Law Review* 99 (1942).

47. Conference notes, February 14, 1942, Douglas Papers, Library of Congress; 316 U.S. at 136.

48. Frankfurter to Murphy, March 5, 1942, Frankfurter Papers, Harvard Law School Library.

49. 316 U.S. at 136. See Bernstein, "The Fruit of the Poisonous Tree."

50. *Katz v. United States,* 389 U.S. 347 (1967).

after the papers of big corporations," but it is more likely that with the war on, the five-man majority did not want to thwart the FBI in its efforts to track down spies and saboteurs. In 1941 and 1942 Congress had held a major debate on wiretapping as it related to national security. Jackson (then attorney general), FBI director J. Edgar Hoover, and President Roosevelt had all urged Congress to legalize eavesdropping in security investigations. Labor and a number of civil liberties groups withdrew their normal opposition to wiretapping and supported a bill that permitted interceptions in security cases. Congress did not enact legislation, but as Justice Jackson knew, the issue had already been resolved. In 1940 President Roosevelt had sent the attorney general a secret executive order directing the use of wiretaps by the FBI "when necessary in situations involving national defense."[51] Even without this information, a majority of the Court still found nothing wrong with wiretapping, and Roberts's opinions are every bit as obtuse on the subject as Taft's had been.

By 1942 the Court had established the rule that federal courts had to provide counsel for indigent defendants and that if the defendant wished to waive that right, the decision had to be "intelligent and competent"— that is, the accused had to be mentally capable of making a decision and had to have the necessary facts on which to evaluate the choice. The Court then faced a series of cases that attempted to determine just how intelligent and competent a waiver had to be.

The first case arrived in January 1942. Daniel Glasser, an assistant U.S. attorney, had been indicted with several other persons on charges of conspiracy to defraud the government. The trial judge had appointed one of Glasser's lawyers—in fact the most able and active of his attorneys—to represent one of the other defendants as well. Glasser had immediately objected but then had remained silent for the rest of the trial. Four months after having been found guilty, however, he filed an appeal claiming that his Sixth Amendment right to counsel had been denied.

Stone did not like the circumstances but at Conference voted to let the verdict stand, a position joined only by Frankfurter. Murphy, writing for the majority, noted that a technical reading of the Sixth Amendment might lead one to the conclusion that Glasser had an attorney, and by not maintaining his protest during the trial, he had in effect waived the right. The

---

51. Sidney Fine, *Frank Murphy: The Washington Years* (Ann Arbor: University of Michigan Press, 1984), 279; Paul L. Murphy, *The Constitution in Crisis Times, 1918–1969* (New York: Harper & Row, 1972), 206, n.112; Alan F. Westin, *Privacy and Freedom* (New York: Atheneum, 1967), 176–77. Jackson recused himself in the cases because as attorney general he had permitted the wiretaps to go forward; Murphy might well have recused since taps also had been initiated during his tenure at the Justice Department.

real issue was not whether or not there had been counsel but how effective that counsel had been; the judge's assignment of another client had seriously hampered the ability of the attorney to act in Glasser's best interest. The court must not only see that the accused has a lawyer but must "refrain from embarrassing counsel in the defense of an accused by insisting, or indeed, even suggesting that counsel undertake to concurrently represent interests which might diverge from those of his first client."[52]

Frankfurter argued in dissent that Glasser had not raised the issue "at any of the critical occasions" during the trial and that the constitutional claim was "obviously a lawyer's afterthought." Hugo Black, however, disagreed; he told Murphy that the "argument that a defendant must iterate, reiterate and then reiterate again his assertion of a Constitutional right has no appeal to me." Murphy agreed. "*Once* is enough," he told Black; a person doesn't have to keep repeating the claim every day of the trial.[53]

On the other hand, if a person really wanted to waive the right to counsel, trial courts had to allow him to do so. Gene McCann had been indicted on six counts of mail fraud and had insisted on acting as his own attorney; when the case came to trial in July 1941, the judge questioned McCann extensively, and the accused said that he knew the facts better than anyone and could defend himself more effectively than a lawyer. Moreover, he wished to have the case tried by the judge rather than a jury. With the consent of the U.S. attorney, a bench trial followed, with McCann found guilty on all counts. As Frankfurter put it in the majority opinion, "An accused, in the exercise of a free and intelligent choice, and with the considered approval of the court, may waive trial by jury, and so likewise may he competently and intelligently waive his Constitutional right to assistance of counsel."[54] Douglas, interestingly enough, joined by Black and Murphy, dissented on the grounds that no layperson could understand the "limited nature of the defenses" available under the mail fraud statute. Murphy, in a separate dissent, went even further, declaring that "the right to a jury trial can [not] be waived in criminal proceedings in federal courts."[55]

Fundamental fairness of a trial involved more than just counsel; jury composition could also affect how fair a trial a defendant received. The

---

52. *Glasser v. United States*, 315 U.S. 60, 76 (1942). Glasser also raised the issue that some women had been deliberately excluded from the jury pool, which made the panel unrepresentative. Local officials included only women on lists supplied by the League of Women Voters. Murphy noted that such a process "did not conform to the traditional requirements of jury trial" but that the record failed to sustain the claim that jury selection had affected the outcome of the trial.

53. *Ibid.* at 88, 89 (Frankfurter dissenting); Fine, *Murphy*, 272.

54. *Adams v. United States ex rel. McCann*, 317 U.S. 269, 275 (1942).

55. *Ibid.* at 286.

Sixth Amendment provides that "in all criminal prosecutions, the accused shall enjoy the right to a speedy and public trial by an impartial jury." Although the words do not appear in the text, it has traditionally meant a trial by one's peers. But in many states of the Union in the 1940s, juries were hardly representative of the local population. In southern states blacks rarely appeared on juries since jury pools were chosen from voter registration records; other states excluded women from the grand jury and/or the petit jury.[56]

Early efforts by southern states to exclude African Americans had met a mixed response in the Court. White defendants never challenged a state law banning black jurors, so the only disputes heard by appellate courts resulted when black defendants raised the question. The Supreme Court heard three cases in 1879 that set the pattern for the next three generations. It struck down a West Virginia law restricting jury duty to whites, but juries selected under that law would be considered valid unless individually challenged.[57] When a state judge barred blacks from serving on a jury, the Court ruled that this constituted state action and violated federal civil rights legislation.[58] But even if general laws excluding the former slaves could not pass judicial muster, particular practices would. In the third case, the high court held that the absence of blacks from any particular jury did not prove the existence of systematic exclusion.[59] The sum result of these cases seemed to be that a black defendant had a right to a trial by a jury that included blacks, but blacks had no right to serve on juries. And since it took resources to challenge the system, over the years southern practice tended to confirm all-white juries.

This began to change with the 1935 decision in *Norris v. Alabama,* a follow-up to the notorious *Scottsboro* case. Evidence showed that no black had served on a jury within the memory of any officer of the court, leading Chief Justice Hughes to find that "this long-continued, unvarying and wholesale exclusion of Negroes from jury service" constituted a pattern of unconstitutional conduct.[60] With this decision, the Court abandoned the practice in which individual defendants would have to show discrimination in specific cases and allowed the evidence of long-term exclusion to establish that fact. In 1938 the Court extended that doctrine to grand juries as well as petit juries.[61]

---

56. Although exclusion of blacks from jury pools was the most blatant form of discrimination dealt with by the justices in this area, the Court also struck down the practice of deliberate exclusion of persons working for a daily wage. *Thiel v. Southern Pacific,* 328 U.S. 217 (1946).

57. *Strauder v. West Virginia,* 103 U.S. 303 (1879).

58. *Ex parte Virginia,* 100 U.S. 339 (1879).

59. *Virginia v. Rives,* 100 U.S. 313 (1879).

60. 294 U.S. 587, 597 (1935).

61. *Pierre v. Louisiana,* 306 U.S. 354 (1938).

Despite these rulings, local practices, conducted by white officials, continued to keep blacks off juries. In one Texas county, where blacks made up 20 percent of the population, the jury commissioner explained why in an eight-year period only 5 out of 384 grand jurors were black: he was "not personally acquainted with any member of the Negro race." The Court avoided questioning the truth of this story and simply held that for a commissioner to limit jury selection to his own acquaintances constituted a discriminatory practice.[62]

Texas proved singularly unwilling to comply with the ruling, and in 1942 the Stone Court had to repeat the lesson. In a unanimous opinion, the Court held that the deliberate exclusion of blacks from grand juries for a sixteen-year period constituted a clear violation of the Equal Protection Clause.[63] The Dallas County jury commissioners then decided that if they could no longer keep all blacks off juries, they could limit the number who actually served to no more than one per sixteen-member grand jury panel. In an amazing decision, a majority of the Court found this practice legitimate.[64] In Dallas County blacks made up 15 percent of the population, and therefore a truly representative jury would have had at least two black members. But the Court had never required mathematical exactitude or even proportional representation in prior jury cases, and Frankfurter at Conference actually praised the county as having made a "conscientious effort to carry out the law." Justice Jackson claimed that by requiring one black member, the commissioners had actually discriminated against whites, and he thought the justices had been "damned fools" to take the case.[65]

Originally only Murphy and Black thought that L. C. Akins, who had been sentenced to death for murder, had been denied equal protection. In his draft for the majority, Reed claimed that history and the record in the case showed that Texas had attempted to comply with the spirit of the *Hill* decision. All three of the jury commissioners, however, had admitted that they had no intention of allowing any more than one black per jury; yet according to Reed, the Court remained "unconvinced" that the commissioners had "deliberately and intentionally limited the number of Negroes on the grand jury list."

Murphy's dissent easily tore apart this casuistry and convinced the chief justice that there had, indeed, been discrimination. Stone suggested to Reed that he add a paragraph meeting Murphy's objection along the lines

62. *Smith v. Texas*, 311 U.S. 128 (1940).

63. *Hill v. Texas*, 316 U.S. 400 (1942).

64. *Akins v. Texas*, 325 U.S. 398 (1945).

65. Fine, *Murphy*, 391.

that this practice, while discriminatory, was "not the kind of discrimination" that came within the reach of the Equal Protection Clause.[66] Reed refused, and Stone joined Murphy's dissent. Five years later, however, the Court reversed *Akins* and without mentioning Murphy's dissent nonetheless validated his argument.[67]

The Court recognized the difficulty of dealing with southern racial practices despite the fact that the nation was then engaged in a war against totalitarian regimes based on racist ideologies. Just as it had chipped away at the exclusion of blacks from juries, so the Court also began eroding segregation in the political process. In 1935 the Court had seemingly validated black disenfranchisement in primaries in *Grovey v. Townsend*,[68] but it soon reversed itself. In *United States v. Classic* (1941), the justices held that Congress could regulate a primary where it constituted part of the overall machinery for choosing elected federal officials.[69] The National Association for the Advancement of Colored People (NAACP) recognized that the latter case had been decided on narrow grounds; it involved a claim by registered white members of the Democratic Party in Louisiana that their votes in the 1940 primary had not been counted. *Classic* looked more like a voting frauds case than a civil rights decision, but Thurgood Marshall gambled that with the liberal makeup of the Court in the 1943 Term he might be able to use the case as a way to get at the all-white primary itself, and his gamble paid off in *Smith v. Allwright*.[70]

At Conference on January 17, 1944, all the justices except Roberts voted to overrule *Grovey*, and Chief Justice Stone assigned the decision to Frankfurter.[71] That afternoon a troubled Robert Jackson came to Frankfurter's chambers and said he had something delicate to discuss, but he would talk with the "customary feeling of freedom" the two friends enjoyed. He urged Frankfurter not to write the decision in *Allwright* since the decision, unpalatable to the South in any event, would be even more so if it came from the pen of a member who, in light of southern prejudices, had three disqualifications.

66. Stone to Reed, May 25, 1945, Stone Papers, Library of Congress.
67. *Cassell v. Texas*, 339 U.S. 282 (1950).
68. 295 U.S. 45 (1935).
69. 313 U.S. 299 (1941).
70. 321 U.S. 649 (1944). For an enthusiastic view, see William H. Hastie, "Appraisal of *Smith v. Allwright*," 5 *Lawyers Guild Review* 65 (1945). Robert E. Cushman considered the decision only a first step. "The Texas 'White Primary' Case—*Smith v. Allwright*," 30 *Cornell Law Quarterly* 66 (1944). For Marshall's strategy, see Mark V. Tushnet, *Making Civil Rights Law: Thurgood Marshall and the Supreme Court, 1936–1961* (New York: Oxford University Press, 1994), 105–7.
71. Conference notes, January 17, 1944, Douglas Papers, Library of Congress.

"You are a New Englander, you are a Jew, and you are not a Democrat—at least not recognized as such." Frankfurter replied that all three accusations were true and asked Jackson what he thought should be done. Jackson said that unless Frankfurter had objections, he would go see Stone and suggest that the chief reassign the case. "Of course, I am primarily interested in this matter for the Court's sake," Jackson added, "but I am also concerned about you. A lot of people are [set] on exploiting Anti-Semitism, as you well know, and I do not think they ought to be given needless materials."

Frankfurter recognized the force of Jackson's argument and agreed that he would do whatever would be best for the Court. Jackson immediately went to see Stone, and the next day the chief justice saw Frankfurter. Stone was evidently embarrassed at the whole thing and understandably did not like the idea of having to make assignments out of fear of arousing prejudice. Frankfurter apparently let him stew in this for a while before offering to return the case to the chief for reassignment.

The case went to Stanley Reed, whose opinion appalled Frankfurter. At conference Frankfurter had argued that the Court ought to overrule *Grovey* "without any pussyfooting" and admit forthrightly that it had changed its mind regarding the policy considerations. Reed, in Frankfurter's view, took exactly the wrong approach, and, as he explained to the chief, "I tried hard to make Reed give the opinion the form and atmosphere of aggressive candor . . . but Reed has his own notions of appeasement which are bound to fail."[72] Reed did in fact reject the earlier ruling, but cautiously; he held the primary to be an integral part of the electoral process, and as such, exclusion of blacks violated the Fifteenth Amendment. Frankfurter prepared a concurring opinion that he suppressed at Jackson's strong insistence. The incident left a sour taste in Frankfurter's mouth (although it did not affect his friendship with Jackson) and no doubt shaped his views in subsequent civil rights cases.[73]

The most notorious civil rights case of the Stone Court must be *Screws v. United States* (1945),[74] which one scholar termed "a decision profoundly important to the cause of civil liberty."[75] Sheriff Claude Screws of Baker County, Georgia, and two of his deputies had arrested a black suspect,

72. Frankfurter to Stone, March 17, 1944, Stone Papers, Library of Congress.

73. Jackson to Stone, January 17, 1944, Stone Papers, Library of Congress; Frankfurter, "Memorandum on Smith v. Allwright," April 10, 1944, Frankfurter Papers, Harvard Law School Library.

74. 325 U.S. 91 (1945).

75. Robert K. Carr, "Screws v. United States: The Georgia Brutality Case," 31 *Cornell Law Quarterly* 48 (1945); see also Julius Cohen, "The Screws Case—Federal Protection of Negro Rights," 46 *Columbia Law Review* 94 (1946).

Robert Hall, handcuffed him, and then beaten him into unconsciousness. Hall died soon after. The Justice Department's civil rights section, which had been established while Frank Murphy was attorney general, could not persuade Georgia officials to prosecute the three men, so the federal government went into court and secured convictions that "under color of law" they had deprived Hall of rights accorded by the Fourteenth Amendment.

The case caused a deep split among the justices, not because any of them approved of the sheriff's brutality but because of differing views on the statute involved. After the Civil War there had been a variety of laws passed to protect the freedmen's newly acquired rights, but many of these had been eviscerated in the *Civil Rights Cases* (1883),[76] in which the Court had severely limited congressional action. In 1940, however, two of these laws still remained on the books in the form of Sections 19 and 20 of the 1909 Criminal Code.[77] Section 19 forbade conspiracies to deny any person the rights assured by the Constitution and laws of the United States, while Section 20, a remnant of the Civil Rights Act of 1866, made it a misdemeanor to willfully deprive any person under color of state law of those rights "secured or protected by the Constitution or laws of the United States or to subject any person to different pains or penalties on account of race."

In cases heard decades earlier, the Court had interpreted Section 19 to mean little more than that a person had a right to be free from violence while in either state or federal custody.[78] The other section had first come before the Court only a few years earlier. In 1941 the justices had upheld the conviction of a New Orleans politician who had been found guilty of the crudest election frauds.[79] Justice Stone, who wrote the opinion, had supported the federal government's taking a more active role in preventing election abuses, but he was unwilling to read a broad interpretation into the old law. The Court had long held that state primaries were not subject to federal oversight, and Stone only wanted to set a minimal level of protection to ensure honesty; otherwise federal action "would end that state autonomy with respect to elections which the Constitution contemplated."[80]

---

76. 109 U.S. 3 (1883).

77. These provisions were kept as sections 51 and 52 of the 1946 revision of the U.S. Code and are now, respectively, sections 241 and 242 of 18 U.S. Code.

78. *Logan v. United States,* 144 U.S. 263 (1892); *United States v. Powell,* 212 U.S. 564 (1909).

79. *United States v. Classic,* 313 U.S. 299 (1941).

80. *Ibid.* at 319–20. Stone's opinion in the case caused a great deal of comment at the time since it appeared to many, especially southerners, that it was exalting federal power over the states in an area reserved to the states. See Alpheus T. Mason, *Harlan Fiske Stone: Pillar of the Law* (New York: Viking, 1956), 588–89; and Noel T. Dowling, "The Methods of Mr. Justice Stone in Constitutional Cases," 41 *Columbia Law Review* 1160, 1177 (1941).

Although all of the justices supported Stone's result, three of them—Black, Murphy, and Douglas, who normally were among the strongest supporters of civil rights—had their doubts. Primaries had not been widespread at the time the Reconstruction statutes had been enacted, and Douglas questioned whether Stone's opinion did not expand the right of a person to vote in a primary at the expense of another right, that of an accused to have the crime with which he is charged clearly defined. "Civil liberties," Douglas wrote, "are too dear to permit conviction for crimes which are only implied."[81]

In the 1943 Term the Court heard another case in which it tried to interpret the Reconstruction laws as they applied to modern elections. In Illinois the State Primary Canvassing Board had failed to certify a black candidate for state senator as one of the two winning candidates even though his vote tally placed him second in the contest. He sued the Board, claiming that his rights had been denied under color of law, but a majority of the Court disagreed. Only Murphy and Douglas agreed with the appellant, Snowden, while Roberts reflected the general view that if the Court upheld Snowden's claim, it would "have to take over every city and state election."[82] Later in the Term the Court held it an offense under Section 51 to stuff the ballot boxes in federal elections, and this elicited a dissent from Douglas, Black, and Reed that ballot stuffing was a state crime under state law, not a federal crime.[83]

So when the Conference came to discuss *Screws,* the justices had very little to guide them. Could Section 52 be applied here, or was it too vague in its references to "any rights, privileges or immunities"? The law used the term "willful," but what exactly did that mean, and how could it be proved? And did a state official acting in an official capacity, but clearly violating the state's own laws, act "under color" of state law?

Though Roberts, Frankfurter, and Jackson were clearly shocked at the sheriff's conduct and believed him guilty of murder, nonetheless they thought the statute unconstitutional because of vagueness; to allow its use in this case would open a Pandora's box for federal interference in matters clearly within the states' purview. Stone thought that the statute was so vague as to "incorporate a law library" into it. Only Murphy seemed convinced that the statute was clearly constitutional.[84]

---

81. 313 U.S. at 336; see also Douglas to Stone, April 24, 1941, Douglas Papers, Library of Congress.

82. *Snowden v. Hughes,* 321 U.S. 1 (1944); see also Fine, *Murphy,* 395–96.

83. *United States v. Saylor,* 322 U.S. 385 (1944).

84. Conference notes, November 4, 1944, Jackson Papers, Library of Congress; Frankfurter to Stone, November 30, 1944, Frankfurter Papers, Harvard Law School Library. For the peregrinations leading up to the final opinion, see Fine, *Murphy,* 396–403.

Stone assigned the case to Douglas, who wrote a very careful and restrictive opinion. Section 52 could be upheld as constitutional, but only if
applied to state officials acting "under color of law." To save the statute
from vagueness grounds, Stone suggested, and Douglas agreed, that they
center the case around the question of whether Screws had acted "willfully."[85] The Court held that the law could be applied but sent it back for
a new trial under clearer criteria of whether Screws had acted "willfully"
and "under color of law."[86]

Because the Court had not struck down Section 52 as unconstitutionally vague, it remained alive for use by the government in later years, and
many of its defects would be corrected in the 1964 and 1965 Civil Rights
Acts. This led scholars such as Robert Carr to hail the decision as "a distinct
victory for the cause of civil liberty."[87] Other scholars, however, saw it differently, and Herman Belz points out that both the *Classic* and *Screws* decisions
set up significant constitutional difficulties in enforcing civil rights. Years
later Justice Thurgood Marshall, who at the time of these decisions had
been head of the NAACP's Legal Fund, said that much as he admired William Douglas, he could never forgive him for the *Screws* decision.[88]

The First Amendment provides basic protections for freedom of expression. There were few speech cases per se during the war years, and all
of them dealt with the problem of picketing. The notion that picketing
enjoyed protection as speech, a doctrine laid down first in *Thornhill v. Alabama* (1940),[89] was then restricted the following year in *Milk Wagon Drivers'
Union v. Meadowmoor Dairies*.[90] In a 6–3 decision, the Court sustained an
injunction against peaceful picketing because, as Frankfurter noted, it
could be found coercive because of "the momentum of fear generated
by past violence."[91] Black, Douglas, and Reed dissented. Black dismissed
Frankfurter's fear of violence, saying that just because a few men had acted

---

85. Stone to Douglas, November 25, 1944, Stone Papers, Library of Congress.

86. The federal government was unsuccessful in its second attempt to convict Screws, who
had in the meantime become something of a local hero. He was later elected to the state
senate.

87. Carr, *Federal Protection of Civil Liberties* (Ithaca: Cornell University Press, 1947), 114. For
a more modern but still quite positive evaluation of the decision, see Stephen B. Duke,
"Justice Douglas and the Criminal Law," in Stephen L. Wasby, ed., *"He Shall Not Pass This
Way Again": The Legacy of Justice William O. Douglas* (Pittsburgh: University of Pittsburgh
Press, 1990), 134–37.

88. Herman Belz et al., *The American Constitution*, 7th ed. (New York: Norton, 1991), 597;
author's interview with Thurgood Marshall, May 17, 1988.

89. 310 U.S. 88 (1940).

90. 312 U.S. 287 (1941).

91. *Ibid.* at 294.

wrongly, one could not assume that all six thousand members of the union would do likewise. Reed actually came much closer to the modern view of the First Amendment in his dissent when he wrote that if "the fear engendered by past misconduct coerces storekeepers during peaceful picketing, the remedy lies in the maintenance of order, not in denial of free speech."[92]

Shortly after Stone had become chief justice, the Court decided two more picketing cases. In one, a sharply divided bench, again speaking through Frankfurter, upheld an injunction against picketing a restaurant based on the state's antitrust law.[93] The picketers' quarrel with the restaurant owner rested on the fact that he had hired a contractor employing nonunion labor to erect another building about two miles from the restaurant site. As usual, Frankfurter was willing to defer to state law, and he found that granting the pickets constitutional protection would force the states to allow the disputants to "conscript neutrals having no relation to either the dispute or the industry" in which the dispute arose.[94] That same day, however, the Court unanimously set aside an injunction against picketing of bakeries by drivers, who protested the practice of independent jobbers purchasing the bakery goods and then retailing them using nonunion drivers. Justice Jackson made no mention of the *Ritter's Cafe* decision but distinguished the two cases on the grounds that there were no neutral parties in this dispute unwillingly dragged into the fray. The drivers had a legitimate complaint, and their picketing thus deserved First Amendment protection.[95] In 1945, in the final labor-speech case heard by the Stone Court, the justices reversed the conviction of a labor union organizer who had failed to secure an organizer's card before soliciting members. Justice Rutledge ruled that such a requirement interfered with freedom of speech and was "a restriction so destructive of the right of public discussion that it could not be upheld."[96]

The First Amendment also provides that "Congress shall make no law . . . prohibiting the free exercise" of religion, and in this area the Stone Court decided some of the most important cases ever to come before the high court regarding religious freedom. Congress, the object of the framers' admonition, had in fact done nothing to restrict religious freedom

---

92. *Ibid.* at 319 (Reed dissenting).
93. *Carpenters and Joiners Union v. Ritter's Cafe*, 315 U.S. 722 (1942).
94. *Ibid.* at 728.
95. *Bakery & Pastry Drivers & Helpers Local 802 v. Wohl*, 315 U.S. 769 (1942). For further discussion of the picketing cases, see David P. Currie, *The Constitution in the Supreme Court: The Second Century, 1888–1986* (Chicago: University of Chicago Press, 1990), 311–13.
96. *Thomas v. Collins*, 323 U.S. 516, 537 (1945). See Francis Powers, "Note: Freedom of Speech for Labor Organizers," 43 *Michigan Law Review* 1159 (1945).

except enact a post–Civil War statute prohibiting bigamy in the territories. A Mormon challenge on the grounds that the ban interfered with their religious beliefs received no sympathy from the Court.[97] Although most states also had bills of rights that included guarantees of religious freedom, some dissident sects complained that a variety of police laws restricted the free exercise of their beliefs. Starting in the late 1930s, one of these groups, the Jehovah's Witnesses, began testing these statutes in court, and in doing so wrote a new chapter into First Amendment jurisprudence.[98]

The first Witness cases had successfully challenged local ordinances that prohibited distribution of pamphlets or door-to-door solicitation without local officials' permission.[99] The Court decided both these cases on traditional First Amendment speech grounds rather than on the Free Exercise Clause, but in the latter case Justice Roberts took the first step in implementing Stone's *Carolene Products* note, calling on courts to scrutinize any regulation of personal rights with heightened attention.[100] Then in 1940 the high court had given the Witnesses their first victory based on the Free Exercise Clause. Roberts, for a unanimous bench, struck down a state law that prohibited solicitation of money for any charitable or religious clause without approval by the secretary of the public welfare council, who alone could determine if the applicants represented a legitimate religion before granting approval. The state had the power to license solicitors, Roberts noted, even for religious causes, but the arbitrary power lodged in the secretary created an impermissible censorship over religion.[101]

Roberts, however, reiterated the doctrine first enunciated by Chief Justice Morrison Waite in the nineteenth-century Mormon case that differentiated belief from action. The First Amendment provided absolute freedom to believe but did not provide equal protection for action, even action taken for religious purposes. In the latter case, courts had to balance that activity against its impact on others, to balance individual rights against the needs of society. Shortly afterward, the Court showed just how relative that balance could be in the most famous of the wartime religion cases, those involving Jehovah's Witnesses' opposition to the flag salute.

The first flag salute case in 1940 presented no new questions to the Court.[102] Whether or not a state could compel school children to salute the

97. *Reynolds v. United States,* 98 U.S. 145 (1879).

98. See Edward F. Waite, "The Debt of Constitutional Law to Jehovah's Witnesses," 28 *Minnesota Law Review* 209 (1944); and Hollis W. Barber, "Religious Liberty v. The Police Power: Jehovah's Witnesses," 41 *American Political Science Review* 226 (1947).

99. *Lowell v. Griffin,* 303 U.S. 404 (1938); *Schneider v. Irvangton,* 308 U.S. 147 (1939).

100. 308 U.S. at 161.

101. *Cantwell v. Connecticut,* 310 U.S. 296 (1940).

102. *Minersville School District v. Gobitis,* 310 U.S. 586 (1940).

American flag had been an issue in twenty states between 1935 and 1940 and had been the subject of major litigation in seven. Prior to *Gobitis* the high court had four times upheld state court decisions validating compulsory flag salute laws.[103] Jehovah's Witnesses objected to the flag salute because of their literal reading of Exodus 20:4–5 and equated the salute with bowing down to graven images. Frankfurter, a naturalized American citizen who always took ideals of citizenship and patriotism very seriously, had little sympathy with those who, as he saw it, refused to meet their civic obligations. During oral argument of the case on April 25, 1940, he passed a note to Frank Murphy questioning whether the framers of the Bill of Rights "would have thought that a requirement to salute the flag violates the protection of 'the free exercise of religion?' "[104]

Chief Justice Hughes assigned the opinion to Frankfurter, who circulated a draft in May. Douglas, who later intimated that he might have voted the other way had Stone circulated his dissent earlier,[105] endorsed not only Frankfurter's original draft but the final version as well. "This is a powerful moving document of incalculable contemporary and (I believe) historical value," he wrote, terming the opinion "a truly statesmanlike job." He scribbled a similar encomium on the recirculation.[106]

In his opinion for the 8–1 majority, Frankfurter framed the "precise" issue in terms of judicial restraint and called upon the Court to defer to the wisdom and prerogatives of local school authorities:

> To stigmatize legislative judgment in providing for this universal gesture of respect for the symbol of our national life in the setting of the common school as a lawless inroad on that freedom of conscience which the Constitution protects, would amount to no less than the pronouncement of pedagogical and psychological dogma in a field where courts possess no marked and certainly no controlling competence. . . . To the legislature no less than to courts is committed the guardianship of deeply cherished liberties.[107]

---

103. The full story of the flag salute cases is told in David Manwaring, *Render unto Caesar: The Flag Salute Controversy* (Chicago: University of Chicago Press, 1962).

104. Fine, *Murphy*, 185.

105. William O. Douglas, *The Court Years: 1939–1975* (New York: Random House, 1980), 45.

106. Comments on circulations, [n.d.], Frankfurter Papers, Harvard Law School Library.

107. 310 U.S. at 597–98, 600. Frankfurter privately commented that he believed the majority opinion would preach "the true democratic faith of not relying on the Court for the impossible task of assuring a . . . tolerant democracy," a task that properly belonged to "the people and their representatives." Quoted in Mason, *Security Through Freedom: American Political Thought and Practice* (Ithaca: Cornell University Press, 1955), 217.

There is almost a formulaic quality about the opinion. Is the legislative end legitimate? Are the means chosen reasonable? If so, then it is not up to the courts to say that a better way exists. Therefore, if the end is legitimate and the means chosen are not unreasonable, the measure—in this case the flag salute—is constitutional.[108] Frankfurter paid practically no attention to the *Gobitis* claim that First Amendment rights of free exercise of religion had been violated, and in a nominal bow to balancing, he found national unity a far more pressing matter.[109]

One might stop for a moment and compare this approach to later First Amendment analysis. Where Frankfurter's lead question was whether the state has a legitimate interest, modern courts would ask whether speech or free exercise rights had been restricted. If yes, then the next question would be whether the state had a *compelling* interest to warrant that restriction. A merely "legitimate" or even an "important" interest will not justify violation of the First Amendment. If, however, the state does have a compelling interest, then the courts will ask whether the limitation has been imposed in the least restrictive manner. The difference between the two approaches is neither semantic nor one of degree; it distinguishes between a view that sees regulations of speech or religion in the same manner as economic rules and an approach that elevates the rights of the individual above the administrative convenience of the state. In terms of balancing, it places far greater weight on individual liberty than on any but the most compelling governmental interest. In short, the modern approach derives directly from Stone's *Carolene Products* footnote in that it requires the courts to look more intensely at issues involving individual rights; Frankfurter's view is that the courts must defer to legislative judgment regardless of the issue.

Only Harlan Fiske Stone dissented in *Gobitis*,[110] and much of the liberal press applauded his opinion and denounced that of Frankfurter. Harold

---

108. 310 at U.S. at 597–98; see also Sanford Levinson, "Skepticism, Democracy, and Judicial Restraint: An Essay on the Thought of Oliver Wendell Holmes and Felix Frankfurter" (diss., Harvard University, 1969), 225–26.

109. There is little question but that Frankfurter's own experience as an immigrant boy Americanized in the New York public school system, and his intense patriotic fervor, played a significant role in how he saw the facts of the two cases. See the interesting discussion in Richard Danzig, "Justice Frankfurter's Opinions in the Flag Salute Cases: Blending Logic and Psychologic in Constitutional Decisionmaking," 36 *Stanford Law Review* 675 (1984).

110. 310 U.S. at 601. Murphy evidently also had some doubts. "This has been a Gethsemane for me," he noted on the circulation. "But after all the institution presupposes a government that will protect itself and therefore I join your beautifully expressed opinion." Murphy to Frankfurter, June 3, 1940, Frankfurter Papers, Harvard Law School Library.

Laski, a close friend of Frankfurter, wrote Stone to tell him "how right I think you are . . . [and] how wrong I think Felix is."[111] Harold Ickes, recognizing Frankfurter's concern about the war in Europe (the decision came down during the Dunkirk evacuation), thought the opinion worse than useless, "as if the country can be saved, or our institutions preserved, by forced salute of our flag by these fanatics."[112]

The three most liberal members of the Court, Black, Douglas, and Murphy, all voted with the majority, but from the start Murphy had been troubled by the decision. Black did not like the law, but he saw nothing in the Constitution to invalidate the measure. When the Court convened after its summer recess, Douglas told Frankfurter that Black had had second thoughts about his *Gobitis* vote. "Has Black been reading the Constitution?" Frankfurter sarcastically asked. "No," Douglas responded, "he has been reading the newspapers."[113] There Black—and everyone else—would have noted the Justice Department reports that in the weeks following the decision, there had been hundreds of attacks on Witnesses, especially in small towns and rural areas. This pattern continued for at least two years.

The first flag salute case had been one of the early struggles in the debate over how far the protection of the Bill of Rights extended to the states and what role the courts had in determining the limits of that protection. In *Gobitis*, despite the 8–1 vote, at least three members of the majority found themselves uncomfortable over Frankfurter's application of *Palko*, and in the next few years this unease expanded. The Witnesses refused to compromise their beliefs despite a great deal of public scorn and even physical attacks, and they pressed litigation to vindicate their religious practices. In *Cox v. New Hampshire* (1941),[114] a unanimous court upheld a state regulation requiring permits for parades, even religious parades, and the following year sustained the conviction of a Witness who had gotten into a fight after calling a city marshall "a God damned racketeer" and "a damned Fascist." Murphy, normally the Court's champion of free speech,

---

111. Mason, *Stone*, 532.

112. Harold L. Ickes, *The Secret Diaries of Harold L. Ickes*, 3 vols. (New York: Simon & Schuster, 1954), 3:199. Frankfurter knew that the opinion troubled some of his friends and seemed to run counter to his earlier reputation as a civil libertarian. To Alice Hamilton he wrote that he could appreciate her concern; "after all, my life has not been dissociated from concern for civil liberties." June 13, 1940, Frankfurter Papers, Harvard Law School Library. In the files concerning the flag salute cases, there is an undated memorandum in Frankfurter's handwriting that reads: "No duty of judges is more important nor more difficult to discharge than that of guarding against reading their personal and debatable opinions into the Case." In this opinion, however, Frankfurter certainly injected his zealous love of country and his belief that all other Americans should be just as patriotic.

113. Fine, *Murphy*, 187.

114. 312 U.S. 569 (1941).

nonetheless found these "fighting words" outside the protection of the First Amendment.[115]

The following term the issue rose again when the Court announced its decision in *Jones v. Opelika*,[116] in which Jehovah's Witnesses had refused to pay a municipal licensing fee for peddlers prior to selling their religious tracts. The issue was essentially the same as in *Gobitis,* the extent to which the government's acknowledged power to maintain public order impinged on the free exercise of religion. A majority voted in favor of the state, but this time four judges dissented—Stone, Black, Douglas, and Murphy. Moreover, in an unprecedented step, the latter three appended a statement acknowledging *Opelika* as a logical extension of *Gobitis* and said they believed this was "an appropriate occasion" to confess they had been wrong in the earlier case. The majority opinions in both decisions, they charged, "put the right freely to exercise religion in a subordinate position in violation of the First Amendment."[117] This recantation infuriated Frankfurter, who pointed out that *Gobitis* had not been challenged in the *Opelika* litigation or even mentioned in conference.

By this time many Americans had begun to rethink the implications of the earlier flag salute case, especially after the country had entered the war against fascism. The flag salute could hardly compare to the repression practiced in Nazi Germany, but it did strike many people as a needless intrusion on personal liberty in the name of the state. Though Black and Frankfurter disagreed on other things, they did agree that, as Frankfurter put it, the Witness cases "are probably but the curtain raisers of future problems of [great] range and magnitude."[118]

When President Roosevelt named Wiley Rutledge to replace James Byrnes in 1942, the dissenters in *Opelika* now had a majority. In May 1943, the Court by a 5–4 majority handed the Witnesses two victories on the same day, striking down a tax on peddlers of religious tracts and an ordinance prohibiting door-to-door distribution of religious materials. In the former, Justice Douglas described the tax as comparable to taxing a minister for the privilege of delivering a sermon, while in the latter Justice Black conceded the need for some police regulation but held that the preferred position of speech and religion took precedence.[119] A furious Frankfurter

---

115. *Chaplinsky v. New Hampshire,* 315 U.S. 568 (1942). Another area then held outside the First Amendment ambit was commercial speech; see *Valentine v. Christensen,* 316 U.S. 52 (1942).

116. 316 U.S. 584 (1942).

117. *Ibid.* at 623–24.

118. Frankfurter to Reed, April 9, 1943, Jackson Papers, Library of Congress.

119. *Murdock v. Pennsylvania,* 319 U.S. 105 (1943); and *Martin v. Struthers,* 319 U.S. 141 (1943).

believed that the majority opinions were full of "large, uncritical, congenial abstractions" that would not only confuse but mislead the American
people. "The dissenting Justices, therefore, have a duty within the bounds
of judicial restraint to make it as clear as they can that they care as much
about the freedoms of the Bill of Rights as those who profess to be their
special guardians and true interpreters."[120]

In light of the spate of attacks on Witness members, the apparent shift
in Court sentiment, and news of Hitler's "Final Solution" of the Jewish
question in Europe, the Court accepted another case dealing with required
flag salutes and free exercise of religion in the October 1942 Term. In
Jackson's original draft of the opinion, he referred to these attacks, and
Chief Justice Stone urged him to delete those lines because they "might
well give the impression that our judgment of the legal question was affected by the disorders which had followed the Gobitis decision."[121] Both
the American Bar Association Committee on the Bill of Rights and the
ACLU, a rare tandem, filed *amici* briefs in support of the Witnesses. Stone
assigned the opinion to Justice Jackson, who, although he rarely voted for
minority rights against a public interest argument, had this time joined the
liberals to strike down the mandatory salute. In his memoirs, after noting
that Black, Douglas, and Murphy had publicly "recanted" their earlier flag
salute vote, Jackson claimed that Stone's assignment of the second flag case
to him "was plainly distasteful. They wanted to do their own recanting."[122]
Jackson wrote one of the most eloquent opinions of his judicial career,
declaring that "if there is any fixed star in our constitutional constellation,
it is that no official, high or petty, can prescribe what shall be orthodox in
politics, nationalism, religion or other matters of opinion or force citizens
to confess by word or act their faith therein."[123]

Frankfurter entered an impassioned dissent that if taken literally would
nearly have denied the Court any role in enforcing the Bill of Rights, and
despite Frankfurter's comment that he belonged to "the most vilified and
persecuted minority in history," he in fact dismissed judicial protection of
minorities. The framers, he said, "knew that minorities may disrupt society."[124] He reiterated the formula he had used in the earlier decision, that
"this Court's only and very narrow function is to determine whether within

---

120. Frankfurter to Reed, April 9, 1943, Jackson Papers, Library of Congress. According
to a memorandum by Frankfurter, Black originally voted to sustain the ordinance and
later changed his mind. "The Story of Struthers," May 6, 1943, Frankfurter Papers, Harvard Law School Library.
121. Stone to Jackson, March 31, 1943, Stone Papers, Library of Congress.
122. Jackson Memoirs, Columbia Oral History Collection.
123. *West Virginia Board of Education v. Barnette*, 319 U.S. 624, 642 (1943).
124. *Ibid.* at 653.

the broad grant of authority vested in legislatures they have exercised a judgment for which reasonable justification can be offered."[125] Because of Jackson's eloquent depiction of the meaning of free exercise of religion, Frankfurter could not pass over it as lightly as he had in *Gobitis,* but he took a minimalist approach. The First Amendment provided "freedom from conformity to religious dogma, not freedom from conformity to law because of religious dogma."[126] Claims of conscience by themselves can never justify exemption from valid laws that have a reasonable basis. Since, as Sanford Levinson points out, the state could always create the nexus of a reasonable justification for its action, the courts would never impose any serious review on state action.[127]

The swing to the side of individual rights marked by the Witness cases did not go unprotested. The minority opinions in *Murdock* and *Struthers* emphasized the importance of the states preserving public order and took a relatively restricted view of the Bill of Rights. In his *Murdock* dissent, Reed argued that the framers had only intended that freedom of speech would ensure the right to be heard and that freedom of religion would ensure the protection of ritual. The First Amendment, he said, should not be interpreted to exclude speech, press, or religion from those general rules that govern society.[128] Jackson, aside from the second flag salute case, normally voted with Frankfurter, Roberts, and Reed, and his dissents indicated disenchantment with the Witnesses, whose intolerance he documented in *Douglas v. Jeannette* (1943). The Constitution, he asserted, did not allow one religious group to ride "roughshod over others simply because their conscience told them to do so."[129]

---

125. *Ibid.* at 649. Frankfurter evidently had a difficult time in writing the opinion— "perhaps," as he told Jackson, "because it is credo and not research . . . the expression of it is so recalcitrant." Frankfurter to Jackson, June 4, 1943, Frankfurter Papers, Harvard Law School Library.

126. 319 U.S. at 653.

127. Levinson, "Skepticism, Democracy, and Judicial Restraint," 232.

128. For an explication of Reed's views, see John D. Fassett, *New Deal Justice: The Life of Stanley Reed of Kentucky* (New York: Vantage, 1994), 352–54; see also F. William O'Brien, *Justice Reed and the First Amendment* (Washington: Georgetown University Press, 1958), especially chap. 1, for the wartime cases.

129. 319 U.S. 157, 166 (1943). In a non-Witness case, leaders of the "I Am" movement had been indicted for mail fraud because of their solicitation of funds, and at the trial the prosecution had attacked the truth of the movement's beliefs. Justice Douglas's majority opinion ruled that the First Amendment barred the questioning of the truth of religious belief. "Men may believe what they cannot prove," he wrote. "They may not be put to the proof of their religious doctrines or beliefs. . . . If one could be sent to jail because a jury in a hostile environment found those teachings false, little indeed would be left of religious freedom." *United States v. Ballard,* 322 U.S. 78, 86–870 (1944). Stone objected to this part of the opinion since he thought it irrelevant in the particular case. Stone to Douglas, March 22, 1944, Stone Papers, Library of Congress.

The Court had not yet moved to the position where it would be the preeminent guardian of constitutional liberties. The Stone Court's record is mixed, and the Japanese detention cases will always remain a blot on the Court's and the nation's history. But during these years, through the process of incorporation, the justices spread at least some of the protections of the Bill of Rights over state as well as federal action; the Court took more than a few steps on the path that would lead it to strike down racial segregation as a violation of the Equal Protection Clause; the justices, perhaps reluctantly, started to make the Court the overseer of criminal procedure in the state systems and to erect the banner of due process as fundamental fairness in all the courts of the land; and they began to flesh out the jurisprudential parameters of the First Amendment, which some of them claimed occupied a "preferred" position in the constitutional pantheon. All in all, civil libertarians looking back at the war years could not only breathe a sigh of relief that rights had not been seriously impaired but could applaud the fact that some significant steps had been taken in expanding the liberties of Americans.[130]

---

130. For evaluations of the wartime record, see the Symposium, "Constitutional Rights in Wartime," 29 *Iowa Law Review* 379 (1944); and Osmund K. Fraenkel, "War, Civil Liberties and the Supreme Court, 1941–1946," 55 *Yale Law Journal* 715 (1946).

# 4

# UMPIRE OF THE FEDERAL SYSTEM

The Roosevelt revolution profoundly altered relations within the federal system. At the time of the founding of the Republic the Framers envisioned a partnership between a strong federal Union, paramount within its sphere of powers and responsibilities, and potent state governments that would have full authority within their prescribed spheres. Although the work of Chief Justice John Marshall did much to build up the strength of the central government, throughout the nineteenth century most Americans saw the Union as one in which the states were at least equal to the government in Washington.

While the federal government experienced periodic surges in power, such as during the Civil War and World War I, nearly all commentators viewed the constitutional system as requiring strong state governments if for no other reason than as a counterweight to central authority. Certainly the Supreme Court, which has often been described as the umpire of the federal system, believed as late as the mid-1930s that states enjoyed a great deal of authority except in those areas that were specifically given over to the national government. Conservative judges, in fact, used the notion of states' rights to defeat federal efforts in areas that were arguably the responsibility of Congress. During the 1920s the Taft Court created a notion of dual federalism in which it carved out a sort of no-man's-land where neither the states nor the federal government could act lest they trespass on the other's responsibility. Efforts by conservative justices to utilize these notions to nullify reform legislation had been at least partly responsible for the 1937 crisis.

Now the questions remained whether the states still had authority and, if so, over what fields they exercised primary responsibility. How far did the federal government's power extend, and to what limits could Congress take the Commerce Clause? The Great Depression and the war that followed created a profound shift in American government, but the Constitution still called for a federal system, a partnership between the states and the national Union. Among its other tasks during the war, the Stone Court had to resolve a number of questions determining where power would now be located.

In 1938 Justice Louis Brandeis realized a long-sought objective when he handed down the majority decision in *Erie Railroad v. Tompkins*,[1] overturning nearly a century of precedent. In 1842, Justice Joseph Story, in his quest to establish a national body of commercial law, had in essence created a federal common law in *Swift v. Tyson*.[2] The Judiciary Act of 1789 had instructed federal courts to follow the decisional rules of the states, and Story interpreted this to mean that federal courts had to follow only statutory law, not state common law. They could thus follow "the general principles and doctrines of common jurisprudence." Initially, the decision gave federal courts a tool by which to forge a somewhat coherent body of national rules in various areas of commercial law. Later on, however, "Old Swifty" opened the door to forum shopping, by which essentially local firms evaded state laws by going into federal courts. By the 1920s forum shopping had become a blatant means to evade state regulations, and both Holmes and Brandeis attacked the practice.[3] In *Erie*, Brandeis's long-term attack finally yielded an unusual opinion in that the Court declared one of its own decisions unconstitutional; there was no federal common law, and federal courts would have to follow not only the statutory law but also the common law of the states.[4]

Brandeis's avowed purpose was to put greater emphasis on state power and to strengthen the idea of federalism at a time when it seemed all power had flowed to the national government. He told his law clerk at the time that he regarded *Erie* as his "last major contribution to the law and a triumph for state power."[5] Others have shared this view. Justice John Marshall Harlan described the Brandeis opinion as "one of the cornerstones of our federalism," while the noted constitutional scholar John Hart Ely has said that "*Erie* is by no means simply a case. . . . It implicates, indeed perhaps it is, the very essence of our federalism."[6]

No one on the Stone Court shared this dedication to the Brandeisian ideal of federalism more than Felix Frankfurter, who while a professor had

---

1. 304 U.S. 64 (1938).
2. 16 Pet. 1 (1842).
3. See *Black & White Taxicab Co. v. Brown & Yellow Taxicab Co.*, 276 U.S. 518 (1928).
4. For the best analysis of the two cases, see Tony Freyer, *Harmony and Dissonance: The Swift and Erie Cases in American Federalism* (New York: New York University Press, 1981); for a shorter analysis, see F. Thornton Miller, "Federal Common Law?" in John W. Johnson, ed., *Historic U.S. Court Cases, 1690–1990: An Encyclopedia* (New York: Garland, 1992), 103–6.
5. Philippa Strum, *Brandeis: Beyond Progressivism* (Lawrence: University Press of Kansas, 1993), 89.
6. *Hanna v. Plumer*, 380 U.S. 460, 474 (1965) (Harlan concurring); John Hart Ely, "The Irrepressible Myth of Erie," 87 *Harvard Law Review* 693, 695 (1974).

done much to argue the need for such a rule.[7] Cases began arriving before the Court testing just how literally the Brandeis opinion should be taken. Complicating matters was the fact that although Brandeis had said that federal courts should in all instances follow both state statutory and common law, there were situations in which such law either did not exist or did not apply, and in those cases, Brandeis said in an opinion handed down the same day as *Erie,* there was a federal common law.[8] The process of limning the parameters of *Erie* began almost immediately and still goes on. In the first case, *Sibbach v. Wilson & Co.,*[9] the Court examined the validity of one of the recently enunciated federal rules of civil procedure, authorizing a district judge to order a medical examination in civil suits. A 5–4 majority upheld the rule, arguing that it involved procedural rather than substantive matters and that the basic test of *Erie* would be "whether a rule really regulates procedure."[10] Frankfurter dissented and charged that merely describing something as "procedural" did not really make it so; one had to examine the matter thoroughly to determine whether the issue at stake involved procedural or substantive matters. Frankfurter did not, however, enunciate what he thought would be a proper test to make this determination.[11]

Four years later Frankfurter did state such a test, and this time he spoke for a 5–2 majority in *Guaranty Trust v. York.*[12] The Court, he said, must put aside abstractions regarding differences between "substance" and "procedure" because the main demand of *Erie* was respect for state law. The rule to preserve this respect required that a party could not secure recovery in a federal court if the state did not provide a right to that recovery—that is, one could not secure in federal court what one could not get in state court. In effect, a federal court sitting in diversity is "only another court of the State."[13]

The *Erie* doctrine is still with us today, and in large part the *York* analysis still holds: federalism discourages forum shopping and tries to avoid inequitable administration of the law.[14] The impact of *Erie,* however, has been vitiated by a number of developments, chief of which is the explosion of

---

7. Mary Brigid McManamon, "Felix Frankfurter: Architect of 'Our Federalism,' " 27 *Georgia Law Review* 697, 749–51, 754–55 (1993).

8. *Hinderliter v. La Plata River Co.,* 304 U.S. 92 (1938).

9. 312 U.S. 1 (1941).

10. *Ibid.* at 14.

11. *Ibid.* at 17 (Frankfurter dissenting).

12. 326 U.S. 99 (1945).

13. *Ibid.* at 108. In this particular case, a state statute of limitations barred recovery, and therefore the federal court could not open its doors for the plaintiff.

14. *Hanna v. Plumer,* 380 U.S. at 467–68 (1965).

federal statutes that have superseded state laws in many areas. In a number of cases, even diversity cases, federal courts look to Congress rather than state legislatures for controlling law. In addition, many states have adopted proposals by the Commission on Uniform State Laws, especially the Uniform Commercial Code, which has in effect achieved what Justice Story sought in the mid–nineteenth century, a uniform body of national law to facilitate commerce.

No case had better exemplified the antagonism of conservatives on the Supreme Court against the New Deal than *United States v. Butler*,[15] in which the majority struck down the Agricultural Adjustment Act (AAA) of 1933. The measure, aimed at eliminating the large crop surpluses that depressed farm prices, placed limits on how much individual farmers could grow and rewarded them for participation in the program through subsidies; financing for the scheme came from a tax on the first processor. Unlike the industrial centerpiece of the first New Deal, the National Industrial Recovery Act, the AAA had been received by farmers with enthusiasm and within a short period of time had significantly improved the economic position of the nation's agricultural sector. Then in the *Butler* case a 6–3 majority, speaking through Justice Roberts, held that Congress had no power in this area since farming was essentially a local activity; moreover, the Court held that Congress had abused its taxing power, and Roberts labeled the processing fee nothing more than a device to take money out of the pockets of one group and place it in the hands of another. The most memorable part of Roberts's opinion remains his wooden and inflexible theory of judging. When an act of Congress is challenged, Roberts wrote, all the Court can do is "to lay the article of the Constitution which is invoked beside the statute which is challenged and to decide whether the latter squares with the former."[16] Stone's powerful dissent, joined by Brandeis and Cardozo, demolished both the factual and theoretical grounds of Roberts's opinion, calling it a "tortured construction of the Constitution," and Stone pleaded with the Court to exercise judicial restraint.[17]

Congress "cured" the tax problem in the second AAA by financing the plan through general rather than particular taxes, and following the Court fight of 1937, the new Court had little difficulty sustaining the act; in fact Roberts wrote the opinion that did so in *Mulford v. Smith* (1939).[18] In the

---

15. 297 U.S. 1 (1936).

16. *Ibid.* at 62.

17. *Ibid.* at 78, 87 (Stone dissenting).

18. 307 U.S. 38 (1939). Roberts was attacked for his opinion in this case as another example of his reversing himself, and he later noted, "Looking back, it is difficult to see how the Court could have resisted the popular urge for uniform standards throughout the country—for what in effect was a unified economy." Owen J. Roberts, *The Court and the Constitution* (Cambridge: Harvard University Press, 1951), 61.

next few years the Court continued to sustain New Deal legislation, and in 1941 Justice Stone effectively killed off the idea of dual federalism, by which the conservatives had managed to block federal legislation on the grounds that the subject matter covered belonged to state control.[19] The question remained, however, whether the states themselves retained any control over local commerce, and the answer appeared to be no.

Roscoe Filburn ran a small chicken farm in Ohio, and each year he planted a few acres of wheat to feed his poultry and livestock. Under the Agricultural Marketing Agreement Act of 1937 (which had been sustained by the Court in 1942),[20] Filburn had signed an allotment agreement allowing him 11.1 acres of wheat, but he actually planted 23 acres and grew 239 bushels beyond his assigned quota. The Agriculture Department invoked the penalty provisions of the law and brought suit to collect the fines.

Filburn defended himself on the grounds that the regulations exceeded the federal powers granted by the Commerce Clause because the excess wheat had not gone into interstate commerce but had been grown for and used by his chickens. This argument caused some doubt among at least five justices—Jackson, Murphy, Roberts, Byrnes, and Frankfurter—who were also dissatisfied with the presentations of both the government and Filburn's attorneys. Three members of the Court saw no problem, but for different reasons. Black and Douglas took an extremely expansive view of the commerce power, claiming it had no limitations except those explicitly mentioned in the Constitution. Stone, while agreeing that the constitutional arguments had not been well presented, nonetheless believed that sufficient precedent existed to sustain the law.[21]

It is interesting that Robert Jackson, who would eventually write the opinion in the case, disagreed and, in language that Stone's biographer terms "reminiscent of the Old Guard,"[22] complained that he did not see it as a simple matter. "The Constitution drew a line between state and federal power," Jackson wrote,

> and here the Congress wants to cross that line admittedly. I suppose that before we give it our approval there must be some finding that it is warranted by facts and conditions. Otherwise, the federal compact was

19. *United States v. Darby*, 312 U.S. 100 (1941).

20. *United States v. Wrightwood Dairy*, 315 U.S. 110 (1942); for a review of the New Deal agricultural laws and their reception in the courts, see Ashley Sellers and Jesse E. Baskette, Jr., "Agricultural Marketing Agreement and Order Programs, 1933–1943," 33 *Georgetown Law Journal* 123 (1945).

21. Stone, Memorandum to Court, May 25, 1942, Jackson Papers, Library of Congress. Reed took no part in the discussion or decision.

22. Alpheus T. Mason, *Harlan Fiske Stone: Pillar of the Law* (New York: Viking, 1956), 594.

pretty meaningless if Congress is to be sole judge of the extent of its own commerce power. . . . If I am wrong about the proposition that whereas regulation of interstate commerce itself requires no justification beyond the will of Congress, but regulation of what is neither interstate nor commerce does depend on at least a reasonably probable effect of some kind, not too indirect, remote or trivial, then we have no function but to stamp this Act O.K.[23]

After rehearing that fall, Stone assigned the case to Jackson, who proceeded to write one of the Court's strongest opinions upholding the federal commerce power. Even though Filburn's wheat had been intended for his own chickens, "such wheat overhangs the market and if induced by rising prices tends to flow into the market and check price increases." Even if it never did enter the market, "it supplies a need of the man who grew it which would otherwise be reflected by purchases in the open market. Home-grown wheat in this sense competes with wheat in commerce."[24]

Jackson, despite his earlier doubts, did have precedent on which to rely. Charles Evans Hughes, in his first tenure on the bench, had written in the *Shreveport Cases* that Congress could regulate intrastate rates of railroads if these rates had a substantial effect upon interstate rates.[25] Later, using a similar argument, Chief Justice Taft—whom no one would accuse of being overly sympathetic to federal regulation—had upheld congressional control over the Chicago Board of Trade because its activities had an impact on interstate commerce.[26] But Jackson's opinion went further since, in the earlier cases, Hughes and Taft had required some evidence besides Congress's saying so that the intrastate activities did in fact have an interstate effect. "If we are to be brutally frank," Jackson wrote shortly after the opinion came down, "I suspect what we would say is that in any case where Congress thinks there is an effect on interstate commerce, the Court will accept that judgment. All of the efforts to set up formulae to confine the commerce power have failed. When we admit that it is an economic matter, we pretty nearly admit that it is not a matter which courts may judge."[27]

---

23. Jackson to Stone, May 25, 1942, Stone Papers, Library of Congress. Douglas believed there were sufficient precedents to uphold the law and believed reargument unnecessary. Douglas to Jackson, May 25, 1942, Douglas Papers, Library of Congress.

24. *Wickard v. Filburn*, 317 U.S. 111, 128 (1942).

25. 234 U.S. 342 (1914).

26. *Chicago Board of Trade v. Olsen*, 262 U.S. 1 (1923).

27. Jackson to Sherman Minton, December 21, 1942, Jackson Papers, Library of Congress. Minton was then still a member of the Court of Appeals. Stone evinced a similar sentiment, noting that while the decision seemed to be "an extreme application of the rule," so long as the power was committed to Congress, reform could be achieved only through

In fact, the notion of an expansive commerce power was hardly new; it had been put forward by Chief Justice John Marshall in the early days of the Republic. But as Paul Murphy points out, in an era of minimal government Marshall had used a broad interpretation of the Commerce Clause to block out state interference without assuming that the federal government necessarily would act; the New Deal Court, on the other hand, intended to clear the path of state regulation so Congress could legislate far-reaching programs. Nonetheless, when Justice Frank Murphy declared that the government's regulatory power under the Commerce Clause "was as broad as the economic needs of the nation," commentators praised the statement as being particularly "Marshallian."[28]

But was there anything left for the states to control, or had the Court really put an end to the whole notion of federalism? The answer came in the same term; it involved a challenge to California's Agricultural Prorate Act. California farmers produced nearly all of the raisins consumed in the United States, and about 90 percent of the crop entered interstate commerce. The Prorate Act created a state-sponsored monopoly for the marketing of raisins, and all growers of grapes for raisins had to comply with its provisions. Each grower could market only 30 percent of the crop in the open market and had to turn over the remainder to a central committee, which controlled the amount of raisins let into the market so as to stabilize prices.

The challenge to the Prorate Act raised three questions for the Court. Did the measure violate the Sherman Antitrust Act? Did it run afoul of the 1937 Agricultural Marketing Agreement Act? Did it transgress the Commerce Clause? Although some of the justices raised the issue of jurisdiction and wanted to remand the case to federal court for a hearing on that issue, Stone prevailed in his views that the Court had jurisdiction and should decide the merits.[29]

In an opinion for a unanimous Court, the chief justice upheld the California statute, and in doing so he completed the work he had begun in the *Darby* case the previous term. The Sherman Act had no applicability since it applied only to private companies, not to the states. In a federal system, Stone warned, courts should not infer applicability of federal legislation to the states in the absence of an explicit congressional directive. The law also did not interfere with the federal statute; Congress had not

---

the ballot and not through the courts. Stone to Sterling Carr, January 11, 1943, Stone Papers, Library of Congress.

28. *American Power & Light Co. v. S.E.C.*, 328 U.S. 90, 141 (1946); Paul L. Murphy, *The Constitution in Crisis Times, 1918–1969* (New York: Harper & Row, 1972), 168.

29. Stone, Memoranda for the Court, October 21 and December 30, 1942, Stone Papers, Library of Congress.

totally preempted the field, and the Secretary of Agriculture had testified that the federal and state plans worked harmoniously together.

The key question, of course, was whether California's plan crossed into terrain reserved for Congress by the Commerce Clause. Stone noted that the state plan dealt primarily with regulation of raisins before shipment into interstate commerce and could legitimately be described as a local activity. But that would have been a mechanistic reading of the Constitution and the situation since there was no question but that the scheme affected interstate commerce. The courts, Stone declared, had to take a realistic view of the facts:

> When Congress has not exerted its power under the commerce clause, and state regulation of matters of local concern is so related to interstate commerce that it also operates as a regulation of that commerce, the reconciliation of the power thus granted with that reserved to the state is to be attained by the accommodation of the competing demands of the state and national interests involved.
>
> Such regulations by the state are to be sustained, not because they are 'indirect' rather than 'direct,' . . . not because they control interstate activities in such a manner as only to affect the commerce rather than to command its operations. But they are to be upheld because upon a consideration of all the relevant facts and circumstances it appears that the matter is one which may appropriately be regulated in the interest of the safety, health, and well-being of local communities, and which, because of its local character and the practical difficulties involved, may never be adequately dealt with by Congress.[30]

In some ways, Stone resurrected a "dual federalism" with this opinion, but one quite different from that used by conservatives in the 1920s and 1930s to strike down both state and federal measures. The conservatives had erected a no-man's-land, an area of activities that had both a local and an interstate character and that in essence could be regulated by neither the states nor the federal government. Stone had put an end to that version of dual federalism in *Darby*, which had given the federal government the power to regulate goods made in local business and then shipped in interstate commerce.[31]

Under Stone's version, the no-man's-land became neutral territory, subject to regulation by either the state or federal government. Obviously,

---

30. *Parker v. Brown*, 317 U.S. 341, 362–63 (1942).

31. See Edward S. Corwin, "The Passing of Dual Federalism," 36 *Virginia Law Review* 1 (1950).

and especially after *Wickard v. Filburn,* federal control took precedence, but until and unless Congress acted, the states remained free to establish whatever measures they saw fit. In many ways, Stone did little more than return to the commonsense rule of the nineteenth century, which the Court had enunciated in *Cooley v. Board of Wardens of the Port of Philadelphia* (1851).[32] That case made the Tenth Amendment what the framers had intended it to be, a statement of the partnership between the states and the federal government, not a means to paralyze them.

In fact, in only two nonunanimous opinions during the Stone years did the Court invalidate state regulation of commerce as impinging on federal authority. In *Southern Pacific Railroad v. Arizona* (1945),[33] the majority voided a state law limiting the size of trains operating within Arizona borders to no more than fourteen passenger cars or seventy freight cars in length. Evidence indicates that the railway unions backing the proposal saw it as a means of increasing jobs, but the official justification emphasized safety concerns, with the hazards to trainmen allegedly greater on overly long trains. The majority deemed the safety rationale slight and dubious and outweighed by a "national interest in keeping interstate commerce free from interferences which seriously impede it and subject it to local regulation which does not have a uniform effect on the interstate train journeys which it interrupts." If there were to be limits on train size, the Court concluded, it would have to come from Congress.[34] The opinion elicited a strong dissent from Justice Black, joined by Douglas, who condemned the majority for attempting to evaluate the probable dangers to trainmen, a task that properly belonged to the state legislature.[35]

Still another area in which the Court attempted to sort out the proper allocation of powers between the states and the national government within the federal system involved taxation, both state taxes on interstate commercial transactions as well as the so-called intergovernmental immunity. One might have thought that the Court would have been stringent in preventing states from interfering with interstate commerce through taxation, but in fact the Court took a very cautious stand. In a 1940 decision, Justices Black, Douglas, and Frankfurter entered a dissent in which they argued that Congress rather than the courts should determine when

---

32. 12 Howard 299 (1851).

33. 325 U.S. 761 (1945).

34. *Ibid.* at 776. The majority also distinguished the case from *South Carolina Highway Department v. Barnwell Brothers,* 303 U.S. 177 (1938), in which it had upheld stringent limits on the width and weight of motor trucks operating within the state, on the grounds that states were the proprietors of their highways and therefore had power to regulate their use.

35. 325 U.S. at 784 (Black dissenting).

state taxes constituted a burden on interstate commerce. Congress alone, they declared, "in the exercise of its plenary constitutional control over interstate commerce, [can] not only consider whether such a tax as now under scrutiny is consistent with the best interests of our national economy, but can also on the basis of full exploration of the many aspects of a complicated problem devise a national policy fair alike to the States and to our Union."[36]

The dissent alarmed some critics, who worried that should a majority adopt its reasoning, the Court might abandon its traditional role as umpire of the federal system. Although this did not happen, the Court for a while took a surprisingly permissive attitude toward state taxation.[37] In 1944, in fact, by a 5–4 vote, the Court went rather far in upholding a state tax. Minnesota had imposed a tax on Minneapolis-headquartered Northwest Airlines on the basis that its entire fleet of planes entered the state, although in fact only one-sixth of the company's total daily mileage was flown within the state's borders. The minority of Stone, Roberts, Reed, and Rutledge protested that the Minnesota tax went beyond the bounds permitted by the Constitution.[38] The case, however, marked the limits of what the Court would permit, and although Rutledge joined the Black-Douglas-Murphy view, Frankfurter and Jackson appeared to have been won over by Stone's reasoning, and later in 1944, the Court began striking down state taxes on goods in interstate commerce.[39]

Control over interstate and foreign commerce did not occupy as much of the Court's docket as the issue had in the 1920s and 1930s; the Roosevelt revolution, the appointment of sympathetic judges throughout the federal system, and Supreme Court decisions such as *Darby* and *Filburn* enabled the vast majority of state and federal regulation of industry to be sustained.

---

36. *McCarroll v. Dixie Grayhound Lines*, 309 U.S. 176, 189 (1940) (Black dissenting). The case involved a challenge to an Arkansas law requiring buses and trucks entering the state to pay a state gasoline tax on all fuel over twenty gallons that they carried in their tanks at the time of entry. The majority considered the tax an unconstitutional burden on interstate commerce.

37. Just before Stone took over as chief, the Court handed down several decisions upholding state taxation on interstate commerce: see *McGoldrick v. Berwind-White Coal Co.*, 309 U.S. 33 (1940); *Nelson v. Sears, Roebuck & Co.*, 312 U.S. 359 (1941); and *Nelson v. Montgomery Ward & Co.*, 312 U.S. 373 (1941).

38. *Northwest Airlines v. Minnesota*, 322 U.S. 292 (1944); the Stone dissent is at 308. See the critical analysis of the majority opinion by Thomas Reed Powell, "Northwest Airlines v. Minnesota: State Taxation of Airplanes—Herein Also of Stamps and Sealing Wax and Railroad Cars," 57 *Harvard Law Review* 1097 (1944).

39. *McLeod v. Dilworth*, 322 U.S. 327 (1944); *Hooven & Allison Co. v. Evatt*, 324 U.S. 652 (1945).

But sometimes new situations arose independent of legislation, requiring the justices to rethink older notions of the commerce power.

Since the 1869 decision of *Paul v. Virginia,*[40] insurance had been considered a matter of state regulation. The Court had held that even though the parties might be domiciled in different states, the actual insurance contract constituted a local transaction. As a result, over the next seventy years the insurance industry—which by 1940 had assets in excess of $37 billion and annual receipts of $6 billion—was completely governed by a patchwork of state regulations. Despite the national nature of insurance, the legal fiction of a "local business" continued. Moreover, Congress had acquiesced in the decision and had not legislatively attempted to bring insurance within the scope of federal action.

Then in 1942 the Justice Department secured antitrust indictments against the 196 members of the South-Eastern Underwriters Association, charging them with conspiracies to fix rates for fire insurance and to monopolize commerce in violation of the Sherman Antitrust Act. The federal district court that heard the initial case felt itself bound by precedent and dismissed the indictments; the government then appealed to the high court.

Three members of the Court—Stone, Frankfurter, and Jackson—believed that the case should be governed by precedent and also by the fact that Congress had not explicitly brought insurance within the compass of the 1890 Sherman Antitrust Act. To overrule *Paul* would mean the dismantling of an elaborate array of state regulation, a result that adherents of judicial restraint feared. But four justices—Black, Douglas, Murphy, and Rutledge—believed that not only had *Paul* been wrongly decided, but the fact that complex arrangements had resulted from that decision should not be a bar to correcting it.[41] After all, just a few terms previously the Court had overturned another ancient and honorable precedent, the venerable decision by Joseph Story in *Swift v. Tyson* (1842); if the Court could overrule "Old Swifty," why could it not as easily overturn *Paul v. Virginia?*

Jackson, who during the original conference had been willing to reverse and hold insurance part of interstate commerce, found that the longer he mulled the issue over in his mind, the less sure he became of his position. On February 12, 1944, he circulated a six-page memorandum designed, as he put it, "only to give you the direction in which my mind is feebly groping in the dark." In the memo he worried that the Court was being asked to make a profound constitutional decision, one that would upset three-quarters of a century of precedent and practice, on the slimmest of records. "We are asked to base our decision on what is charged,

---

40. 8 Wall. 168 (1869).
41. Reed and Roberts took no part in the case.

not on what has been proved." He noted that in his book, *The Struggle for Judicial Supremacy*, he had criticized courts that had reached major constitutional decisions on an inadequate factual basis.

The government, Jackson noted, had not yet proven either that insurance was in fact interstate commerce or that the defendants, as they engaged in the insurance business, had been involved in activities that were interstate commerce or affected it. The insurance companies, on the other hand, were arguing that even if it could be proven factually that they were engaged in interstate commerce, they could not be held to have done so illegally, because of the *Paul* decision and its subsequent development. This made no sense, but neither did Jackson like the idea of reaching an important constitutional decision on so slim a basis. Would it not be better to remand to the district court with instructions that *Paul* was not binding and let the government proceed in its attempts to prove that the defendants had engaged in interstate commerce and that in doing so they had transgressed the Sherman Act?[42]

Frankfurter immediately responded, picking up on Jackson's doubts and urging him to consider that the best way to get *Paul* reversed was not by a Court decision but by an explicit statement by Congress that it considered insurance subject to the Sherman Act. The Court would be serving the Constitution best by forcing Congress to meet its legislative responsibilities.[43] A week later Frankfurter again played on Jackson's doubts and portrayed the men who had drafted the Sherman Act as lawyers "of considerable stature [who] did not think of exempting that which they never thought was included."[44]

By mid-April it appears that a majority of the Court wanted to return the case to the district court with orders to proceed on the assumption that *Paul* did not control and to reserve decision on the constitutional questions until a fuller record had been developed regarding both the interstate nature of the insurance business as well as whether any antitrust violations had occurred. The chief justice drew up a *per curiam* in the *South-Eastern* case, and Justice Douglas drafted one for the companion *Polish Alliance* litigation.[45] In both instances the memoranda noted that a majority of the Court could not agree on the basic constitutional issue.[46]

42. Jackson, Memorandum, February 12, 1944, Jackson Papers, Library of Congress.

43. Frankfurter to Jackson, February 15, 1944, *ibid.*

44. Frankfurter to Jackson, February 23, 1944, Frankfurter Papers, Harvard Law School Library.

45. Tied in with *South-Eastern* was a related case, *Polish National Alliance v N.L.R.B.*, 322 U.S. 643 (1944), which raised the issue of whether or not the Wagner Labor Relations Act applied to employees of insurance companies. If the Court held insurance as part of interstate commerce, then the Wagner Act would apply.

46. Memorandum, Stone to Court, n.d., Douglas Papers, Library of Congress; Douglas, Memorandum to Court, n.d., Rutledge Papers, Library of Congress.

But this was not completely accurate. Actually a majority and perhaps all seven of the justices who took part in the decision agreed on the fact that insurance constituted part of interstate commerce. They could hardly think otherwise after the expansive interpretation of what constituted or affected such commerce in *Wickard v. Filburn*. If a farmer growing an extra few bushels of wheat for the consumption of his own chickens could be said to affect interstate commerce, then surely billions of dollars worth of insurance contracts issued each year must also be part of that commerce. The issue dividing the justices was not whether insurance could be categorized as interstate commerce but who should remedy the problems that had resulted from the 1869 *Paul* decision—the Court or the elected members of the Congress.

It is not surprising that Stone and Frankfurter would choose the Congress or that Jackson, from the lawyerly position that the current case did not provide sufficient grounds for a judicial determination, would join them. Black and Douglas initially seemed willing to go along, but the more Black thought about it, the more he believed the Court should correct its own error and then leave the other ramifications up to Congress and the states. On May 16, Black informed the chief justice that he believed the insurance case should be decided on its merits, even though only four members of the Court, not an absolute majority, supported his position.[47]

In his opinion for the 4–3 majority, Black went back and examined the line of cases extending from *Paul* and discovered that all of them had involved the validity of state laws and the extent to which the Commerce Clause deprived states of the power to regulate insurance. In all of these cases, the Court had consistently upheld state power; now for the first time the Court had to adjudge whether a federal statute applied to insurance companies doing interstate business. With what the conservatives labeled an activist disdain for precedent, Black noted that "past decisions of this Court emphasize that legal formulae to uphold state power cannot uncritically be accepted as trustworthy guides to determine Congressional power under the Commerce Clause."[48]

Rather than looking at decisions regarding *state power*, Black now looked at the record in determining *federal authority*, and over the years the Court had upheld the power of Congress to regulate transactions across state lines involving lottery tickets, kidnapped persons, women for immoral purposes, and even radio waves. Given this record, "it would indeed be difficult to hold that no activities of any insurance company can ever consti-

---

47. Black to Douglas, n.d., Douglas Papers, Library of Congress; Black to Stone, May 16, 1944, Stone Papers, Library of Congress.
48. *United States v. South-Eastern Underwriters Association*, 322 U.S. 533, 545 (1944).

tute interstate commerce." Whether or not one held the actual contract to be local in nature, there could be no question but that insurance involved a chain of transactions that crossed state lines. Black concluded that "no commercial enterprise of any kind which conducts its activities across state lines has been held to be wholly beyond the regulatory power of Congress under the Commerce Clause. We cannot make an exception of the business of insurance."[49]

Stone entered a dissent joined by Frankfurter; the two men disagreed with the majority primarily on the question of whether Congress had intended the Sherman Act to apply to insurance. Both Stone and Black looked at the historical record, the congressional debates and reports, and neither of them could point to any definitive evidence. For Stone, this lack of proof meant that one could not assume that Congress had intended the act to apply, and therefore the courts had to proceed on the assumption that it did not; for Black, lack of evidence meant that the Congress of 1890 had not "intended to freeze the proscription of the Sherman Act within the mold of then current judicial decisions."[50]

For Stone, an even weightier consideration involved overturning the vast scheme of state regulation that had arisen in the previous seventy-five years. While the chief justice had always argued that the Court should not be shy in rectifying its own errors, here practical problems made reversing *Paul* inexpedient. Such a decision "cannot fail to be the occasion for loosing a flood of litigation and of legislation, state and national, in order to establish a new boundary between state and national power, raising questions which cannot be answered for years to come, during which a great business and the regulatory officers of every state must be harassed by all the doubts and difficulties inseparable from a realignment of the distribution of power in our federal system."[51]

The decision triggered a chorus of protest, not so much at the rationale of the Black opinion but at the chaos that many people believed would surely follow. The *Washington Post* applauded Stone's dissent and his point that Congress had "refused to venture into this field, while the States have built up elaborate systems to control the insurance business. . . . This has been the settled law of the land." While national controls might be a good

---

49. *Ibid.* at 553. For further discussion, see C. Herman Pritchett, *The Roosevelt Court: A Study in Judicial Politics and Values, 1937–1947* (New York: Macmillan, 1948), 63–66.
50. 322 U.S. at 557.
51. *Ibid.* at 562, 583 (Stone dissenting). For an analysis of the dissent, see Mason, *Stone,* 620–22. Jackson entered a separate dissent, admitting that insurance constituted interstate commerce but adhering to the legal fiction that it was local in nature. If a change should be made, he argued, Congress should indicate that it wished the Sherman Act to apply to insurance. 322 U.S. at 584 (Jackson dissenting).

idea, surely, the paper concluded, "that decision should be left to Congress, as Justice Jackson suggests, and not thrust upon the Federal Government in wartime by the Supreme Court."[52]

Professor Thomas Reed Powell of the Harvard Law School complained in a jocular fashion about the Court's upsetting established doctrine. In a letter to his friend William O. Douglas, he wrote: "I am looking forward to teaching this summer for twelve weeks when your body is not in session. It is a very nerve-wracking enterprise to run a class [in constitutional law] Monday afternoon, as I have been doing this term, without knowing what I was saying is still so."[53]

The turmoil predicted by the dissenters did not materialize. Congress declined the invitation to regulate insurance and in the McCarran Act permitted the states to continue regulation and taxation of the insurance business despite its interstate character. In addition, the act exempted the industry from any federal statute not specifically covering insurance, with the exception of the Sherman Act and three other laws. In 1946 the Court unanimously upheld the McCarran Act's notion that insurance, even though interstate in nature, could be jointly governed by the states and the federal government.[54]

It would not be unfair to say that the majority opinion caused exactly the results desired by the minority, namely that Congress should make its intentions clear. One may even wonder if the dire warnings of chaos by Stone and Jackson were at least in part hyperbole, designed to spur the legislature to action. In a letter to Jackson, Frankfurter proclaimed his belief in reason,[55] but one must wonder at the sort of reason that acknowledged that in *fact* insurance constituted interstate commerce—and could not be anything else—and yet clung to the admitted *fiction* that it was local. Stone himself had often commented on the slowness of Congress to act in situations requiring uniform regulation of commerce,[56] and he may have worried that if the Court held insurance to be interstate, Congress would not act—in which case there surely would have been confusion.

---

52. *Washington Post,* June 6, 1944.

53. Powell to Douglas, May 23, 1944, Powell Papers, Harvard Law School Library. Powell attacked the majority's logic in "Insurance as Commerce in Constitution and Statute," 57 *Harvard Law Review* 937 (1944). After reading the article, Frankfurter told Powell that he hoped his colleagues would read it "and be in a chastened mood after having read it to the extent of realizing what intellectual responsibility means and above all that 'law' is not the same thing as a result that one likes." Frankfurter to Powell, October 24, 1944, Powell Papers, Harvard Law School Library.

54. *Prudential Insurance Co. v. Benjamin,* 328 U.S. 408 (1946); *Robertson v. California,* 328 U.S. 440 (1946).

55. Frankfurter to Jackson, February 23, 1944, Frankfurter Papers, Harvard Law School Library.

56. Mason, *Stone,* 621 n.

Much of the criticism of the decision, though, was aimed at the new majority's willingness to abandon precedent and ignore the practical difficulties its rulings might have. None of the articles,[57] however, could match the dissents in their warnings of doom and gloom, and none of them even hinted that the solution might be as simple as Congress's merely indicating its approval of and permission for the states to continue their prior regulation. Black and the majority insisted that the Court ought to face the facts, something that liberals—including Stone, Frankfurter, and Jackson—had demanded of the conservative Court in the 1920s and 1930s. That there might be a dislocation did not escape the notice of the activist wing, and they did worry about the consequences. Yet in terms of intellectual honesty—of the reason that Frankfurter claimed to hold so dear—it is hard to see how the Court could have reached any other conclusion.

The Court's role as umpire in the federal system extended well beyond matters of commerce, and in one of the livelier cases to come before it in these years, the justices had to deal with a question involving moral as well as legal values. Otis B. Williams and Lillie S. Hendrix met, fell in love, and wanted to marry, a not unusual occurrence except that at the time both happened to be married to other people. So they packed their bags, left North Carolina, and went to Las Vegas, where, after the requisite six weeks of residence, they secured divorces from a Nevada court. They immediately married and returned to North Carolina, where local authorities arrested, tried, and convicted them for "bigamous cohabitation." The state considered the Nevada divorce decrees invalid because their spouses had not appeared in person in the Nevada courts to contest them, and North Carolina did not recognize divorces based on substituted service—that is, cases in which notice of the action had been sent to agents of the parties. North Carolina also charged that Williams and Hendrix had not gone to Nevada to establish a legitimate residence but simply to secure a divorce, and therefore they had committed a fraud on that state's courts. On appeal, the Supreme Court of North Carolina had upheld the conviction based on the 1906 case of *Haddock v. Haddock.* There the Supreme Court, over a dissent by Justice Holmes, had ruled that the Constitution's Full Faith and Credit Clause did not require one state to recognize a divorce granted by another state when one of the parties to that divorce was a "nonresident who did not appear and was only . . . served with notice of the pendency of the action."[58]

---

57. See, for example, Symposium, "South-Eastern Underwriters," 1944 *Insurance Law Journal* 387.

58. 201 U.S. 562 (1906). The case was narrowly decided, 5–4, with Holmes, Harlan, Brewer, and Brown dissenting. Article IV, Section 1 of the Constitution directs that "Full

At conference a majority of the Court quickly reached the conclusion that *Haddock* had to be overruled, and the chief justice assigned the case to Douglas. In his opinion, Douglas held that decrees of the state of one spouse's domicile had to be recognized throughout the nation under the Full Faith and Credit Clause, even if such decrees conflicted with the policy of another state. Moreover, Douglas noted the problems that would result if *Haddock* remained in force:

> Under the circumstances of this case, a man would have two wives, a wife two husbands. The reality of a sentence to prison proves that there is no mere play on words. Each would be a bigamist for living in one state with the only one with whom the other state would permit him lawfully to live. Children of the second marriage would be bastards in one state but legitimate in the other. . . .
>
> Certainly if decrees of a state altering the marital status of its domiciliaries are not valid throughout the Union . . . a rule would be fostered which could not help but bring "considerable disaster to innocent persons" and "bastardize children hitherto supposed to be the offspring of lawful marriage" or else encourage collusive divorces. . . . These intensely practical considerations emphasize for us the essential function of the full faith and credit clause.[59]

There is little doubt that in terms of comity within a federal system, one state must recognize decrees of another, or else the nation would be racked by unresolvable legal conflicts. But the case involved more than just law, and Justice Roberts noted in conference that while *Haddock* was not "good law," it was "good morals." Frankfurter agreed with Roberts, but when Douglas in his draft opinion referred to the "sanctity of marriage," Frankfurter urged him to drop that phrase; the Court must not express personal views but "the compulsions of governing legal principles."[60]

While Douglas believed *Haddock* had to be overruled, a more troubling legal question bothered him: whether or not Williams and Hendrix had in fact established a legitimate residence in Nevada. If they had not, as the North Carolina authorities claimed, then that would have served as a jurisdictional basis for invalidating both the Nevada divorces and the marriage. But the chief justice persuaded Douglas not to deal with this issue, on the grounds that the North Carolina court had based its opinion solely on the

---

Faith and Credit shall be given in each state to the public Acts, Records and Judicial Proceedings of every other State."

59. *Williams v. North Carolina*, 317 U.S. 287, 299, 301 (1942); the quotes in the second paragraph are from Holmes's dissent in *Haddock*, 201 U.S. at 628.

60. Frankfurter to Douglas, November 19, 1942, Douglas Papers, Library of Congress.

*Haddock* precedent; overrule that case, Stone urged, and leave the domicili-ary question for further proceedings in state court.[61]

But if a majority saw this simply as a legal question, Frank Murphy did not. Murphy believed that law embodied morality and that a ruling that went against moral values could not be considered "good law." The justice began referring to *Williams* as the "free love case" and condemned the Nevada divorce law as "a raucous fraud, a pure tourist racket." He had no intention, he told his clerk, of giving "extra-territorial effect to Nevada's *lustful* decree." But while he personally abhorred the Nevada arrange-ments, he recognized that his dissent would have to be based on legal rather than moral grounds, and he fastened on the same issue that had caused Douglas some doubts—the jurisdictional question arising out of the legitimacy of the Nevada residence. Six weeks in a hotel, he believed, did not constitute a bona fide domicile sufficient to meet the requirements of the Full Faith and Credit Clause.[62]

Robert Jackson agreed, and in a witty and brilliant dissent he charged that the Court had repealed the divorce laws of forty-seven states and had substituted for them "the law of Nevada as to all marriages one of the parties to which can afford a short trip there." Along with Murphy, Jackson stressed the domicile issue, noting that "the only suggestion of a domicile within Nevada was a stay of about six weeks at the Alamo Auto Court, an address hardly suggestive of permanence." As for the practical considera-tions Douglas mentioned in his opinion, he agreed there were serious con-sequences if a Nevada court without proper jurisdiction says that "the sojourn of two spouses gives four spouses rights to acquire four more, but I think it far more serious to force North Carolina to acquiesce in any such proposition." As for the problem of bastard children, Jackson wrote that he "had supposed that our judicial responsibility is for the regularity of the law, not the regularity of pedigrees."[63]

According to Murphy's biographer, the justice did not ordinarily allow his religion to affect his behavior on the bench, but in this case the Catholic Church's opposition to divorce may well have influenced him, and he sent copies of his dissent to a number of priests.[64] As he told Jackson, he had tried to write in a "non-churchy and austere way—which is not easy for me." But Jackson, who had an admirable writing style, had created a very

---

61. Stone to Douglas, November 4, 1942, Frankfurter Papers, Harvard Law School Li-brary. Frankfurter entered a concurrence expanding on this theme. See his undated mem-orandum to the Court, Douglas Papers, Library of Congress; and his concurrence at 317 U.S. at 304.
62. Fine, *Murphy*, 362–63; Murphy's dissent is at 317 U.S. at 308.
63. 317 U.S. at 311, 312, 321, 324 (Jackson dissenting).
64. Fine, *Murphy*, 365.

favorable impression with his dissent. "I hope you are not embarrassed that my brethren of the Faith are singing your praises. In Detroit the Archbishop and Bishop spoke to me about your views." Of course, Murphy said, "we are concerned with the law and not the Church." But in fact it was morality, not the law, that governed Murphy's views. Nevada's catering to the rich, he charged, "compels sister states to an acceptance of her degraded morality about something we can view as sacred without being hypocrites."[65]

Many people saw the case as more a moral question than a legal dispute. At that time most states made divorce difficult, often requiring stringent evidentiary rules that one partner had committed adultery. The notion that divorce should be granted because the marriage had not worked out and that one or both partners no longer wanted to stay married did not receive widespread acceptance until the 1960s. At this time Nevada did a land-office business thanks to what we would now call its no-fault divorce law. While in some instances the divorce was secured by one partner against the wishes of the other, in many, perhaps even a majority, of the cases, both partners had worked out the terms of the settlement, and then one person would move to Nevada for the required six weeks and secure the divorce that both wanted. Liberalization of divorce laws in other states eventually made it unnecessary for unhappy persons to undertake the Nevada route.[66]

Despite the effort by the majority to frame the issue in narrow legal standards, moral and indeed legal ethics played a major part in the proceedings and in how the public perceived it. Erwin Griswold told his friend Felix Frankfurter that the case "was in fact about the crudest sort of low-dealing with the marriage relation." Griswold believed the domicile issue had been buried in the opinion, and "if there is *ever* going to be a case when there is no domicile in Nevada, it would seem to be this case." As a result, the Court's approval of the divorce would appear to most people to be approval of Nevada's domiciliary laws, and if the Court should ever decide that a Nevada divorce is not good without actual domicile, "the public will be likely to feel that it is simply another case of Supreme Court vacillation."[67]

---

65. Murphy to Jackson, n.d. [October 1942], Jackson Papers, Library of Congress.

66. See Glenda Riley, *Divorce: An American Tradition* (New York: Oxford University Press, 1991), especially chap. 6.

67. Griswold to Frankfurter, February 15, 1943, Frankfurter Papers, Harvard Law School Library. Frankfurter wrote back hotly that the domicile issue had not been decided because it had not been before the Court; the North Carolina decision had specifically not raised that question. As for the matter of public impressions, it was not for the Court to explain its technical decisions to the public; that was the job of the law schools. Frankfurter to Griswold, February 19, 1943, *ibid.*

In fact, the case did come back to the Court, this time on the domicili-
ary issue that had so concerned the dissenters in the first case. Taking its
cue from the majority opinion that the matter of domicile had not been
adjudicated, the North Carolina Supreme Court ordered a second trial on
that question. The jury found Williams and Hendrix guilty of bigamous
cohabitation since they had not established a bona fide residence in Nevada and thus had not secured a valid divorce. Once again the couple appealed, but this time the Supreme Court, speaking through Justice
Frankfurter, sustained the conviction in an opinion that seemed to abandon all notions of full faith and credit.

"A judgment in one State," Frankfurter wrote, "is conclusive upon the
merits in every other State but only if the court of the first State had power
to pass on the merits—had jurisdiction, that is, to render the judgment."[68]
But he then went on to give the second state the power to make the judgment whether or not the courts of the first state had jurisdiction, regardless
of what the first state decided. Thus whether or not Nevada considered six
weeks' residence sufficient to establish domicile made no difference; North
Carolina could evaluate what had happened in Nevada and decide for itself
whether there had been adequate residence. In effect, the Frankfurter
opinion undermined the Full Faith and Credit Clause, which required one
state to recognize the decrees of another, on the basis that the state issuing
its decrees did so upon a finding that its requirements had been met. Here
Nevada had said, "A person staying within our borders for six weeks is
considered a resident." Under *Williams II*, North Carolina could and did
say, "We don't care whether you think six weeks a resident makes; we do
not, and therefore will not recognize your divorce decrees."

Frankfurter believed that the two decisions taken "together give not
only a coherent body of law with reference to decrees of divorce as between
the States but also does justice to correct legal analysis without sacrificing
social morality."[69] Not all of his brethren agreed. Reed reluctantly went
along with the majority, albeit with considerable misgivings, and declared
that "one revolts at North Carolina's requirement that parties to a sister
state divorce prove their domicile."[70]

Although Jackson agreed with Frankfurter's conclusion, he pointedly
noted that domicile had been an issue in *Williams I;* that, after all, had
been what he and Murphy had written about. It is interesting to compare
comments by Jackson in a speech given that year. "By the full faith and
credit clause," he said, the framers of the Constitution "sought to federal-

68. *Williams v. North Carolina,* 325 U.S. 226, 229 (1945).

69. Frankfurter to Stone, February 20, 1945, Stone Papers, Library of Congress.

70. Reed to Frankfurter, April 26, 1945, Frankfurter Papers, Harvard Law School Library.

ize the separate and independent state legal systems by the overriding principle of reciprocal recognition of public acts, records, and judicial proceedings. It was placed foremost among those measures which would guard the new political and economic union against the disintegrating influence of provincialism in jurisprudence, but without the aggrandizement of federal power at the expense of the states." Yet by allowing a state to question the jurisdiction underlying other states' actions, the second *Williams* decree did allow for just such "provincialism in jurisprudence."[71]

Justice Rutledge thought the domicile question a sham and asserted that "the Constitution does not mention domicil." In his view the majority opinion transformed a valid legal transaction in one state into perjury, for which people could be sent to prison. The whole Nevada operation, he believed, was also a sham. The parties, their lawyers, and the judges all recognized that even while a person suing for divorce claims that she intends to remain in Nevada "indefinitely," she already has a paid reservation on the next flight home. No one had been misled, and everyone knew it was a legal ruse and nothing more. It was certainly not good public policy or good law, Rutledge claimed, but if one believed in the Full Faith and Credit Clause, then Nevada divorce proceedings had to be sustained. For himself, he could find no evidence that the Constitution had "confided to the caprice of juries the faith and credit due the laws and judgments of sister states."[72]

The strongest blast came from Hugo Black, joined by William O. Douglas, who originally had indicated his willingness to go along with the Frankfurter opinion.[73] Black pointed out that Williams and Hendrix had been jailed despite the fact that the Supreme Court had never held that they had engaged in fraud or that their divorces were invalid under Nevada law. That state had accepted their residence as fulfilling the domiciliary requirement, and the majority of the Court, ignoring the Full Faith and Credit Clause, now found the Nevada court lacking jurisdiction because a North Carolina court had ruled domicile lacking in Nevada. In a swipe at Frankfurter's notion of what the Due Process Clause meant, Black declared

---

71. Jackson to Frankfurter, February 24, 1945, *ibid.*; Jackson, "Full Faith and Credit—The Lawyer's Clause," 45 *Columbia Law Review* 1, 17 (1945).

72. 325 U.S. at 244, 245 (Rutledge dissenting); see also Fowler V. Harper, *Justice Rutledge and the Bright Constellation* (Indianapolis: Bobbs-Merrill, 1965), 295–99. Murphy also worried about the fact that people could be sent to prison when they believed they had received a legal divorce. Fine, *Murphy*, 367–68. Murphy filed a concurrence, 325 U.S. at 239.

73. Douglas to Frankfurter, February 28, 1945: "I have nothing to add in Williams, no changes to suggest. I will agree with it. But I *may* file . . . a short concurring opinion which I will show you." Douglas to Frankfurter, March 20, 1945: "Contrary to my earlier expectation I now doubt if I can join you in your opinion in Williams v. North Carolina." Frankfurter Papers, Harvard Law School Library.

that the majority viewed that clause as "a blank sheet of paper provided for courts to make changes in the Constitution and the Bill of Rights in accordance with their ideas of civilization's demands."[74]

The two *Williams* cases did not show the Court at its best as umpire of the federal system, and contemporary commentators pointed out the inherent contradictions in the two opinions.[75] The Court's decisions did not, as Black had charged, put every divorce granted in the United States in jeopardy, nor did it even put all Nevada proceedings at risk. *Williams* involved two couples, and at least one partner in each marriage had had no chance to speak up in a Nevada court. Most of the divorces granted by Nevada and Florida, another state with minimal requirements, involved only one marriage, in which both partners agreed on the desirability of ending their union. As a result, neither one would have any reason to call the divorce into question, and without a private complaint, most state governments preferred to look the other way.

Frankfurter, on jurisprudential grounds, and Murphy, on moral grounds, continued to oppose applying the Full Faith and Credit Clause to quickie divorces. When in 1947 a majority held that Massachusetts had to recognize a Florida divorce in dividing the former couple's property, the two men dissented, and Frankfurter exclaimed in conference, "I cannot bring myself to believe that the Full Faith and Credit Clause gave to the few states which offer bargain-counter divorces constitutional power to control the social policy governing domestic relations of the many states which do not."[76]

At the same time it decided this case, the Court also gave its approval to so-called divisible divorce. A New York man had obtained a Nevada divorce that a New York court recognized as valid, but the court held that he had to continue paying alimony to his wife under a decree issued to her in her separation suit filed in New York since she had not appeared in the Nevada proceeding or been served notice of that proceeding. In this case Frankfurter and Jackson dissented, and Jackson mocked the majority decree for reaching the conclusion that the Nevada decree was "half good and half bad." He also noted the confusion spawned by the Court's various rulings, and while he felt bound by the ruling in *Williams I,* he charged that "if there is one thing that people are entitled to expect from their lawmak-

---

74. 325 U.S. at 239, 261, 274 (Black dissenting).

75. See, for example, William J. Barnhard, "Haddock Revised," 31 *Georgetown Law Journal* 210 (1943); Edward S. Corwin, "Out-Haddocking Haddock," 93 *University of Pennsylvania Law Review* 341 (1945); and Thomas Reed Powell, "And Repent at Leisure, an Inquiry into the Unhappy Lot of Those Whom Nevada Hath Joined Together and North Carolina Hath Put Asunder," 58 *Harvard Law Review* 930 (1945).

76. *Sherrer v. Sherrer,* 334 U.S. 343 (1948); Fine, *Murphy,* 369–70.

ers, it is rules of law that will enable individuals to tell whether they are married and, if so, to whom."[77]

Perhaps worn out by the confusion they themselves had generated, the five-justice majority in *Rice v. Rice* (1949) issued a *per curiam* opinion sustaining a Connecticut ruling regarding another Nevada decree. A Connecticut man had obtained a Nevada divorce, remarried, and then died without leaving a will. The Connecticut court ruled that the deceased's property should go to his first wife, who lived in that state. Jackson spoke for the four dissenters and again mocked the results of the Court's rulings. The judgment, he declared, "permits Rice to have a wife who cannot become his widow and to leave a widow who was no longer his wife." Murphy almost joined the dissenters, but in the end he could not bring himself to give any validity to a Nevada proceeding.[78]

The Court's role as umpire of the federal system is critical to any effective functioning of the constitutional scheme, but by the 1940s problems had arisen that went far beyond the simple categories utilized by the framers. Commerce in the mid–twentieth century was vastly more complex than it had been in the late–eighteenth century, and efforts by both the national and state governments to regulate commerce made it difficult to determine exactly where the Commerce Clause drew the line of authority.

Moreover, new issues, or older ones in new guises, such as divorce, also raised questions about how the system should work. That the justices often failed to agree is hardly surprising, given the complexity of the questions and the widely diverse views that had fragmented the Stone Court. In some areas, such as the recognition of divorce decrees under the Full Faith and Credit Clause, the justices reached opinions, although those opinions often lacked intellectual consistency. In other areas, such as intergovernmental tax immunity—the issue of whether the federal and state governments could levy taxes on property held by the other—the justices could not even reach agreement.[79]

But despite shifting interpretations of the limits and meanings of particular constitutional clauses, all the justices believed that the judiciary had been entrusted with a unique role and that if the notion of federalism were to survive, then the Supreme Court had no choice but to continue in the always difficult and often unenviable position of umpire to the system.

---

77. *Estin v. Estin*, 334 U.S. 541, 553–54 (1948) (Jackson dissenting).

78. *Rice v. Rice*, 336 U.S. 674, 676, 680 (1949) (Jackson dissenting).

79. *New York v. United States*, 326 U.S. 572 (1946). The case involved federal taxation of water bottled from the state-owned Saratoga Springs. For a discussion of the issues, see Mason, *Stone*, 780–82.

# 5

# TRANSITION

Shortly after the Court adjourned in the spring of 1946, Frankfurter summed up what he considered one of the stormiest five-year periods in the Court's history. If he had to go into a classroom, he told Frank Murphy, and explain these five terms, he would have to say:

1. Never before in the history of the Court were so many of its members influenced in decisions by considerations extraneous to the legal issues that supposedly control decisions.
2. Never before have members of the Court so often acted contrary to their convictions on the governing legal issues in decisions.
3. Never before has so large a proportion of the opinions fallen short of requisite professional standards.[1]

Frankfurter might well have added that never before had collegial relations within the Court been so poor, and for that he would have been in large part responsible. By the end of the war the normal level of polite give-and-take within the Court had been seriously poisoned by the ongoing feuding among Frankfurter, Roberts, and Jackson on one side and Black, Douglas, and Murphy on the other. The extent of this bitterness can be seen from two incidents, both seemingly minor, which mushroomed out of all proportions. One involved the normal courtesy of a retirement letter to Owen J. Roberts, which has been discussed earlier[2]; the other led to one of the most acrimonious fights in the Court's history.

During the 1944 Term, the Court heard a case requiring an interpretation of the Fair Labor Standards Act of 1938, otherwise known as the Black-Connery Act, one of Hugo Black's last legislative accomplishments before his appointment to the bench.[3] The Court had to decide the "portal-to-portal" question, whether the law required that miners' pay be calculated from the time they entered the portal of the mine rather than from the moment they actually started to work the coal. In large mines with deep

---

1. Frankfurter to Murphy, June 10, 1946, Frankfurter Papers, Library of Congress.
2. See above, pp. 45–46.
3. William E. Leuchtenburg, *Franklin D. Roosevelt and the New Deal, 1932–1940* (New York: Harper & Row, 1963), 261–62.

shafts requiring extensive travel time, the amount of additional wages involved could be substantial. Arguing for the United Mine Workers was
Crampton Harris, who had once been Black's law partner in Alabama.[4]
The Court initially split 5–4 against the union position, and Stone assigned
the opinion to Jackson; Stanley Reed then changed his mind, and Black,
now the senior justice in the majority, designated Frank Murphy to write
the decision.[5]

Jackson turned what would have been his majority opinion into a dissent and buttressed his interpretation of the Black-Connery Law by reference to statements that Black, then a senator, had made in the *Congressional
Record*. An angry Black charged that Jackson had quoted him out of context, a view Murphy incorporated into his opinion, but Jackson's dissent
still stung.[6] This should have been the end of the issue, but the coal company petitioned for a rehearing on the grounds that Black ought to have
disqualified himself because of the involvement of his former law partner.

Chief Justice Stone saw no merit in this argument. Holmes, Brandeis,
and many other justices—including Stone himself—had not recused when
the Court heard arguments by lawyers with whom they had at one time or
another been professionally involved. It had always been left to the individual justice's sense of propriety whether a conflict of interest existed with a
particular counsel in any given case.[7] The Chief Justice therefore prepared
a *per curiam* denying the petition, but knowing how strongly Frankfurter
and Jackson felt about this issue, he suggested a statement be added that
no question of disqualification is ever open for consideration by the Court.
Frankfurter immediately objected, saying this raised new matters; Black insisted that the denial be issued without any explanation. "Any opinion
which discussed the subject at all," Black told the Conference, "would

---

4. The personal and professional relations between Black and Harris are explained in
Gerald T. Dunne, *Hugo Black and the Judicial Revolution* (New York: Simon & Schuster,
1977), 234.

5. Murphy had written an expansive interpretation of the same act a year earlier in another case in which the union had also been represented by Harris, *Tennessee Coal, Iron &
Railroad Co. v. Muscada Local 123,* 321 U.S. 590 (1944).

6. *Jewell Ridge Coal Corp. v. Local 6167 United Mine Workers,* 325 U.S. 161 (1945); Frankfurter
voted with Jackson, whose dissent is at 325 U.S. 170. Justice Roberts tried, without success,
to get Jackson to change this part of his dissent in order, as he put it, to "avoid Black's
feeling of wrongful use of his language." Roberts to Jackson, n.d. [May 1945], Jackson
Papers, Library of Congress.

7. Stone himself had a highly developed sense of propriety in these matters even though
he had not been in private practice since the early 1920s. In 1943 he recused when one of
the litigants was represented by his old law firm, Sullivan & Cromwell; Stone to Roberts
(as senior justice), May 19, 1943. He also recused himself when friends argued cases or
sometimes for what he termed personal reasons. See Stone to Black (as senior justice),
September 29, 1945 and March 29, 1946, all in Stone Papers, Library of Congress.

mean a declaration of war." Stone tried to negotiate a compromise, but to no avail. Jackson believed a simple denial would imply the Court's approved of Black's conduct, and encouraged by Frankfurter, he prepared a two-page concurrence to the *per curiam,* implicitly criticizing Black's conduct.[8] Evidently aware that his signature along with Jackson's might be misinterpreted as merely a personal attack, Frankfurter sent a letter to Black explaining his position:

> It happens to be one of my deepest convictions that the world's difficulties are due to no one cause more than to the failure of men to act on that which they believe to be true. I had no share in creating the situation whereby Bob felt it his duty to make clear the issue of disqualification. But since he had done so, I could withhold joining him only by suppressing my belief in the truth. I do not propose to do that—and that is the sole reason why I join him.[9]

In the ensuing brouhaha in the press, no doubt Frankfurter suffered from conflicting emotions—the pleasure of seeing Black portrayed as an unprincipled judge and the anguish of having the Court's dirty linen aired in public.[10]

For Jackson, vindication came from Congress. In light of the *Jewell Ridge* decision, unions began pressing suit for alleged back wages and compensation for times they claimed employers required their workers to be on the premises.[11] Companies complained to Congress that they faced billions in

8. *Jewell Ridge Coal Corp. v. Local 6167, United Mine Workers,* 325 U.S. 897 (1945). The story of the internal friction on the Court arising from this case can be found in Alpheus T. Mason, *Harlan Fiske Stone: Pillar of the Law* (New York: Viking, 1956), 642–45; Dunne, *Hugo Black,* 233–40; and Joseph Lash, *From the Diaries of Felix Frankfurter* (New York: Norton, 1975), 265.

9. Frankfurter to Black, June 9, 1945, Frankfurter Papers, Library of Congress. Frankfurter circulated this letter to the brethren, and Murphy tried to use it to delay the announcement of the Court's decision in order to give Black and Jackson time to cool down, a ploy Frankfurter considered patently false. Memorandum by Frankfurter, June 9, 1945, Jackson Papers, Library of Congress. Murphy then withdrew his request for a delay, and the Court denied rehearing in an unsigned *per curiam,* which stated that the "Court is without the authority and does not undertake, to pass upon the propriety of the participation, by its members, in the decision of cases brought here for review."

10. See, for example, the editorial in the *New York Times,* June 12, 1945, in which the writer says, "It seems to us that Justice Jackson has committed an error in taste and that Justice Black has committed the worse offense of lowering judicial standards."

11. One such case reached the Supreme Court, which by a 5–2 vote upheld the workers' claims. *Anderson v. Mt. Clemens Pottery Co.,* 328 U.S. 680 (1946). Murphy wrote the majority opinion, from which Burton and Frankfurter dissented. Jackson was overseas and did not take part in the decision, and Stone died before the result was announced.

losses should these suits prove successful, and Congress responded by amending the Fair Labor Standards Act to incorporate the view Jackson had taken in dissent, thus overriding the majority holding. In its preamble to the revision, Congress noted that "the Fair Labor Standards Act, as amended, has been interpreted judicially in disregard of long established customs, practices and contracts between employers and employees, thereby creating wholly unexpected liabilities immense in amount and retroactive in operation."[12] Jackson might well gloat that "the Supreme Court had never had such a rebuke at the hands of Congress." He took additional satisfaction from the fact that Congress amended the United States Code to make more explicit conditions under which judges should disqualify themselves, including "relationship to a party's attorney."[13]

The denial for rehearing had come down on the last day of the term, and soon afterwards, Owen J. Roberts decided to retire after fifteen years on the bench. Roberts had had enough of the strife among the brethren and also felt himself increasingly out of step with the Roosevelt appointees;[14] in his last term, Roberts dissented fifty-three times. Jackson also found the atmosphere poisonous and fled to Europe, not sure, as he later confessed, whether he would ever come back to the disagreeable climate of the Court.[15]

During the war, Roosevelt and Winston Churchill had pledged that following an Allied victory, those who had committed crimes against humanity would be brought to justice. To keep this promise, the Allies subsequently convened an International Military Tribunal in Nuremberg, Germany, the city where the infamous Nazi racial laws had been proclaimed. President Harry S Truman asked Jackson to serve as the American prosecutor, and Jackson, without consulting Stone, quickly accepted.[16] Jackson saw the Nuremberg trials not only as the greatest challenge of his career but also as a noble endeavor to replace the rule of law for the

---

12. 61 *Stat.* 84 (1947).

13. 28 U.S.C. 455; Jackson Memoirs, Columbia Oral History Collection.

14. See, for example, his bitter dissent in *Mahnich v. Southern Steamship Co.*, 321 U.S. 96, 113 (1944), encouraged and joined in by Frankfurter.

15. Jackson Memoirs, Columbia Oral History Collection.

16. In his memoirs, Jackson candidly noted why he did not discuss the president's request with the chief justice: "I knew that he would disapprove of my doing it. I didn't have to ask him to know that. I knew that I would disapprove it if anyone else were doing it. If internal matters at the Court had been pleasant and agreeable, and if I had not already considered leaving the Court, I probably would not have undertaken it. All things considered I didn't know but that it might prove to be a good exit from the Court, and I wasn't at all sure that if I took it on I would ever return to the Court." Jackson went on to note, however, that he totally misjudged how long the assignment would take. *Ibid.*

vengeance that victors had traditionally inflicted on the vanquished. The
trial, Jackson declared in his opening statement, comprised "one of the
most significant tributes that Power has ever paid to Reason."[17]

Not everyone shared this view, and there has been an ongoing debate
over the legitimacy of the Nuremberg trials and whether they did in fact
represent a rule of law or merely a legal fiction to rationalize vengeance.[18]
The Court rejected all efforts to file writs of *habeas corpus* by the Nuremberg
defendants since that tribunal had been created by a four-power agreement and therefore was not subject to review by American courts.[19]

The real impact the war crimes trials had on the Court was not jurisprudential but the havoc they wreaked among the brethren. Although Jackson
had been eager to take on the assignment, he realized that it created both
practical and theoretical problems for the Court. His departure left the
bench evenly divided in a number of cases so that decisions had to be
deferred until after Jackson returned; it also put additional burdens on the
other members, a situation deeply resented by Black in particular. When
Jackson returned to the United States for a brief visit in the fall of 1945, he
recognized the strain his absence had put on the Court and suggested to
the president that it might be better if he resigned from the Court; Truman
immediately rejected the idea.[20] Whatever one might have felt about the
rightness or wrongness of the war crimes trial, one might well question the
appropriateness of having a member of the United States Supreme Court
act as a prosecutor.

As the trials stretched out far longer than had been anticipated, Jackson grew increasingly uneasy about his role. He knew that Chief Justice
Stone disapproved of the war crimes trials, Jackson's role in them, and the
extra work caused by his absence.[21] Stone wrote on several occasions to

---

17. Quoted in James F. Simon, *The Antagonists: Hugo Black, Felix Frankfurter and Civil Liberties in Modern America* (New York: Simon & Schuster, 1989), 158.

18. The debate is beyond the scope of this book, but the reader is referred to Telford
Taylor, *The Anatomy of the Nuremberg Trials: A Personal Memoir* (New York: Knopf, 1992);
William J. Bosch, *Judgment on Nuremberg: American Attitudes Toward the Major War-Crimes
Trials* (Chapel Hill: University of North Carolina Press, 1970); H. Tusa and J. Tusa, *The
Nuremberg Trial* (New York: Atheneum, 1983); and the highly polemical and critical Rich-
ard H. Minear, *Victor's Justice: The Tokyo War Crime Trials* (Princeton: Princeton University
Press, 1971).

19. The justices did agree to hear an appeal from the court set up to try Japanese accused
of war crimes because that had been established by General Douglas MacArthur in his
capacity as military commander under the aegis of the allied powers. In the end, however,
the Court denied the appeal and in a brief *per curiam* held that as an international tribunal,
it could not have its decisions reviewed by American courts. *Hirota v. MacArthur*, 338 U.S.
197 (1948).

20. Jackson Memoirs, Columbia Oral History Collection, Columbia University.

21. Mason, *Stone*, 714–19.

Jackson, and underneath the pleasantries there were sharp barbs about the extra work Jackson's absence caused. "I found myself doing some work on both Christmas and New Year's day in order to keep up," he wrote early in January. "At the moment all of my opinions are written, but I think there is no one else in the Court in that fortunate situation. . . . We are continuing to develop four-to-four votes in cases which will, for that reason, have to be reargued."[22]

Criticism of the need to carry over cases soon became public (a fact that Jackson attributed to Black), and Jackson wrote from Nuremberg offering to return for the April sitting of the Court so that he could vote on all the tied cases, thus clearing the docket.[23] Stone had evidently initially approved of this idea but then changed his mind; in early March he wrote to Jackson that attendance at the April session for the purpose of voting would not be satisfactory. "It would, I think, be preferable not to return to the work of the Court until you are ready to take it up in the regular way without further interruptions, even at the cost of putting over cases which might otherwise be disposed of this term."[24] In other words, Stone said, do not come back until you can fully carry your part of the load.

Jackson understood the chief's message and also knew that Frankfurter shared at least some of Stone's doubt about the propriety of his role. His letters to Frankfurter took on a strained, self-justifying tone, and Frankfurter tried to reassure his friend, urging him to "dismiss all concern" since the complaints "neither in volume nor in quality really amount to a hill of beans."[25] When Jackson remained perturbed, Frankfurter wrote to him again: "Whatever I may think about a Justice of the Supreme Court taking on other jobs—and I am afraid I am impenitent on that subject—I never had any doubt about the profound importance of your enterprise and equally no doubt that you would discharge the task according to the finest professional standards both intellectually and ethically. That you have done so I have said again, and again, and again."[26]

Then on April 22, 1946, attendees in the Court were stunned when Chief Justice Stone, about to deliver the three decisions he had prepared for the Court that week, suddenly began to mumble. Wiley Rutledge saw "the Chief, sitting back, holding his opinions in reading position, his right hand fumbling through the pages. Then I heard him say in a low voice

---

22. Stone to Jackson, January 2, 1946, Stone Papers, Library of Congress.

23. Jackson to Attorney General Tom Clark, January 12, 1946, Jackson Papers, Library of Congress.

24. Stone to Jackson, March 1, 1946, Stone Papers, Library of Congress.

25. Frankfurter to Jackson, February 6, 1946, Frankfurter Papers, Harvard Law School Library.

26. Frankfurter to Jackson, May 11, 1946, *ibid.*

something like 'this case should be stayed . . .' Still it did not occur to me that he was ill." Hugo Black, however, sitting at Stone's right hand, immediately saw that something serious had happened. At 1:45 Black grabbed the gavel and announced that Court would be adjourned until 2:30. Black and Reed assisted Stone from the bench and helped him to a couch; an ambulance took him home at 3:30, and at 6:45 the twelfth chief justice of the United States died quietly from a massive cerebral hemorrhage.[27] The nation mourned, and newspaper editors, congressmen, and lawyers praised Stone's career and especially his twenty years on the bench. But as Robert Jackson once said, "Washington adores a funeral—especially if it ushers in a vacancy."

It was no secret that Jackson wanted the center chair, and supposedly he had been Franklin Roosevelt's first choice to succeed Charles Evans Hughes. At that time it had been Frankfurter who had convinced Roosevelt to name Stone, arguing that with war approaching, naming the Republican Stone as chief would foster national unity.[28] Jackson had then taken Stone's place as associate justice, with Roosevelt's assurances that when Stone, by then almost seventy years old, stepped down, Jackson would take his place. But Harry Truman, not Franklin Roosevelt, now occupied the Oval Office, and even though Truman thought highly enough of Jackson to name him chief American prosecutor at Nuremberg, he had serious and legitimate doubts about naming him chief justice. The internal strife during Stone's tenure had become general knowledge, and following the *Jewell Ridge* battle,[29] Truman might well have questioned Jackson's ability to unify the Court.

On May 16, Doris Fleeson's column in the *Washington Star* carried a report on the confrontation between Black and Jackson over *Jewell Ridge*, with details that could have been provided only by someone who had been at the conference—one of the members of the Court. In addition, Fleeson reported that Truman had been told that if he did appoint Jackson, both Hugo Black and William O. Douglas would resign. Less than a month later, Truman named Fred Vinson as chief justice, and the following day the president received a blistering fifteen-hundred-word cable from Jackson purporting to set the record straight. In the cable Jackson touched on a number of matters affecting, as he put it, the integrity of the Court, but the heart of the message consisted of Jackson's version of the *Jewell Ridge*

---

27. Mason, *Stone*, 806. The initial diagnosis had been indigestion, which the doctor thought would clear up after some rest. Handwritten note from a clerk or secretary, TEW to Black, April 22, 1946, Black Papers, Library of Congress.

28. Mason, *Stone*, 566–67; see also Jackson's recollection in his Memoirs, Columbia Oral History Collection, in which he claims that Stone also saw him as his successor.

29. See above, pp. 137–39.

controversy and a bitter attack on Hugo Black, whom Jackson accused of meddling with the president's choice of a chief justice.[30] In his oral history memoir, Jackson noted that Black had resented him from the time he came on the Court:

> It wasn't long after I came on the court that I realized that Justice Black felt that he was entitled to be the leader of the New Deal group on the court. The story got around that I had been promised the chief justiceship. . . . The result of it was that not only Black, but others who might have ambitions to be promoted, couldn't help but regard me as one who stood in the way.[31]

Despite Truman's plea to hold up publication of the cable until he had a chance to talk to Jackson about it, the infuriated justice made its contents public the next day in the form of a letter to the chairmen of the House and Senate Judiciary Committees.

What had riled Jackson up and led him to such an ill-considered outburst? A few years later, Robert S. Allen and William V. Shannon published an account blaming Frankfurter for stirring up the pot:

> Frankfurter wrote [Jackson] that Black had gone to Truman and declared that he would not serve under Jackson. That accusation was a lie. There was not an atom of truth in it. Black had neither said nor done anything to influence Truman's decision. The story was solely the product of Frankfurter's scheming and devious imagination. But to Jackson, seething and raging in Nuremberg, Frankfurter's letter was like putting an acetylene torch to a powder keg.[32]

An outraged Frankfurter personally denied the story to Black and threatened to sue the two columnists for libel. In a letter to Black, Frankfurter declared that "neither directly nor indirectly did I send any communication whatever to Jackson regarding the vacancy created by Stone's death." Whether Black believed Frankfurter at the time is questionable; but later, after the two men had grown closer in the late 1950s and early 1960s, Black seems to have accepted the story.[33]

---

30. *New York Times,* June 11, 1946.

31. Jackson Memoirs, Columbia Oral History Collection.

32. Robert S. Allen and William V. Shannon, *The Truman Merry-Go-Round* (New York: Vanguard, 1950), 366–67.

33. Frankfurter to Black, September 30, 1950, Frankfurter Papers, Library of Congress; Black at the time told his son that he was sure Felix had in fact done it; Simon, *The Antagonists,* 169; Black, "Mr. Justice Frankfurter," 78 *Harvard Law Review* 1521 (1965).

In fact, despite his great affection for Jackson and his dislike of Black at that time, Frankfurter did not instigate the incident. Frank Shea, who had been in the Justice Department under Jackson and had assisted in the preparation for the Nuremberg trials, wrote to Jackson on May 17, 1946, recounting the spate of events in Washington and speculation about Stone's successor. "I understand that for a few hours it seemed a sure thing for you," Shea said. "Then Black got word to the President that there would be a row if you were appointed. At this, [Truman] began to make wide inquiries and to appreciate, perhaps exaggerate, the rifts in the Court." It was this letter from Shea, not anything from Frankfurter, that pushed Jackson into indiscretion.[34]

Frankfurter seemed to have played no role in the selection of Vinson, and his activity during this time appears to have been limited to trying to sustain his friend's sagging spirits and defending him from attack.[35] Jackson considered resigning from the Court, a thought that horrified Frankfurter, who knew that in the years ahead he would need all the help he could get to fight off what he considered Hugo Black's wrong-headed assault on the Constitution. As a grace note to this whole affair, consider Jackson's comment in his memoirs: "When I came back to the Court, Vinson, of course, was the chief justice. From that day to this, Justice Black has treated me with respect as one gentleman to another. We've never had a word. Relations were never as harmonious between us they have been since. I don't know what they would have been without the letter. Mr. Crampton Harris has never appeared in court since."[36]

During the interim between Stone's death and Vinson's appointment, the Court decided a case that reflected the growing chasm between Frankfurter and Black. Although Frankfurter spoke for a majority over Black's dissent, in the end Black's view prevailed.

In March 1946 the Court heard argument in a suit begun by Professor

Bruce Murphy is a bit more skeptical; although he admits to a lack of specific evidence, he implies that it would have been perfectly in character for Frankfurter to have done just what Allen and Shannon charged. *The Brandeis/Frankfurter Connection* (New York: Oxford University Press), 306–7.

34. Dennis J. Hutchinson, "The Black-Jackson Feud," 1988 *Supreme Court Review* 203, 216–17. Hutchinson also presents evidence supporting his claim that William O. Douglas, in his effort to sink the Jackson candidacy, had leaked information about the *Jewell Ridge* confrontation to Doris Fleeson and also to Drew Pearson.

35. See, for example, Frankfurter to Paul A. Freund, October 29, 1946, Frankfurter Papers, Harvard Law School Library, objecting to a letter, critical of Jackson, that was published in the *Washington Post* by Louis L. Jaffe, a former Frankfurter student and Brandeis clerk.

36. Jackson Memoirs, Columbia Oral History Collection.

Kenneth W. Colegrove of Northwestern University against Illinois Governor Dwight H. Green. Colegrove sought to invalidate all elections held under the state's antiquated apportionment system, which, despite massive population shifts, had not been revised since 1901. As a result, legislative power remained entrenched in the rural districts; efforts to secure reform through state judicial and political methods had failed, and Colegrove had appealed to the federal courts. He argued that the Illinois system, which affected the election of congressmen as well as state representatives, violated the Fifteenth Amendment ban against abridgement of the right to vote as well as guarantees in Article I regarding apportionment of congressmen and Article IV, which decrees that the United States "shall guarantee to every State in this Union a Republican Form of Government."

Colegrove could point to recent decisions protecting the right to vote. The Court had ruled that white primaries designed to thwart black participation in the electoral process violated the Equal Protection Clause,[37] and in a case directly resting on Article I grounds, it held that states could not set different electoral criteria for state legislators and congressional representatives.[38] However, these decisions had involved the special case of discrimination against blacks, and the Court in 1932 had specifically denied that the Constitution required compactness, contiguity, or equality of population in congressional districts. Moreover, a majority of the Court had expressed its belief that such issues comprised "political" questions and were therefore nonjusticiable.[39]

The political question doctrine dates back to the Dorr Rebellion of 1842, when defeated rebels attacked the legitimacy of the old Rhode Island state government under the Guaranty Clause. Chief Justice Roger Taney denied their claim and held that enforcement of the Article IV clause "belonged to the political power and not to the judicial." In such situations, the courts would not intervene because the judicial branch had neither the authority to resolve the dispute nor the means to enforce such a decision.[40] Although Justice Holmes had indicated that he thought the political question doctrine "little more than a play on words,"[41] it nonetheless allowed the Court to evade certain types of cases. For an advocate of judicial re-

37. *Nixon v. Herndon*, 273 U.S. 536 (1927); *Nixon v. Condon*, 286 U.S. 73 (1932); *Smith v. Allwright*, 321 U.S. 649 (1944).

38. *United States v. Classic*, 313 U.S. 299 (1941).

39. *Wood v. Broom*, 287 U.S. 1, 8 (1932).

40. *Luther v. Borden*, 7 How. 1 (1849). See also Charles Gordon Post, Jr., *The Supreme Court and Political Questions* (Baltimore: Johns Hopkins University Press, 1969); and Philippa Strum, *The Supreme Court and "Political Questions": A Study in Judicial Evasion* (University: University of Alabama Press, 1974), especially 41–54.

41. In *Nixon v. Herndon*, 273 U.S. at 540.

straint, such as Felix Frankfurter, the political question doctrine could be invoked as an absolute bar to judicial involvement in the Illinois dispute.

A "bob-tailed Court" of seven justices handed down its decision on June 10, 1946; Chief Justice Stone had died a month after oral argument, and Jackson, still in Nuremberg, had not participated. Frankfurter, speaking for himself, Harold Burton (who had taken Roberts's seat), and Stanley Reed, declared that

> the petitioners ask of this Court what is beyond its competence to grant. This is one of those demands on judicial power which cannot be met by verbal fencing about "jurisdiction." It must be resolved by considerations on the basis of which this Court, from time to time, has refused to intervene in controversies. It has refused to do so because due regard for the effective working of our government revealed this issue to be of a peculiarly political nature and therefore not meet for judicial determination.[42]

The Constitution, Frankfurter concluded, had conferred sole authority in Congress to assure fair representation among the states in the House of Representatives. Courts, he warned in a famous phrase, "ought not to enter this political thicket." Frankfurter got his fourth vote, and the majority, through the concurrence of Wiley Rutledge, who, although he disagreed about the nonjusticiability of such issues, voted to dismiss for want of equity. With the next elections so close, Rutledge believed, it would be impossible to implement any workable remedy.[43]

Black, Douglas, and Murphy dissented. Black believed a clear constitutional violation existed and that federal courts had not only the power but the obligation to protect rights secured by the Constitution. Legislative malapportionment violated Black's beliefs in the popular sovereignty implicit in the Constitution and that he considered had been the basis for its adoption.[44] No one, he asserted in his dissent, "would deny that the equal protection clause would also prohibit a law that would expressly give certain citizens a half-vote and others a full vote." Why, then, should courts tolerate a system that gave certain citizens a vote only one-ninth as effective as that of other citizens in choosing their state and congressional representatives? "Such discriminatory legislation," he concluded, "seems to me exactly the kind that the equal protection clause was intended to prohibit."[45]

---

42. *Colegrove v. Green*, 328 U.S. 549, 552 (1946). For details on this case, see Richard C. Cortner, *The Apportionment Cases* (New York: Norton, 1970), chap. 1.

43. 328 U.S. at 565–66.

44. Tinsley E. Yarbrough, *Mr. Justice Black and His Critics* (Durham: Duke University Press, 1988), 229–30.

45. 328 U.S. at 569.

Although only four members of the Court found against Colegrove, and only three members actually believed apportionment nonjusticiable, the case served as a barrier to election reforms in the states for the next sixteen years. For Frankfurter, *Colegrove* stood for exactly the type of restraint the Court should exercise, but his analysis suffered a serious flaw. In cases involving supposedly "political" questions, courts had assumed that if a legitimate grievance existed, then the political process would be amenable to its rectification. But malapportioned legislatures not only constituted the grievance; they barred any change through the political process. So long as a minority of a state's population could elect a majority of the state assembly, it would not voluntarily give up that power, and the majority will would continue to be thwarted.[46]

After the Court adjourned in early June, Harry Truman named Frederick Moore Vinson the next chief justice of the United States. It is difficult to say whether the president ever gave any serious thought to naming Robert Jackson to succeed Stone, but given the well-known discord that had marred the last few terms of the Court, Truman no doubt wanted a chief who he believed might impose some control and unity on a fractured bench. Whether anyone could have done that with the group that Stone had called his "wild horses" is doubtful, but it was certainly beyond Fred Vinson's talents.

Born the son of a jailer in a small Kentucky town, the able and ambitious Vinson had studied law and then gone into politics. In 1924 the Ninth Congressional District sent him to Congress, where, with the exception of one term, he served for the next fourteen years. Gifted with mathematical acumen, Vinson soon became a key figure on the powerful House Ways and Means Committee, the one person there who really understood all the ramifications of complex tax measures. As such, he became indispensable to the Roosevelt administration, who valued Vinson not only for his abilities but also for his loyalty. Vinson played a key role in the drafting of several important New Deal measures, including the Social Security Act of 1935 and the Revenue Act of 1937. With only one exception, which involved administration efforts to reduce veterans' benefits, Vinson proved a down-the-line supporter of White House proposals. In 1938 President Roosevelt rewarded him with an appointment to the Court of Appeals for the District of Columbia circuit, the second most important court in the

---

46. The Court finally abandoned the *Colegrove* position at the end of Frankfurter's tenure on the bench, first voting that the issue was justiciable (over a bitter dissent by Frankfurter) in *Baker v. Carr,* 369 U.S. 186 (1962), and then adopting Black's position that malapportionment violated the Constitution in *Reynolds v. Sims,* 377 U.S. 533 (1964), in which Chief Justice Earl Warren enunciated a "one man, one vote" rule.

nation.There Vinson compiled a respectable record, but when war broke out, Roosevelt needed someone with Vinson's skills to help with the enormous problems associated with mobilization. At first the president left him on the bench, but in 1942 he had him named chief judge of the wartime Emergency Court of Appeals. The following year Vinson resigned to become director of the Economic Stabilization Board, and before Roosevelt died in April 1945 he had moved Vinson to ever-increasing positions of responsibility, including head of the Office of War Mobilization and Reconversion. Harry Truman tapped him to be secretary of the treasury, and it was from the Cabinet that Vinson moved to the Supreme Court.

The new chief's experience in both the legislative and executive branches of the government had not, however, been the main reason Truman selected him, nor had it been for any reputation as a legal scholar. Rather, Vinson had been a loyal supporter of both the New Deal and the Fair Deal, and Harry Truman valued loyalty. The president called Vinson a "devoted and undemonstrative patriot" with "a sense of personal and political loyalty seldom found among the top men in Washington."[47] Perhaps more important, Vinson had a reputation as friendly, sociable, humorous, patient, and able to get along with other people; the president hoped these qualities would allow him to lead and unite the court. Thomas Emerson, who worked for Vinson at this time, recalled that during Vinson's tenure at the Office of Economic Stabilization, he had gotten on very well with his former colleagues in Congress. "He used to play golf and poker and associate with them a great deal. He was 'one of the boys' and was very well liked in Congress."[48] In fact, Frankfurter, Douglas, and Black personally liked Vinson, but because of their independence and strongly held views, they would not be any more amenable to following Vinson's direction than they had been to following that of Stone, whom they respected far more.

Moreover, Vinson's experience in the executive branch in some ways may have unfitted him for his new role. Fred Rodell speculates that the "one-man power he held in his high administrative posts perhaps led him to believe that he could boss the Supreme Court in the same firm-but-gentle way."[49] More to the mark is the fact that Vinson's experience in government led him to be an almost unquestioning supporter of federal policies. As James Thomson has noted, Vinson did not think in terms of legal theory but in specifics; he formulated responses designed to meet present contingencies. Where a judge ought to consider cases in terms of

47. David McCullough, *Truman* (New York: Simon & Schuster, 1992), 507.

48. Thomas Emerson Memoirs, Columbia Oral History Collection. According to David McCullough, the fact that Vinson was an expert poker player "was not incidental to Truman's high regard for [him]." *Truman*, 511.

49. Fred Rodell, *Nine Men* (New York: Random House, 1955), 307.

long-range impact on the development of legal doctrines, Vinson thought like the administrator he had been—how do we solve this question—without thought of how it might affect future cases.[50] Judge Albert B. Maris, who served with Vinson on the Emergency Court of Appeals, described Vinson's work there: "He was not a Holmes or a Cardozo or a Brandeis. He was more of a judge of the type [that] some of the rest of us are, I guess, that carried on and met our problems as they arose without trying to write too much for the future."[51] Vinson's decisions in the seven years he headed the Court nearly always favored the power of the federal government over that of the states, and the power of government in general over that of the individual. In fact, even on the bench Vinson continued to serve his president, and as Richard Kirkendall wrote, the chief justice "in a sense remained a part of the administration. . . . Truman continued to admire Vinson's ability as an adviser and tapped it frequently, often in late-evening telephone conversation."[52] In terms of legal theory, he left practically no mark on American jurisprudence.[53]

That Vinson was not an original thinker did not by itself disqualify him from the chance of becoming a good or even a great chief justice. For all of Earl Warren's many fine attributes, no one has ever claimed that he

50. James A. Thomson, "Frederick Moore Vinson," in Melvin I. Urofsky, ed., *The Supreme Court Justices: A Biographical Dictionary* (New York: Garland, 1994), 489.

51. Quoted in Frances Howell Rudko, *Truman's Court: A Study in Judicial Restraint* (Westport. Conn.: Greenwood, 1988), 64–65. See also William O. Douglas's characterization of Vinson and the other Truman appointees as "small-town people . . . the stuff out of which the populist movement was fashioned. . . . [Their philosophy] at bottom was the philosophy of Main Street." *The Court Years: 1939–1975* (New York: Random House, 1980), 245–46.

52. Richard Kirkendall, "Frederick M. Vinson," in Leon Friedman and Fred L. Israel, eds., *The Justices of the Supreme Court, 1789–1969: Their Lives and Opinions,* 4 vols. (New York: Chelsea House, 1969), 4:2648. The president frequently consulted Vinson on a number of issues, including the firing of Douglas McArthur, and in 1951 Truman tried to talk Vinson into becoming the 1952 Democratic presidential candidate. McCullough, *Truman,* 840, 887. While such conduct would no doubt be condemned under current standards of judicial propriety, it was hardly unusual not only in the long history of the Court but especially during the war years, when Frankfurter, Jackson, Douglas, and Murphy regularly consulted with and on occasion worked for Franklin Roosevelt.

53. There has been relatively little written about Vinson, although his career would seem to warrant a biography. General studies of Vinson include Francis A. Allen, "Chief Justice Vinson and the Theory of Constitutional Government: A Tentative Appraisal," 49 *Northwestern University Law Review* 3 (1954), and John P. Frank, "Fred Vinson and the Chief Justiceship," 21 *University of Chicago Law Review* 212 (1954), both written shortly after his death. For analyses of the Vinson Court, see C. Herman Pritchett, *Civil Liberties and the Vinson Court* (Chicago: University of Chicago Press, 1954), and Rudko, *Truman's Court.* A somewhat different type of analysis can be found in Jan Palmer, *The Vinson Court Era: The Supreme Court's Conference Votes: Data and Analysis* (New York: AMS Press, 1990).

contributed a great deal to jurisprudential thought. Vinson had, in fact, many of the qualities that Warren had. As Thomas Emerson described him, Vinson "was a person of considerable ability. He had the capacity to grasp problems rather quickly, and had a rather good capacity to get to the heart of a problem rather quickly. . . . He was an excellent negotiator, however, and a very good mediator."[54] Given another lineup at a different time, Vinson might well have been considered a good chief, but he proved unable to control or guide his colleagues.

Within the Court, while his colleagues liked Fred Vinson, they did not think much of him as a chief. Vinson assigned relatively few opinions to himself, leading Jackson to call the chief justice "just plain lazy," and he tended to spend more time with Truman and his friends in Congress—with whom he felt far more comfortable than with the brethren. Black considered Vinson so ineffective that he declared "there should be no chief justice. The job should be rotated among the justices as some state courts do."[55]

Vinson's lack of distinction as a jurist matched that of the other three Truman appointees. Fred Rodell predicted accurately that "fifty years hence, none of the Truman Justices . . . will be any better remembered—or deserves to be better remembered—than the nameless Justices (save Johnson and Story) who sat with [Chief Justice John] Marshall are remembered today."[56] Whatever their abilities may have been in their pre-Court careers, none of them proved to be in the same league as the men Roosevelt had named to the bench.

Vinson was, in fact, the second person Truman named to the Court; the president had made his first appointment a year earlier, naming Harold Hitz Burton to the bench when Owen Roberts had retired. Born in Jamaica Plain, Massachusetts, Burton had spent his early years in Switzerland, where his ailing mother was convalescing. After her death he returned to the United States and compiled an excellent academic record at both Bowdoin College and the Harvard Law School, from which he graduated in 1912. He then practiced law with his wife's uncle, first in Cleveland and then in Salt Lake City, where his abilities led to his becoming counsel for the Utah Power and Light Company. After distinguished army service in France and Belgium during World War I, he returned to Cleveland and resumed law practice.

A Republican, the affable Burton succeeded in politics and held a

---

54. Emerson Memoirs, Columbia Oral History Collection.

55. Roger K. Newman, *Hugo Black: A Biography* (New York: Pantheon, 1994), 419.

56. Rodell, *Nine Men*, 306. Black once told a nephew that "Truman's appointments were mediocre at best. We didn't get the best people." Newman, *Black*, 419.

number of positions ranging from member of a local school board to mayor of Cleveland on up to United States senator, which Ohioans elected him in 1940. Burton was not, however, a party ideologue; in state politics he had represented the "good government" interests and had supported Roosevelt's relief programs. In the Senate he broke with traditional Republican isolationists to favor an active American role in shaping the postwar world. His road to the Court also included service on Harry Truman's committee investigating the defense procurement programs, and like Vinson, he became one of the more adept members of the Senate in tax matters.

No doubt cronyism played some role in Burton's appointment, but as Eric Rise notes, the nomination satisfied several mandates. The retirement of Owen Roberts left Chief Justice Stone the Court's only Republican member, and by naming Burton, the president satisfied the demands of Republican congressional leaders that he restore some political balance on the high court. Moreover, Truman believed that Burton's moderate and pragmatic politics would make him a judge who would be neither strongly partisan nor a staunch ideologue. Beyond that, Truman could expect that the Senate would quickly confirm one of its sitting members, and on this his intuition proved accurate; the Senate unanimously confirmed Burton the day after receiving his name from the White House.[57]

Burton came in for heavy criticism, much of it unfounded, during the Vinson years. In terms of the Court's output, he was never a prolific opinion writer, which led some columnists to charge that he shirked his obligations. In June 1947, Drew Pearson, in his national column, not only attacked Burton for his "meager" output but also characterized him as an inveterate partygoer and implied that his social life interfered with his duties on the bench. According to Pearson, Burton seemed "to think that being on the Supreme Court is not for the purpose of handing down opinions but to enjoy a continued round of parties."[58]

Felix Frankfurter, who detested Pearson, immediately came to Burton's defense and told his colleague, "I have known every man who sat on this Court since 1906—many of them well and half a dozen intimately. It is on that basis that I can say to you what I have said behind your back, that this Court never had a Justice who was harder working or more conscientious." William O. Douglas, at the other end of the jurisprudential spectrum, shared this view; he called Burton "as conscientious a man as ever sat on the Court, God-fearing, and painfully slow in his work. He spent night after

---

57. Eric W. Rise, "Harold Hitz Burton," in Urofsky, ed., *Supreme Court Justices*, 77. According to Burton's diary entry, the president told him: "I want someone who will do a thoroughly judicial job and not legislate. You are fitted for the court, you have a judicial temperament." Entry for September 17, 1945, Burton Papers, Library of Congress.

58. The Pearson column is in the *Washington Post*, June 23, 1947.

night, way after midnight, in his office."[59] Black, writing to a former clerk in late 1949, acknowledged that Burton had been a little slow to adapt to the demands of the Court but stated that experience had solved that problem. Now, Black said, "he writes opinions with much more rapidity. . . . He can discuss cases in conference with considerable clarity due I think to the fact that he studies and understands the points raised."[60]

Evaluations of Burton as a judge have varied. His biographer Mary Frances Berry noted that Burton's overriding trait appeared to have been judicial restraint. His background gave him a "generally conservative mindset," but his conscientiousness made him a "lawyer's judge," and Berry argued that he attempted to decide cases objectively and dispassionately.[61] Frances Rudko also gives Burton high marks, noting that "he saw both sides of a legal problem, carefully weighed the issues and played the game of making judicial decisions by the self-imposed rules of judicial restraint."[62]

Eric Rise agrees that Burton sided with those on the Court who, like Frankfurter, advocated judicial restraint, but Rise suggests he did so more from his political views and experience than from firm jurisprudential beliefs:

He supported national security measures because he subscribed to Cold War Politics; he favored desegregation because he found racial discrimination personally abhorrent; and he urged restrictions on the right to picket because he feared the effect of organized labor on corporate power. In short, he deferred to legislative judgments because he agreed with them, not necessarily because he believed the political branches had the exclusive power to formulate policy.[63]

It is difficult to chart a consistent path through Burton's opinions; they range the gamut from liberal to conservative. He may not have been a results-oriented jurist, as Berry claims, but it seems clear that he voted his

---

59. Frankfurter to Burton, June 23, 1947, Burton Papers, Library of Congress. According to Douglas, Truman told him that Burton had been "the most conscientious and hardworking committee member I ever did know." Douglas, *Court Years*, 247–48. One reason Burton worked so hard is that he evidently wrote most of his opinions by himself, with relatively little help from clerks other than research. In "Justice Harold H. Burton and the Work of the Supreme Court," 27 *Cleveland State Law Review* 69 (1978), David N. Atkinson provides a portrait of Burton's work habits drawn from interviews with clerks.
60. Black to John Frank, November 17, 1949, Black Papers, Library of Congress.
61. Mary Frances Berry, *Stability, Security and Continuity: Mr. Justice Burton and Decision-Making in the Supreme Court (1945–1958)* (Westport, Conn.: Greenwood, 1978), 231.
62. Rudko, *Truman's Court*, 57.
63. Rise, "Burton," 77.

beliefs as much as anything, as can be seen in his dissent in *Louisiana ex rel. Francis v. Resweber* (1947), in which he objected to the state's effort to electrocute a black man a second time after the first effort had failed to kill him.[64] Like Vinson, he had a pragmatic mind, one that did not tend toward jurisprudential consistency. But he did fulfill at least part of Truman's hopes for him: while on the bench Burton proved a point of calm and stability, liked and even respected by all his colleagues. That by itself was no mean feat on a Court that included Black, Douglas, Murphy, Frankfurter, and Jackson.[65]

Truman made his third appointment to the Court in the summer of 1949 when he named Tom Campbell Clark to succeed Frank Murphy, who had unexpectedly died in July of that year. Later on Truman reputedly said of this appointment:

> Tom Clark was my biggest mistake. . . . He was no damn good as Attorney General, and on the Supreme Court . . . he has been even worse. He hasn't made one right decision that I can think of. . . . it isn't so much that he's a *bad* man. It's just that he's such a dumb son of a bitch. He's about the dumbest man I think I've ever run across. . . . Being dumb's just about the worst thing there is when it comes to holding high office, and that's especially true when it's on the Supreme Court of the United States.[66]

Given Truman's warmth toward Clark both during his years in the White House and after, it is hard to reconcile this statement with anything other than pique at Clark's vote against presidential seizure of the steel mills, which dealt a sharp blow to Truman's policy during the Korean conflict.[67]

Clark was born in Dallas, Texas, and after army service in World War I, he returned there to enter the family law practice. Though he was success-

---

64. 329 U.S. 459 (1947); see below, pp. 223–24.

65. There is no good biography of Burton; the standard work by Berry, *Stability, Security and Continuity*, is useful primarily for its description of the internal politics of the Court during Burton's tenure. A substantive analysis of his decisions is in Ronald Marquardt's unpublished dissertation, "The Judicial Justice: Mr. Justice Burton and the Supreme Court" (University of Missouri, 1973). Articles by Atkinson in 9 *Houston Law Review* 271 (1971) and 27 *Cleveland State Law Review* 69 (1978) are quite illuminating as to Burton's Cold War views and his work habits respectively.

66. Merle Miller, *Plain Speaking: An Oral History of Harry S. Truman* (New York: Berkeley, 1974), 225–26.

67. *Youngstown Sheet & Tube Co. v. Sawyer*, 343 U.S. 579 (l952); see below, pp. 206–11. For a discussion of the preceding quote, see Dennis D. Dorin, "Truman's 'Biggest Mistake': Tom Clark's Appointment to the Supreme Court," in William F. Levantrosser, ed., *Harry S. Truman: The Man from Independence* (Westport, Conn.: Greenwood, 1986), 323–55.

ful, Clark was restless, and in 1937 he eagerly accepted an offer to join the Justice Department. He started as an assistant in the war risk litigation section, and his ability quickly moved him up. Following Pearl Harbor, President Roosevelt named him civilian coordinator of the Western Defense Command, in which role he handled all the legal aspects of the Japanese relocation program. After that assignment, he took over the war frauds unit in Justice and worked closely with the Truman committee. When Truman became president, he named Clark attorney general.

Clark's record as head of the Justice Department indicates the different aspects of the man. He energetically enforced the antitrust laws, initiating 160 new prosecutions, and also proved a warm friend of the emerging civil rights movement. Clark pressured the FBI to investigate lynchings and called on Congress to make lynching a federal crime. The department filed an *amicus curiae* brief with the Supreme Court in the case testing restrictive covenants.[68] While advocating fairness in criminal procedure matters, Clark was also a Cold Warrior and personally authorized prosecution of the top leaders of the Communist Party.[69]

According to Harold Gosnell, Truman appointed Clark "at the urging of Chief Justice Vinson, who wanted a colleague who would support his point of view."[70] In Clark's first years on the Court that view seems justified, as Clark did become an ally of Vinson, especially in civil liberties cases. Clark rejected civil liberties claims 75 percent of the time, a little below Vinson's rate of 83 percent, and was a strong supporter of the government position in the Cold War cases that came before the high court. But Clark was not a Red-baiter, and over the years he moved away from the conservative wing of the Court. William O. Douglas praised Clark, who, he said, unlike the other Truman appointees, "was different in the sense that he changed. He had the indispensable capacity to develop so that with the passage of time he grew in stature and expanded his dimensions."[71]

Truman's last appointment came just a few months later, when Wiley Rutledge died and the president named to the Court another good friend, Sherman Minton of Indiana. According to William Douglas, "Shay" Min-

---

68. *Shelley v. Kraemer*, 343 U.S. 1 (1948); see below, pp. 249–50.

69. The prosecutions eventually reached the Court in the case of *Dennis v. United States*, 341 U.S. 494 (1951); see below, pp. 169–75.

70. Harold F. Gosnell, *Truman's Crises: A Political Biography of Harry S. Truman* (Westport, Conn.: Greenwood, 1980), 419.

71. Douglas, *Court Years*, 245. See also the complimentary remarks about Clark in Hugo Black to John Frank, November 17, 1949, Black Papers, Library of Congress. There is no biography of Clark, and much of the writing on him focuses on his later decisions during the Warren years. In fact, Clark left little of a legacy in terms of jurisprudence; his most important contribution came in the form of his service with the American Bar Association's section on judicial administration, which he revivified and led for many years.

ton, then a member of the Court of Appeals for the Seventh Circuit, had flown to Washington upon hearing of Rutledge's death and gone to the White House to see his old buddy. The following conversation then reportedly took place:

> "What can I do for you, Shay?"
> "Harry, I want you to put me on the Supreme Court to fill that new vacancy."
> "Shay, I'll do just that," Truman replied. And he did.[72]

Whether or not this actually happened is difficult to determine because Minton was, among other things, a great storyteller. But there is no question about the depth of the Truman-Minton friendship, or that the president considered the Minton appointment his finest. Years later Truman wrote that there "never was a finer man or an abler public servant than the Honorable Sherman Minton."[73]

Born in a small Indiana town, Minton had excelled in academics as well as sports. While he was in the army in France during World War I, he had found time to study law at the Sorbonne. He finished his law work after the war and then practiced in New Albany, Indiana, where he also became active in the Democratic Party. This led to his appointment to the position of counsel with the Indiana Public Service Commission, where he soon achieved a reputation as a champion of the consumer and the nemesis of the utilities. In 1934 he successfully ran for the United States Senate on the slogan "You can't offer a hungry man the Constitution."

In the Senate Minton proved a staunch supporter of the Roosevelt administration and wholeheartedly endorsed the president's court reform plan in 1937; he also became a close friend of another first-term senator, Harry Truman of Missouri. In 1940 Minton lost his bid for reelection when Indiana went solidly for another native son, Wendell Willkie, whose coattails swept a number of Republican candidates into office. But Roosevelt rewarded Minton for his past loyalty by naming him to the Seventh Circuit.

Once on the Court, Minton, more than any of the other Truman appointees, committed himself to the philosophy of judicial restraint. His beliefs grew out of his political experience in Indiana and in the Senate during the Great Depression, and especially from his reaction to the conservative justices who had sought to block New Deal measures. He firmly believed that, barring a specific constitutional prohibition, the legislature had almost unlimited powers and should not be second-guessed by the

---

72. Douglas, *Court Years*, 247.
73. Harry Truman to Sherman Minton, July 19, 1961, cited in Rudko, *Truman's Court*, 111.

courts. While in the Senate he had introduced a measure that would have required the vote of seven justices to declare a federal statute unconstitutional.

On the bench Minton adhered strictly to precedent, took narrow interpretive views of both the Constitution and statutes, and deferred to the judgment of the executive and legislative branches. He proved to be a natural ally of Felix Frankfurter, although in many instances Frankfurter's willingness to look beyond formalistic application of precedent led him to disagree with Minton.

Minton was well aware of the internecine feuding that had taken place on the high court and wanted no part of it. He believed that, whenever possible, the Court should act as a unified deliberative body and that an opinion should reflect the judgment of the Court, not that of an individual justice. As a result, he proved amenable to altering passages of his opinions in order to garner support. He eschewed what had become the common practice of writing concurring opinions, because he believed they confused the public about what the Court had in fact decided; he wrote only three concurrences in his seven years on the bench. When writing for the majority, he attempted to lay out the line of decision as neatly as possible and ignored opposing arguments. Minton's writings do not contain any of the jurisprudential musings that Frankfurter loved.

The one exception to Minton's deference to the other branches of government involved race relations. From the start he showed himself an ardent opponent of any form of government-sponsored racial discrimination. He considered the landmark decision of *Brown v. Board of Education* (1954) to be the most important case in which he participated.

At another time, Minton might have been a leader of the Court, for he had a politician's skill in getting people together and a well-articulated belief in judicial restraint. But during his tenure, he often stood in the shadow of the greatest advocate of judicial restraint in modern times, Felix Frankfurter, and he lacked Frankfurter's ability to expand the notion beyond doctrinal rigidity into a larger theory of jurisprudence. Moreover, the agenda with which he felt most comfortable, the economic questions of the New Deal era, had been settled; and aside from racial matters, about which he felt strongly, Minton often found himself uncomfortable with many of the issues confronting the Court. When ill health forced him to retire after only seven years on the bench, he noted presciently that "there will be more interest in who will succeed me than in my passing."[74]

---

74. Quoted in Rise, "Sherman Minton," in Urofsky, ed., *Supreme Court Justices*, 325. There is no full-length biography of Minton, but two articles are very useful. Atkinson discusses his pre-judicial career as well as the origins of his judicial philosophy in "From New Deal Liberal to Supreme Court Conservative," 1975 *Washington University Law Quarterly* 361. The

The four Truman appointees, along with Reed, Frankfurter, and Jackson, would give the Vinson Court a decidedly conservative slant compared to its more activist character in the Stone years. But "conservative" in this context does not refer to the antistatism of the Taft era or the unremitting opposition to government regulation by the Four Horsemen who opposed the New Deal. Following its notions of judicial restraint, the majority of the Vinson Court approved practically anything the government did in regulating the economy. But as noted earlier, the Court's agenda had been changing since the late 1930s, and cases involving civil rights and liberties had taken center stage. Just as they would not go against the state in economic matters, so the Truman appointees proved reluctant to vote against the government in these areas as well. John P. Frank, in his study of the Vinson era, found a high rate of correlation on civil liberties among the Truman appointees in that they routinely voted against such claims. Between 1946 and 1953 Chief Justice Vinson voted 83 percent of the time to deny a claimed right, Harold Burton 74 percent, Tom Clark 75 percent, and Sherman Minton 87 percent. Frank, writing in 1954, thought that the Court's record indicated a turning point in the course of American jurisprudence.[75]

But then came Earl Warren. Considering the Court's record after his arrival, William Swindler's appraisal of the Vinson years as an "interlude" between the reforms of the late 1930s and those launched following the *Brown* decision seems more accurate.[76] In fact, as we shall see, much of the jurisprudential groundwork for the Warren era was articulated in the postwar years, but for those living through the era, the Supreme Court certainly did not appear to be a bastion of reform or a protector of individual liberties. This proved especially true for those caught up in the witch-hunt mentality of the Cold War.

---

best account of his tenure on the Court is by one of his clerks, Harry L. Wallace: "Mr. Justice Minton—Hoosier Justice on the Supreme Court," 34 *Indiana Law Journal* 145, 377 (1959).

75. John P. Frank, "Fred Vinson and the Chief Justiceship," 21 *University of Chicago Law Review* 212, 243 (1954).

76. William F. Swindler, *Court and Constitution in the 20th Century, The New Legality, 1932–1968* (Kansas City: Bobbs-Merrill, 1970), 182.

Chief Justice Harlan Fiske Stone at his desk. (Collection of the Supreme Court of the United States.)

The Stone Court in 1943. Seated (left to right): Stanley F. Reed, Owen J. Roberts, Chief Justice Harlan Fiske Stone, Hugo L. Black, Felix Frankfurter; standing: Robert H. Jackson, William O. Douglas, Frank Murphy, Wiley B. Rutledge. (Collection of the Supreme Court of the United States.)

Justice Hugo L. Black stepping out of a cab on his way to the
Court. (Collection of the Supreme Court of the United States.)

Nominee Felix Frankfurter testifying at his confirmation hearings.
(Photograph by Harris & Ewing, Collection of the Supreme Court of the
United States.)

The Vinson Court in 1951. Seated (left to right): Felix Frankfurter, Hugo L. Black, Chief Justice Fred M. Vinson, Stanley F. Reed, William O. Douglas; standing: Tom C. Clark, Robert H. Jackson, Harold H. Burton, Sherman Minton. (Photograph by Fabian Bachrach, Collection of the Supreme Court of the United States.)

Justice William O. Douglas walking to the Court on his first day as a justice. (Collection of the Supreme Court of the United States.)

Chief Justice Fred M. Vinson. (Photograph by Harris & Ewing, Collection of the Supreme Court of the United States.)

# 6

# THE COLD WAR

The fear of communist expansion in Europe and Asia in the late 1940s and early 1950s triggered a new Red Scare in the United States, one even worse than the hysteria following the Great War. Then the bugaboo had been far more imaginary than real, and calm, rational people had soon realized that a minuscule group of anarchists posed no real threat to the body politic. But while false fears and the incitement of demagogues fanned the flames of nativism and paranoia in the 1940s and 1950s, even the most levelheaded person could find much to worry about. In a relatively short period of time one witnessed the Berlin blockade, the triumph of Mao Tse-tung and the communists in China, the first Soviet atomic bomb, the discovery that British and American scientists had spied for the Russians, the invasion of South Korea, and the exposure and subsequent conviction of the Rosenbergs.

In response to both real and imagined threats, federal and state governments established a number of so-called loyalty and security programs that affected nearly everyone who worked for government. Congress passed various laws, and its committees attempted to ferret out "security risks." All of these measures led to numerous court challenges, primarily under the First Amendment and, to a lesser extent, under the Fifth. Judges during the Vinson era had to balance the perceived needs of national security against the individual rights guaranteed in the Constitution, and Cold War issues dominated much of the Vinson Court's docket.

Unlike earlier radical movements, communism during the 1930s appealed to a number of Americans. Between 1930 and 1935, the rolls of the Communist Party had increased from seventy-five hundred to around thirty thousand, and that in turn generated legislative efforts both in Congress and in the states to make party membership a crime. In March 1940 Congress had reenacted the Espionage Act of 1917, and then in June it had passed the Alien Registration or Smith Act, which drew together a variety of antialien and antiradical proposals. Although it was aimed primarily at the communists, its broadly phrased terms applied to anyone conspiring to overthrow the government or even conspiring to advocate an overthrow. The measure required the registration of aliens, and within a short time the government had fingerprinted and registered over five million of them.[1]

The Smith Act had had little immediate impact because none of the men serving as attorney general during the war sympathized with its provisions.[2] Moreover, following the German invasion of Russia and American entry into the war, the United States had found itself allied with the Soviet Union in a common war against fascism, and no Americans, it seemed at the time, had supported that war with greater fervor than the communists.[3] The Smith Act came before the Court indirectly a few months after its passage, when the justices invalidated a Pennsylvania alien registration act on grounds that the federal law had preempted state legislation,[4] and it also figured in the efforts to deport Harry Bridges.[5]

After the war, however, anticommunist sentiment within the United States built as the iron curtain descended across Europe. Harry Truman established a Temporary Committee on Employee Loyalty in November 1946 and, following criticism that he had not gone far enough, set up a full-scale federal loyalty and security program the next year. Under Executive Order 9835, the attorney general and the FBI launched a massive investigation of all federal employees. The attorney general compiled a list of allegedly subversive organizations, with membership in any of these groups constituting "reasonable doubt" about a person's loyalty.[6] As Robert McCloskey noted, the "growing national awareness of the totalitarian threat

---

1. The genesis and provisions of the Smith Act are detailed in Michal R. Belknap, *Cold War Political Justice: The Smith Act, the Communist Party, and American Civil Liberties* (Westport, Conn.: Greenwood, 1977), chap. 1.

2. See, for example, Francis Biddle, *In Brief Authority* (Garden City, N.Y.: Doubleday, 1962), 233–51.

3. The Justice Department did invoke the Smith Act against a group of Troskyites and convicted them for activities designed to effect insubordination in the armed forces. *Dunn v. United States*, 138 F.2d 137 (8th Cir. 1941), cert. denied, 329 U.S. 790 (1941).

4. *Hines v. Davidowitz*, 312 U.S. 52 (1941). The decision allayed the fears of Justice Department officials that state action might not only impede the federal program but lead to the heavy-handed purges that had marked World War I state efforts.

5. See above, p. 56. The Court did have the chance to deal with the Smith Act directly in the October 1943 Term in a case entitled *Dunne v. United States*, 320 U.S. 790 (1943); but only three members of the Court—Murphy, Rutledge, and Black—voted to grant certiorari. Douglas later explained his decision to vote against hearing the case on the grounds that the remaining five members of the Court would have voted to affirm the Smith Act's constitutionality. "It seemed to me at that particular point in history unwise to put the Court's seal of approval of that doctrine." *The Court Years: 1939–1975* (New York: Random House, 1980), 94.

6. Paul L. Murphy, *The Constitution in Crisis Times, 1918–1969* (New York: Harper & Row, 1972), 256–57; see also David Caute, *The Great Fear: The Anti-Communist Purges Under Truman and Eisenhower* (New York: Simon & Schuster, 1978).

in the years after 1945 generated a national mood toward 'subversion' that sometimes approached hysteria."[7]

The Court's record in reviewing the loyalty cases that came before it show that the judiciary, like the other branches of government, got caught up in the anticommunist fever of the times. The tale begins with the Court's decision in 1950 upholding Section 9(h) of the Taft-Hartley Act denying access to the National Labor Relations Board to those unions whose officers had refused to swear they were not communists. In *American Communications Association v. Douds*,[8] Chief Justice Vinson admitted that the statute discouraged the lawful exercise of political freedom by requiring oaths related to individual political beliefs. This abridgement of free speech, however, had to be weighed against the government's power to regulate commerce, and by utilizing the Commerce Clause the chief justice managed to evade the First Amendment issues. Frankfurter and Jackson, while concurring in the result, nonetheless objected to imposing a test on beliefs. Jackson in particular, while clearly laying out the dangers of communism, argued that Congress had no power to proscribe opinions that had not yet led to overt acts. In words that the majority should have recalled in later cases, Jackson concluded that "under our system, it is time enough for the law to lay hold of the citizen when he acts illegally, or in some rare circumstances where his thoughts are given illegal utterance. I think we must let his mind alone."[9] For Justice Black, this infringement upon personal beliefs went beyond constitutional bounds, and he would have held Section 9(h) void; the Commerce Clause, he concluded, does "not restrict the right to think."[10]

The problem with Vinson's opinion lay not in his argument that rights could sometimes be abridged in return for government benefits, since he recognized that in some circumstances the condition might be a denial of the right itself. Rather he totally disregarded the First Amendment issues raised by Black, Frankfurter, and Jackson and also ignored the overly broad sweep of the Taft-Hartley provision. Section 9(h) could disqualify unions whose officers were Communist Party members regardless of whether they shared all of the party's goals or were merely intellectual adherents of socialism. That the chief justice wanted to balance national security interests against free expression is not unusual, but by relying on the commerce

---

7. Robert G. McCloskey, *The American Supreme Court* (Chicago: University of Chicago Press, 1960), 196.

8. 339 U.S. 382 (1950). Vinson spoke for himself, Reed, and Burton; Frankfurter and Jackson partially concurred; Black dissented; and Douglas, Clark, and Minton did not participate.

9. *Ibid.* at 422, 444 (Jackson concurring).

10. *Ibid.* at 445, 446 (Black dissenting).

power he tipped the scales far more than if he had used a free speech analysis.

Within a short time the fruits of *Douds* could be seen in a series of cases in which the Court upheld a variety of measures precluding alleged subversives from running for public office,[11] holding municipal jobs,[12] and even teaching in the public schools.[13] In 1952 a majority agreed that even a longtime resident alien could be deported for membership in the Communist Party in the distant past.[14] It looked for a while as if a majority of the Court would validate any measure in the name of national security. But it reached its limit when it was confronted by the blacklist cases.

The Court managed to evade the First Amendment issues involved in the blacklists when it granted a declaratory judgment removing three organizations from the attorney general's list. The Joint Anti-Fascist Refugee Committee claimed to be nothing more than a charity providing aid to Spanish Republicans, victims of the Spanish Civil War. It and two other groups denied that they were communist or engaged in any subversive activities, and they charged that their inclusion on the list had been an arbitrary act devoid of due process. The district and circuit courts had rejected their claim, but five members of the Supreme Court agreed with the petitioners, although they could not settle on a common rationale.[15]

Justice Burton, supported in part by Douglas, took the narrowest approach; he acknowledged that the case "bristled with constitutional issues" that he believed the Court should avoid, and he disposed of the case on procedural grounds. Frankfurter concurred in the result but did not avoid the constitutional questions. The attorney general's arbitrariness had violated the Fifth Amendment's Due Process Clause, which Frankfurter praised as "perhaps the most majestic concept in our whole constitutional system." Due process, he claimed, did not operate as a mechanical yardstick but as a process for evaluating facts and determining truth. The attorney general had neither given notice nor established criteria for inclusion on the list nor held hearings at which the accused could respond, and thus he had failed to meet the constitutional test.[16]

While Frankfurter condemned the practices that had been followed, he did not deny that the attorney general could draw up such lists provided he followed correct procedures. Black, joined by Douglas, denied that the executive branch had any such authority no matter what methods it used.

---

11. *Gerende v. Board of Supervisors*, 341 U.S. 56 (1951).

12. *Garner v. Board of Public Works*, 341 U.S. 716 (1951).

13. *Adler v. Board of Education*, 342 U.S. 485 (1952).

14. *Harisiades v. Shaughnessy*, 342 U.S. 580 (1952).

15. *Joint Anti-Fascist Refugee Committee v. McGrath*, 341 U.S. 123 (1949).

16. *Ibid.* at 149, 171–72.

"Officially prepared and proclaimed governmental blacklists possess almost every quality of bills of attainder, the use of which was from the beginning forbidden to both national and state governments."[17] Although Black did not cast his opinion in First Amendment terms, he and Douglas seem to have been the only ones to inquire even indirectly into the right of the government to regulate ideas through proscriptive lists.

Just a few months before Vinson's death, however, the Court handed down a unanimous decision in *Wieman v. Updegraf,*[18] involving an Oklahoma statute denying public employment to anyone not willing to swear that he or she was not a member of any organization on the attorney general's list. Deciding the case on the narrowest possible grounds, the Court, speaking through Justice Clark, held that such a sweeping provision caught up too many people and could exclude people who had joined an organization of whose communist nature they were unaware. Clark attempted to distinguish the earlier cases, such as *Douds,* on the grounds that in those instances the proscription had been read to apply only to people who knowingly participated in subversive organizations or personally sought to destroy the government. Mere membership in an organization was not enough to prove that a person was a subversive.

The road from *Douds* to *Wieman* is somewhat circular. *Douds* relied on an analysis of the effect that political strikes would have on interstate commerce, and while it may have overreacted to the potential threat of communist union leaders' tying up the nation's industry, at least there was a rational basis for its conclusion. In the subsequent oath cases, however, the Court could not come up with any coherent basis for justification, not in the Commerce Clause and certainly not in the First Amendment; the majority relied on fear of a potential evil to justify an admitted infringement on personal liberties. In those cases, an increasing number of justices began to feel uncomfortable, especially under Justice Black's constant dissents regarding freedom to think. Also, by the time the Court decided *Wieman,* the peak of the anticommunist hysteria had passed, and a more clearheaded analysis had begun to reappear in the Court's decisions. In the later 1950s nearly all these earlier decisions would be either overturned or, in most instances, quietly buried.

Despite the fact that the Court would in all likelihood have upheld even a rigorous loyalty program, the Truman administration did move carefully in seeking out communists in the federal government. By 1951 the Civil Service Commission had cleared more than three million federal em-

---

17. *Ibid.* at 142, 143.
18. 344 U.S. 183 (1952). Justice Burton concurred in the result, and Justice Jackson did not participate in the case.

ployees. The FBI had initiated 14,000 full-scale investigations, which led to the resignation of some 2,000 persons, although it is unclear how many of them resigned solely because of the investigations. Only 212 persons were dismissed because of "reasonable doubt" as to their loyalty.[19] While actively seeking "security risks" inside the government, the administration also went after the Communist Party directly, and on July 20, 1948, the Justice Department secured a grand jury indictment against twelve members of the party's national board, including Eugene Dennis and William Z. Foster, for conspiring with one another and with unknown persons to

> organize as the Communist Party of the United States, a society, group, and assembly of persons who teach and advocate the overthrow and destruction of the Government of the United States by force and violence, and knowingly and willfully to advocate and teach the duty and necessity of overthrowing and destroying the Government of the United States by force, which said acts are prohibited by . . . the Smith Act.[20]

It would take nearly three years from this initial indictment for the case to reach the Supreme Court on appeal from one of the most bombastic political trials in American history. During that time the Court had the opportunity to review several speech cases that would point the way to the fractured opinions in *Dennis v. United States.*

The Supreme Court entered the postwar era with relatively little Speech Clause jurisprudence aside from the "clear and present danger" test developed by Holmes and Brandeis in the 1920s. But Holmes's famous aphorism about falsely shouting fire in a crowded theater is not a very useful analytical tool to determine when a danger is real, and if real, when it is proximate, and if proximate, if it is of the magnitude that justifies state intervention.

Justices Black and Douglas became increasingly unhappy with the test, especially as it was applied by the conservative majority after the war. Douglas believed that had Holmes and Brandeis had the opportunity to develop their ideas more fully in additional cases, they would have eventually abandoned clear and present danger in favor of free and unrestricted speech except in the most dire emergency. Douglas, in fact, claimed that the Holmes dissent in *Gitlow v. New York* (1925) "moved closer to the First Amendment ideal."[21]

---

19. Murphy, *Constitution in Crisis Times,* 256–57.

20. Belknap, *Cold War Political Justice,* 51.

21. Douglas made his comment in his concurrence in *Brandenburg v. Ohio,* 395 U.S. 444, 452 (1969). The Holmes dissent is at 268 U.S. 652, 672 (1925). Philippa Strum indicates her agreement with Douglas's evaluation of where Brandeis was heading; see her *Brandeis: Beyond Progressivism* (Lawrence: University Press of Kansas, 1993), 116–31.

Black and, to a lesser extent, Douglas began to develop a new jurisprudence that viewed the First Amendment, particularly the Speech Clause, as occupying a "preferred" position among constitutionally protected rights. They also argued for an "absolutist" interpretation of the First Amendment's prohibition against the abridgement of speech. The First Amendment, in their view, barred all forms of governmental restriction on speech, so "there was no place in the regime of the First Amendment for any 'clear and present danger' test."[22] The reason, as Black explained elsewhere, was that the test "can be used to justify the punishment of advocacy." It can function only as a balancing test, and rights protected under the First Amendment cannot be balanced; thus it had become "the most dangerous of the tests developed by the justices of the Court."[23]

For Frankfurter, on the other hand, the evaluation and balancing implicit in the clear and present danger test fitted perfectly with his conception of the judicial function. By applying rigorous tools of analysis and clearheadedly evaluating the circumstances, judges would be able to say with reasonable certainty when a clear and present danger existed and warranted state action and when it did not. But by this view, explicating First Amendment issues did not differ at all from explicating Commerce Clause questions. In a letter to Stanley Reed, Frankfurter asked:

When one talks about "preferred," or "preferred position," one means preference of one thing over another. Please tell me what kind of sense it makes that one provision of the Constitution is to be "preferred" over another. . . . The correlative of "preference" is "subordination," and I know of no calculus to determine when one provision of the Constitution must yield to another, nor do I know any reason for doing so.[24]

Comments like this led Douglas to charge that Frankfurter saw the First Amendment not as a protection against state regulation of speech but as an invitation to limit speech, with "the constitutional mandate being construed as only a constitutional admonition for moderation."[25]

It is not so clear, however, that Frankfurter actually meant what he said, as evidenced in his opinions in the loudspeaker cases. In 1948 and 1949 two cases reached the Court involving the use of loudspeakers on sound trucks. In the first case, *Saia v. New York,* a 5–4 majority invalidated a local ordinance prohibiting the use of amplification devices without the consent

---

22. Douglas in *Brandenburg,* 395 U.S. at 454.
23. Hugo L. Black, *A Constitutional Faith* (New York: Knopf, 1968), 50, 52.
24. Frankfurter to Reed, February 7, 1956, Frankfurter Papers, Library of Congress.
25. Douglas, *Court Years,* 47.

of the police chief. Speaking for the Court, Douglas found the restriction unconstitutional for establishing a standardless "prior restraint." While volume, time, and place regulations could be established, no public official should have the power to cut off speech at his uncontrolled discretion. Frankfurter, joined by Reed and Burton, dissented on the ground that the city had made a reasonable decision that with amplification devices so easy to get, some sort of controls had to be imposed to prevent unwanted "intrusion into cherished privacy."[26]

The following year, in another 5–4 decision, *Kovacs v. Cooper*, the Court sustained a local ordinance because this one involved subsequent punishment rather than prior restraint and, according to Justice Reed, punished only the emission of "loud and raucous noises." In passing, however, Reed mentioned "the preferred position of freedom of speech." Frankfurter immediately recognized the danger to "correct analysis" of speech questions if he allowed this phrase to pass unchallenged, so he entered a lengthy concurrence, a close reading of which would lead one to conclude that Frankfurter did put speech on a higher plane.[27]

The Court did have opportunities to examine whether and how it should balance free speech against other interests. A good example is the case of Father Arthur Terminiello, a defrocked priest arrested for disturbing the peace. Terminiello specialized in attacking the Jews and the Roosevelt administration, and he went after both before eight hundred sympathizers in a Chicago auditorium in 1946. Outside more than a thousand protesters rioted, throwing rocks and stink bombs through the windows, and police had all they could do to prevent the mob from storming the hall. After managing to get Terminiello and his party safely out of the building, the police arrested him on a disorderly conduct charge under an ordinance prohibiting "making any improper noise, riot, disturbance, breach of the peace, or diversion tending to a breach of the peace."

The case seemed custom-made for the Court to reexamine the question of whether "fighting words," those that by their very offensiveness tended to disrupt the social order, qualified for protection under the First Amendment.[28] But a majority of Black, Reed, Douglas, Murphy, and Rutledge, speaking through Douglas, evaded the constitutional issue and voided the conviction on an allegedly improper charge by the judge, even though the attorneys for Terminiello had never raised this issue.[29]

---

26. 334 U.S. 558 (1948).

27. 336 U.S. 77 (1949); Frankfurter's concurrence is at 89.

28. The Court had unanimously held, in *Chaplinsky v. New Hampshire*, 315 U.S. 568 (1942), that insults and "fighting" words "are no essential part of any exposition of ideas" and of so little social value as to waerant no First Amendment protection.

29. *Terminiello v. Chicago*, 337 U.S. 1 (1949).

Jackson's dissent, joined by Frankfurter and Burton (Vinson dissented separately), described the inflammatory situation and noted that the episode bore a startling resemblance to the prewar struggle between totalitarian groups for what Hitler had called "the conquest of the streets . . . [as the] key to power in the state." With the memories of the Nazi atrocities he had prosecuted so recently at Nuremberg still fresh in his mind, Jackson compared the rioting that Terminiello had incited to the street battles between fascists and communists that preceded Hitler's grab for power. Jackson asked whether the anti-Semitic garbage spewed out by Terminiello constituted the free discussion, the tool of democracy, that the First Amendment had been designed to protect. He doubted it, and he believed that Terminiello's speech had created the clear and present danger of a riot that the state had the right and obligation to prevent.[30]

Although Douglas's opinion received wide notice in the press as proof of the high level of tolerance in America, it provided the lower courts with no guidelines by which to decide future cases of a similar nature. On January 15, 1951, the Court handed down three decisions involving local restrictions on speech that did little to clarify the situation. The justices upheld, in one decision,[31] the right of religious groups to speak in public parks and, in another, their right to speak on street corners,[32] even, as in the latter case, if the speaker preached a doctrine of hate against other religious groups. However, the Court upheld the conviction of Irving Feiner, a procommunist college student whose aggressive rhetoric to a hostile streetcorner crowd raised the same issue as in *Terminiello*. Feiner called President Truman a "bum" and condemned the American Legion as "a Nazi Gestapo." Since blacks did not have equal rights, he urged them to "rise up in arms." Two police officers, fearing the crowd would attack Feiner, asked him to stop. When he refused, they arrested him, and he was later convicted for disorderly conduct. Speaking for a 6–3 majority, Chief Justice Vinson upheld the conviction, and in a distortion of the clear and present danger test, held that Feiner had been arrested not for the content of his speech but "for the reaction which it actually engendered."[33]

---

30. *Ibid.* at 13, 23, 37 (Jackson dissenting).

31. *Niemotko v. Maryland,* 340 U.S. 268 (1951).

32. *Kunz v. New York,* 340 U.S. 290 (1951).

33. *Feiner v. New York,* 340 U.S. 315, 320 (1951). In concurrence, Frankfurter urged courts not to second-guess the officials who had been on the scene; the Court should defer to the state court's knowledge of local conditions rather than impose an "abstract or doctrinaire" interpretation of the Fourteenth Amendment. Frankfurter also had a high opinion of the New York Court of Appeals and its sensitivity to civil liberties. Since it had ruled unanimously against Feiner, he would not question that decision. *Ibid.* at 273; C. Herman Pritchett, *Civil Liberties and the Vinson Court* (Chicago: University of Chicago Press, 1954), 62.

The balancing in this case totally ignored the values of free speech. Vinson's ruling lumped together two types of speakers who presented quite different constitutional issues—the person who incites the audience to violence and the speaker whose audience wishes to silence him. By applying the clear and present danger test to the latter, the chief justice validated the so-called "heckler's veto," by which evidence or fear of hostile audience reaction justifies silencing the speaker, and Frankfurter endorsed that position in his concurrence. "It is no constitutional principle," he declared, "that in acting to preserve order, the police must proceed against the crowd, whatever its size and temper, and not against the speaker." By this reasoning, police could always suppress an unpopular speaker. Any group that did not like what they heard could create a disturbance in the audience, and, rather than maintain order, the police could then stop the speaker. Aware of this danger, Vinson and Frankfurter suggested that the courts would not allow abuse of this practice, but they advanced no criteria to guide lower courts in their decisions.

The following term Frankfurter delivered the Court's opinion in a decision involving so-called group libel. Joseph Beauharnais, head of the White Circle League, distributed antiblack leaflets on Chicago streetcorners in the form of petitions to the mayor and city council asking them to use the police to halt the further encroachment of blacks into previously all-white neighborhoods. The pamphlets referred to the need "to prevent the white race from becoming mongrelized by the negro" and to the "rapes, robberies, knives, guns and marijuana of the negro." Police arrested Beauharnais under an Illinois statute prohibiting the portrayal of "depravity, criminality, unchastity, or lack of virtue of a class of citizens, of any race, color, creed or religion."[34] Following conviction and a $200 fine, he appealed on grounds that the law violated liberty of speech and press. The Supreme Court upheld the conviction and the law by a 5–4 vote.[35]

Frankfurter noted for the majority that every state had laws protecting individuals from libel, and he saw no problem with attempting to protect groups as well.[36] The question, then, was whether the Due Process Clause

---

34. For background on group libel laws, written before this case and keyed closely to events in Nazi Germany in the 1930s, see David Riesman, "Democracy and Defamation: Control of Group Libel," 42 *Columbia Law Review* 727 (1942).

35. *Beauharnais v. Illinois*, 343 U.S. 250 (1952); the four dissenters were Jackson, Reed, Douglas, and Black. For a later critique of the case and of the various opinions, see Hadley Arkes, "Civility and the Restriciton of Speech: Rediscovering the Defamation of Groups," 1974 *Supreme Court Review* 181, 287–305.

36. David P. Currie raises the interesting question of whether defaming an entire race is worse than defaming an individual. While the attack is broader, group libel may do less actual harm to specific individuals. *The Constitution in the Supreme Court: The Second Century, 1888–1986* (Chicago: University of Chicago Press, 1990), 351.

of the Fourteenth Amendment prohibited such laws. (Frankfurter framed many of his speech opinions of this time in terms of due process rather than the First Amendment because it provided an easier context in which to place his balancing test. As Black constantly pointed out, the First Amendment did not mandate a balance; it prohibited all abridgment of speech.)

Going into the state's past, Frankfurter noted a long history of racial tension, "from the murder of the abolitionist Lovejoy in 1837 to the Cicero riots of 1951." In the face of this history, he said, "we would deny experience to say that the Illinois legislature was without reason in seeking ways to curb false or malicious defamation of racial and religious groups." The Court had to trust legislative judgment and allow the states some room for a "choice of policy," for the "trial-and-error inherent in legislative efforts to deal with obstinate social issues." And should the states abuse this discretion, "while this Court sits" it could "nullify action which encroaches on freedom of utterance under the guise of punishing libel."[37]

But it was this very Court that, in its failure to articulate a clear standard for the protection of speech, allowed the travesty of the Dennis conviction to stand.

The *Dennis* case constituted the final judicial validation of the government's loyalty and security program. Unions had been purged of known or admitted communists under Section 9(h) of the Taft-Hartley Act, sustained by the Court in *Douds,* and the government loyalty program had been upheld in *Bailey v. Richardson.*[38] In *Dennis* the Court pondered the constitutionality of the Smith Act as applied to leaders of the Communist Party. They had been indicted for (1) conspiring to organize as an assembly of persons who teach and advocate the overthrow and destruction of the government of the United States by force and violence, and (2) advocating and teaching the duty and necessity of overthrowing the government by force and violence.

The government never claimed that any revolutionary acts other than teaching and advocacy had taken place, and although "seditious conspiracy" remained a crime on the statute books, the Justice Department did not charge the eleven men with conspiring to overthrow the government. Because the government would have been unable to show that the speech itself had raised a clear and present danger, it resorted to the conspiracy

---

37. 343 U.S. at 253–64; for a critique of the Frankfurter opinion, see Loren P. Beth, "Group Libel and Free Speech," 39 *Minnesota Law Review* 167, 169ff. (1955).

38. 341 U.S. 918 (1951). *Bailey* relied heavily on the attorney general's list of suspected organizations, which had been upheld in *Joint Anti-Fascist Refugee Committee v. McGrath.*

charge. In essence, the men had been tried and convicted for a conspiracy to form a party to teach and advocate the overthrow of the government. The First Amendment test, as articulated by Holmes and Brandeis, declared that the government had to wait for the evil to mature before acting, but the conspiracy doctrine, as Harry Kalven pointed out, "enables the government 'to move the clock back' so as to reach a prior stage of preparation to speak." Thus all the government had to show was that the speech *might* be dangerous, an easy task in the Cold War atmosphere, and the parties would then be guilty of conspiracy to bring about that evil, even if they had never actually spoken.[39] By a vote of 6–2 (with former attorney general Tom Clark not participating), the Court confirmed the conviction.

The central issue involved reconciling the constitutional guarantee of free speech with a conviction for no more than speaking and teaching. The trial judge, Harold Medina, had solved the problem by the bridge of intent and had instructed the jury that it could find the defendants guilty if it believed they intended to overthrow the government as soon as the opportunity arose. The highly respected Learned Hand had sustained the conviction on appeal, arguing that courts had to balance a number of factors in applying a version of the clear and present danger test. "In each case they must ask whether the gravity of the 'evil,' discounted by its improbability, justifies such invasion of free speech as to avoid the danger."[40] Given recent events in Europe and Asia, it seemed evident that Russia intended to conquer the world, and the American Communist Party, as a highly disciplined arm of the international movement, stood ready to act at a moment's notice. The conspiracy existed, and the government could act to avert the evil.

The conference saw little acrimony among the brethren because, as Douglas noted, "those wanting to affirm had minds closed to argument or persuasion. The conference discussion was largely *pro forma*. It was the more amazing because of the drastic revision of the 'clear and present danger' test which affirmance requires."[41] The task of modifying or perhaps even abandoning the Holmes-Brandeis test fell to the chief.

Vinson closely followed Hand's reasoning in his plurality opinion for

39. Harry Kalven, Jr., *A Worthy Tradition: Freedom of Speech in America* (New York: Harper & Row, 1988), 193.

40. *United States v. Dennis*, 183 F.2d 201, 212 (2d Cir. 1950). Hand personally disliked the Smith Act and under his own earlier formulation of the test would have limited restriction of speech only to those instances when the speech constituted a direct incitement to illegal action. But that test had never won acceptance by the Supreme Court. For a thorough analysis and a partial defense of Hand's decision, see Gerald Gunther, *Learned Hand: The Man and the Judge* (New York: Knopf, 1994), 593–600.

41. Conference notes, December 9, 1950, Douglas Papers, Library of Congress.

the Court, which was joined by Burton, Minton, and Reed. Although he paid lip service to the Holmes test, Vinson pointed out that communism posed a far different and more menacing danger than the anarchism and socialism Holmes and Brandeis had dealt with in the 1920s cases. Therefore, the clear and present danger test could not possibly mean that before the government could act, it had to wait "until the *putsch* is about to be executed, the plans have been laid and the signal is awaited."[42] By this line of reasoning, the government could not only reach speech directly inciting unlawful action, or conspiring to promote such action, or teaching that such action should occur, but also penalize conspiring to organize a group that would teach that such action ought to occur.[43] The justices might well have remembered Brandeis's powerful cautions that clear heads had to prevail in (cold) wartime as well as peacetime, and that suppression was impermissible while there was time for discussion.[44]

Harry Kalven, one of our century's most perceptive critics of the Court's First Amendment jurisprudence, has wondered why the Court had to "work so hard to affirm the convictions." After all, the trial court had already determined the factual basis for guilt, and the highly respected Second Circuit had upheld the verdict. The Smith Act had been modeled after laws upheld by earlier courts, and the defendants were hardly nonentities; they were, in fact, the leaders of the Communist Party, a group dedicated to the overthrow of the government. Kalven suggests two reasons. First, the trial had been a highly volatile and highly visible public event and had prompted charges that the United States was engaging in exactly the type of political trials it had condemned in the Soviet Union. Dennis and his colleagues had been put on trial not for their actions but for their political ideas, and the majority looked long and hard to make this appear anything but a political trial.

Second, according to Kalven, "the justices had to make peace with the stringent version of the clear and present danger test they had inherited from Holmes and Brandeis by way of the Stone Court." The one lasting

---

42. *Dennis v. United States*, 341 U.S. 494, 509 (1951).

43. For an attack on this distortion of the original Holmes-Brandeis formulation, see Louis B. Boudin, " 'Seditious Doctrines' and the 'Clear and Present Danger' Rule," 38 *Virginia Law Review* 143 and 315 (1952). The decision is defended by Wallace Mendelson, "Clear and Present Danger—From Schenck to Dennis," 52 *Columbia Law Review* 52 (1952).

44. *Schaefer v. United States*, 251 U.S. 466, 482, 483 (1920) (Brandeis dissenting); *Whitney v. California*, 274 U.S. 357, 376–77 (Brandeis concurring); Douglas did quote from the *Whitney* opinion in his dissent, 341 U.S. at 585–86. For a sharp critique (by a former Brandeis clerk) of the notion that application of the clear and present danger doctrine would leave the government powerless to defend itself, see Nathan Nathanson, "The Communist Trial and the Clear-and-Present-Danger Test," 63 *Harvard Law Review* 1167 (1950).

effect of *Dennis*, therefore, is "that it made the Court sweat so much to affirm the conviction."[45] From this point of view, the chief justice's opinion becomes more intelligible since he is working very hard to prove something that is impossible to prove—namely, that thinking about ideas, or even thinking about teaching and discussing ideas, without anything else, without any overt action, constitutes a clear and present danger to the state. To prove this, he had to read evil intent into the record, a notion that Holmes and Brandeis had specifically disavowed.

Michal Belknap claims that Frankfurter realized that the Hand-Vinson modification of the clear and present danger test "could produce harmful results in future cases which had nothing to do with communism" and therefore refused to join in the plurality opinion, not because he objected to the results but because he disagreed with Vinson's reasoning.[46] Frankfurter personally detested the Smith Act and feared that its heavy-handedness would silence not only those who sought to overthrow the government but honest and loyal critics of its policies as well. But his devotion to judicial restraint, and his refusal to accept a preferred position status for speech or a special role for the courts in protecting civil liberties, left him limited room to maneuver. He tried to do so by reserving to the judiciary the right to review the application of laws that otherwise appeared facially valid.

That is what the Court had done in this case, and Frankfurter emphasized that the seriousness of the communist danger far outweighed the "puny anonymities" that Holmes had defended in *Abrams* or the "futile" advocacies in *Gitlow*. The Communist Party, with its extensive organization, membership, and discipline, constituted a serious threat to the nation. On the other hand, of course, one valued freedom of speech. But not "every type of speech occupies the same position on the scale of values," and "it is not for us to decide how we would adjust [this] clash of interests. . . . Congress has determined that the danger created by advocacy of overthrow justifies the ensuing restriction of freedom of speech."[47] Frankfurter's opinion in *Dennis*, read in the light of history, smacks more of judicial abdication of responsibility than measured deference and restraint.

Had Rutledge and Murphy still been on the Court, it is possible that *Dennis* might have gone the other way since there would have been four solid votes against the government's position. Instead the conservative Tom Clark and Sherman Minton now held those seats, and Jackson, after his experience at Nuremberg, looked on potential dictatorial groups with far less tolerance than he had displayed in some of his wartime opinions.

---

45. Kalven, *A Worthy Tradition*, 195–96.
46. *Cold War Political Justice*, 145.
47. 341 U.S. at 517, 550 (Frankfurter concurring).

Black and Douglas tried in vain to tone down the Court's opinion, pointing out the fallacies in Vinson's reasoning and the fact that the dreaded conspiracy was, in Black's words, a "ghost conspiracy." Every time Vinson raised the specter of a communist *putsch,* Black would respond, "The goblin'll get you!"[48] The two men sat down and divided up the response. Black entered a brief opinion since they had agreed that in this case Douglas would carry the major burden of dissent.

To Black, the indictment for conspiracy amounted to a "virulent form of prior censorship of speech and press." Referring in particular to Frankfurter's concurrence, Black said he could not believe that the First Amendment "permits us to sustain laws suppressing freedom of speech and press on the basis of Congress' or our own notions of mere 'reasonableness.' " Such a doctrine "waters down the First Amendment to little more than an admonition to Congress." He could only hope that in calmer times "this or some later Court will restore the First Amendment liberties to the high preferred place where they belong in a free society."[49]

Douglas, perhaps more than any other member of the Court, worried constantly about the effects of the new Red Scare on American society. "The great danger of this period," he wrote in a popular article, "is not inflation, nor the national debt, nor atomic warfare. The great, critical danger is that we will so limit or narrow the range of permissible discussion and permissible thought that we will become victims of the orthodox school."[50] In the *Dennis* case he searched the voluminous record to find evidence—any evidence—that the defendants had engaged in actual acts of terror or seditious conduct that fell outside the ambit of First Amendment protection. But he found only that they had attempted to teach Marxist-Leninist doctrine, and the First Amendment, he believed, fully protected instruction.[51] Teaching, as he pointed out in his dissent, may have been the reason communism had been rejected in the United States:

Some nations less resilient than the United States, where illiteracy is high and where democratic traditions are only budding, might have to

---

48. Howard Ball and Phillip J. Cooper, *Of Power and Right: Hugo Black, William O. Douglas and America's Constitutional Revolution* (New York: Oxford University Press, 1992), 144.

49. 341 U.S. at 579, 580, 581 (Black dissenting). Writing some years later, Harry Kalven expressed the belief that Black's dissent "wears well. He has touched all the points, has sounded the long-term concern with the value of free speech against the anti-Communist excitements of the moment, and has compressed it all into a statement of just two pages." *A Worthy Tradition,* 202–3.

50. William O. Douglas, "The Black Silence of Fear," *New York Times Magazine,* January 13, 1952, VI, 7.

51. James F. Simon, *Independent Journey: The Life of William O. Douglas* (New York: Harper & Row, 1980), 294.

take drastic steps and jail these men for merely speaking their creed. But in America they are miserable merchants of unwanted ideas; their wares remain unsold. The fact that their ideas are abhorrent does not make them powerful. . . . The First Amendment reflects the philosophy of Jefferson "that it is time enough for the rightful purposes of civil government, for its officers to interfere when principles break into overt acts against peace and good public order."[52]

Much as he believed in an absolutist interpretation of the First Amendment,[53] Douglas drew a clear distinction between thought and speech on the one hand and action on the other: the first enjoyed absolute protection; the second did not. *Dennis* involved only speech, not "speech plus acts of sabotage or unlawful conduct. Not a single seditious act is charged in the indictment." He did not deny that communism posed a threat on the world stage, but the witch-hunt launched against the Communist Party leaders constituted an even greater threat to American values. "The crime," he charged, "depends not on what is taught but on who the teacher is. That is to make freedom of speech turn not on what is said, but on the intent with which it is said. Once we start down that road we enter territory dangerous to the liberties of every citizen."[54]

The Douglas opinion, for which he was roundly criticized at the time, later came to be seen as one of the great defenses of free thought during the McCarthy era. Thomas Emerson, one of the leading theorists of the First Amendment, noted an essential ingredient in Douglas's thought, a "remarkable ability to grasp the realities of the system of freedom of expression."[55] For Douglas free speech could be understood only in the larger context of facts. The power of the Douglas dissent is not in its rhetoric nor in it Holmesian pithy phrases; it is more Brandeisian in that it is fact-specific, and the facts it specifies clearly show that the government did not prove that Dennis and the other defendants posed the clear and pres-

---

52. 341 U.S. at 581, 588, 590 (Douglas dissenting). In another forum Douglas would later write: "[The communists'] lack of success . . . when the platform and press are open to them is notorious. They thrive under suppression, not in exposure. . . . Better that they be forced into open debate." "The Bill of Rights and the Free Society: An Individual View," 13 *Buffalo Law Review* 1, 3 (1963).

53. Douglas did not start out as an absolutist. See Lucas A. Powe, Jr., "Evolution to Absolutism: Justice Douglas and the First Amendment," 74 *Columbia Law Review* 371 (1974). See also Powe's later elaboration, "Justice Douglas, the First Amendment, and the Protection of Rights," in Stephen L. Wasby, ed., *"He Shall Not Pass This Way Again": The Legacy of Justice William O. Douglas* (Pittsburgh: University of Pittsburgh Press, 1990), 69–90.

54. 341 U.S. at 584, 583.

55. Thomas Emerson, "Mr. Justice Douglas' Contribution to the Law: The First Amendment," 74 *Columbia Law Review* 354 (1974).

ent danger that, at the very least, was required before government could stifle expression. Alone of all the justices, Douglas told the country the gravamen of the government's case—the teaching of four books about Marxist-Leninist doctrine. The books themselves had never been banned in the United States, yet the defendants had been convicted for believing in and teaching the contents of those books. With more than a touch of irony Douglas noted that the government of the United States had employed the tactics of communism itself, and he quoted Andre Vishinsky's assertion in *The Law of the Soviet State* (1938) that there could be no freedom of speech for foes of socialism. Douglas warned that "our concern should be that we accept no such standard for the United States."[56] Although his *Dennis* opinion led to a great deal of scorn from the academic protégés of Felix Frankfurter,[57] in the end it would be Douglas and Black who would be hailed as the true defenders of free thought in the postwar Red Scare. The majority opinion would have practically no doctrinal significance, and within a few years the Court moved to bury *Dennis* with almost indecent haste. About the only positive thing that might be said of it is that the clear and present danger test never recovered from the beating it received at the hands of the majority; when the Court next faced the issue of seditious conspiracy, it did not apply the test but instead formulated a much more liberal interpretation of free speech.[58]

The Dennis trial, at the federal courthouse in New York's Foley Square, had been one of the most unruly in American history, thanks to nearly all of the participants. The defendants viewed the Smith Act charges as political persecution and wanted to use the opportunity to preach their gospel. Judge Harold Medina and the defense attorneys engaged in a constant and acrimonious interchange over procedure and the admissibility of certain types of evidence, and reporters covering the trial began referring to it as the "battle of Foley Square." Immediately after the jurors had returned their verdict of guilty, Medina avenged himself for what he believed to have been a deliberate effort to sabotage the judicial process. He called the defense lawyers before the bar and judged them guilty of contempt. He attributed twenty-three offenses to Harry Sacher, eighteen to Richard Gladstein, nine to George Crockett, seven to Abraham Isserman, and six

---

56. 341 U.S. at 591.

57. Powe, "Evolution to Absolutism," 82–83.

58. *Brandenburg v. Ohio*, 395 U.S. 444 (1969). In the short run, the Justice Department relied upon *Dennis* to convict and imprison roughly forty state and local communist leaders under the Smith Act. See Robert Mollan, "Smith Act Prosecutions: The Effect of the Dennis and Yates Decisions," 26 *University of Pittsburgh Law Review* 710 (1965).

each to Eugene Dennis and Lewis McCabe; he then imposed sentences ranging from thirty days to six months.[59]

The bar has a long tradition of defending unpopular defendants, and the American Bar Association's canon of professional responsibility notes that "history is replete with instances of distinguished and sacrificial services by lawyers who have represented unpopular clients and causes. Regardless of his personal feelings, a lawyer should not decline representation because a client or a cause is unpopular or community reaction is adverse."[60] Similarly, judges are expected to rise above political considerations and perform the duties of their office "unswayed by partisan interests, public clamor, or fear of criticism."[61]

By any fair reading of the trial, Harold Medina violated the canons of judicial propriety. The lawyers, certainly zealous in the defense of their clients, matched Medina's abrasiveness, and while they were probably deserving of some rebuke, their conduct did not seem to warrant the heavy-handed vengeance Medina meted out. Moreover, in the anticommunist climate of the early 1950s, their persecution had only just begun. In addition to the contempt citations and jail terms, local bar associations moved to strip the Dennis attorneys of their right to practice law.[62] The attorneys appealed their contempt citations, and their case eventually reached the Supreme Court.

Several of the justices might have liked to say, "A plague on all your houses," for the defendants, their attorneys, and the judge had all in some ways made a mockery of the judicial process. A larger issue faced the Court, however: the integrity of the legal system. If a judge as intemperate as Medina could provoke defense attorneys and afterward sentence them to prison for contempt,[63] then unpopular defendants would be denied the constitutional protection of counsel since few lawyers would be willing to jeopardize career or freedom. While the attorneys' behavior had been far from ideal, it seemed clear to Frankfurter at least that Medina, whom he had long disliked as a "most insufferable egotist," had to be reprimanded as well.[64]

---

59. Belknap, *Cold War Political Justice,* chap. 4, details the trial; Dennis not only was one of the defendants but had served as his own lawyer.

60. American Bar Association, *Model Code of Professional Responsibility and Code of Judicial Conduct* (Chicago: ABA, 1980), Canon 2, Ethical Consideration, 2–27.

61. *Ibid.,* Canon 3.A.1.

62. For the travail of the lawyers, see Stanley I. Kutler, *The American Inquisition: Justice and Injustice in the Cold War* (New York: Hill & Wang, 1982), chap. 6.

63. Medina, however, appeared a hero to many Americans at the time, and mail came addressed to him as "The *American* Judge." For a sympathetic portrait, see Daniel Hawthorne, *Judge Medina: A Biography* (New York: Funk, 1952).

64. Kutler, *American Inquisition,* 267, n21.

The majority of the Court, however, did not share Frankfurter's agitation, and in May 1951 it voted to deny review.[65] Only Black and Douglas had initially agreed with Frankfurter, but after considerable lobbying by Frankfurter, Robert Jackson changed his mind and agreed to a limited review. Upon reconsideration, he told his colleagues, he believed that the earlier refusal had had the undesired effect of making it difficult for unpopular defendants to secure adequate counsel. But unlike the others, Jackson wanted to examine the case on the narrowest possible basis— whether Medina, in passing judgment and punishing the lawyers, had violated Rule 42(a) of the Federal Rules of Criminal Procedure, which seemingly required a separate hearing in these circumstances.

The full-scale review did not change the outcome. Five members of the Court, speaking through Jackson, upheld Medina's ruling and noted that Rule 42(a) permits "summary disposition" by a judge if he heard or witnessed the conduct constituting the contempt, and that it gave the judge the discretion to deal with contempt either at the time it took place or at the end of the trial. Jackson avowed that the Court would "unhesitatingly" defend lawyers in the "fearless, vigorous and effective performance of every duty" pertaining to their responsibilities to their client, but not if they overstepped these bounds and interfered with the orderly processes of justice. For Jackson, the leading trial lawyer on the Court, all other considerations seemed secondary to protecting the orderly process and the powers of the judge to maintain that order.[66]

Black, joined by Douglas, entered a short dissent that zeroed in on Medina's prejudicial behavior. Evidence throughout the trial indicated the judge's distrust of and hostility toward the attorneys. No lawyers who had been called "liar," "brazen," or "mealy-mouthed," as these men had, should then be tried for contempt before the very judge who had so denounced them. In Black's opinion, at the very least the petitioners should have a jury trial on the contempt charges.[67]

Only Frankfurter, to his credit, dealt in his accompanying dissent with the substantive question of judicial misconduct and its potentially disruptive effect on securing counsel for unpopular defendants. In this case Frankfurter, for the first time since he had come on the bench, seemed like the Felix of old, the Harvard professor willing to stand up to public contumely for the sake of men he despised but knew, no matter what their beliefs, to be entitled to a fair trial under the American judicial system.

---

65. *Sacher et al. v. United States,* 341 U.S. 952 (1951).

66. *Sachar et al. v. United States,* 343 U.S. 1, 5, 11–14 (1952). As the attorney general at the time of the *Dennis* case and therefore nominally responsible for its prosecution, Clark did not participate either in the certiorari or decisional aspects of this case.

67. *Ibid.* at 14.

Although he initially asserted that the case involved only questions of procedural regularity, Frankfurter went rapidly beyond that narrow issue. He appended forty-seven pages of excerpts from the trial transcript, consisting of exchanges between Medina and the attorneys, to show that "the contempt of the lawyers had its reflex in the judge." He then proceeded, chapter and verse, to detail Medina's misconduct. The trial judge, he declared, had engaged in "dialectic, in repartee and banter, in talk so copious as [to] inevitably" weaken his own authority. Medina, Frankfurter charged, had so failed to exercise "moral authority" during the trial that for him to be the one to adjudicate the contempt did violence to the belief "that punishment is a vindication of impersonal law."[68]

The *Sacher* decision fortunately had few of the dire consequences that Frankfurter had feared, and three years later the Court in effect overruled the holding.[69] More important, the Red Scare itself would soon pass its zenith, after which the country would resume some semblance of sanity in dealing with the threat of communist subversion. But before that happened, the justices endured one of the most emotionally trying cases in this or any other era.

Without doubt the most controversial Cold War cases to come before the Supreme Court involved the various appeals of Julius and Ethel Rosenberg, convicted in March 1951 under the Espionage Act of 1917 of passing atomic secrets to the Soviet Union in wartime. In April, Judge Irving Kaufman sentenced the two to death, and the Court of Appeals upheld the sentence in February 1952. Then began the convoluted series of petitions for review that did not end until the Rosenbergs died in the electric chair at Sing Sing prison on the evening of June 19, 1953, the only persons ever executed for espionage in American history.

Between June 7, 1952, and June 18, 1953, the Court had at least six opportunities to accept the case for review on its merits, and in each case it declined to do so. Only Felix Frankfurter and Hugo Black, the two men who in the previous decade had so often opposed each other, voted in every instance for the Court to hear the case.

The Rosenbergs' attorneys attempted to raise a number of procedural

---

68. *Ibid.* at 25.

69. *Offutt v. United States*, 348 U.S. 11 (1954). The Court heard one more case involving a Dennis attorney, an appeal from the New York disbarment ruling of Abraham J. Isserman, on the basis of his conviction for contempt of court. The Court declined to overturn the disbarment and under its own rules also disbarred Isserman from Supreme Court practice. The justices split on the issue, with Vinson, Reed, Burton, and Minton upholding the disbarment, while Black, Frankfurter, Douglas, and Jackson voted to reverse. Clark recused, and the 4–4 split left the state ruling intact. *In re Isserman*, 345 U.S. 286 (1953).

and substantive issues and claimed that their clients had been tried and sentenced to death for treason without the constitutional protections afforded persons accused of that crime. They also charged that the federal prosecutors had not met certain responsibilities under the federal criminal code and that Judge Kaufman had been prejudiced against them. The Court of Appeals for the Second Circuit had upheld the trial court, but by a split vote, and had in effect urged the Supreme Court to resolve the pending legal questions.[70]

Had the appeal come to the Court earlier, when Frank Murphy and Wiley Rutledge still sat, there is no question but that certiorari would have been granted. But they had both died in 1949, and the Truman appointees proved to be politically cautious as well as conservative. With the Korean War and the Red Scare going on, the majority of the Vinson Court wanted nothing to do with such a potentially explosive issue.

In the first round of appeals, Frankfurter and Black expressed their concerns about the imposition of the death sentence without Supreme Court review and about the question of whether they had in fact been tried for treason, not espionage, and thus been denied constitutional protection. Harold Burton voted with Black and Frankfurter the first two times because of how strongly the two senior justices felt about the necessity of the Court's reviewing the case, but thereafter he voted against granting certiorari.

As the months went by, Frankfurter grew increasingly concerned that the Rosenberg case would become another Sacco and Vanzetti cause célèbre, and the two convicted spies would become martyrs for the communists to hold up as examples of capitalist injustice. The country could not go through another such spasm; the Court, he believed, had to review the case and assure the nation that justice had been done. Whether the convictions stood or fell made no difference by itself; the Rosenbergs might be guilty, but they were entitled to all the protections the Constitution afforded to those accused of crimes, including review of the case when legitimate legal issues existed.

---

70. *United States v. Rosenberg,* 195 F.2d 583 (2d Cir. 1952). The literature on the Rosenberg case is enormous, and there is still controversy over whether the Rosenbergs were in fact innocent or guilty and whether they, like Sacco and Vanzetti in the 1920s, had been convicted and executed not for their alleged crime but for their political beliefs. We are here primarily concerned with how the Supreme Court responded to their appeals. For this section I have relied on Michael E. Parrish, "Cold War Justice: The Supreme Court and the Rosenbergs," 82 *American Historical Review* 805 (1977), in which he strongly criticizes Justice Douglas; that criticism is challenged by William Cohen, "Justice Douglas and the *Rosenberg* Case: Setting the Record Straight," 70 *Cornell Law Review* 211 (1985). See also Parrish's rejoinder, *ibid.* at 1056.

The attorneys for the Rosenbergs introduced new evidence in an appeal in April 1953, including claims that one witness had committed perjury and the prosecutor had prejudiced the case by making statements out of court. This time only Frankfurter and Black voted to grant certiorari; Burton did not consider the new arguments very persuasive, and he voted with the majority. This third refusal upset Frankfurter to the point that he took what was for him the unusual step of writing a dissenting opinion to the Court's denial of certiorari. He then reconsidered this step, worried that it might further embroil the Court in the growing national controversy over the case. After conferring with Black, the two issued a one-sentence statement noting that they still believed the Court should review the case.

Frankfurter did, however, distribute a memorandum within the Court. He begged the brethren's pardon for bothering them again with this question, which he described as "the most anguishing situation since I have been on the Court," but he literally pleaded with them to reconsider their decision. He did not know whether the conviction itself should be overturned, but the only way to determine that would be by a full-scale review. The attorneys for the Rosenbergs had, he asserted, raised sufficient procedural questions for the Court to consider their validity.

Most important, Frankfurter declared, by not hearing the case, the Court in effect abandoned the field to demagogues like Senator Joseph McCarthy of Wisconsin. He had no fear of what he termed "the puny force of Communist influence in this country." But he did worry about the good men and women in the country "who feel as I do that it is a concession to Communism, not a safeguard against it, to retreat from reason and to compromise those cherished traditions which one likes to think of as the peculiar characteristics of an Anglo-American justice."[71]

Shortly afterward, on May 22, 1953, William O. Douglas circulated a memorandum in which he said that he had given further study to the allegations about prosecutorial conduct and had decided to vote for certiorari. This made three for review, still one shy of the number needed, but Douglas upset the other members of the Court by indicating that he planned to issue a statement that he believed review necessary because "some of the conduct of the United States Attorney was 'wholly reprehensible' . . . [and] that it probably prejudiced the defendants seriously."[72]

71. Frankfurter, Memorandum to the Conference, May 20, 1953, Frankfurter Papers, Harvard Law School Library.

72. Douglas, Memorandum to Conference, May 22, 1953, Douglas Papers, Library of Congress. The Court of Appeals had agreed that some of the U.S. attorney's conduct had been inappropriate but had concluded that it had not prejudiced the defendants' case. Leonard Boudin has suggested that in this case Douglas let his very strong anticommunist feelings influence him. "He was an American liberal who hated Communism. Also hated anything that threatened the United States Government. Like Espionage. And he let those feelings control him." Boudin Memoirs, Columbia Oral History Collection.

Frankfurter immediately asked Chief Justice Vinson to reopen discussion, and he did so fuming inwardly at Douglas's turnabout. While he no doubt welcomed another vote, he believed it wholly unethical for Douglas to issue a statement in which, in essence, he prejudged the merits of the case. The Rosenberg attorneys wanted the review to decide just this issue—whether the United States attorney's conduct had prejudiced the trial. The Court's grant of certiorari in a case signifies no more than that four justices believe sufficient questions have been raised to warrant further study, not that a majority has been convinced that error exists. By threatening to go public in a way that might embarrass the Court, Douglas seemed to be blackmailing his colleagues into granting review. Justice Jackson told Frankfurter that he considered the Douglas memorandum "the dirtiest, most shameful, most cynical performance that I have ever heard of in matters pertaining to law."[73]

Frankfurter immediately began lobbying both Jackson and Burton, who had voted with him and Black on the first two ballots. Douglas, he claimed, had "put the whole Court in a hole," but "we cannot ostrich-like bury our heads in the sand."[74]

Jackson reluctantly agreed to change his vote, providing the necessary fourth vote for certiorari, and he did so, he told the Court, because of Douglas's proposed dissent. At a specially called conference the next day, Douglas stunned everyone by announcing that he wanted to withdraw his memorandum. It had been badly drawn, he conceded, and he had not realized it would embarrass anyone. Jackson, who had been prepared to vote for review to block Douglas, now changed his vote back, but Douglas said nothing. The conference dissolved with only Black, Frankfurter, and Douglas voting for review.

The last scenes of the drama played out in the middle of June. The Rosenberg attorneys made one last appeal, asking for a stay of execution and for oral argument before the Court on the stay. Moreover, they brought in new evidence of perjury,[75] and they brought some new legal talent to assist them, including the legendary John Finerty, a longtime defender of civil liberties who had argued for Sacco and Vanzetti and had also played a role in the Mooney case. Unlike petitions for certiorari, petitions for a stay require a majority vote. Black, Frankfurter, and Jackson voted both to hear oral argument and to stay the execution. Douglas voted to stay the execution but not to hear the oral argument, while Burton was willing to hear oral argument but not stay the execution without the argument. As a result, the Rosenbergs lost both appeals by a 4–5 vote.[76]

---

73. Simon, *Independent Journey*, 303.
74. Frankfurter to Burton, May 23, 1953, quoted in Parrish, "Cold War Justice," 824.
75. For details of this evidence, see *ibid.* at 828–31.
76. *Rosenberg et ux. v. United States*, 345 U.S. 989 (1953).

It seemed as if the Rosenbergs had run out their legal string, but then in a totally unexpected move, two lawyers, Fyke Farmer and Daniel Marshall, representing a coalition of civil libertarian and church groups, intervened with a claim that the Rosenbergs had been indicted, tried, and sentenced under the wrong law.[77] They brought this evidence to Douglas on June 15, two days after the last conference, and he pored over the materials for the next two days, consulting, among others, Frankfurter and the chief justice. Vinson told him that Farmer had no standing to intervene and that the Court had already disposed of the question of the Atomic Energy Act. Frankfurter thought the issue worth looking into, but he refused to review Douglas's draft of a stay of execution.[78] Moreover, Frankfurter lectured him, do what your conscience tells you, not what the chief justice says.

Frankfurter's coolness toward Douglas at this stage derived not from any desire to hasten the Rosenbergs to their doom but from distrust of Douglas's motives. The man had had more than one opportunity to provide the crucial fourth vote for certiorari, or the fifth vote for a stay, and had flip-flopped from one side to the other. Frankfurter and Jackson suspected that Douglas did not want the Court to review the case; he just wanted to score points with the liberals and keep his political ambitions alive by writing militant but ineffective dissents.

On June 17—two days before the scheduled execution—Douglas issued an order staying execution pending further proceedings in the district court on the question of the applicability of the Atomic Energy Act. Douglas assumed this would hold things up for a while, and his order also provided for review of the district court's findings by the court of appeals. He signed and released the papers and immediately left by car for his summer vacation in the West.

Unknown to either Douglas or Frankfurter, Jackson had met on June 16 with the chief justice and Attorney General Herbert Brownell to discuss what to do should Douglas issue the stay. Vinson said that if Douglas issued a stay, he would call the Court into special session to vacate it. Douglas issued the stay, Brownell immediately petitioned the Court to vacate the stay, and Vinson called a special session on June 18. Although Douglas had left his itinerary with the chief justice, he only heard about the special

---

77. They claimed that the 1917 Espionage Act had been superseded by the Atomic Energy Act of 1946. Under terms of the latter statute, a death sentence for espionage could be imposed only after jury recommendation and if it had been proved that the crime had been committed with the intent to injure the United States.

78. Individual justices can, if they believe circumstances warrant it, issue stays of execution pending review by the full Court. At this point only an individual stay could possibly save the Rosenbergs.

session on his car radio near Pittsburgh. He immediately turned around and headed back to Washington.[79]

On June 18, for the only time in this long and convoluted process, the justices heard arguments in open court about the Rosenberg case, but arguments restricted to whether the Atomic Energy Act provision on the death penalty raised sufficient questions to support the stay. At different times five members of the Court had voted in one way or another to give the Rosenbergs their full day in court, but in the end only Black and Frankfurter voted to sustain Douglas's stay; the other six voted to vacate. The Court then announced that the order had been lifted; after a last-minute appeal for clemency to President Eisenhower had been denied, the Rosenbergs were executed shortly after eight o'clock that evening. Frankfurter, Jackson, and their clerks kept a somber deathwatch in Jackson's chambers, awaiting the news that Ethel and Julius Rosenberg were dead.

At the conference earlier that day, an angry Frankfurter had questioned the Court's right to vacate a stay issued in chambers and in such an unusual manner. He believed that everyone's mind had been made up even before the special session had met and that the brethren had given in to the mob. In his dissent, issued a month later, he expressed these views and charged that the Court had rushed to judgment without adequate study or reflection. Can it be said, he asked, "that there was time to go through the process by which cases are customarily decided here?"[80] Certainly the judgment of history has been that, whatever the guilt or innocence of the Rosenbergs, their less than fair trial received inadequate review by the appellate courts. But that is hardly surprising considering the attitudes of a majority of the justices during the Cold War.

---

79. Douglas, *Court Years*, 80–81.

80. *Rosenberg v. United States*, 346 U.S. 273, 309 (1953). One might question why Frankfurter even bothered to enter a dissent, and he himself noted that doing so after the deaths of the Rosenbergs had "the appearance of pathetic futility." But history also had its claims, and he proceeded to write a moving and eloquent essay on the dangers of allowing personal prejudice or political emotionalism to intrude on the legal process. Michael Parrish notes that Frankfurter's skepticism of absolutes yielded a philosophy of caution and restraint in most areas of the law, but it also yielded a special sensitivity to human failings. In the Rosenberg case, as in Sacco and Vanzetti a generation earlier, he tried to warn against the "terrible possibility of judicially sanctioned death through error, bias or deceit." Parrish, "Cold War Justice," 842.

# 7

# THE RIGHTS OF LABOR

No group benefited more from the New Deal than organized labor. In contrast to the antiunion animus of the 1920s, the Roosevelt Administration committed itself to securing for workers the right to organize and to bargain collectively. The first step in this process had been Section 7(a) of the 1933 National Industrial Recovery Act, but that law had been struck down by the Supreme Court in the *Schechter* decision.[1] The administration did not, however, abandon labor, and in 1935 Congress passed the Wagner Labor Relations Act.

The Wagner Act not only reestablished 7(a) but changed the entire posture of government vis-à-vis labor and industry. The old ideas of laissez-faire in labor-management relations went by the boards; the government would now serve as the protector of labor's right to organize and to bargain collectively. Advocates of the Wagner Act argued that in a highly industrialized economy, only government support would allow labor to meet management on roughly equal terms. Moreover, where previously laws and court decisions had benefited management almost exclusively,[2] the Wagner Act's list of unfair labor practices applied entirely to management; the law imposed no restraints on labor. Congress established a National Labor Relations Board (NLRB) to administer the act, and this board had sole authority to determine a whole range of issues dealing with labor-management relations. It could order elections to choose a bargaining agent, issue "cease and desist" orders when it found unfair labor practices, and go to court to secure judicial enforcement of its decisions.[3]

---

1. *Schechter v. United States*, 295 U.S. 495 (1935). Franklin Roosevelt himself was no ardent exponent of unionism; he saw himself more as a "patron" of labor and initially had no strong feelings on labor demands. But the growing intransigence of employers to New Deal programs and the support labor gave Roosevelt in his campaigns for reelection led him to become organized labor's champion. William E. Leuchtenburg, *Franklin D. Roosevelt and the New Deal, 1932–1940* (New York: Harper & Row, 1963), 107–8.

2. See William E. Forbath, *Law and the Shaping of the American Labor Movement* (Cambridge: Harvard University Press, 1991), for the course of labor in the courts up to the Norris-LaGuardia Act.

3. For a sympathetic analysis of the Wagner Act, see Harry A. Millis and Emily Clark Brown, *From the Wagner Act to Taft-Hartley: A Study of National Labor Policy and Labor Relations* (Chicago: University of Chicago Press, 1950), part 1.

In the midst of the 1937 Court-packing debate, the Supreme Court upheld various provisions of the Wagner Act in a series of 5–4 decisions. Chief Justice Charles Evans Hughes managed to skirt the narrow definition of interstate commerce that had been handed down in *Schechter* and the *Carter Coal* case and revive the traditionally broad interpretation of the commerce power.[4] In *N.L.R.B. v. Jones & Laughlin Steel Company*,[5] Hughes used the "stream of commerce" theory to justify government regulation of labor relations in particular plants. "When industries organize themselves on a national scale, making their relation to interstate commerce the dominant factor in their activities," he declared, "how can it be maintained that their industrial labor relations constitute a forbidden field into which Congress may not enter when it is necessary to protect interstate commerce from the paralyzing consequences of industrial war?"[6] The federal commerce power gave Congress the authority to protect interstate commerce no matter the source of the dangers. In a companion case, the Court extended this ruling to small manufacturers whose business had a negligible effect on interstate commerce; in doing so, however, Hughes did not look at single firms but at the interstate nature of the industry.[7]

These two rulings had important and immediate consequences. The Wagner Act had been the most controversial of the Second New Deal measures, for it had not only injected the federal government into a new field but had substantially changed the rules of the marketplace, giving more power to workers and their unions. Freedom of contract, one of the main conservative weapons against reform labor legislation, gave way to a seemingly unlimited view of the commerce power, which could apparently be used to justify a large spectrum of regulatory legislation. Although there would be many more NLRB cases before the Court in years to come, none of them would deal with the agency's legitimacy; rather the justices would be asked to determine the reach of the enabling legislation, and, for the most part, they found that reach quite extensive.[8]

---

4. *Carter v. Carter Coal Company*, 298 U.S. 238 (1936).

5. 301 U.S. 1 (1937).

6. *Ibid.* at 41.

7. *N.L.R.B. v. Friedman-Harry Marks Clothing Co.*, 301 U.S. 58 (1937).

8. See in general Christopher L. Tomlins, *The State and the Unions: Labor Relations, Law, and the Organized Labor Movement in America, 1880–1960* (Cambridge: Cambridge University Press, 1985), part 2. See also C. Herman Pritchett, *The Roosevelt Court: A Study in Judicial Politics and Values, 1937–1947* (New York: Macmillan, 1948), 199–208, for a review of both the NLRB cases and those arising under the Fair Labor Standards Act. In both cases, as Pritchett shows, the Court was extremely deferential to the fact-finding conclusions of the administrators, and because much of the law is fact-based, the justices therefore had few occasions to overturn agency decisions. A more minute review of the Fair Labor Standards Act cases can be found in Sidney Fine, *Frank Murphy: The Washington Years* (Ann Arbor: University of Michigan Press, 1984), chap. 14.

Labor also benefited from another series of Court decisions dealing with the First Amendment's protection of speech. In 1936 the American Civil Liberties Union declared that the greatest threat to liberty came from "the resort to force and violence by employers, vigilantes, mobs, troops, private gunmen, and compliant sheriffs and compliant police" against workers.[9] That same year, a Senate subcommittee chaired by Robert M. LaFollette, Jr., of Wisconsin began investigating charges that workers' rights, particularly those of free speech and assembly, had been violated. The LaFollette committee detailed the lengths to which management had gone to crush labor unions, including the use of private armies, spies, intimidation, and agents provocateurs as well as the involvement of corrupt local officials. Following the violence of the Little Steel strike of 1937, the committee publicized the way employers had continuously flouted the Wagner Act, broken the laws, and disregarded civil liberties.[10]

But now for the first time the power of the federal government swung over to protect labor. The Department of Labor and the NLRB actively supported organized labor; the Roosevelt appointees to the Court fully sympathized with labor goals, unlike the antiunion justices of the Taft era; and the young lawyers who flocked to Washington to staff New Deal agencies had imbibed the prolabor and pro–civil liberties views of teachers such as Ernst Freund, Felix Frankfurter, and Zechariah Chafee, Jr. Moreover, the Justice Department under Frank Murphy established a civil liberties unit and staffed it with men and women committed to the protection of labor rights as a component of individual liberties. "I am anxious," Murphy told civil liberties activist Roger Baldwin, that the Justice Department "should be a force for the protection of the people's liberties."[11]

The changes on the Court following 1937 also led labor to look for help from the judiciary, which had been its traditional enemy. Both Justice Cardoza, in the *Palko* case,[12] and Justice Stone, in his *Carolene Products* footnote,[13] had invited dissident groups and individuals to seek out a broader interpretation of constitutionally protected rights. Organized labor initiated one series of cases testing the reach of the First Amendment's Speech Clause. As he had done in so many areas, Louis Brandeis had pointed the way in this matter in *Senn v. Tile Layers' Protective Union* (1937) when he had suggested that picketing, aside from its role as a tool in labor disputes,

9. Paul L. Murphy, *The Constitution in Crisis Times, 1918–1969* (New York: Harper & Row, 1972), 171.

10. Jerald S. Auerbach, "The LaFollette Committee: Labor and Civil Liberties in the New Deal," 51 *Journal of American History* 435 (1964).

11. *Ibid.* at 455.

12. *Palko v. Connecticut,* 302 U.S. 319 (1937).

13. *United States v. Carolene Products Company,* 304 U.S. 144, 152.n4 (1938).

might also be a form of speech.[14] Then in his first opinion for the Court, Frank Murphy wrote an extremely broad interpretation of picketing as speech in *Thornhill v. Alabama* (1940).[15] Picking up on Brandeis's suggestion as well as the implications of Stone's *Carolene Products* footnote, Murphy declared that if freedom of discussion were to "fulfill its historic function, it must embrace all issues about which information is needed or appropriate." Free discussion about labor disputes "appears to be indispensable to the effective and intelligent use of the processes of popular government to shape the destiny of modern industrial society."[16]

As the labor movement gained strength under the protective arm of the New Deal, its frequent resort to litigation expanded the meaning of the First Amendment. The Congress of Industrial Organizations challenged the iron grip Mayor Frank Hague had on Jersey City, where police frequently broke up union meetings, destroyed labor literature, and ran union organizers out of town. By a 5–2 vote the Court invalidated a municipal ordinance requiring permits for public meetings that had been used arbitrarily against unions.[17] Then in 1941 the Court categorized picketing as speech in striking down an Illinois law prohibiting picketing by persons not directly involved in the labor dispute.[18] The following year the Court ruled that a union could not be prohibited from peaceful picketing even in the absence of a normal type of labor dispute.[19]

A majority of the Court did not, however, view picketing per se as a fully protected constitutional right. In the *Meadowmoor Dairies* case, Justice Frankfurter held that freedom of speech, while basic to American democracy, could in the context of violence "lose its significance as an appeal to reason and become part of an instrument of force." States could therefore restrain picketing that led to violence or destruction of property. Black,

---

14. The case involved the validity of a Wisconsin law making peaceful picketing lawful and nonenjoinable and also providing for publicity in labor disputes. Union members did not have to rely on such a statute to make the facts of a labor dispute public, Brandeis declared, "for freedom of speech is guaranteed by the Federal Constitution." 301 U.S. 468, 478 (1937).

15. 310 U.S. 88 (1940). For an analysis of the case, see Fine, *Murphy*, 168–77.

16. 310 U.S. at 102, 103.

17. *Hague v. C.I.O.*, 307 U.S. 496 (1939).

18. *American Federation of Labor v. Swing*, 312 U.S. 321 (1941).

19. *Carpenters & Joiners Union v. Ritter's Cafe*, 315 U.S. 722 (1942). The series of cases beginning with *Thornhill* led to a very active debate in the law journals over the correctness of the Court's decisions viewing picketing as a form of protected speech. See as just one example the exchange between Ludwig Teller and E. Merrick Dodd. Teller argued that "since picketing is a form of economic pressure and not simply the exercise of free speech, its legality and enjoinability may best be solved under the law of torts." "Picketing and Free Speech," 56 *Harvard Law Review* 180, 204 (1942). Dodd's rejoinder, backing the Court's view of picketing as speech, is at *ibid.* at 513 (1943).

joined by Reed and Douglas, dissented and claimed that the injunction that had been issued by the state court went beyond merely prohibiting violence and had, in fact, prevented public discussion of important issues.[20] Then in 1943 the Court again took a broad view of picketing rights in a unanimous decision upholding the peaceful picketing of a restaurant where the union grievance was that the restaurant was operated by its owners and so hired no employees that the union could organize.[21]

In similar reasoning, the Court refused to exempt public meetings from all state control, although it stood ready to intervene when local laws clearly discriminated against groups such as labor. In *Thomas v. Collins* (1945), for example, Justice Rutledge spoke for the 5–4 majority in voiding a Texas statute requiring labor union officials to secure an organizer's card before soliciting for members. In this case, a Congress of Industrial Organizations organizer had addressed a mass meeting of oil workers to seek members, despite a restraining order from a local court. Rutledge held the law an invalid interference with the rights of free speech and assembly, which as protected under the First Amendment had "a sanctity and a sanction not permitting dubious intrusions."[22] But four members of the Court—Roberts, joined by Frankfurter, Stone, and Reed—dissented, claiming that a state could license public meetings in order to maintain peace and order provided it administered the rules in a neutral manner.[23] Within a few years the dissenters on the Stone Court would become the majority on the Vinson Court.

During World War II the administration leaders saw all labor issues taking a back seat to the necessity to win the war and maintain the highest

---

20. *Milk Wagon Drivers Union v. Meadowmoor Dairies*, 312 U.S. 287, 293 (1941); the Black dissent is at 299. Interestingly, Frank Murphy, labor's staunchest champion on the bench, voted with the majority and told Frankfurter that his opinion "puts this court in a correct position in regard to activities about which we can encourage or discourage responsible conduct. Free speech and the other freedoms will not and have not been left either friendless or impoverished by this court." Murphy to Frankfurter, n.d., Frankfurter Papers, Harvard Law School Library.

21. *Cafeteria Employees Union v. Angelos*, 320 U.S. 293 (1943).

22. 323 U.S. 516, 530 (1945); for a discussion of the case, see Fowler V. Harper, *Justice Rutledge and the Bright Constellation* (Indianapolis: Bobbs-Merrill, 1965), 118–22. William O. Douglas entered a short concurrence at 323 U.S. at 543, joined by Black and Murphy. It is interesting to note that Douglas had not yet reached the absolutist view of the First Amendment he would propound; he held that once speech involves action, no matter how incidental, it may be regulated. In a note to Rutledge, Douglas had said that once a person "does more than speak and engages in conduct such as getting subscriptions, signatures, etc., he steps into a realm which the state may regulate." Douglas to Rutledge, May 26, 1944, Rutledge Papers, Library of Congress.

23. 323 U.S. at 548.

level of production. By the end of 1941 union leaders had become concerned that the government's pressure on them to subordinate trade union goals to the needs of defense production would lead to growing apathy and resentment among union members and to the possible collapse of the union movement.[24] But the administration, through the various war production agencies, did its best to maintain union standards and protect the gains labor had made in the 1930s. For the most part, union officials tried to work with the administration and to be responsible in carrying out what they perceived as their wartime duties, and as the war drew to an end, "there was hardly a political or military leader who did not take occasion to pay glowing tribute to the role which labor had played." In President Roosevelt's words, labor had made possible "the greatest production achievement in the world's history."[25]

Yet despite all the praise and the undeniable role labor had played in war production, antilabor sentiment grew considerably during the war. In broad terms, much of management remained unreconciled both to the idea of having to deal with organized labor and to the power of the federal government to back up demands that companies recognize unions and then bargain collectively with them. Conservatives saw the unions as a pillar of political and electoral strength for the Democrats, and in fact labor became and remained central to the New Deal coalition until it fell apart in the 1980s.

But some events in the war also left a sour taste. The National War Labor Board had been empowered to handle all labor controversies affecting war production, and the number of workdays lost to strikes and other labor disputes dropped dramatically. The Board, however, saw its prime mission as maintaining the continuity of production, and while it tried to work out fair and equitable guidelines for pay adjustments, its decisions did not always sit well with particular groups of workers. A number of strikes took place in 1943 in protest against government wage guidelines, which union leaders claimed did not keep up with inflation.

The most notorious of these strikes was led by the flamboyant and colorful John Llewellyn Lewis, head of the United Mine Workers and the man responsible for creating the Congress of Industrial Organizations (CIO). When Lewis led his men out on strike in April 1943, Roosevelt immediately seized the coal mines and blamed the breakdown in contract negotiations on Lewis. Although the president came in for some criticism

---

24. Nelson Lichtenstein, *Labor's War at Home: The CIO in World War Two* (Cambridge: Cambridge University Press, 1982), 67–81.

25. Foster Rhea Dulles and Melvyn Dubofsky, *Labor in America: A History,* 4th ed. (Arlington Heights: Harlan Davidson, 1984), 322–23.

for his role in the strike negotiations, for the most part the press and the country blamed Lewis for acting against the national interests in the midst of war.[26]

As a result of the coal strikes, Congress passed the Smith-Connally Act, also known as the War Labor Disputes Act, over Roosevelt's veto in June 1943. The measure empowered the president, following the failure of government mediation, to take control of plants or even industries critical to the war effort and provided criminal penalties for persons who instigated or promoted a strike.[27] It did not place any ban on strikes in areas the government considered nonessential, but it did provide for a thirty-day cooling-off period in which the NLRB would hold a strike vote among the plant workers. Among other provisions, the law also forbade union contributions to political campaigns. Although critics termed the Smith-Connally measure hasty and ill-conceived, it embodied the federal government's labor law for the balance of the war.

For the most part, even without the Smith-Connally Law, the War Labor Board proved to be extremely successful in keeping labor relations during the war peaceful and the production lines rolling. No serious challenge to the board's authority reached the courts, so there are no important wartime labor decisions involving it.[28] The delicate equilibrium among labor, management, and the government fell apart, however, in the postwar conversion. Congress moved quickly to remove wage and production controls after V-J Day; prices shot upward, and labor strikes increased as workers demanded higher wages. Although a variety of factors contributed to the 30 percent increase in retail prices between June 1946 and August 1948, conservatives saw the main cause of inflation as the "unreasonable" demands by labor unions.[29] Congressional critics of labor were already at work on efforts to repeal all or part of the Wagner Act provisions when

---

26. See Dubofsky and Warren Van Tine, *John L. Lewis: A Biography*, abridged ed. (Urbana: University of Illinois Press, 1986), chap. 18.

27. During the war, starting with a proclamation of national defense on May 27, 1941 until Roosevelt's death on April 12, 1945, the federal government seized thirty-eight plants or industries. John L. Blackman, Jr., *Presidential Seizure in Labor Disputes* (Cambridge: Harvard University Press, 1967), 259–70.

28. A few cases involving interpretations of the Wagner Act reached the circuit courts of appeals. In *N.L.R.B. v. Ohio Calcium Company*, 133 F.2d 721 (6th Cir. 1943), the Sixth Circuit held that the Wagner Act's protection of the right to strike applied only to lawful strikes. The Third Circuit ruled that employers could dismiss wildcat strikers without committing an unfair labor practice in *N.L.R.B. v. Condenser Corp. of America*, 128 F.2d 67 (3rd Cir. 1942); a similar ruling can be found in *N.L.R.B. v. Draper Corp.*, 145 F.2d 199 (4th Cir. 1944).

29. In the twelve months following the end of the war there had been 4,630 work stoppages involving 5 million strikers, leading to more than 120 million lost days of work. Dulles and Dubofsky, *Labor in America*, 340.

John L. Lewis, whose activities had led to the Smith-Connally Act, gave antilabor groups fresh ammunition, and this time the issue did come to the high court.

The decision in *United States v. United Mine Workers of America*,[30] according to C. Herman Pritchett, "was about as bitter a pill as a Court, generally sympathetic to labor and ardently believing in strict adherence to constitutional procedure in criminal cases, could have been called upon to swallow."[31] On May 21, 1946, the federal government had seized control of the country's bituminous coal mines to end a strike that had crippled coal production. Eight days later Secretary of the Interior Julius Krug and United Mine Workers president John L. Lewis announced agreement on wages and working conditions and signed a contract that specifically applied only to the period during which the government ran the mines. By October, however, Lewis believed that his people deserved a better deal, so he informed the government that he intended to terminate the contract under provisions of the agreement signed with the bituminous coal operators in April 1945, which he argued carried over into the arrangement with the government. On November 15, Lewis informed Krug that the contract would be terminated five days later, and he sent a copy of the letter to union members, effectively calling a strike since the United Mine Workers traditionally would not work without a contract.

Although the administration indicated its willingness to renegotiate the contract, Krug insisted that as long as the government held the mines, the May 29 agreement remained in effect. The government then went to court, where federal district judge Alan T. Goldsborough issued a temporary restraining order on November 18 to prevent the strike. The union ignored the order and claimed that the Norris-LaGuardia Act of 1932, which precluded the courts from issuing injunctions in private labor disputes, also applied to the federal government.

Judge Goldsborough rejected this argument; on December 4 he made the temporary order permanent and also found both the union and its president in civil and criminal contempt. He fined the United Mine Workers $3.5 million and John L. Lewis $10,000 and imposed an additional fine on the union for every day it remained on strike. Three days later Lewis ordered his people to return to work until the end of March, in order, as he said, to give the Supreme Court the opportunity to hear the issues free from the hysteria that surrounded the strike.[32]

---

30. 330 U.S. 258 (1947).

31. Pritchett, *Roosevelt Court*, 232.

32. For details of the strike and the administration's response, see Dubofsky and Tine, *John L. Lewis*, 331–36; and Blackman, *Presidential Seizure*, 33–36.

Although the government had "won" in the district court, it immediately asked the Supreme Court to grant certiorari and bypass the appellate court stage in order to get definitive approval of its power to secure an injunction against the union. The justices debated the issue first on December 6 and at that time agreed to hear the appeal; then came the announcement that the strike had ended. Supposedly union lawyers and the attorney general had met with Chief Justice Vinson in his chambers to discuss the matter while the strike was still on. Union lawyers had asked for twenty-five days in which to prepare their arguments; the attorney general claimed there was a national emergency and wanted the Court to hear the case in nine days. Vinson then stunned both sides by saying he was ready to put it down for argument in five days. According to Drew Pearson, who published this account in his "Washington Merry-Go-Round" column of December 6, 1946, "two hours later John L. Lewis called off his strike."[33] A majority of the Court now wanted to have the case follow the usual route, but the justices eventually agreed to hear the expedited appeal and to consolidate the union case with that of its president.

The central issue seemingly could not have been clearer: did the Norris-LaGuardia Act apply to government? And no matter how the Court decided this question, it still had to determine other matters. Could the union and Lewis be held in contempt, and if so, had Judge Goldsborough improperly mixed civil and criminal contempt proceedings and imposed an excessive fine? Did the government takeover substantively transform the labor contract the miners had signed earlier? The answers to these question split the Court in several directions. Probably no one knew more about the Norris-LaGuardia Act than Felix Frankfurter, who had helped to draft it, and he believed that it did apply to government, a view shared by Frank Murphy and Wiley Rutledge. Chief Justice Vinson, joined by Stanley Reed and Harold Burton, argued that the statute did not apply to the government. Black and Douglas "leaned that way," and Jackson was "in a bog" on the matter. As for the fines, Murphy and Rutledge thought the defendants could not be held in contempt, Black thought they could be guilty only of civil and not criminal contempt, Douglas and Reed thought the fines excessive, and on no issue could a clear majority agree.[34]

Although the Court theoretically does not take notice of public feeling, the justices could hardly have been unaware of the antilabor sentiment then sweeping the country, which would come to fruition in the Taft-

---

33. The account and other details are in Harper, *Justice Rutledge and the Bright Constellation*, 218–19.

34. Fine, *Murphy*, 528; Jan Palmer, *The Vinson Court Era: The Supreme Court's Conference Votes: Data and Analysis* (New York: AMS Press, 1990), 187.

Hartley Act that June. All of the members of the Court shared in the Roosevelt administration's generally favorable attitude toward organized labor and remembered how earlier conservative courts had cooperated with management to defeat union efforts to organize and to strike. But at the same time, as members of the nation's highest court, they also recognized the need to protect the integrity of the judiciary. Judge Goldsborough may have been wrong, but a court order had to be obeyed until proven unlawful. John L. Lewis, in defying the temporary restraining order, had in effect thumbed his nose at the federal courts, a condition that could not be tolerated. The chief justice kept muttering during the conference that Lewis was getting "too big for his britches," while Rutledge, in counterpoint, warned his colleagues not to let public emotion against the defendants affect their decision.[35] After weeks of intense lobbying by Frankfurter and Vinson and efforts by Burton and Reed to reach some sort of compromise,[36] the Court issued a highly fragmented opinion on March 6, 1947. No fewer than seven separate questions divided the justices.

First, five members of the Court—Vinson, Reed, Burton, Black, and Douglas—found that the Norris-LaGuardia Act did not apply to the government since its language and legislative history did not indicate that Congress had intended it to do so. Moreover, a general rule of statutory interpretation is that limitations upon the sovereign may not be imposed without the sovereign's assent; Congress could have given this assent in the law but had not done so, and the Court could not read that permission into the statute. Frankfurter led the dissenters and claimed that the majority had misread the legislative history.[37] The same five justices ruled that the government in seizing the mines had become the de facto proprietor and that the Krug-Lewis agreement thereby superseded any previous labor contracts signed by the mines' actual owners.

Justice Jackson joined the majority on the third issue. The War Labor Disputes Act of 1943 had provided the justification for the administration's seizure of the mines. The legislative history of that act showed that Congress had specifically considered, and then rejected, the use of injunction as a remedy against interference with seized plants. As Frankfurter archly

---

35. Fine, *Murphy*, 528–29.

36. John D. Fassett, *New Deal Justice: The Life of Stanley Reed of Kentucky* (New York: Vantage, 1994), 428–31.

37. On this ground Frankfurter may have been correct about the intent of Congress since he had had such a major hand in drafting the legislation. Moreover, Frankfurter had been generally acknowledged as one of the foremost scholars of labor law prior to his appointment to the Court, and the book he wrote with one of his students, Nathaniel Greene, *The Labor Injunction* (New York: Macmillan, 1930), had been the bible of reformers who sought and secured the Norris-LaGuardia Act.

noted, "the whole course of legislation indicates that Congress withheld the remedy of injunction. This Court now holds that Congress authorized the injunction." For Frankfurter, if the government had become the private employer the majority said it had, then the Norris-LaGuardia Act applied and denied injunctive relief; if it had not, then Congress in the Smith-Connally Act had reached a similar conclusion regarding government as employer.[38] Frankfurter's reasoning here is much stronger than the legal gymnastics Chief Justice Vinson was attempting to perform, and one has to conclude that Vinson's judicial restraint nonetheless still permitted him to find in favor of the government on almost any issue, even when the foundation for such a ruling was shaky.

Seven justices agreed that Lewis and the United Mine Workers had been properly convicted of criminal contempt for ignoring the temporary restraining order, and this would have been true even if the high court had later determined that the district court had no authority to issue such an injunction. The proper way to determine if an injunction is lawful is by legal appeal, not defiance. The district court had been trying "to preserve existing conditions while it was determining its own authority to grant injunctive relief. The defendants, in making their private determination of the law, acted at their peril. Their disobedience is punishable as criminal contempt."[39] Even Frankfurter joined this point; whatever his views on the authority of the court to grant an injunction, an order of a court must be obeyed, and challenges to it must be mounted within the legal system and not on the streets. "The greater the power that defies law the less tolerant can this Court be of defiance."[40] Only Rutledge and Murphy dissented from this holding, as they did from the fifth ruling that the district court's failure to describe the alleged contempt as criminal did not constitute prejudicial error.

Sixth, the Court had to overlook Judge Goldsborough's trying the union and John L. Lewis for both civil and criminal contempt in the same proceeding. While it noted that it would always be better to separate civil and criminal charges, there had been no "substantial prejudice"; in fact,

---

38. 330 U.S. at 307, 328; Frances Howell Rudko, *Truman's Court: A Study in Judicial Restraint* (Westport, Conn.: Greenwood, 1988), 75–76.

39. 330 U.S. at 293.

40. *Ibid.* at 312. In a memorandum to the Conference, March 11, 1947, Frankfurter had written that the Court could not treat this case "as though it were the common garden variety ordinary situation." Lewis had to be told that this had been a lawful order and he had to obey it; but if they did not impose some sanctions, then in essence the Court would be saying that Lewis had been a naughty boy, but he would be allowed to be a good boy and even given time to do it. Frankfurter believed this would send the wrong message. Douglas Papers, Library of Congress.

the defendants had enjoyed in both trials the heightened protections of criminal proceedings. Again Murphy and Rutledge dissented, the latter quite vehemently, and claimed that commingling the two proceedings "in a single criminal-civil hodgepodge would be shocking to every American lawyer and to most citizens."[41]

Finally, the Court had to decide whether the fines levied upon the defendants, especially the $3.5 million on the United Mine Workers, should be deemed excessive. The Court spent a great deal of time on this issue in conference since all the members agreed that the fine exceeded any reasonable relation to the alleged crime. Some members wanted to send the matter back to the district court for adjudication, but in the end Vinson prevailed, and the Court ordered the amount reduced to $700,000, with the balance to be imposed only if the union failed to comply with the lower-court order by withdrawing its November 15 strike notice. Lewis's $10,000 fine remained intact, although some justices apparently thought this excessive as well, since the maximum fine permitted under the Smith-Connally Act would have been $5,000 (plus a possible year in prison).[42]

The reaction to the decision split between those who favored the cause of organized labor and those who wanted to restrict what they saw as unbridled power unleashed by the New Deal's Wagner Act. In terms of constitutional reasoning, Vinson's majority opinion was roundly criticized, and as Sidney Fine noted, Frankfurter's concurring opinion "demolished Vinson's blundering treatment of the Norris-LaGuardia Act."[43] Commentators at the time tended to treat the Murphy and Rutledge dissents as better reasoned and better law than the majority holdings.[44]

Those looking for some trend in the Court's labor rulings thought they had spotted one when three months later a 5–3 majority handed down its decision in *United States v. Petrillo*.[45] In 1946 Congress had passed the so-called Petrillo Act, aimed at the featherbedding practices of the American Federation of Musicians and its leader, James "Caesar" Petrillo. The measure made it illegal to compel radio stations to employ more people than were necessary to do the actual work; thus it cut down on the musicians' union's power to require stations to hire large studio orchestras.

The district court found the statute constitutionally flawed on the

---

41. 330 U.S. at 342, 364.

42. When the mines were returned to private operation on the expiration of the Smith-Connally Act in June 1947, Lewis succeeded in winning a new contract that met virtually all his demands in respect to both wages and contributions to the union welfare fund.

43. Fine, *Murphy*, 532.

44. For criticism of this decision, see Charles O. Gregory, "Government by Injunction Again," 14 *University of Chicago Law Review* 363 (1947).

45. 332 U.S. 1 (1947); Justice Douglas did not participate in this decision.

grounds that it was too vague to meet the standards of a criminal law. The Supreme Court, speaking through Justice Black, reversed the district judge's decision and remanded the case for trial. The majority did not find the statute vague; it relegated the union's questions about free speech and involuntary servitude to the trial, where the union could attempt to show that the statute had been used to achieve an unconstitutional result. Reed, joined by Murphy and Rutledge, dissented and characterized the statute as "too indefinite in its description of the prohibited acts to support an information or indictment for violation of its provisions."[46]

While many conservatives would have liked the Wagner Act repealed entirely, a majority of Americans and of the Republican Eightieth Congress believed that unions had grown too powerful and that the Wagner Act had to be modified to provide greater protection in labor disputes to management and to the public. By outlawing unfair management practices only, without any corresponding curtailment of unfair union activities, the Wagner Act, according to critics, had left labor free to act in a coercive manner. If there were to be a federal labor policy, then it should treat both labor and management in an evenhanded manner.

The first effort came in 1945 and 1946 during the initial wave of post-war strikes. In June 1945 Senators Carl A. Hatch (Democrat, New Mexico), Harold Burton (Republican, Ohio), and Joseph Ball (Republican, Minnesota) introduced a bill that would have placed all federal mediation and conciliation activities under a new federal labor relations board, established an unfair labor practices board to hear and rule on complaints by either labor or management, made the closed shop (an arrangement in which only union members could be hired) illegal except when the union had been selected by an overwhelming percentage of the plant's workers, provided for compulsory arbitration in certain circumstances, and made penalties applicable equally to unions and management.[47]

Neither the Hatch-Burton-Ball bill nor the milder measure proposed by Senator Brien McMahon (Democrat, Connecticut) received sufficient support to get out of committee, but the much tougher Case bill did. Introduced by Representative Francis Case (Republican, South Dakota), the measure would have established a federal mediation board, decreed a sixty-day cooling-off period before any strike could be called, and provided that workers who quit their jobs during the cooling-off period would lose their Wagner Act rights. The Case bill also called for banning secondary boycotts

---

46. *Ibid* at 16.
47. Arthur F. McClure, *The Truman Administration and the Problems of Postwar Labor, 1945–1948* (Rutherford: Fairleigh Dickinson University Press, 1969), 108–13.

and jurisdictional strikes and would have authorized courts to issue injunctions to prevent violence or obstructional picketing. Truman promptly vetoed the measure, and antilabor forces could not muster sufficient votes for an override.[48]

Three months later Congress passed and Truman signed the Hobbs Act, which resulted directly from a Supreme Court interpretation of the Anti-Racketeering Act of 1934. Speaking through Justice Byrnes, eight members of the Court did not deny that the teamsters had engaged in extortion of drivers coming into New York from New Jersey, but they held that the Anti-Racketeering Act had been aimed primarily at organized crime. "Congress plainly attempted to distinguish militant labor activity from [criminal activity] and to afford it ample protection." This did not mean, however, that "such activities are beyond the reach of federal legislative control."[49] The original measure, proposed by Representative Samuel Hobbs (Democrat, Alabama), had been passed twice by the House but bottled up in the Senate. Then in the reaction to the postwar labor turmoil, it had been made part of the Case bill. When Congress failed to pass that measure over Truman's veto, the original Hobbs proposal had been resurrected and enacted.

All these proposals, however, laid the foundation for the sweeping changes in the 1947 Taft-Hartley Act, which clearly sought to redress what its proponents saw as the prolabor bias in the Wagner Act. The law gave management new rights and imposed limits on various trade union practices such as the closed shop. Union officials, in order to call upon the services of the National Labor Relations Board, had to sign affidavits denying not only membership in the Communist Party but also communist beliefs. Unions, but not management, faced prohibitions against contributions to political campaigns. In addition, the Taft-Hartley law incorporated some features of earlier measures, such as an eighty-day cooling-off period. Harry Truman denounced the bill and vetoed it, but the Republican-controlled Congress easily overrode the veto.[50]

Congress, it should be noted, merely reflected a more generalized antiunion animus. Thirty states also enacted a number of laws restricting labor, including "right to work" and antipicketing measures. One might have expected that the Supreme Court, with members whose personal history and experience had been prolabor, would have been more sympathetic to

---

48. *Ibid.,* 124–34.

49. *United States v. Local 807, International Brotherhood of Teamsters,* 315 U.S. 521, 535, 536 (1942). Chief Justice Stone disagreed in a long and impassioned dissent at 539.

50. For details of Taft-Hartley, see Millis and Brown, *From the Wagner Act to Taft-Hartley,* part 3.

the unions' cause, but labor faced one setback after another in the Vinson Court.[51]

In early 1949 Justice Black spoke for a unanimous Court upholding a Nebraska constitutional amendment and a North Carolina law prohibiting closed-shop labor agreements. The CIO counsel, Arthur Goldberg, failed to persuade the justices that these provisions violated labor's freedom of contract, speech, and assembly.[52] Black tried to reassure labor that the Court was not reversing itself and going back to the days when the judiciary had been a stalwart opponent of unions; rather it intended to reaffirm basic principles of federalism. Beginning at least as early as 1934, he wrote, the Court

> has steadily rejected the due process philosophy enunciated in the *Adair-Coppage* line of cases. In doing so it has consciously returned closer and closer to the earlier constitutional principle that states have power to legislate against what are found to be injurious practices in their internal commercial and business affairs, so long as their laws do not run afoul of some specific federal constitutional prohibition, or of some valid federal law.[53]

A few months later Black again spoke for the majority and noted that picketing could not be considered as solely speech since it involved elements of coercion, restraint of trade, and other types of pressure upon the public at large. The case involved an injunction issued by a Missouri court prohibiting a union from picketing an ice company because the firm had refused to enter into an agreement the union had signed with other wholesale ice distributors not to sell to nonunion retailers. The state court ruled that the union wanted to force the company to take an action that would be criminal under the state's antitrust policy. The right to picket, Black noted, had to be balanced against other social values. Here the picketers did more than just exercise their freedom of expression; they had attempted to use economic influence to coerce the employer in a manner contrary to state policy.[54]

---

51. The only specific challenge to the Taft-Hartley Act involved its anticommunist provisions, which the Court sustained in *American Communications Association v. Douds,* 339 U.S. 382 (1950); see above, pp. 161–62.

52. *Lincoln Federal Labor Union v. Northwestern Iron & Metal Co.,* 335 U.S. 525 (1949). The case was decided along with two other cases also dealing with the closed shop, *Whitaker v. North Carolina,* 335 U.S. at 525, and *American Federation of Labor v. American Sash & Door Co.,* 335 U.S. at 538.

53. 335 U.S. at 536.

54. *Giboney v. Empire Storage and Ice Co.,* 336 U.S. 490 (1949); the case involved only the state law, but it should be noted that the Taft-Hartley Act took a much more restrictive

Black took great pains to distinguish the facts in *Giboney* from those of earlier cases and tried to reassure labor that the Court did not intend to abandon its views on protected speech. But despite his views on the absolute nature of First Amendment coverage of speech, Black always distinguished between speech and action. The First Amendment did not mean that "conduct otherwise unlawful is always immune from state regulation because an integral part of that conduct is carried on by display of placards by peaceful picketers."[55]

Ironically, during the first discussion of the case, the five most liberal members of the Court—Black, Douglas, Reed, Murphy, and Rutledge—wanted to reverse the state court on grounds that the injunction was too broad. Black said the injunction against picketing differed little from an injunction against a newspaper prohibiting it from publishing something that might violate a law; there could be no prior restraint, although the newspaper—and the picketers—could be punished under appropriate criminal measures. When Frankfurter argued that picketing here was "more than speech," Douglas said that all speech was intended to influence or perhaps even coerce people to act. As Black mulled the case over, however, he came to emphasize the conduct part more than the speech, and in the end the whole Court, including a somewhat reluctant Rutledge, went along.[56]

The early decisions of 1942 and 1943, broadly supporting picketing rights, seem to indicate that the Court followed Brandeis's suggestion in *Senn* that picketing comprised a form of speech if its purpose was to inform the public of the nature of a labor dispute. Surely a union had a right, if it wished, to take out advertisements in newspapers informing the public that a labor dispute existed between certain workers and their employers; marching around a business with signs carrying this information, then, should also deserve constitutional protection. But there is another element of picketing—coercion—and unions such as the Teamsters could shut off all deliveries to a plant by merely posting one picket at each entrance.[57] As

view of picketing as protected expression than the Court's earlier decisions. See Millis and Brown, *From the Wagner Act to Taft-Hartley,* 422–23; and the discussion on picketing and free speech, above at pp. 186–88.

55. 336 U.S. at 498.

56. Palmer, *Vinson Court Era,* 239; Fine, *Murphy,* 538–39; Tinsley E. Yarbrough, *Mr. Justice Black and His Critics* (Durham: Duke University Press, 1988), 178–81; and Roger K. Newman, *Hugo Black: A Biography* (New York: Pantheon, 1994), 369–70.

57. See Archibald Cox's influential article "Strikes, Picketing and the Constitution," 4 *Vanderbilt Law Review* 574, especially 591–97 (1951), in which he drew a distinction between "publicity" picketing (the type Brandeis had in mind in *Senn,* of which the purpose is primarily to inform the public about the details of a labor dispute) and "signal" picketing (which is intended to warn off union members from dealing with the company in any

labor had grown stronger in the 1940s, many people believed that picketing had come to have less informational value and had taken on more of a coercive nature. (Picketing, of course, always had something of a coercive nature; even when it was designed primarily to inform the public of a labor dispute, the picketers hoped to influence the public to stay away from a business. Merely having to cross a picket line exerts a coercive effect on would-be customers that is obviously intended by the protesters.)[58]

The Court's new circumspection regarding picketing appeared in several other cases,[59] and while it did not mark a return to the days before Norris-LaGuardia, it did indicate that just as labor no longer enjoyed a privileged position with Congress, so too the courts believed that time had come to strike a balance. But Black did not fully abandon the unions or their right to picket, and in a 1950 case he dissented when he thought the Court had gone too far. Frankfurter, speaking for the majority, held that a state might prohibit picketing even when the union's goal was legal.[60]

Two used-car businesses in Seattle had been picketed by the Teamsters, who wanted them to become union shops, even though in both instances the owners operated the businesses without additional employees. The union wanted to establish maximum hours for workers in the used-car industry, which included closing all stores evenings and weekends. The self-employed owners said they could not afford to stay in business on that schedule. The state courts enjoined the picketing and noted that all but 10 of the 115 used-car lots in the area were self-employers.

But unlike the statutes at issue in some of the other cases, where the unions sought objectives contrary to state policy, Washington law did not prohibit the union demands; the court merely did not approve of the union's objectives. The Court split 4–4, with Douglas not participating. Frankfurter, joined by Vinson, Jackson, and Burton, affirmed the state court ruling on the grounds that Washington could strike whatever balance it chose between competing economic interests.

As Herman Pritchett pointed out, Frankfurter managed to take Brandeis's *Senn* opinion and stand it on its head to support just the contrary

---

form). A good example of the latter would be when the Teamsters posted a single picket at every entrance to a business so that other union drivers would refuse to make deliveries to that business.

58. See the exchange on this issue between Edgar A. Jones, Jr., and Charles O. Gregory in 39 *Virginia Law Review* at 1023 and 1053 (1953).

59. See *Building Service Employees Union v. Gazzam*, 339 U.S. 532 (1950); *Hughes v. Superior Court of California*, 339 U.S. 460 (1950); and *Local Union No. 10 v. Graham*, 345 U.S. 192 (1953). See Joseph Tanenbaum, "Picketing as Free Speech: The Growth of the New Law of Picketing from 1940 to 1952," 38 *Cornell Law Quarterly* 1 (1952).

60. *International Brotherhood of Teamsters v. Hanke*, 339 U.S. 470 (1950).

opinion. In *Senn* Brandeis had held that Wisconsin could elect to allow picketing, even in unique situations, and thus put picketing on a par with newspaper advertisements. Here, Frankfurter said, "If Wisconsin could permit such picketing as a matter of policy it must have been equally free as a matter of policy to choose not to permit it and therefore not to 'put this means of publicity on a par with advertisements in the press.' "[61] But Frankfurter stopped short and managed to avoid the whole thrust of Brandeis's argument—namely, that even without state approval, members of a union had a constitutional right to make known the facts of a labor dispute. Black reaffirmed his position in the *Ritter's Cafe* case of 1942 that unions could not be enjoined from peaceful picketing in pursuit of a lawful objective.[62] Justice Minton also dissented, and he cut right to the heart of the matter: Frankfurter had distorted the meaning of Brandeis's *Senn* opinion. The earlier cases, he declared, had been "rooted in the free speech doctrine. I think we should not decide the instant cases in a manner so alien to the basis of our prior decisions."[63]

The Court's picketing decisions are far from clear, and part of the problem may be the evolving nature of First Amendment jurisprudence. It is possible that had these cases come up a decade or two later, after the Court had moved to a more protective position on speech and speech-related conduct, there might have been a more consistent pattern.[64] But by the time the Vinson Court handed down the last of its picketing decisions, a no-man's-land had been created that left the public, the unions, and the lower courts more than a little confused. On the one hand, indiscriminate bans against picketing clearly violated the Constitution. On the other, peaceful picketing could be enjoined if it constituted part of an activity that the state, speaking through either its legislature or its highest court, had declared contrary to public policy. In between one found a vast gray area in which, as Osmund Fraenkel noted, "no safe prediction can be made."[65] It would take a number of years before the Court finally sorted out some of these problems, and by then it had achieved a much more sophisticated understanding both of labor speech and of commercial speech. The fact that coercion was present did not automatically invalidate

61. *Ibid.* at 476–77.

62. *Carpenters and Joiners Union v. Ritter's Cafe,* 315 U.S. 722 (1942); the Black dissent in *Hanke* merely points to his dissent in *Ritter* at 729.

63. 339 U.S. at 481, 483 (Minton dissenting).

64. Black, however, despite his absolutist views on speech, remained firm in his insistence on treating conduct, even expressive conduct, differently; see his dissent in *Bell v. Maryland,* 378 U.S. 226, 318 (1963).

65. Osmund K. Fraenkel, "Peaceful Picketing—Constitutionally Protected?" 99 *University of Pennsylvania Law Review* 1, 11 (1950).

picketing, although certain levels of coercive picketing were forbidden by federal labor law.[66] When a conservative National Labor Relations Board attempted to restrict peaceful picketing during the Reagan era, the Court unanimously stopped it. According to Justice White, such an interpretation of the law "would make an unfair labor practice out of any kind of publicity or communication to the public urging a consumer boycott of employers. . . . newspaper, radio, and television appeals not to patronize the mall would be prohibited."[67] Such restrictions could not stand the scrutiny of the First Amendment; in many ways, the messages of *Senn* and *Thornhill* had not been abandoned.

The same pattern of inconsistency can be noted in other areas as well, such as the Court's treatment of labor in the contexts of criminal and antitrust law.

The question of labor's status under the Sherman Antitrust Act of 1890 had been a thorny issue during the Progressive era and had seemingly been resolved by the 1914 Clayton Act's exemption of labor from antitrust prohibitions. But the wording of Section 6 of the Clayton Act said little more than that labor unions would not be considered illegal per se and that the antitrust laws should not be interpreted to prevent unions from lawfully carrying out their legitimate goals. The Taft Court seized on this wording and in 1921 ruled that the Clayton Act did little more than state the obvious and had not freed unions from injunctive restraint by the courts when their actions so warranted, which meant that judges could continue to enjoin picketing and boycotts under the guise that these activities violated the antitrust laws.[68]

The Norris-LaGuardia Act of 1932 effectively stopped federal courts from interfering in nonviolent labor disputes, and a number of states adopted similar statutes applying to their courts. But the question of whether or not particular union activities could come under antitrust proscriptions remained unanswered. The courts had little occasion to deal with the matter during the 1930s, since several New Deal measures

---

66. See *N.L.R.B. v. Fruit and Vegetable Packers, Local 760*, 377 U.S. 58 (1964), and *N.L.R.B. v. Retail Store Employees Local 1001*, 447 U.S. 607 (1980). For two broad, and quite different, overviews of the development of picketing as speech doctrine, see Mark D. Schneider, "Note: Peaceful Labor Picketing and the First Amendment," 82 *Columbia Law Review* 1469 (1982); and "Note: Labor Picketing and Commercial Speech: Free Enterprise Values in the Doctrine of Free Speech," 91 *Yale Law Journal* 938 (1982), especially 940–44.

67. *DeBartolo Corp. v. Florida Gulf Coast Building and Construction Trades Council*, 485 U.S. 568, 583 (1988).

68. See, among other cases, *Duplex Printing Press Co. v. Deering*, 254 U.S. 443 (1921); *Coronado Coal Co. v. United Mine Workers*, 268 U.S. 295 (1925); and *Bedford Cut Stone Co. v. Journeymen Stone Cutters' Association*, 274 U.S. 37 (1927).

seemed—at least temporarily—to put the Sherman and Clayton Acts in abeyance.

The Roosevelt appointees had heard their first antitrust labor case in 1940. Employees had seized a nonunion hosiery plant in Philadelphia in a sit-down strike and then locked the doors, barring managers and all non-union workers. In addition, they had broken windows and machinery and had refused to turn over more than 1.5 million pairs of stockings for ship-ment around the country. The company sued the union for triple damages under the Sherman Act, but a majority of the Court, speaking through Justice Stone, held that while the particular acts may have been illegal under state law, they did not comprise the type of interference with inter-state commerce envisioned under the Sherman law.[69]

Although Stone had a 6–3 majority, he tried to distinguish the ruling from earlier antitrust cases involving labor rather than simply overruling them. He did, in fact, present a strong argument that the courts, instead of using the earlier vague test of intent to obstruct interstate commerce, should use an easier and more clearly defined test of intent to monopolize supply, control prices, or discriminate among consumers in a manner that repressed competition. While this fit with Stone's well-known penchant against overruling precedent, it did not grapple with the economic realities of the case; and as Herman Pritchett suggests, it would have been better for the Court had it come out and said that "elimination of competition between union and nonunion made goods was a normal and lawful objec-tive of nationally organized labor unions, and not subject to the prohibi-tions of the Sherman Act."[70]

Felix Frankfurter tried to clear up some of the confusion later that year in a case the Justice Department had brought against the carpenters' union, growing out of a jurisdictional dispute between the carpenters and machinists over who would control certain jobs in a St. Louis brewery. The company decided in favor of the machinists, and the carpenters went on strike, picketed the plant, and organized a boycott of the company's beer. Thurman Arnold, the head of the Justice Department's Antitrust Division, filed a complaint against the head of the carpenters' union under the Sher-man Act.

The same 6–3 majority held that there had been no violation, but Frankfurter, instead of trying to distinguish prior decisions, ignored them on the ground that the Norris-LaGuardia Act had restored the Clayton Act's labor provisions to their full coverage. Whether a union violates fed-eral antitrust policy, he wrote, "is to be determined only by reading the

69. *Apex Hosiery Co. v. Leader,* 310 U.S. 469 (1940).

70. Pritchett, *Roosevelt Court,* 212.

Sherman Law and section 20 of the Clayton Act and the Norris-LaGuardia Act as a harmonizing text of outlawry of labor conduct."[71] Frankfurter then expanded upon Stone's rule in *Apex Hosiery* by holding that union activities would be acceptable providing that labor did not combine with nonlabor groups to achieve its ends. This seemed a clear test, for Frankfurter probably did not envision a situation in which this would occur.

But it did, and as unions flexed their muscles following World War II, the Court heard a variety of cases in which union activities went beyond traditional labor practices and affected commerce in ways that clearly impinged on antitrust policy.

In 1945 the Court heard a case in which an electrical workers' union had entered into closed-shop agreements with both manufacturers and distributors of electrical equipment in the New York city area, and the terms of the agreement made it impossible for new competitors to enter the market. This combination of labor and nonlabor groups clearly violated the one proscription Frankfurter had handed down, and, in *Allen Bradley Co. v. Local Union No. 3*, an 8–1 Court held the union to have violated the antitrust laws.[72] While only Frank Murphy dissented, Justice Roberts in concurrence pointed out that nothing prohibited the union from achieving the same end if it acted on its own, so that there would still be a suppression of competition, but under the *Hutcheson* rule it would be immune from prosecution.[73]

Two years later the Court heard *United Brotherhood of Carpenters and Joiners v. United States*,[74] an appeal of a criminal prosecution of both employers and unions for conspiring to monopolize parts of the finished lumber business in the San Francisco Bay area, using methods similar to those in the New York case. Under the earlier ruling the Sherman Act clearly covered such practices, but the unions claimed that Section 6 of the Norris-LaGuardia Act protected their officers. That section exempted unions from being held liable for the acts of individual officers without clear proof that the unions had ratified such actions. The provision had been drafted to cover the situation of the old *Danbury Hatters* decision, in which the unions had been held liable for triple damages for the actions of their leaders.[75]

---

71. *United States v. Hutcheson*, 312 U.S. 219, 231 (1941). See Frankfurter to Stone, January 21, 1941, Frankfurter Papers, Harvard Law School Library. Although the Justice Department's Antitrust Division had initiated the suit, by the time the Court handed down its decision, a new attorney general, Robert Jackson, apparently believed the case should never have been brought. Frankfurter noted that on the day the Court handed down its decision, Jackson called him at home and said that "it isn't often that the losing client phones to the author of the adverse opinion to thank him for it." *Ibid.*

72. *Allen Bradley Co. v. Local Union No. 3*, 325 U.S. 797 (1945).

73. *Ibid.* at 813, 814–15; the Murphy dissent is at 820.

74. 330 U.S. 395 (1947).

75. *Loewe v. Lawler*, 208 U.S. 274 (1908).

There was no doubt that the unions had engaged in anticompetitive and perhaps even criminal activity; the chief justice, at the conference, declared that this was not a labor dispute at all, since the union had acted not to help workers but to help employers in their "piratical activities."[76] But a 5–3 majority, speaking through Justice Reed, interpreted Section 6 to mean that liability applied only to those unions or their officers who actually participated in unlawful acts, unless it could be proven that the acts had been approved after knowledge of their occurrence became available. Since the jury had not been instructed on the meaning of this form of limited liability, the Court reversed all of the convictions for both employers and unions.

Frankfurter, joined by Vinson and Burton, dissented in a biting attack in which he charged that the Court had totally misinterpreted the congressional intent behind Section 6. Given the legislative history of Norris-LaGuardia and Frankfurter's role in its drafting, his point is well taken: the law was meant to do no more than prevent courts from misusing the antitrust laws to punish unions for the actions of particular members who did not have the authority to represent the union. By its new interpretation, Frankfurter charged, the Court had made it impossible to hold unions responsible for clearly illegal activities. "Practically speaking," he claimed, the decision "serves to immunize unions, especially the more alert and powerful, as well as corporations involved in labor disputes, from Sherman Law liability."[77]

The Court seemed reluctant to apply the Sherman Act to unions except in cases of grossly illegal activity, and some of the decisions make little or no sense. On the same day it handed down its decision in *Allan Bradley*, the Court ruled in *Hunt v. Crumboch*.[78] In 1937, during an organizing strike, a member of the teamsters' union had been killed, and the man accused of the murder, a partner in a trucking firm, had been tried and acquitted. The union eventually won its strike and secured a closed shop, and the company sought union membership for its employees. The union, however, would not deal with the firm because it blamed the owners for the death of the organizer, despite the fact that a jury had acquitted the man accused of the crime. As a result of being shut out of the agreement, the firm lost its interstate contracts and went out of business; it then sued the teamsters under the Sherman Act.

---

76. Douglas, Conference notes, March 10, 1941, Douglas Papers, Library of Congress.

77. 330 U.S. at 413, 422. See also Frankfurter to Vinson, December 10, 1946, Frankfurter Papers, Harvard Law School Library; and Douglas, Conference notes, May 4, 1946, Douglas Papers, Library of Congress. The case, originally argued in the spring of 1946, was held over and reargued that fall.

78. 325 U.S. 821 (1945).

By a 5–4 vote the majority held that there had been no violation of the antitrust law because nothing more had occurred than that laborers in lawful combination had refused to sell their services. Roberts and Jackson wrote stinging dissents, joined by Stone and Frankfurter. One wonders if Frankfurter failed to write because he realized that the majority decision, illogical as it sounded, was in fact a direct consequence of his *Hutcheson* rule; perhaps that is why his friend Justice Jackson tactfully refrained from mentioning that opinion.[79]

But Jackson's opinion did carry the following paragraph, which in some ways can stand for the entire effort of the Court during these years to work out a consistent policy toward labor. With this decision, Jackson wrote,

> the labor movement has come full circle. The working man has struggled long, the fight has been filled with hatred, and conflict has been dangerous, but now workers may not be deprived of their livelihood merely because their employers oppose and they favor unions. Labor has won other rights as well, unemployment compensation, old-age benefits and, what is most important and the basis of all gains, the recognition that the opportunity to earn his support is not alone the concern of the individual but is the problem which all organized societies must contend with and conquer if they are to survive. This Court now sustains the claim of a union to the right to deny participation in the economic world to an employer simply because the union dislikes him. This Court permits to employees the same arbitrary dominance over the economic sphere which they control that labor so long, so bitterly and so rightly asserted should belong to no man.[80]

It is this sense that labor had grown too powerful, a development that the Court had in no small way facilitated, that played such an important role in the passage of the Taft-Hartley Act two years later.

The only other case involving labor that the Vinson Court decided had relatively little to do with the rights of labor and a great deal to do with the distribution of powers in the federal government to deal with problems raised by labor disputes.

Throughout the late 1940s there had been a constant fear that the Cold War might erupt into a shooting war, and in June 1950 that fear turned into reality. After the Allies had liberated Korea from Japanese oc-

---

79. Roberts dissented at *ibid.* at 826, and Jackson at 828.
80. *Ibid.* at 830–31.

cupation at the end of World War II, they had "temporarily" divided the country along the 38th parallel: communist North Korea came under the influence of China, while South Korea aligned itself with the United States. In 1950 North Korean troops invaded the south, which immediately appealed to the United Nations for help. Because the Soviet Union had temporarily walked out of the international body, its representative was not present to veto a Security Council resolution that branded North Korea an aggressor, called for the withdrawal of its forces, and asked United Nations members to render assistance. On June 27, President Truman ordered American troops into the fight in Korea. Termed a "police action," the conflict cost 33,000 American lives, 104,000 Americans wounded or missing, and billions of dollars, yet it never constituted a war in the legal sense because Congress never passed a declaration of war. By enacting empowering legislation as well as appropriating funds to support military operations, however, Congress in fact approved presidential policy, much as it would a decade and a half later in Vietnam.

In the spring of 1952, the United Steel Workers threatened to strike after the Wage Stabilization Board failed to negotiate a settlement between the union and the mill owners. Harry Truman believed that with American troops fighting in Asia, whether it was a "war" or a "police action," he had the same broad authority to mobilize the country that Roosevelt had used between 1941 and 1945. In early April 1952, Truman issued Executive Order 10340 directing Secretary of Commerce Charles Sawyer to seize and operate the nation's steel mills to assure continued production of steel for defense needs.[81]

Although the president had no statutory authority for this action, he did have another option, one with express legislative approval, that he could have used to forestall the strike. The Taft-Hartley Act of 1946 included procedures by which the government could secure an eighty-day cooling-off period to postpone any strike that might adversely affect the public interest. Truman had vetoed the measure, only to have the Republican Congress override his veto. Taft-Hartley would not have provided a permanent solution, but at the least it enjoyed statutory legitimacy and might have bought time in which a settlement could be negotiated. Truman, however, did not want to use a law that he had condemned and vetoed. Instead, he simply seized the steel mills, informed an astounded

---

81. For the steel strike, see Maeva Marcus, *Truman and the Steel Seizure Case: The Limits of Presidential Power* (New York: Columbia University Press, 1977). For an "inside" view of the steel case in the Supreme Court, see William H. Rehnquist, *The Supreme Court: How It Was, How It Is* (New York: William Morrow, 1987), chaps. 2 and 3. Rehnquist served as a law clerk to Justice Jackson during the term in which the Court heard the case.

Congress of what he had done, and invited them to take legislative action
if they thought it necessary.

The steel operators immediately appealed the action, but few contemporary commentators gave them much chance at success. After all, both
the lower benches as well as the Supreme Court were staffed by judges
appointed by either Roosevelt or Truman, men (and a handful of women)
who believed that the government had few limits in terms of its powers to
regulate private property.

Moreover, the companies framed their argument in a way that allowed
the courts an easy way to avoid deciding the case on its merits. The steel
operators conceded that an emergency existed and that in an emergency
the government had the right and the power to take over their businesses.
They objected *that the wrong branch of government had proceeded against them.*
In essence, they complained that the executive had unconstitutionally in-
fringed upon the powers of the legislative branch. Rarely does a private
party sue on behalf of a branch of government, and the courts could have
dismissed the suit for lack of standing.

Nonetheless, the steel companies secured an injunction against the
seizure in federal district court, at least in part because of the Justice Department's poor handling of the case.[82] Judge David A. Pine ruled that the
government lacked any authority to seize the mills, in either statutory or
constitutional form.[83] The government immediately went to the Court of
Appeals seeking a stay of the restraining order, and in an unusual step the
entire nine-member court heard arguments by the government and the
steel companies. By a bare 5–4 vote on May 2, the appeals court granted a
forty-eight-hour stay so that both sides could seek certiorari from the Supreme Court.[84]

Although the rules of the Supreme Court allow a direct appeal for
certiorari from a district court ruling, in practice the Court prefers not to
hear a case until it has traversed the full gamut of lower court hearings and
a so-called final decision has been handed down. In unusual cases, however, the Court will accept a case when the issues are "of such imperative
public importance as to justify the deviation from normal appellate processes as to require immediate settlement in this Court." At its regular Saturday conference on May 3, 1952, less than a month after Truman had
ordered the seizure, the Court granted certiorari by a vote of 6–2; only
Frankfurter and Burton voted against hearing the case, and Jackson
passed.[85]

---

82. Marcus, *Steel Seizure Case,* 120–23.

83. *Youngstown Sheet & Tube Co. et al. v. Sawyer,* 103 F.Supp. 569 (D.C. 1952).

84. 197 F.2d 582 (D.C. Cir. 1952).

85. Palmer, *Vinson Court Era,* 347; other sources give the vote as 7–2, counting Jackson as
voting for the granting of certiorari.

Truman might well have been forgiven if he assumed the government would triumph in the high court. He had based his decision to seize the mills in part upon a memorandum prepared at an earlier time by Tom Clark, then attorney general, which spoke expansively about the "inherent" powers of the presidency.[86] Moreover, according to Robert J. Donovan, Truman had met with Chief Justice Fred Vinson before issuing his executive order, and Vinson had "privately advised the president to go ahead with the seizure, basing the recommendation on legal grounds."[87] With four members of the Court his own appointees, Truman might well have assumed that a majority would bless his expansive use of presidential authority as Roosevelt's appointees had blessed their appointer's.

On Monday, May 12, the Court heard oral argument and at conference on Friday, May 16, spent an unusual four hours debating the case. Harold Burton thought initially that he might be the only one to vote against the president, but by the end of the discussion he could note that the justices had discussed the steel case "with a most encouraging result."[88]

According to Justice Douglas's extensive conference notes, a clear majority emerged fairly quickly on the view that the president had overstepped his authority, but no consensus developed as to what limits actually existed on presidential authority. Only Chief Justice Vinson, who had earlier told Truman that he had the necessary power, joined by Stanley Reed and Sherman Minton, supported the government's seizure of the steel mills.[89] Felix Frankfurter suggested that everyone ought to write in this case, and for once the brethren took his advice; every member of the majority issued a separate opinion, while the minority all joined in the chief justice's dissent.

The Court handed down its decision in *Youngstown Sheet & Tube Co. v. Sawyer* on June 2, 1952,[90] barely a month after it had voted to grant certiorari and three weeks after it had heard oral argument. Four members of the majority agreed that Congress had prohibited the seizure. The legislative history of the Taft-Hartley Act showed that Congress had rejected a proposed amendment that would have authorized seizure of plants in na-

86. Howard Ball and Phillip J. Cooper, *Of Power and Right: Hugo Black, William O. Douglas, and America's Constitutional Revolution* (New York: Oxford University Press, 1992), 131.

87. Robert J. Donovan, *The Tumultuous Years* (New York: Norton, 1982), 386. See also David McCullough, *Truman* (New York: Simon & Schuster, 1992), 897; McCullough reports that the chief justice was a regular visitor at the White House, and "out of friendship and loyalty" Vinson had offered advice on a subject that he must have known would wind up facing a challenge in court.

88. Burton Diary, diary entry for May 16, 1952, Burton Papers, Library of Congress.

89. Conference notes, May 16, 1952, Douglas Papers, Library of Congress.

90. 343 U.S. 579 (1952).

tional emergencies in favor of a provision to enjoin strikes. According to
Justice Frankfurter, "the authoritatively expressed purpose of Congress to
disallow such power to the President could not be more decisive if it had
been written into . . . the Labor Management Relations Act."[91]

Justice Black, as the ranking senior member of the majority, had assigned himself the opinion for the Court and took a broader approach. In
this view, neither statute nor constitutional provision gave the president
power to act as he had done; the constitutional provisions of the commander in chief, which had always been used by executives to justify wartime acts, did not extend this far. While Black's strict constructionist
interpretation of the Constitution led to an expansion of the protections
guaranteed in the Bill of Rights, here it led to a narrow view of presidential
power. In essence, Black took a Jeffersonian position: if neither the Constitution nor an act of Congress specifically gave the chief executive the
power, then the president did not have the power. The "President's power,
if any," Black asserted, "must stem either from an act of Congress or from
the Constitution itself."[92] Power to authorize seizure of the mills did exist,
but in the legislative branch, and when the president acted on his own
authority in this manner he encroached on congressional responsibility
and violated the separation of powers. Douglas, who joined Black's opinion, also developed the separation of powers argument. The seizure of the
mills constituted a taking of private property for which the owners had to
be compensated. Only Congress could authorize such expenditures, and a
seizure not authorized by statute would go against the express constitutional requirement of congressional appropriation of funds to compensate
the taking.[93]

If in Black's view the president could do only what statute or Constitution authorized, Chief Justice Vinson in dissent took the exact opposite
stance: that the president could, in response to a national emergency, do
everything except what had been specifically prohibited. Taking an expansive reading of Article II, Vinson read broad authority into the Constitution's delegation of the "executive power," which he interpreted to go far
beyond the few examples the framers had enumerated.[94] Truman himself,

---

91. *Ibid.* at 602 (Frankfurter concurring). Justice Jackson also noted that Congress had
made clear its intentions not to give the president extensive power; *ibid.* at 634, 639 (Jackson concurring).

92. *Ibid.* at 585; see discussion of Black's position in Yarbrough, *Black and His Critics,*
39–42.

93. 343 U.S. at 631 (Douglas concurring). For an analysis of the Douglas opinion, see
Michael J. Glennon, "Douglas the Internationalist: Separation of Powers and the Conduct
of Foreign Relations," in Wasby, ed., *"He Shall Not Pass This Way Again,"* 267–69.

94. 343 U.S. at 681 (Vinson dissenting).

writing a few years later, took a similar position in justifying his actions. "The President must always act in a national emergency. A wise President will always work with Congress, but when Congress fails to act or is unable to act in a crisis, the President, under the Constitution, must use his power to safeguard the nation."[95]

For Jackson, the issue was not whether specific statutory authority or implied constitutional powers existed to justify the seizure; in this case Congress had specifically said that it did not want to delegate such a power to the president. While this had not been spelled out in the Taft-Hartley Act and other laws, the legislative history clearly showed congressional intent. By consciously omitting giving the president this power, Congress intended that he should not have it.

Presidential authority, Jackson held, stood at its height when the chief executive acted at the direct or implied command of Congress, and in such situations the president relied on his own powers as well as those given to him by the legislature. In circumstances in which Congress had not acted, the president might act relying on his own powers, but here a twilight zone existed in which it would not be clear who had the ultimate responsibility. Presidential authority was weakest, Jackson said, when the executive acted in defiance of either express or implied legislative intent, and in such circumstances the Court could uphold the president only by ruling that Congress lacked power to legislate on the subject. In this instance, Congress did have the power, and it had spoken quite clearly as to its intent.[96]

Frankfurter set out another position, one that rightly caught the practice of government as well as its theory. In many instances, he noted, Congress has been silent but has acquiesced in presidential actions. If there has been a tradition of the legislature's going along with a particular policy, then such acceptance adds a "historical gloss" on the Constitution, and the Court had often relied in the past on the understanding of the other two branches to evaluate the constitutionality of specific actions. But there had been only three somewhat similar presidential seizures prior to 1952, a number insufficient to provide the "gloss."[97]

---

95. Harry S. Truman, *Memoirs*, 2 vols. (Garden City, N.Y.: Doubleday, 1955–56), 2:478. After the decision, as a peace gesture, Hugo Black invited the president and the justices to a party at his home in Alexandria. At the start, Truman was polite but seemed "a bit testy," according to William O. Douglas; "but after the bourbon and canapes were passed, he turned to Hugo and said, 'Hugo, I don't much care for your law, but, by golly, this bourbon is good.' " McCullough, *Truman*, 901.

96. 343 U.S. at 637 (Jackson concurring). Louis Jaffe described Jackson's concurrence as "a most brilliant exposition of 'undefined presidential powers' and their relation to legislation. "Mr. Justice Jackson," 68 *Harvard Law Review* 940, 989 (1955). For a differing view, see Sylvester Petro, "The Supreme Court and the Steel Seizure," 3 *Labor Law Journal* 451, 494 (1952).

97. 343 U.S. at 610 (Frankfurter concurring).

The story of labor in the Supreme Court in the Stone and Vinson era is one that reflected general attitudes and in fact had little to do with constitutional matters. The men who sat on the bench had all come out of the New Deal milieu, which had accepted as a given that something had to be done to redress the imbalance of power between labor and management. The Wagner Act gained immediate acceptance by the Court, and for a while it appeared that the justices would expand the notion of protected speech to include picketing as well.

But the justices, like Franklin Roosevelt, may have had more of a patronizing attitude toward organized labor than a real commitment to its goals. After the war, no one emerged on the Court as a champion of the rights of labor, not even Douglas or Black, and the judiciary, like Congress and to a lesser extent the executive, seemed to feel that the balance of power had now swung too far in the other direction. From a constitutional point of view, neither the Stone nor the Vinson Court left positive markers regarding the rights or limitations of labor unions.

# 8

# INCORPORATION AND DUE PROCESS

The Vinson Court's handling of what was rapidly becoming the prime focus of its postwar agenda, a concern for individual liberties that replaced the older concern for property rights, is indicative of the changes that mark the passing of the so-called Old Court and the emergence of modern jurisprudential issues. The basic idea of a stricter judicial scrutiny of state action affecting protected rights had been set forth in Stone's *Carolene Products* footnote, and the notion of incorporation—the application of the Bill of Rights to the states through the Fourteenth Amendment—had been adumbrated in Cardozo's *Palko* opinion. During the Stone years there had been a number of cases that had begun the exploration of these issues, but that process had of necessity taken a back seat to matters directly related to the war. With the advent of peace, the Court faced one case after another challenging older notions of how far the Constitution protected individual liberties. The Court not only had to decide specific cases; it also had to come up with a jurisprudential rationale for its decisions. In this debate the chief justice did not play a significant role. It is not that Fred Vinson was a cipher, because in some cases, especially those discussed in chapter 6, he had strong views. But unlike Stone, who exercised influence primarily through his well-developed jurisprudential views, and Earl Warren, who led the Court by his extraordinary political skill, Vinson had neither strong intellectual influence nor political influence over his colleagues. In the debates that took place from 1946 to 1953, the important views are those of Hugo Black and Felix Frankfurter.

Frankfurter and Black, as noted earlier,[1] had for several years carried on a debate on the meaning of the Fourteenth Amendment's Due Process Clause. Both men started from the same place—their opposition to the use of substantive due process by earlier courts to strike down reform legislation. For Frankfurter, the answer to this abuse of power lay in judicial restraint and appropriate deference to the policy decisions of the political branches. But the Due Process Clause obviously meant something, and as interpreters of the Constitution, judges had to define what this something was.

---

1. See above, pp. 36–39.

Black had just gone onto the Court when the *Palko* decision came down, and at first he subscribed to it. But he grew increasingly uncomfortable with the philosophy and method of selective incorporation and the great power it lodged in the courts. Over the next decade he thought about this problem endlessly and finally reached his solution in 1946.

By then Black identified the heart of his differences with Frankfurter as centering on the great discretion the Frankfurter-Cardozo approach vested in the Court. If judges could strike down state laws that failed to meet "civilized standards," then the courts had reverted to a "natural law concept whereby the supreme constitutional law becomes this Court's view of 'civilization' at a given moment." This philosophy, he declared, made everything else in the Constitution "mere surplusage" and allowed the Court to reject all of the provisions of the Bill of Rights and substitute its own idea for what legislatures could or could not do.[2] Black, however, still had difficulty articulating the standards he would apply.

The answer for Black came in a California murder case. Admiral Dewey Adamson (his real name) was a poor, illiterate black who had twice served time for robbery. He had, however, been out of prison for seventeen years when police arrested him for the murder of an elderly white widow. The only evidence linking Adamson to the crime consisted of six fingerprints on a door leading to the garbage container in the woman's kitchen, which police identified as his. On the advice of his attorney, a veteran of the Los Angeles criminal courts, Adamson did not take the stand in his own defense. Had he done so, the prosecutor could have brought up Adamson's previous record, and that would have resulted in a sure conviction. But the prosecutor, as he was allowed to do under California law, pointed out to the jury Adamson's failure to testify and claimed that this surely proved his guilt. If he had been innocent, the prosecutor declared, it would have taken fifty horses to keep him off the stand. The jury convicted Adamson, and his lawyer on appeal challenged the California statute as violating the Fourteenth Amendment. Allowing comment on the failure to testify was equivalent to forcing a defendant to take the stand, he contended; both violated due process.[3]

In conference Frankfurter convinced a majority of his colleagues that the issue had already been decided, and correctly. In *Twining v. New Jersey* (1908) the Court had ruled that a state law permitting comment on a defendant's refusal to testify did not violate procedural fairness.[4] Justice Reed,

---

2. Black to Conference, March 23, 1945, Frankfurter Papers, Harvard University Law School.

3. *Adamson v. California*, 332 U.S. 46 (1947).

4. 211 U.S. 78 (1908).

assigned the opinion, conceded that such behavior by the prosecutor in a federal proceeding would be unacceptable and a violation of the Fifth Amendment. But it was "settled law" that the self-incrimination law did not apply to the states; it was not "a right of national citizenship, or . . . a personal privilege or immunity secured by the Federal Constitution as one of the rights of man that are listed in the Bill of Rights." In short, it was not one of the fundamental principles inherent in "the concept of ordered liberty" test of *Palko*. "For a state to require testimony from an accused," Reed concluded, "is not necessarily a breach of a state's obligation to give a fair trial."[5]

Black dissented and set forth his belief in the "total incorporation" of the first eight amendments by the Fourteenth. He would consider it the most important opinion of his career. "There I laid it all out. . . . I didn't write until I came to the complete conclusion that I was reasonably sure of myself and my research. It was my work from beginning to end."[6] Just as the Bill of Rights applied objective standards to the behavior of the federal government, so the application of the first eight amendments to the states would provide equally ascertainable criteria by which to judge state action. In a lengthy appendix he presented the historical evidence he had assembled to support this position, an essay that most scholars find less than convincing. As might be expected from a former senator, Black relied entirely on the congressional history of the Fourteenth Amendment, the account of what Congress did in drafting it. But amending the Constitution requires ratification by the states, and Black neglected to look at the debates there; nor did he look at the abolitionist antecedents of the amendment. As Roger Newman notes, "Black's was an advocate's history: he proved too much and ignored or swept away all doubtful evidence."[7]

What is most interesting in Black's rationale is that in many ways it

---

5. 332 U.S. at 50–51, 54.

6. Roger K. Newman, *Hugo Black: A Biography* (New York: Pantheon, 1994), 352.

7. *Ibid.*, 354. Black's essay in history started a minicontroversy of its own. Charles Fairman attacked Black's interpretation in "Does the Fourteenth Amendment Incorporate the Bill of Rights? The Original Understanding," 2 *Stanford Law Review* 5 (1949), which in turn triggered a response from William W. Crosskey in his *Politics and the Constitution in the History of the United States* (Chicago: University of Chicago Press, 1953). Black also responded to Fairman more than twenty years later in his concurrence in *Duncan v. Louisiana*, 391 U.S. 145, 162 (1968). (The interrelationships between the two justices and the two scholars is explored in Richard L. Aynes, "Charles Fairman, Felix Frankfurter, and the Fourteenth Amendment," 70 *Chicago-Kent Law Review* 1197 (1995). A number of historians have found the evidence far from conclusive on either side; for two recent expositions, see Michael Kent Curtis, *No State Shall Abridge: The Fourteenth Amendment and the Bill of Rights* (Durham: Duke University Press, 1986); and William E. Nelson, *The Fourteenth Amendment: From Political Principle to Judicial Doctrine* (Cambridge: Harvard University Press, 1988).

resembled Frankfurter's own views on limiting judicial power. Black rejected Cardozo's criteria as too vague since phrases like "civilized decency" and "fundamental liberty and justice" could be interpreted by judges to mean many things. This "natural law" theory of the Constitution "degrade[s] the constitutional safeguards of the Bill of Rights and simultaneously appropriate[s] for this Court a broad power which we are not authorized by the Constitution to exercise." The only way to avoid this abuse of judicial power would be to carry out the original intent of the framers of the Fourteenth Amendment and apply all the protections of the Bill of Rights to the states.[8]

Douglas joined Black's opinion, but Murphy filed a separate dissent, in which he attempted to combine elements of both the Frankfurter and Black approaches. He had found Black's essay "exciting reading," but, he said, "I think you go out of your way—as you always do—to strike down natural law." Murphy wanted to incorporate all of the Bill of Rights, as Black proposed, but he objected to what he saw as the rigidity in Black's approach. There were times when one had to be flexible, when a strict reading of the first eight amendments would not suffice to provide justice. In those instances Frankfurter's use of due process would allow judges to secure justice. Murphy's reading of Black's opinion was not that wrong. Although Black would later adopt some of Frankfurter's views regarding due process as fundamental fairness, at the time of the *Adamson* case he told a group of clerks with whom he was having lunch that the Due Process Clauses of the Fifth and Fourteenth Amendments had "*no* meaning, except that of emphasis."[9]

Black had his clerk, Louis Oberdorfer, deliver the first draft to Frankfurter, who on reading it flung it on his desk and declared, "At Yale they call this scholarship?" Oberdorfer, a recent Yale Law School graduate, picked up the pages and excused himself. To his own clerk, Frankfurter fumed that "Hugo is trying to change the world and misreading history in the attempt, just making things up out of whole cloth."[10] Frankfurter, who had originally written a brief concurrence, now set to work to respond to Black, and the results must surely rank as one of his most forceful and important opinions. In probably no other statement, either for the Court or in dissent, do we get such a clear exposition of Frankfurter's philosophy of judging, one which scholars have termed "process jurisprudence." Relying on his own historical research, Frankfurter denied that the framers of

8. 332 U.S. at 68, 70.

9. Sidney Fine, *Frank Murphy: The Washington Years* (Ann Arbor: University of Michigan Press, 1984), 503–4; the Murphy dissent is at 332 U.S. at 123.

10. Newman, *Black*, 354.

the Fourteenth Amendment had intended to subsume all of the Bill of Rights. He also responded to what he took as the most serious of Black's charges, that the vague criteria of *Palko* left judges too much discretion, and protection of rights relied on the mercy of individual subjectivity. The real issue, he declared,

> is not whether an infraction of one of the specific provisions of the first eight Amendments is disclosed by the record. The relevant question is whether the criminal proceedings which resulted in conviction deprived the accused of the due process of law. Judicial review of that guaranty of the Fourteenth Amendment inescapably imposes upon this Court an exercise of judgment upon the whole course of the proceedings in order to ascertain whether they offend those canons of decency and fairness which express the notions of justice of English-speaking peoples even toward those charged with the most heinous offenses. These standards of justice are not authoritatively formulated anywhere as though they were prescriptions in a pharmacopoeia. But neither does the application of the Due Process Clause imply that judges are wholly at large. The judicial judgment in applying the Due Process Clause must move within the limits of accepted notions of justice and is not to be based upon the idiosyncrasies of a merely personal judgment. The fact that judges among themselves may differ whether in a particular case a trial offends accepted notions of justice is not disproof that general rather than idiosyncratic standards are applied. An important safeguard against such merely individual judgment is an alert deference to the judgment of the State court under review.[11]

Frankfurter portrayed judging as a process removed from the fray of daily pressures. Protected in their sanctum, justices may engage in that process of discovery that will yield *the* right answer—not an objective, eternally fixed answer, but the right answer for the time. Frankfurter did not espouse a moral relativism but believed that judges in their decisions should reflect the advances that society has made, so that the Due Process Clause does not mean fairness in terms of 1868 but fairness today. Courts thus help keep the Constitution contemporary, but they must do so cautiously, always following strict intellectual processes and always deferring to those who are in the thick of the battle—the state courts and legislatures—who must in turn be left free to reform their procedures according to their standards of fairness. As Frankfurter noted in another case, "due process of law requires an evaluation based on a disinterested inquiry pursued in the spirit

---

11. 332 U.S. at 67–68.

of science, on a balanced order of facts exactly and fairly stated, on the detached consideration of conflicting claims, on a judgment not ad hoc and episodic but duly mindful of reconciling the needs both of continuity and change in a progressive society."[12] Thus if the judge adheres to certain methods and standards, it does not matter what the result will be in a particular case, because the process will assure ultimate fairness across the spectrum of cases. "Whatever shortcut to relief may be had in a particular case," Frankfurter wrote a year after *Adamson*, "it is calculated to beget misunderstanding and friction and to that extent detracts from those imponderables which are the ultimate reliance of a civilized system of law."[13] The *process*, not a particular *result*, is the desideratum of judging.

The great appeal of process jurisprudence is that it attempts to remove idiosyncracy and individuality from judicial decision making and replace them with objectivity and consistency. Public faith in the judicial process is enhanced if the public believes the judges are acting fairly and adhering to a common set of methods and principles in all cases, regardless of the results in specific instances.

Yet can judging ever be quite this impersonal? Would scientific analysis really produce the right results? Oliver Wendell Holmes had declared that the prejudices of judges had as much if not more to do with determining the law than the logic of the syllogism.[14] As Black asked, how did one objectively determine the "canons of decency and fairness" that everyone accepted? Moreover, while one might say that due process is meaningful over a whole gamut of cases, individuals are on trial; individuals must cope with the criminal justice system; individuals must pay the penalties if found guilty; individuals suffer if deprived of their rights.

For Black, total incorporation provided at least a partial answer in that judges would no longer subjectively determine what rights met the "canons of decency and fairness." There were still questions to answer. Even if one applied the Fourth Amendment to the states, one still had to determine what constituted an "unreasonable search." But the basic rights, the ones enshrined in the Constitution, would be in force and not dependent on whether a handful of judges determined that they met the canon.

Neither approach is without merit, and neither is without flaw. If Frankfurter's method refused to face up to the fact that process jurisprudence involved subjective evaluation, it did have the virtue of recognizing an acceptable diversity in a federal system and acknowledging that one could have more than one model of a fair and workable system. Its open-

---

12. *Rochin v. California*, 342 U.S. 165, 172 (1952).
13. *Uveges v. Pennsylvania*, 335 U.S. 437, 449–50 (1948).
14. Oliver Wendell Holmes, *The Common Law* (Boston: Little, Brown, 1881), 5.

ended approach to fairness also permitted judges, always exercising caution, to help keep basic constitutional guarantees current with the times.

Black's approach did do away with some but not all subjectivity, and
debates over the reach of the exclusionary rule and expectations of privacy
show that interpreting the "canons of decency and fairness" is an ongoing
judicial function. Moreover, in many ways Black's rigid adherence to the
text led to a cramped view of individual liberty. He would take an uncompromising stand that the First Amendment permitted no abridgement of
speech, but since he could find no mention of privacy in the Constitution,
he could not support the judicial claim that such a right existed.[15]

In the end Frank Murphy's approach, almost ignored in the battle between Black and Frankfurter, prevailed, and it came into effect in the landmark 1965 case of *Griswold v. Connecticut*, which established a right to
privacy that eventually came to be embedded in due process. Although the
Court adopted the Cardozo-Frankfurter approach of selective incorporation, during the Warren years nearly all of the first eight amendment guarantees were applied to the states. But Black's approach proved too rigid, as
Murphy had argued, and Frankfurter's notion of due process as fundamental fairness became a useful tool for judges confronting new and unusual
situations in the Warren, Burger, and Rehnquist eras.[16]

In the meantime, it soon became clear that *Adamson* had not resolved
the issue but was merely the opening scene of what would be an ongoing
debate within the Court. Less than a year later the Court heard a Michigan
case in which a local judge had sat as a one-man grand jury, indicted the
suspect, and then convicted him in a secret trial without giving the defendant any opportunity to defend himself. The Court almost unanimously
condemned this travesty in *In re Oliver*,[17] and Justice Rutledge pointed out
that much of the problem lay in the *Adamson* doctrine of allowing the states
to experiment without hindrance. This case, he said,

demonstrates how far this Court departed from our constitutional plan
when, after the Fourteenth Amendment's adoption, it permitted selec-

---

15. See Black's dissent in *Griswold v. Connecticut*, 381 U.S. 479, 507 (1965).

16. Both *Twining* and *Adamson*, it should be noted, were eventually overruled, the former
in *Malloy v. Hogan*, 378 U.S. 1 (1964), and the latter in *Griffin v. California*, 380 U.S. 609
(1965). See Richard C. Cortner, *The Supreme Court and the Second Bill of Rights: The Fourteenth
Amendment and the Nationalization of Civil Liberties* (Madison: University of Wisconsin Press,
1981), 228–29.

17. 333 U.S. 257 (1948). Frankfurter and Jackson dissented from the opinion on technical
grounds, although Frankfurter did tell Harold Burton that he did not believe that "things
like grand jury procedure," unlike the search and seizure provisions of the Fourth Amendment, had "the vindication of history and experience behind them so as to be deemed
indispensable for a free society." Frankfurter to Burton, March 5, 1948, Frankfurter Papers, Harvard Law School Library.

tive departure by the states from the scheme of ordered personal liberty established by the Bill of Rights. In the guise of permitting the states to experiment with improving the administration of justice, the Court left them free to substitute, "in spite of the absolutism of continental governments," their "ideas and processes of civil justice" in place of the old time-tried "principles and institutions of the common law" perpetuated for us in the Bill of Rights. . . .

So long as the Bill of Rights is regarded here as a strait jacket of Eighteenth Century procedures rather than a basic charter of personal liberty, like experimentation may be expected from the states.[18]

In the late 1940s, the Truman appointees looked to Frankfurter for leadership and followed his call for judicial restraint and deference to the states. In the area of criminal procedure, as in no other, Felix Frankfurter dominated the Court during the Vinson era. The justices heard a fair number of these cases and set the groundwork for the great due process revolution of the Warren era. But they did so hesitatingly, and in the end it would be the dissents of Black and Douglas that would carry the day.

Related to the debate over incorporation was that over due process. Here the key question is not whether the framers of the Fourteenth Amendment intended to apply the Bill of Rights to the states but the meaning of the phrase itself, used in both the Fifth and the Fourteenth Amendments. Both Frankfurter and Black had rebelled against the conservative use of so-called substantive due process to protect property rights and defeat reform legislation. In regard to *procedural* due process, most often associated with criminal prosecutions, the two men also differed, and their views have shaped the modern debate.

The question of due process is crucial in criminal procedure because if the police are not restrained by procedural safeguards, then persons suspected or accused of crimes are totally at the mercy of the state. To protect against police abuse, the Bill of Rights spelled out restrictions on the national government; one did not have to incorporate those protections, Frankfurter believed, because the Due Process Clause by itself governed state police practices. Relying on Cardozo's *Palko* opinion, Frankfurter spoke often of "those canons of decency and fairness which express the notions of justice of English-speaking peoples even toward those charged with the most heinous offenses."[19] The courts should not tolerate police tactics that "offend the community's sense of fair play and decency" or conduct that "shocks the conscience."[20] Due process, then, equated with

---

18. *Ibid.* at 286.
19. *Adamson v. California*, 332 U.S. at 67–68.
20. *Rochin v. California*, 342 U.S. 165, 172, 173 (1952).

fundamental fairness; but one can argue that fairness, like beauty, may be in the eye of the beholder, and that upset Hugo Black. If judges had the discretion to determine fairness on the basis of what shocked them, then due process would vary from judge to judge and court to court. The guarantees of the Constitution had to be absolute, not dependent upon any one judge's notions of fairness. "Due Process for me," said Black, "means the first nine amendments and nothing else."[21] Frankfurter could not accept so rigid a view; for him the Due Process Clause by itself provided a sufficient limit on state abuse. Judges "knew" what was fundamentally fair and what was not; judges had the power and the duty to pronounce what was fair and what offended that fairness.

Not everyone, however, not even all judges, defined "fairness" in precisely the same way, and so within rather broad parameters, Frankfurter stood ready to defer to state legislatures in their determination of proper procedure. The Fourteenth Amendment, he argued, should not be applied "so as to turn this Court into a tribunal for revision of criminal convictions in the State courts." Due process did not restrict the states "beyond the narrow limits of imposing upon them standards of decency deeply felt and widely recognized in Anglo-American jurisdictions."[22] The problem with this approach is that it had few if any objective standards.

The debate over the meaning of due process almost came to a head in a 1945 confession case, *Malinski v. New York*.[23] Malinski and two accomplices had been arrested on suspicion of a police officer's murder. The police took Malinski not to a station house but to a hotel room, where they stripped him naked and subjected him to intense questioning until he confessed. A few days later, he confessed a second time. Five members of the Court considered the first confession to have been coerced and thus to have tainted the conviction. However, one of the codefendants, a man named Rudish, had been convicted of murder at least in part on the basis of the second confession, which the jury, following the judge's instructions, had accepted as voluntary. Douglas, Black, and Frankfurter all voted to void Malinski's conviction but then voted to affirm that of Rudish.[24]

Douglas had initially been willing to affirm both convictions, but then

---

21. Mark Silverstein, *Constitutional Faiths: Felix Frankfurter, Hugo Black and the Process of Judicial Decision Making* (Ithaca: Cornell University Press, 1984), 151, n.60.

22. *Stein v. New York*, 346 U.S. 156, 199 (1953), Frankfurter dissenting.

23. 324 U.S. 401 (1945).

24. They voted to do so on the basis of the first confession; the second confession appears to have been secured under far less onerous circumstances. As Douglas noted, "I could find nothing worthy of the label 'inquisition.' There is not a shred of evidence that he was examined more than casually." Douglas to Rutledge, January 23, 1945, Rutledge Papers, Library of Congress.

Black and Frankfurter indicated they would dissent, Black on grounds that the forced confession violated the Fifth Amendment's ban against self-incrimination, and Frankfurter because the police behavior appalled him. "I think the requirements of due process," he told Douglas, "are an independent constitutional demand and not merely the compendium of some of the specific 'ten amendments.' Therefore, for me, the prosecutor's performance and general conduct of a trial may offend, for me, 'due process' even without my considering that such incidents help establish self-incrimination."[25] Frankfurter went on to spell this out further in a concurring opinion. His predecessors on the Court, he noted, had been correct in refusing to hem in the meaning of due process by limiting it to the first eight amendments. Due process possessed a "potency different from and independent of the specific provisions contained in the Bill of Rights." Due process was "not a stagnant formulation of what had been achieved in the past but a standard for judgment in the progressive evolution of the institutions of a free society." Within its scope it included steadily evolving "notions of justice of English-speaking people" and "a demand for civilized standards of law."[26] According to Tinsley Yarbrough, this concurrence provoked Black to promise that he would soon answer Frankfurter's "natural law" exposition, a promise he kept in his *Adamson* dissent.[27]

The problem, as Black pointed out, is that the rigorous analysis Frankfurter called for required some objective criteria, and as Frankfurter admitted, "these standards of decency are not authoritatively formulated anywhere."[28] But is there a scientific means of determining what society, or even a large part of it, considers civilized behavior? Looking at the not too distant past, we cannot but be shocked at the large number of what we consider petty crimes that could be punished by death in England, or the tortures routinely applied to suspected "enemies of the state," or the inanity of imprisonment for debt. At what point did society determine that such punishment violated civilized standards?

Frankfurter personally opposed the death penalty,[29] and yet in a 1947

---

25. Frankfurter to Douglas, n.d., Douglas Papers, Library of Congress.

26. 324 U.S. at 414–17.

27. Tinsley E. Yarbrough, *Mr. Justice Black and His Critics* (Durham: Duke University Press, 1988), 90. In commenting on Frankfurter's draft, Black told his colleagues that it appeared to be "a restoration of the natural law concept whereby the supreme constitutional law becomes this Court's view of 'civilization' at a given point." Black to Conference, March 23, 1945, Jackson Papers, Library of Congress.

28. 324 U.S. at 417.

29. In 1950 Frankfurter testified before the Royal Commission on Capital Punishment in London and explained that he opposed the death penalty not on humanitarian or even penological grounds but because of its deleterious effects on the trial system caused by the sensationalism surrounding a potential death sentence. Copy of testimony, July 21, 1950, Frankfurter Papers, Harvard Law School Library.

case he exercised the restraint he considered an essential limit on judicial interpretation of due process. Willie Francis, a young black man, had been convicted of murder and sentenced to death in Louisiana. He had been strapped into the electric chair, the switch had been closed, and the device malfunctioned. Francis then sued to block Louisiana from trying again, on grounds that a second attempt would violate due process.[30]

The Court voted 5–4 to send Francis back to the electric chair. In conference Frankfurter told his colleagues that the state's action, while hardly defensible, did not shock his conscience. To Harold Burton, who prepared a powerful dissent in the case, Frankfurter wrote an anguished letter noting his opposition to the death penalty and explaining his vote:

> I have to hold on to myself not to reach your result. I am prevented from doing so only by the disciplined thinking of a lifetime regarding the duty of this Court. . . . Holmes used to express it by saying he would not strike down state action unless the action of the state made him "puke." . . . And that being so, I cannot say it so shocks the accepted, prevailing standards of fairness not to allow the state to electrocute . . . that we, as this Court, must enforce that standard by invocation of the Due Process Clause. . . . And when I have that much doubt I must, according to my view of the Court's duty give the state the benefit of the doubt and let the state action prevail.[31]

Frankfurter, although with the majority, wrote separately after Reed made several concessions to Black regarding the implied applicability of Fifth and Eighth Amendment standards to the state. In his concurrence, Frankfurter again declared that if he had voted to deny Louisiana a second chance at executing Francis on due process grounds, "I would be enforcing my private view rather than the consensus of society's opinion, which for purposes of due process, is the standard enjoined by the Court."[32]

---

30. *Louisiana ex rel. Francis v. Resweber,* 329 U.S. 459 (1947); the full story of the incident is told in Arthur S. Miller, *Death by Installments: The Ordeal of Willie Francis* (New York: Greenwood, 1988).

31. Frankfurter to Burton, December 13, 1946, Burton Papers, Library of Congress. A year later he told Learned Hand that he deemed it personally shocking that the state would insist on a "second go for a pound of flesh"; but while he considered it "barbaric," he knew that the community, either in Louisiana or in the country at large, did not share his view, and "therefore, I had no right to find a violation of the Due Process Clause." Frankfurter to Learned Hand, December 6, 1947, Frankfurter Papers, Library of Congress.

32. 394 U.S. at 471. See also Frankfurter to Conference, January 11, 1947, urging the Court not to try to overturn the standards of *Palko* or try to tie the Fifth Amendment's protections to the broader umbrella of the Due Process Clause of the Fourteenth Amendment.

Other members of the Court also found the circumstances emotionally painful. Jackson, for example, drafted a concurring opinion that began, "If I am at liberty, in the name of due process to vote my personal sense of 'decency,' I not only would refuse to send Willie Francis back to the electric chair, but I would not have sent him there in the first place. If my will were law, it would never permit execution of any death sentence."[33] Nonetheless, Jackson and a majority of the Court could find no justification that the failed execution attempt violated either the spirit or the letter of the prohibition against double jeopardy. Black also prepared a concurrence, in which he developed an incorporation argument (primarily in response to the Frankfurter concurrence), but he decided not to publish it. Rutledge prepared a dissent describing the state's actions as "torture," but in the end he also decided not to publish, and he, along with Douglas and Murphy, joined in Burton's dissent.[34]

Herman Pritchett found Frankfurter's entire due process rationale in this case untenable. Frankfurter had claimed to rely on society's consensus. "But how did he know what the consensus of opinion was on a subject that had never risen before?" Pritchett asked. "Instead of the result at which he arrived, could he not have assumed with equal validity that his own personal aversion at sending this man on a second trip to the electric chair was what any normally sensitive human being would have felt?"[35]

The *Francis* opinion came down about two months after *Adamson*, and a few weeks later Frankfurter again cast the fifth and deciding vote in a capital punishment case, but this time to overturn the conviction. A fifteen-year-old black youth had confessed to murder after police had subjected him to hours of intense interrogation without allowing him to see a lawyer, friends, or even his family. Frankfurter's separate opinion approached the sanctimonious in its tones of congratulatory self-righteousness:

Humility in this context means an alert self-scrutiny so as to avoid infusing into the vagueness of a Constitutional command one's merely private notions. Like other mortals, judges, though unaware, may be in the grip of prepossessions. The only way to relax such a grip, the only way

33. Draft opinion, December 1946, Rutledge Papers, Library of Congress. To this Rutledge shot back, "I consider it to be more than absurd for the prosecutor at Nuremburg to say that he doesn't approve of capital punishment. If he didn't approve, he should never have taken the job. Rutledge to Jackson, n.d., *ibid.*

34. Newman, *Black,* 351; the Rutledge draft can be found in Fowler V. Harper, *Justice Rutledge and the Bright Constellation* (Indianapolis: Bobbs-Merrill, 1965), 355–56. Fine, *Murphy,* 515, also reports that Murphy prepared a dissent but decided not to publish.

35. C. Herman Pritchett, *Civil Liberties and the Vinson Court* (Chicago: University of Chicago Press, 1954), 246.

to avoid finding in the Constitution the personal bias one has placed in it, is to explore the influences that have shaped one's unanalyzed views in order to lay bare prepossessions.[36]

One seeks in vain in these two concurrences for any hint of an objective standard by which to make the appropriate judgment. As in the speech cases discussed earlier, Frankfurter stood willing to allow the states great leeway in delimiting individual liberties, provided they did not go so far as to shock his conscience. Wallace Mendelson, in a book defending Frankfurter and belittling Black, makes an interesting comment: for Black, "plainly the essence of law is Justice—as he sees it." In contrast, "the essence of law for Mr. Justice Frankfurter is regularity and uniformity. To emphasize these—along with neutrality as the crux of the judicial function—and to leave the other elements of Justice largely to the lawmaking branches of government is to emphasize the Separation of Powers."[37] Mendelson asserts, although not using these words, that Frankfurter had abandoned justice to the elective branches, where it properly belonged. If this is true, then Frankfurter's pride in judicial restraint, in reining in his own biases in favor of community standards, is not judicial statesmanship but judicial abdication, and Frankfurter himself at one point came close to recognizing this. In 1953 he conceded that "the duty of deference cannot be allowed imperceptibly to slide into an abdication by this Court."[38]

Frankfurter always considered himself something of an expert on the Fourth Amendment and admitted his passion for its provisions. "I am nuts about it," he is reported to have said, "because there is no provision of the Constitution more important to be nuts about."[39] In a letter to Frank Murphy he suggested that Fourth Amendment rights needed greater protection by the Court than did First Amendment guarantees. Freedom of speech, he noted, would always attract powerful defenders against encroachment. "But the prohibitions against unreasonable search and seizure is normally invoked by those accused of crime and criminals notoriously have few friends."[40] "Unreasonable" is the key word in Fourth

---

36. *Haley v. Ohio,* 332 U.S. 596, 603 (1947).

37. Wallace Mendelson, *Justices Black and Frankfurter: Conflict in the Court* (Chicago: University of Chicago Press, 1961), 41.

38. *Stein v. New York,* 346 U.S. 156, 200 (1953). For further elaboration on this theme, see Melvin I. Urofsky, *Felix Frankfurter: Judicial Restraint and Individual Liberties* (Boston: Twayne, 1991), chap. 9.

39. Quoted in Newman, *Black,* 371. One wonders how this sort of statement squares with his objections to the Black-Douglas view of a preferred First Amendment.

40. Frankfurter to Murphy, February 15, 1947, Frankfurter Papers, Library of Congress.

Amendment cases since the meaning of the term is very subjective. Judges must strike a balance between the individual's right of privacy and security in the home against the need of society to investigate crimes and bring wrongdoers to justice.

The law has always held that in connection with a proper arrest, a search without a warrant can include only those objects "in plain sight" of the arresting officers. In *Harris v. United States* (1947),[41] FBI agents conducted a five-hour search of the four-bedroom apartment in which they arrested Harris, looking for evidence related to his alleged check-forging operation. In what one commentator described as "the most extensive search without warrant ever to receive the Court's sanction,"[42] they found some selective service classification cards unlawfully in Harris's possession, and on this charge they secured his conviction. Chief Justice Vinson wrote for the 5–4 majority that upheld the conviction on a "totality of the circumstances" rationale. Frankfurter entered a passionate dissent, claiming that the protection of the Fourth Amendment "is not an outworn bit of Eighteenth Century romantic rationalism but an indispensable need for a democratic society."[43]

Although the Court seemed to have adopted at least part of Frankfurter's *Harris* argument in subsequent cases,[44] the conservative Truman appointees swung the pendulum back, and in *United States v. Rabinowitz* (1950) Justice Minton essentially allowed an extensive warrantless search at the time of a proper arrest.[45] Frankfurter again entered a strong dissent, calling on the Court to establish the highest standards of conduct for federal agents. Two years later he dissented once again in a case in which a Chinese laundry operator had been convicted of smuggling opium on the basis of a conversation recorded by a supposed friend wired for sound.

41. 331 U.S. 145 (1947).

42. Jacob W. Landynski, *Search and Seizure and the Supreme Court* (Baltimore: Johns Hopkins University Press, 1966), 103.

43. 331 U.S. at 161. The dissent brought forth letters of praise from Judge Calvert Magruder and Judge Learned Hand. The latter especially deplored the majority opinion, which he condemned as "the kind of thing in which Totalitarianism lives." Magruder to Frankfurter, May 14, 1947, and Hand to Frankfurter, 10 May 1947, Frankfurter Papers, Harvard Law School Library. Evidently in conference Frankfurter had grown quite heated, and later he circulated a memorandum in which he said that if "I spoke with too much vehemence and intensity, I apologize." He then went on for thirteen pages expounding on the history of the Fourth Amendment. Frankfurter to Conference, April [26], 1947, Rutledge Papers, Library of Congress.

44. *United States v. Di Re*, 332 U.S. 581 (1948); *Johnson v. United States*, 333 U.S. 10 (1948); and *Trupiano v. United States*, 334 U.S. 699 (1948). In all three cases the majority took a strict view of the Fourth Amendment's search provision and voted to restrict the seized evidence.

45. 339 U.S. 25 (1950).

Frankfurter, like Brandeis and Holmes before him, considered wiretapping a "dirty business," especially when conducted without an appropriate warrant.[46]

But severe as he might be regarding federal agents' violation of the Fourth Amendment, Frankfurter took a completely different tack when it came to the states, where, as Fred Graham noted, as late as the 1960s "search warrants ha[d] been oddities."[47] With state officers Frankfurter applied the "shock the conscience" test. While values of federalism are certainly important, one wonders if widely disparate standards of police conduct—especially when they flout the spirit if not the letter of the constitutional command—are either an indispensable or valuable aspect of a pluralist system.

The Supreme Court had begun to hold federal agents to a strict accountability under the Fourth Amendment when it imposed the exclusionary rule in the 1914 case of *Weeks v. United States*.[48] The exclusionary rule prohibited the use of evidence seized illegally and provided a simple prophylactic standard. As a result, the government, especially the Federal Bureau of Investigation, trained its officers well in the proper procedures required by the Constitution. The Fourth Amendment, however, does not mention an exclusionary rule; in fact, it does not mention any means by which to enforce its ban against unreasonable searches and seizures. There has been considerable debate about the wisdom of this judge-made rule, but there is also general agreement that it is the only rule that makes the Fourth Amendment effective. Exclude the evidence, and police will have to be more careful; allow illegally seized evidence into court, and there is no incentive for police to obey the search and seizure clause.

Justice William Day, the author of the *Weeks* opinion, explicitly noted that the exclusionary rule applied only to federal agents, not to state or local police. In the next thirty years not only did officials in some states ignore the warrant clause, but an active collusion developed between state and federal officials under the "silver platter doctrine." Dicta in two 1927 cases held that evidence seized in an illegal state search would be admissible in federal court provided there had been no "federal participation."[49] As a result, in circumstances where federal agents could not meet the war-

---

46. *On Lee v. United States*, 343 U.S. 747 (1952).

47. Fred Graham, *The Self-Inflicted Wound* (New York: Macmillan, 1970), 208.

48. 232 U.S. 383 (1914). The Court reiterated its opposition to violation of the Fourth Amendment in *Silverthorne Lumber Co. v. United States*, 251 U.S. 385 (1919), when Justice Holmes, branding the government's actions an "outrage," blocked any use of the illegally seized materials by the government in any court action.

49. *Byars v. United States*, 273 U.S. 28 (1927), and *Gambino v. United States*, 275 U.S. 310 (1927).

rant requirement, a quiet word to state friends could result in a state raid, with the evidence then turned over to federal prosecutors.

This anomalous situation came to the Court's attention in *Wolf v. Colorado* (1949).[50] Dr. Julius Wolf had been convicted twice for conspiring to perform abortions, and the indictment had been based partly on the list of patients in his appointment books, which police had seized without a search warrant during a warrantless arrest. Frankfurter's opinion for the Court highlighted his devotion to the idea of privacy as well as his willingness to tolerate state invasions of that privacy. The case is significant in that Frankfurter, applying his and Cardozo's standards, incorporated part of the Bill of Rights and applied it to the states through the Fourteenth Amendment without actually saying so. Noting that the incorporation thesis had been rejected by the Court "again and again," Frankfurter declared that unreasonable searches and seizures on the part of state officials nonetheless ran afoul of the Constitution. This was not because the Fourteenth Amendment's Due Process Clause incorporated the Fourth Amendment but because such searches violated the *Palko* test for due process. The security of one's privacy, he wrote,

> against arbitrary intrusion by the police—which is at the core of the Fourth Amendment—is basic to a free society. It is therefore implicit in "the concept of ordered liberty" and as such enforceable against the States by the Due Process Clause. The knock at the door, whether by day or by night, as a prelude to a search, without authority of law but solely on the authority of the police, did not need the commentary of recent history to be condemned as inconsistent with the conception of human rights enshrined in the history and the basic constitutional documents of English-speaking peoples.[51]

But if the core of Fourth Amendment's search and seizure policy now applied to the states (whether through incorporation or straight out due process), that did not mean that the methods used to enforce that right also applied. The exclusionary rule, effective as it might be, remained judge-made law and not part of the Fourth Amendment. Therefore, states could develop their own minimal standards to ensure compliance with due process requirements. However, "in a prosecution in a State court for a State crime the Fourteenth Amendment does not forbid the admission of evidence obtained by an unreasonable search and seizure."[52] In other

---

50. 338 U.S. 25 (1949).

51. 338 U.S. at 27.

52. *Ibid.* at 33. All nine members of the Court agreed that the search and seizure policy should apply to the states; Douglas, Murphy, and Rutledge, however, believed that the exclusionary rule should also apply, for without it the Amendment was essentially a dead letter.

words, states could ignore the Fourth Amendment even though it now applied to them, provided they did not act so unreasonably as to shock the conscience.

A fair reading of the majority opinion is that Frankfurter would have liked the states to maintain the same high standards as federal criminal procedure and that he hoped applying the Fourth Amendment to the states would get them to establish high standards; if they did not, however, that would still be acceptable because a federal system allowed diversity, and almost any practice that did not "shock the conscience" would be permissible under this double standard. Despite the high tone of the majority opinion, the ruling left it up to the states to decide whether or not they would follow the example of the federal government. As Paul Murphy noted, "it thus became a classic example of a basic right for which no judicial remedy was provided."[53]

Totally missing is a sense that rights without enforcement are not rights at all. Justice Douglas, in his dissent in *Wolf*, argued that even without judicial articulation of the exclusionary rule, it existed implicitly in the Fourth Amendment by a simple commonsense reading: if the Amendment protected against search and seizure without an appropriate warrant, then it could do so only by making any evidence seized—even incontestably reliable evidence—inadmissible.[54] Justice Murphy wrote that the "conclusion is inescapable that but one remedy exists to deter violations of the search and seizure clause. That is the rule which excludes illegally obtained evidence."[55] The exclusionary rule served primarily as a prophylactic caution to the police—namely, obey the rules, or you cannot use what you find.

Here again the voice of the dissenters eventually prevailed, and the Court explicitly overruled *Wolf* in *Mapp v. Ohio* in 1961. Black, who had concurred in *Wolf* because he could find no justification in the Bill of Rights for the exclusionary rule, recanted that position in a concurrence in *Mapp*. Douglas, in another *Mapp* concurrence, acidly commented that the voice of the majority in *Wolf* was "not the voice of reason or principle." Felix Frankfurter, who had of course been that "voice," dissented in *Mapp*.[56]

In the next decade, the Court heard additional cases in which it reaffirmed the Frankfurter approach. In one in particular, all of the Court

---

53. Paul L. Murphy, *The Constitution in Crisis Times, 1918–1969* (New York: Harper & Row, 1972), 270; see also Francis A. Allen, "The Wolf Case: Search and Seizure, Federalism, and Civil Liberties," 45 *Illinois Law Review* 11 (1950).

54. 338 U.S. at 40.

55. *Ibid.* at 44.

56. *Mapp v. Ohio,* 367 U.S. 643 (1961). The Black concurrence is at 661, Douglas's at 666; Frankfurter joined in Harlan's dissent at 672.

agreed that police conduct had indeed "shocked the conscience." Antonio Rochin and his wife were in bed on the second floor of their California home when police burst into the room without a warrant. Rochin quickly swallowed two cellophane-wrapped capsules on the nightstand, and after police failed in trying to manually force him to regurgitate, they took him to a hospital and had his stomach pumped against his will. The remains of the capsules proved to be morphine and controlled substances that Rochin illegally had, and the trial court sentenced him to two months in jail. The Court found the police conduct so shocking that the evidence had to be excluded from a state trial.[57]

Black ached to write this opinion in order to show how the absolute criteria he had proposed in *Adamson* would have cut this case off at the state level and how vague notions of due process would only lead to more such police atrocities. As he had suspected it would, Frankfurter's opinion danced around the issue and called upon judges to apply due process in an exact and fair manner. "Prosecutions cannot be brought about by methods that offend 'a sense of justice.' . . . Conduct that shocks the conscience" required Rochin's conviction be reversed. This language infuriated Black, and nearly twenty years later he told Roger Newman, "Imagine 'shocks the conscience' as a constitutional basis. Could you imagine that? How does your conscience shock? Mine can get shocked pretty easily."[58] In his concurrence Black went out of his way to be sarcastic. Why, he wondered, should only the standards of English-speaking peoples determine what constitutes the immutable standards of justice? Where did the courts get power to invalidate every state law judges deemed unreasonable? As he had in *Adamson*, Black wanted objective standards, not something that could change depending on which judge drew the lot for a trial.[59]

In matters of religious freedom, Black and Frankfurter found themselves agreeing more often than not on the results but not on the methods. Prior to the 1930s there had been practically no case law involving the Religion Clauses of the First Amendment. In 1879 a Mormon challenge to a federal law prohibiting bigamy in the territories had received no sympathy from the Court, which drew a sharp distinction between *belief* and *action*. The former would receive full protection under the Constitution, but practices, even religious in character, had to conform to general laws.[60]

---

57. *Rochin v. California*, 342 U.S. 165 (1952).

58. Newman, *Black*, 358, n. During the conference discussion of the case, according to Douglas's notes, Frankfurter had declared that the police conduct "makes him puke," a standard that Black found less than precise. Conference notes, October 20, 1951, Douglas Papers, Library of Congress.

59. 342 U.S. at 174.

60. *Reynolds v. United States*, 98 U.S. 145 (1879).

Although nearly every state's bill of rights contained some guarantee of religious freedom, dissident sects complained that a variety of police laws effectively denied them religious freedom.

Jehovah's Witnesses in particular constantly ran afoul of these laws, and starting in the late 1930s they began challenging various statutes as violating their free exercise of religion. Many of the early cases involved pamphleteering or door-to-door solicitation, and the Court found in the Witnesses' favor by relying on the more familiar jurisprudence of the Speech Clause. But in *Schneider v. Irvington* (1939), Justice Roberts pointed to Stone's *Carolene Products* footnote and called on courts to scrutinize regulations of personal rights with heightened attention.[61]

The Court gave the Witnesses a victory based on the Free Exercise Clause in *Cantwell v. Connecticut* (1940), and in doing so they incorporated that clause to apply to the states as well as the federal government.[62] In this case the Court also modified somewhat the belief-action dichotomy so that some actions, if religious in nature or mandated by the religion, would come within constitutional protection. The Vinson Court heard only one major Free Exercise case, *Kedroff v. St. Nicholas Cathedral* (1952), in which an 8–1 majority, speaking through Justice Reed, held that New York could not transfer authority over the Russian Orthodox Church in America to local dissidents to avoid communist influences after the Russian Revolution of 1917.[63] But in the flag salute cases during World War II, the Court, despite the language of Justice Jackson in *Barnette,* had still relied more on a speech rationale than on the Religion Clauses.[64]

Observers had assumed that when the Court incorporated the Free Exercise Clause, the Establishment Clause would also apply to the states.[65] The first of the modern Establishment Clause cases reached the Court in

---

61. 308 U.S. 147 (1939).

62. 310 U.S. 296 (1940).

63. 344 U.S. 94 (1952). For a discussion of the case, see Philip Kurland, *Religion and the Law of Church and State and the Supreme Court* (Chicago: Aldine, 1962), 96, in which he questioned why the Court forced the state to withdraw in favor of ecclesiastical government when the basic issue was which of two competing ecclesiastical governments had the legitimacy to decide the question.

64. See above, pp. 106–12.

65. There is, of course, a lively debate over just what the Framers meant by the phrase "Congress shall make no law respecting an establishment of religion" and whether the First Amendment requires a high wall of separation or allows accommodation between the state and religion. See Leonard W. Levy, *The Establishment Clause: Religion and the First Amendment* (New York: Macmillan, 1986). See also David P. Currie, *The Constitution in the Supreme Court: The Second Century, 1888–1986* (Chicago: University of Chicago Press, 1990), 339–40, in which the author claims that the text of the Establishment Clause, like that of Free Exercise, does not lend itself to incorporation because the clauses do not speak of "freedom."

1947 and involved a challenge to a New Jersey law allowing townships to reimburse parents for bus fare for their children attending private or parochial schools. A local taxpayer then challenged the payments as a form of establishment of religion, and the Supreme Court had to deal with the question of just what constituted an establishment of religion.[66]

In *Everson* Justice Black made that incorporation clear and also set down what still remains basic jurisprudence for Establishment Clause cases:

> The "establishment of religion" clause of the First Amendment means at least this: Neither a state nor the Federal Government can set up a church. Neither can pass laws which aid one religion, aid all religions, or prefer one religion over another. Neither can force nor influence a person to go to or to remain away from church against his will or force him to profess a belief or disbelief in any religion. No person can be punished for entertaining or professing religious beliefs, for church attendance or nonattendance. No tax in any amount, large or small, can be levied to support any religious activities or institutions, whatever they may be called, or whatever form they may adopt to teach or practice religion. Neither a state nor the Federal Government can, openly or secretly, participate in the affairs of any religious organizations or groups and vice versa. In the words of Jefferson, the clause against establishment of religion by law was intended to erect a "wall of separation between Church and State."[67]

Black went on to write a brilliant exposition of the historical forces that had led to the adoption of the First Amendment, and his opinion leads the reader to expect him to hold the New Jersey statute constitutional. Irving Brant, a biographer of Madison, a journalist, and a civil libertarian, certainly thought so, and he wrote to Rutledge, "When I started to read the Everson case I flipped the leaves and missed the break in it, therefore thought it was a unanimous opinion. . . . Then, by gosh, on a point negatived by his own prior reasoning, he jumped over and affirmed the decision."[68] Indeed Black had upheld the program, leading to one of the great judicial epigrams, Justice Jackson's comment comparing Black's reasoning

---

66. *Everson v. Board of Education*, 330 U.S. 1 (1947). For a full exploration of the case, see Theodore Power, *The School Bus Law: A Case Study in Education, Religion, and Politics* (Middletown, Conn.: Wesleyan University Press, 1960).

67. 330 U.S. at 15. Black took much of the wording here from a book he greatly admired, Charles Beard's *The Republic* (1943), a "great book," according to Black, and one whose "title might almost have been 'The Origin and Aim of the American Constitution.' " Newman, *Black*, 363.

68. Brant to Rutledge, March 11, 1947, Rutledge Papers, Library of Congress.

to Byron's Julia, who "whispering 'I will ne'er consent,'—consented."[69] Justice Rutledge took the logic of Black's historical argument and reached the inevitable conclusion that if "the test remains undiluted as Jefferson and Madison made it, [then] money taken by taxation from one is not to be used or given to support another's religious training or belief, or indeed one's own. The prohibition is absolute."[70]

One is surprised to find Black, famous for his absolutist position, here taking a balancing approach, finding the state's subsidy of bus fare a "reasonable" means of promoting the welfare of the children. He evidently had believed from the start that the New Jersey law did not violate the Constitution, and he never changed his mind about his *Everson* opinion.[71]

Felix Frankfurter, who had found no problem with the state's forcing Jehovah's Witnesses to violate their conscience by saluting the flag and had preached deference to state legislative authority and reasonableness in constitutional interpretation, here took an absolutist approach that separation means just that—separation, full and complete. Frankfurter fought Black's conclusion vociferously but, at least in this first case, not publicly.

Four justices—Frankfurter, Jackson, Rutledge, and Burton—dissented. Frankfurter joined in Jackson's dissent as well as in the one filed by Rutledge. A possible reason for his declining to write himself is suggested by a letter he had written a friend a decade earlier explaining his silence during the Court-packing fight in 1937. "I am the symbol of the Jew, the 'red,' the 'alien,' " he told Grenville Clark. "Instead of bringing light and calm and reason . . . [I] would only fan the flames of ignorance, of misrepresentation, and of passion."[72] In the conference room, however, as Black later recalled, Frankfurter "fought long, hard, and loud."[73]

Initially only Frankfurter and Rutledge voted against the New Jersey law, then Jackson and Burton joined them. Frankfurter now went after Frank Murphy, the only Catholic member of the Court, who had passed when the conference discussed the case. And, as happened so often, Frankfurter overplayed his hand. He told Murphy he had "false friends" who flattered him for their own purposes. "What follows is written by one who cares about your place in history, not in tomorrow's columns." Follow your

---

69. *Ibid.* at 19. The *Washington Post*, February 13, 1947, noted that Black's argument "favoring this small encroachment upon a constitutional principle reminds us of the young woman who tried to excuse transgression of the moral law by saying that her illegitimate child was 'only a small one.' "

70. 330 U.S. at 44–45.

71. Gerald T. Dunne, *Hugo Black and the Judicial Revolution* (New York: Simon & Schuster, 1977), 264; Yarbrough, *Black and His Critics*, 154.

72. Frankfurter to Grenville Clark, March 6, 1937, quoted in Dunne, *Hugo Black*, 264–65.

73. Hugo Black, "Mr. Justice Frankfurter," 78 *Harvard Law Review* 1521 (1965).

conscience, Frankfurter urged, and uphold the great American doctrine of separation of church and state. "You have a chance to do for your country and your Church such as never came to you before—and may never again. . . . No one knows better than you what *Everson* is about. Tell the world—and shame the devil."[74] When Murphy refused to join, Frankfurter lambasted him for failing to live up to his responsibilities as a judge and declared that Murphy's biographers would have to explain away how Murphy had allowed his Catholicism to take precedence over his responsibilities as an American and as a justice of the high court.[75]

Thwarted in his efforts to convert Murphy, Frankfurter urged Jackson and Rutledge to strengthen their dissents. Rutledge, under constant pressure from Frankfurter, wrote and rewrote his draft six times to take account of all the suggestions, and in the end it was one of his best opinions. In it Rutledge took the theme of a high wall of separation and showed that if one really believed in separation of church and state, then the New Jersey bus law could not be sustained.[76] Black, aware of Frankfurter's campaign, kept revising his opinion as well, bolstering the basic theme that the First Amendment required a high wall of separation—but still approving the reimbursement law.[77] An angry Frankfurter later called the decision "characteristic of Black to utter noble sentiments and depart from them in practice."[78]

The *Everson* decision brought in a flood of mail to the Court—more, according to Rutledge, than about any other case since he had been on the Court.[79] The next term the Court provoked even greater public outcry when it decided another Establishment Clause case, *McCollum v. Board of Education*,[80] and Frankfurter tried to undo what he considered the damage of *Everson*. The Champaign, Illinois, school system had, like many systems

---

74. Frankfurter to Murphy, n.d., Frankfurter Papers, Library of Congress.

75. Fine, *Murphy*, 569. Fine notes that "although Murphy did not normally permit his religion to influence his behavior as a public official, his *Everson* vote may have been one of those rare instances when his Catholicism tipped the scales for him." *Ibid.* at 571. Since a majority of parochial schools in the country at that time were run by the Catholic Church, the case did have some overtones of a Catholic-Protestant clash. Ironically, Black told Max Lerner two years later, "the most severe and consistent criticisms of the [*Everson*] opinion have come from leading Catholics . . . on the ground that it accorded the members of the Catholic church something which they were not constitutionally entitled to receive." Black to Lerner, March 11, 1949, quoted in Newman, *Black*, 364.

76. 330 U.S. at 28; see also the lengthy memorandum Rutledge dictated after the conference discussion, n.d., Rutledge Papers, Library of Congress.

77. Newman, *Black*, 362.

78. Joseph Lash, *From the Diaries of Felix Frankfurter* (New York: Norton, 1975), 343.

79. Rutledge to Irving Brant, March 18, 1947, Rutledge Papers, Library of Congress.

80. 333 U.S. 203 (1948). See Vashti McCollum, *One Woman's Fight* (Garden City, N.Y.: Doubleday, 1951).

across the country, put aside one hour a week (released-time) when clergy-men from all denominations could come into the schools and provide religious instruction to adherents of their sects. Only Reed thought the plan constitutional,[81] and Vinson assigned Black the opinion for the Court. By this time Black had moved to the absolutist position outlined in Rutledge's *Everson* dissent, and in his opinion for the Court he wrote that the issue could not have been clearer: "Here not only are the state's tax-supported public school buildings used for the dissemination of religious doctrines. The State also affords sectarian groups an invaluable aid in that it helps to provide pupils for their religious classes through use of the state's compulsory public school machinery."[82]

Although Black and Frankfurter agreed that the released-time plan violated the First Amendment, the former was unwilling to overturn or abandon the opinion he had written barely a year earlier, while Frankfurter wanted the Court's decision to avoid any reliance on *Everson*. Frankfurter called the four dissenters from *Everson* together in his chambers, and they all agreed that "it would be stultification for us" to join in Black's draft and its approving references to the earlier case.[83] Frankfurter then circulated a memorandum that he would not agree to any opinion that mentioned *Everson;* Black shot back that he would not agree to one that did not.[84] Even before this exchange took place, Harold Burton had embarked on what would be a long and futile effort to reconcile the two opinions since he believed in essence that they were saying the same thing.[85] But where Frankfurter dug in at this point and refused to compromise, Black agreed to omit certain references to *Everson* that offended Burton and Rutledge, and they signed on to his opinion. A furious Frankfurter decided that much as he preferred to remain silent on this issue and let others make his case, he had to write his own concurrence.

Frankfurter began by noting that he had dissented in *Everson* because he believed that "separation means separation, not something less." In his initial draft, Frankfurter painted such broad strokes that Reed and Burton

81. Conference notes, December 13, 1947, Douglas Papers, Library of Congress. Reed's lone dissent is sympathetically discussed in F. William O'Brien, *Justice Reed and the First Amendment: The Religion Clauses* (Washington: Georgetown University Press, 1958), chap. 8.

82. 333 U.S. at 212.

83. Lash, *Frankfurter Diaries,* 343; Frankfurter to Jackson, January 6, 1948, Jackson Papers, Library of Congress.

84. Frankfurter to Conference, February 11, 1948; Black to Conference, 11 February 1948, both in Rutledge Papers, Library of Congress.

85. See Burton to Frankfurter and Black, February 7, 1948, Black Papers, Library of Congress; Burton to Conference, February 11, 1948, Douglas Papers, Library of Congress; Burton to Rutledge and Minton, February 12, 1948, and to Rutledge, March 2, 1948, Rutledge Papers, Library of Congress.

questioned whether he also opposed released-time programs that met off school property. Frankfurter said he did not, and he made it explicit that he was only discussing religious education that occurred in public school buildings, a central consideration in the justices' vote on the Illinois plan.

One key to Frankfurter's decision to write in *McCollum* is his view of the public school as an Americanizing and unifying force, a place where children from all backgrounds developed a common American outlook. He always remembered the effect that Miss Hogan had on him at P.S. 25 in New York,[86] and he feared that religious education in the schools would destroy that "most powerful agency for promoting cohesion among a heterogeneous democratic people. The public school must keep scrupulously free from entanglement in the strife of sects."[87]

The *McCollum* decision stirred up a nationwide furor among religious groups, nearly all of whom operated some form of released-time program. One indication of the emotion involved is that the eminent constitutional scholar Edward S. Corwin, normally a voice of reason, charged that the Court was trying to set itself up as a national school board.[88] Hugo Black somewhat laconically commented that "few opinions from this Court in recent years have attracted more attention or stirred wider debate."[89] Enforcement of the opinion varied. In northern states where religious instruction actually took place in public school classrooms, there seems to have been general compliance. But in most southern states and in areas where local school boards could differentiate between the Illinois model and theirs, religious instruction continued.[90]

That reaction is often pointed to as the reason behind the Court's 6–3 vote in 1952 to uphold a New York released-time program that took place off school grounds, a ruling that can properly be called the Court's first "accommodationist" decision. To continue the released-time program, a number of states had moved religious instruction off school property; New York officials, for example, established times in which students left the school grounds and went to religious facilities for instruction. Taxpayers challenged the program on grounds that it still involved the state in promoting religion. The authority of the school supported participation in the program; public school teachers policed attendance; and normal classroom activities came to a halt so students in the program would not miss their secular instruction.

---

86. Harlan B. Phillips, ed., *Felix Frankfurter Reminices* (New York: Reynal, 1960), 4–5.

87. 333 U.S. at 216–17. Rutledge, Jackson, and Burton joined in the concurrence.

88. Edward S. Corwin, "The Supreme Court as National School Board," 23 *Thought* 665 (1948).

89. Quoted in Pritchett, *Civil Liberties and the Vinson Court*, 12.

90. Stephen L. Wasby, *The Impact of the United States Supreme Court: Some Perspectives* (Chicago: Dorsey, 1970), 127.

Justice Douglas, writing for the 6–3 majority in *Zorach v. Clauson*,[91] seemed to go out of his way to note that the First Amendment did not require a total separation (a reasonableness argument not unlike that used by Frankfurter in due process cases). Such a separation, he believed, would be impossible, for "we are a religious people whose institutions presuppose a Supreme Being." Total separation of church and state in such an environment could only lead to antagonism between the two, a result obviously not contemplated by the framers.[92] Douglas was trying to do more than merely blunt the criticism of *McCollum*. Although he would later become as absolute a separationist as Black, Douglas worried, as Black did not, that trying to maintain a strict wall of separation would harm religion, and he wanted to find some grounds that would allow incidental benefits to religion yet would not create a situation in which tax dollars underwrote sectarian programs.[93]

Black and Jackson dissented, and the latter thought the Court opinion a disaster. In an emotional letter to Frankfurter, he declared that "the battle for *separation* of Church and State is lost. From here on it is only a question of how far the intermixture will go."[94] Frankfurter, while concurring in Jackson's opinion, submitted a separate dissent in which he charged that the school system did not "close its doors" when some of its pupils went off to religious instruction. Those who remained were deprived of their opportunity for instruction since teachers did not plan substantive work, knowing a significant portion of their classes would be absent.[95]

The dissenters had no trouble exploiting the weakness of the majority opinion, and commentators are agreed that the Court wanted to quiet down the storm of criticism that had greeted the *McCollum* decision. Just three months earlier, in fact, the Court had ducked another controversial issue, a New Jersey statute that required five verses from the Old Testament

---

91. 343 U.S. 306 (1952).

92. *Ibid.* at 313–14.

93. See Howard Ball and Phillip J. Cooper, *Of Power and Right: Hugo Black, William O. Douglas, and America's Constitutional Revolution* (New York: Oxford University Press, 1992), 245–47.

94. Jackson to Frankfurter, April 30, 1952, Frankfurter Papers, Library of Congress. The Black dissent is at 343 U.S. at 315, and that of Jackson at 323.

95. 343 U.S. at 320, 321. Although disconcerted by the vote in *Zorach*, Frankfurter took great pleasure in the fact that both he and Black had dissented, one more step down their road to reconciliation. Frankfurter dropped Black a note proudly reporting that they were both being attacked by religious groups for their dissents. "And for good measure," he added, there is "some rancid Billy Graham stuff whereby we shall be reviled as atheists. But then, it wouldn't be the first time that you and I are reviled." Frankfurter to Black, March 5, 1952, quoted in James F. Simon, *The Antagonists: Hugo Black, Felix Frankfurter and Civil Liberties in Modern America* (New York: Simon & Schuster, 1989), 202.

to be read daily, without comment, in each public school classroom. At the conference discussing the case, Chief Justice Vinson gave the brethren the out that a majority sought by questioning the standing of the plaintiffs.[96] What is confusing, however, is that the three dissenters in the *Doremus* case, Douglas, Reed and Burton, had constituted half the majority in *Zorach*. Why should they want to have the Court hear this case on its merits when they had wanted to calm down public opinion by their position in regard to released time? Unfortunately, the record provides no answer, and their motivation remains unclear.

In one other area of civil liberties, free speech, the Court's most important decisions came in connection with the Cold War cases and are discussed in chapter 6. But there were a few additional speech cases that deserve a brief mention. In *Saia v. New York* (1948),[97] the Court struck down an ordinance requiring a permit for the use of loudspeakers that might inconvenience people in public places. Then the following year in *Kovacs v. Cooper*,[98] it sustained an ordinance that totally forbade loudspeakers on the streets and did not authorize any permits at all. Both cases were decided by a 5–4 vote, and only the chief justice seemed to think them distinguishable. Black and Jackson thought the Court had it backward, for the ordinance the Court upheld was actually far more restrictive than the one invalidated in *Saia* since that at least allowed the police to issue permits.

The *Saia* case found Jehovah's Witnesses back in the Court protesting a Lockport, New York, ordinance that required them to get the permission of the police chief to use loudspeakers. At first a majority of the Court voted to uphold the ordinance; then Chief Justice Vinson changed his mind, saying that he could not distinguish this case from *Cantwell*.[99] This turned Justice Douglas's dissent into the majority opinion, and he ruled that the ordinance provided no standards for the police and therefore left the issuance of the permits to an arbitrary authority. "The right to be heard," he wrote, "is placed in the uncontrolled discretion of the Chief of Police," and ever since the 1930s the Court had steadfastly refused to allow such discretionary power to choose among potential speakers.[100] Given this

---

96. *Doremus v. Board of Education,* 342 U.S. 429 (1952); conference notes, February 2, 1952, Douglas Papers, Library of Congress.

97. 334 U.S. 558 (1948).

98. 336 U.S. 77 (1949).

99. Conference notes, April 2, 1948, Douglas Papers, Library of Congress; Vinson to Frankfurter, 22 May 22 and June 1, 1948, Frankfurter Papers, Harvard Law School Library.

100. 334 U.S. at 560–61. Among the precedents Douglas noted *Schneider v. State,* 308 U.S. 147 (1939); *Hague v. CIO,* 307 U.S. 496 (1939); and *Cantwell v. Connecticut,* 310 U.S. 296 (1940).

precedential trail, it is somewhat surprising that Frankfurter, Reed, Jackson, and Burton dissented. In Frankfurter's case, the reason may have been a blend of concern for privacy as well as a personal distaste for intrusive noise, and his stance brought forth praise from E. B. White and H. L. Mencken, both of whom objected to the intrusiveness of modern sound amplification.

The next year in *Kovacs*, the Court upheld a Trenton, New Jersey, ordinance that completely barred sound trucks and sound devices that emitted "loud and raucous noises" from the city streets. A union organizer had been arrested for operating a sound truck in violation of the ordinance. Reed, joined by Vinson and Burton, seized upon the "loud and raucous" phrase and upheld the ordinance on the grounds that it constituted nothing more than a time, place, and manner regulation that was content-neutral—that is, that bore no relation to the substance of the speech. He distinguished the facts from *Saia* in that here there was no arbitrary authority choosing from among potential speakers. Frankfurter entered a concurrence arguing that *Saia* had been wrongly decided and objecting to Reed's use of a preferred position terminology for speech issues, while Jackson claimed that it had in fact been repudiated.[101]

In dissent, Black agreed that the state could limit sound volume and impose other time, place, and manner regulations but could not ban any form of speech altogether. Sound trucks, he held, were the poor man's press, and barring them gave people with more money and other opportunities a greater say in the public debates.[102] Douglas joined the Black dissent, Rutledge dissented separately, and Murphy dissented without comment.

The two decisions, while seemingly contradictory, do make the point that content regulation would not be permitted by the Court. The fact that Trenton banned all loudspeakers might be viewed as a restriction on speech, which it was, but it differed in that under its terms, no bureaucrat could arbitrarily determine who would or would not speak; in the New York case, it was just that issue that called down the verdict of unconstitutionality. The Court followed this rationale in two additional cases, striking down standardless requirements for park permits in one,[103] invalidating standardless procedures for securing street permits in the other,[104] with the majority opinions by the chief justice in both cases.

Few of the decisions rendered by the Vinson Court in these areas of civil liberties are still in force today, but the basic issues they raised con-

---

101. The Frankfurter opinion is at 336 U.S. at 89, and that of Jackson at 97.

102. *Ibid.* at 102–3.

103. *Niemotko v. Maryland,* 340 U.S. 268 (1951).

104. *Kunz v. New York,* 340 U.S. 290 (1951).

tinue to fuel debate over the proper interpretation of the Constitution. *Everson* in particular is at the heart of a major controversy over the meaning of the Establishment Clause, and the Frankfurter/Black debate over due process has reverberated in the criminal procedure cases of the Warren, Burger, and Rehnquist Courts. As in so many other areas, the Court in transition stepped further away from the issues that had dominated its agenda for the previous seventy years and toward modern questions that required a rethinking of traditional jurisprudence.

# 9

# THE ROAD TO *BROWN*

The theme of transition can clearly be seen in the cases dealing with racial classification, an issue that would come to fruition in the Warren Court's landmark decision in *Brown v. Board of Education* in 1954.[1] The decisions handed down by the Vinson Court clearly pointed the way to *Brown*, although the justices avoided as long as they could tackling the doctrine of "separate but equal," which provided the foundation for the South's pervasive system of racial segregation.[2]

The Thirteenth, Fourteenth, and Fifteenth Amendments had been drafted primarily to free the slaves and to guarantee them the same rights and legal privileges enjoyed by whites. One might have expected that the southern states would have moved immediately to create some system to segregate the races, but in fact, as C. Vann Woodward has shown, a full-scale pattern of state-enforced segregation did not take hold until the 1890s.[3] By then not only had northerners abandoned southern blacks, but the Supreme Court had given the process a green light. In the *Civil Rights Cases* (1883),[4] the Court denied Congress any but the most limited remedial powers under the Fourteenth Amendment to combat racial prejudice. In the 1890s the Court decided several cases involving state statutes establishing formal segregation of the races. In the most famous of these, *Plessy v. Ferguson* (1896),[5] Justice Henry Billings Brown asserted that the Four-

---

1. 347 U.S. 483 (1954).

2. The Vinson Court, with one exception, did not look at equal rights for other groups. In the case of *Goesaert v. Cleary*, 335 U.S. 464 (1948), Justice Frankfurter spoke for a 6–3 Court in upholding a Michigan law denying women bartender licenses unless they were "the wife or daughter of the male owner." The state could, he declared, "beyond question, forbid all women from working behind a bar. This is so despite the vast changes in the social and legal position of women. . . . The Constitution does not require legislatures to reflect sociological insight, or shifting social standards, any more than it requires them to keep abreast of the latest scientific standards." Women would not receive any significant relief under the Equal Protection Clause until the Burger Court.

3. C. Vann Woodward, *The Strange Career of Jim Crow*, 2d ed. (New York: Oxford University Press, 1966), chaps. 2 and 3.

4. 109 U.S. 3 (1883).

5. 163 U.S. 537 (1896). There are many accounts and analyses of this case, the best of which is Charles A. Lofgren, *The Plessy Case: A Legal-Historical Interpretation* (New York: Oxford University Press, 1987).

teenth Amendment had never been intended to abolish "distinctions based upon color." Although nowhere in the opinion can one find the phrase "separate but equal," the Court's ruling approved legal segregation provided the law did not make facilities for blacks inferior to those for whites. Within a short time, Jim Crow had become dominant throughout the southern and border states.

In the 1930s the National Association for the Advancement of Colored People (NAACP) began its campaign to eliminate segregation and made a deliberate decision that the only way it could be successful would be by attacking racial prejudice through the courts.[6] In the first major case to reach the Court, Chief Justice Hughes had startled the South by insisting that if it wanted to keep segregated schools, it would have to make them equal as well.[7] The war temporarily prevented the NAACP from aggressively pursuing its goals, but the *Gaines* decision had given the organization its first real tactical victory.

In World War II the nation's declared goal of fighting intolerance abroad led black Americans to a greater determination to end racial injustice at home. President Roosevelt took the first step in an executive order on June 25, 1941, directing that blacks be accepted into job training programs in defense plants. The order also forbade discrimination by employers holding defense contracts and set up a Fair Employment Practices Commission (FEPC) to investigate charges of racial discrimination. But aside from this one step, civil rights remained a low priority during the Roosevelt administration.

Harry Truman, overwhelmed at the multiplicity of problems facing him when he suddenly inherited the presidency in April 1945, put up no protest when Congress killed the wartime FEPC. But although Truman came from a segregated border state, he believed discriminating on the basis of race to be wrong. He asked Congress to create a permanent FEPC, and in December 1946 he appointed a distinguished panel to serve as the President's Committee on Civil Rights to recommend "more adequate means and procedures for the protection of the civil rights of the people of the United States."[8] The commission issued its report, "To Secure These Rights," in October 1947 and defined in it the nation's civil rights agenda for the next generation. The commission noted the many restrictions on

---

6. Mark V. Tushnet, *The NAACP's Strategy Against Segregated Education, 1925–1950* (Chapel Hill: University of North Carolina Press, 1987); see also Loren Miller, *The Petitioners: The Story of the Supreme Court of the United States and the Negro* (Cleveland: World, 1966), and above all, the magisterial study by Richard Kluger, *Simple Justice: The History of Brown v. Board of Education and Black America's Struggle for Equality* (New York: Knopf, 1976).

7. *Missouri ex rel. Gaines v. Canada*, 305 U.S. 339 (1938).

8. *New York Times*, December 6, 1946.

African Americans and urged that every American, regardless of race, color, creed, or national origin, should have access to equal opportunity in securing education, decent housing, and jobs. Among its proposals, the commission suggested passing antilynching laws, abolishing poll taxes, establishing a permanent FEPC, and strengthening the civil rights division of the Justice Department.[9]

In a courageous act, the president sent a special message to Congress on February 2, 1948, calling for prompt implementation of the commission's recommendations. The southern delegations promptly blocked any action by threatening to filibuster. Unable to secure civil rights legislation from Congress, Truman moved ahead by using his executive authority. He bolstered the Justice Department's civil rights section and ordered it to assist private litigants in civil rights cases. He appointed the first black judge, William H. Hastie, to a U.S. Court of Appeals and named several blacks to high-ranking positions in the administration. Most important, by Executive Order 9981, he abolished segregation in the armed forces and ordered full racial integration of the nation's military.

While Congress refused to create a federal FEPC, a number of states set up agencies to enforce civil rights. New York acted first in 1945, establishing a State Commission Against Discrimination to investigate and stop prejudice in employment. In the next decade other northern states passed similar laws so that nearly two-thirds of the entire population of the country came under some form of governmental protection against discrimination in the labor market.

Against this backdrop the NAACP resumed its campaign—or, to be more accurate, intensified its efforts, because even during the war it had not been quiescent, and one of its suits had led the Court to strike down the all-white primary in *Smith v. Allwright*.[10] The NAACP always had as its ultimate goal the elimination of the "separate but equal" doctrine, but its leaders, especially Thurgood Marshall, realized that in terms of tactics, it would initially have to attack the South's failure to provide equal facilities. In a wide range of cases, decided primarily in lower courts on the basis of *Gaines,* Marshall and his colleagues forced southern states to improve the physical facilities of all-black schools and to pay black teachers on a par with white teachers.[11]

---

9. *To Secure These Rights: The Report of the President's Committee on Civil Rights* (Washington: Government Printing Office, 1947).

10. 321 U.S. 649 (1944); see above, pp. 100–101.

11. The strategy had first been outlined by Nathan Margold in the early 1930s; see Tushnet, *Making Civil Rights Law: Thurgood Marshall and the Supreme Court, 1936–1961* (New York: Oxford University Press, 1994), chap. 8.

In the spring of 1946 Marshall and William Hastie came before the Supreme Court to argue a transportation case. Irene Morgan, a black woman, had boarded a Greyhound bus in Virginia to go to Baltimore and had been ordered to go to the back of the bus as Virginia state law required. Morgan refused, claiming that since she was an interstate passenger, Virginia's law did not apply to her. The bus driver had her arrested, the court fined her ten dollars, and the NAACP took the case on appeal. The Virginia state courts rejected Marshall's arguments that a nineteenth-century Supreme Court ruling, *Hall v. DeCuir* (1878),[12] governed the case. In that case the high court had invalidated a Louisiana reconstruction statute *prohibiting* discrimination on account of race as a burden on interstate commerce. Chief Justice Morrison R. Waite considered it important that there be uniformity of practice. "No carrier of passengers," he wrote, "can conduct his business with satisfaction to himself, or comfort to those employing him, if on one side of a State line his passengers, both white and colored, must be permitted to occupy the same cabin, and on the other side be kept separate."[13] Only Congress, declared Waite, could regulate interstate commerce.

However, a few years later the Court refused to void a Mississippi law *requiring* segregation on intrastate railroads,[14] although the rationale of *Hall v. DeCuir* should have been controlling. As Loren Beth has suggested, the cases may have been less about racial segregation than about the distribution of state and national powers under the Commerce Clause. In 1878 the Waite Court believed that national regulation prevented the states from acting, while a little over a decade later the Fuller Court believed that states should be given more latitude.[15] And it was in a transportation case, also decided by the Supreme Court, that the justices formally endorsed the doctrine of separate but equal.[16]

*Hall v. DeCuir*, however, had not been overruled in the Mississippi case; the justices had merely "distinguished" it on the grounds that the Mississippi statute applied solely to intrastate passengers, conveniently overlooking the fact that so too did the Louisiana law. Later courts also avoided dealing with the issue by finding some technicality. In a Kentucky case, for example, the justices attributed the segregation to the regulations of an

---

12. 95 U.S. 485 (1878).

13. *Ibid.* at 489.

14. *Louisville, New Orleans & Texas Railway Co. v. Mississippi*, 133 U.S. 587 (1890).

15. Loren P. Beth, *The Development of the American Constitution, 1877–1917* (New York: Harper & Row, 1971), 145–46.

16. *Plessy v. Ferguson*, 163 U.S. 537 (1896). For the road away from this decision, see Catherine A. Barnes, *Journey from Jim Crow: The Desegregation of Southern Transit* (New York: Columbia University Press, 1983).

interstate carrier, ignoring the fact that a Kentucky law requiring separate coaches for black passengers had been the reason for the carrier's rule.[17] A few years later the Court upheld an Oklahoma statute on the grounds that no case for relief had been made out, but Justice Charles Evans Hughes insisted that the railroad had to provide first-class cars for black passengers desiring such accommodations, no matter how small that demand.[18]

The tide began to change in 1941, when the Court for the first time since 1873 upheld a black plaintiff's challenge to segregated transportation. Arthur W. Mitchell, a congressman from Illinois, had bought Pullman accommodations, and he and some white passengers had enjoyed the luxury coach until the train crossed the Arkansas border. There the conductor ejected him from the Pullman car on the grounds that Arkansas state law required segregation. Mitchell filed a complaint, not in court but with the Interstate Commerce Commission, claiming that he had been discriminated against in violation of the Interstate Commerce Act. The Commission ruled that the railroad's failure to provide anything except second-class cars for Negroes did not constitute an "unjust or undue" discrimination, but the Supreme Court upheld Mitchell's complaint. The ruling did not directly affect the *Plessy* doctrine, but following the Hughes dictum in *Gaines*, the Court again warned southern states that if they wished to sustain segregation, truly equal facilities would have to be provided by public carriers for their nonwhite customers.[19]

By the time the Morgan case reached the Vinson Court, it appeared that the justices had decided to take a closer look at racial classification. Justice Reed, writing for a 7–1 majority (Justice Jackson was still in Nuremberg), declared that he was merely following the rule of *DeCuir* and that "seating arrangements for the different races in interstate motor travel require a single, uniform rule to promote and protect national travel."[20] The careful wording of the decision applied only to passengers on interstate buses; it did not affect intrastate Jim Crow laws. But it can hardly be doubted that the justices had paid close attention to the NAACP brief, which concluded:

---

17. *Chiles v. Chesapeake & Ohio Railway*, 218 U.S. 71 (1910).

18. *McCabe v. Atcheson, Topeka & Sante Fe Railway Co.*, 235 U.S. 151 (1914). See also *South Covington & Cincinnati Street Railway Co. v. Kentucky*, 252 U.S. 399 (1920), in which the Court held that a railroad operating from Cincinnati, Ohio, into Kentucky, carrying 80 percent of its passengers interstate, was nonetheless an intrastate carrier despite the fact that five years earlier the Court, in a different type of case, had ruled the same traffic by the same carrier as interstate commerce in *South Covington & Cincinnati Street Railway Co. v. Covington*, 235 U.S. 537 (1915).

19. *Mitchell v. United States*, 313 U.S. 80 (1941).

20. *Morgan v. Virginia*, 328 U.S. 373, 386 (1946).

Today we are just emerging from a war in which all of the people of the United States were joined in a death struggle against the apostles of racism. . . . How much clearer, therefore, must it be today than it was in 1877, that the national business of interstate commerce is not to be disfigured by disruptive local practices bred of racial notions alien to our national ideals, and to the solemn undertakings of the community of civilized nations as well.[21]

Only Justice Burton dissented, but he did so not to defend segregation but to uphold a notion of federalism in which state laws had to be given due respect.[22] Although the majority had claimed to be following *DeCuir,* Burton said that the precedent did not require this result. He attacked the lack of evidence to support the claim of an undue burden on interstate commerce, and he reviewed various state practices to show how divergent they were: eighteen states prohibited segregation by public motor carriers, twenty made no provision, and ten contiguous states required segregation. He disputed the need for a court-ordered uniformity; the fact that eighteen states had already prohibited segregation marked "important progress in the direction of uniformity."[23] Moreover, he warned, the Commerce Clause used here to strike down discrimination might well have to be used in other circumstances to protect such bias.

The case had first been discussed while Stone had been alive, and evidently the chief justice had also disagreed with the majority. Burton wanted to include the following statement in his dissent: "The late Chief Justice . . . participated in the hearing and consideration of this case and although his sudden death took him from the Court before the opinions in it were written, it is appropriate, in the light of his many decisions in this field, to record that he dissented from the result reached by the majority." His colleagues, however, convinced him that such a statement would be inappropriate.[24]

Burton's warning almost materialized two years later in *Bob-Lo Excursion Co. v. Michigan.*[25] A Detroit amusement park company operated a steamboat to Bois-Blanc Island on the Canadian side of the Detroit River,

---

21. Quoted in Kluger, *Simple Justice,* 238.

22. Burton would have been happy if his colleagues had been willing to tackle the separate-but-equal issue directly, and in the discussions over the school cases (see below) he stood with Black and Douglas ready to overturn *Plessy.* Frances Howell Rudko, *Truman's Court: A Study in Judicial Restraint* (Westport, Conn.: Greenwood, 1988), 56.

23. 328 U.S. at 72.

24. Burton, Memorandum for the Conference, n.d., Rutledge Papers, Library of Congress.

25. 333 U.S. 28 (1948).

a location, as was noted during oral argument of the case, that had once been the end of an underground railroad line for escaping slaves before the Civil War. The company had refused to allow a young black woman, Sarah Elizabeth Ray, in a group outing with a number of white classmates, to accompany them on the ride. The assistant general manager later testified that company policy excluded "so-called 'Zoot suiters,' the rowdyish, the rough and the boisterous, and it also adopted the policy of excluding colored." The company claimed that the Michigan Civil Rights Act had no applicability since the steamboat ran in foreign commerce.

Under both *DeCuir* and *Morgan* the Court should have upheld the company's claim, but instead a majority led by Justice Rutledge evaded the precedents by ruling that the commerce, although technically foreign, was actually "highly local" with the island "economically and socially, though not politically, an amusement adjunct of the city of Detroit." The Court thus distinguished the earlier cases because they supposedly did not involve "locally insulated" situations; moreover, in neither of the earlier cases had anyone tried to exclude blacks totally as Bob-Lo had done here. Rutledge evidently had wanted to make his opinion much more an attack on segregation in general, but Frankfurter convinced him that this was not the case, and the time not yet ripe. He got Rutledge to bolster the section dealing with the indignities visited upon Ray, but, he said:

> By all means let us decide with fearless decency, but express our decisions with reserve and austerity. It does not help toward harmonious race relations to stir our colored fellow citizens to resentment by even pertinent rhetoric or by a needless recital of details of mistreatment which are irrelevant to a legal issue before us. Nor do we wean whites, both North and South, from what so often is merely the momentum of the past in them.[26]

Justice Jackson and the chief justice dissented, not to support discrimination but because the majority opinion allowed state power to control interstate commerce. "The Court admits," wrote Jackson, "that the commerce involved in this case is foreign commerce, but subjects it to the state police power on the ground that it is not very foreign."[27]

As Herman Pritchett noted, *Bob-Lo* "highlighted the Court's problem in attempting to achieve equalitarian goals through the cold-blooded and

---

26. Frankfurter to Rutledge, January 2, 1948 (2 letters), Rutledge Papers, Library of Congress.
27. *Ibid.* at 44; see also Douglas, Conference notes, December 20, 1947, Douglas Papers, Library of Congress.

clumsy constitutional concept of commerce."[28] Justice Douglas picked up
on this theme in his concurrence, in which he suggested that a revived
Equal Protection Clause would be a far better ground on which to base a
decision since in essence what the young woman wanted was the opportunity to ride on the boat. "If a sister State undertook to bar Negroes from
passage on public carriers, that law would not only contravene the federal
rule but also invade a 'fundamental individual right which is guaranteed
against state action by the Fourteenth Amendment.' Nothing short of at
least 'equality of legal right' in obtaining transportation can satisfy the
Equal Protection Clause."[29]

The Vinson Court heard one more transportation case in which it
could have abandoned the separate-but-equal doctrine. Elmer Henderson,
traveling on the Southern Railway between Atlanta, Georgia, and Washington, D.C., in May 1942, had wanted to eat dinner. Upon reaching the din-
ing car he found ten tables reserved for white passengers and one, shielded
from the others by a curtain, for blacks. The separated table was full, and
the conductor refused to allow Henderson to sit in an empty seat at one
of the white tables. He filed a complaint with the Interstate Commerce
Commission, and once again the Court proved reluctant to take the bold
step. It unanimously struck down the practice on the principle established
in the *Mitchell* case; the arbitrary arrangement interfered with the equal
access of passengers in violation not of the Constitution but of the Interstate Commerce Act.[30] The opinion by Justice Burton very carefully avoided
any implication that the statute prohibited segregation since, as Frankfurter pointed out, it would be inconceivable that the Congress that had
passed the act could have intended such a result. By relying on *Mitchell*,[31]
the Court still supported the separate-but-equal doctrine, but it made it
more difficult and expensive for interstate carriers to meet the standard.[32]
In transportation, *Plessy* remained alive and well, albeit slightly restricted.

African Americans had been discriminated against in housing as well
as other areas of private life, and in confronting this issue the justices struck

---

28. *Civil Liberties and the Vinson Court* (Chicago: University of Chicago Press, 1954), 128.

29. 333 U.S. at 42. Justice Black joined in the concurrence.

30. *Henderson v. United States,* 339 U.S. 816 (1950).

31. At the Conference there appeared to be no question that Henderson should prevail
but a great deal of discussion on whether or not *Mitchell* would be the controlling case. In
the end the Justices decided to stick with the precedent rather than break new ground on
the meaning of the Fourteenth Amendment's Equal Protection Clause. Douglas, Conference notes of April 8, 1950, Douglas Papers, Library of Congress.

32. Frankfurter, Memorandum for the Conference, May 31, 1950, Frankfurter Papers,
Harvard Law School Library.

a blow against racial bias that would have far-reaching effects later on. In 1917 the Court had voided local residence ordinances enforcing racial segregation as a deprivation of property rights in violation of the Fourteenth Amendment.[33] To get around this ruling, white property owners turned to restrictive covenants, which, as private agreements between buyers and sellers, presumably did not come within the reach of the Due Process or Equal Protection Clauses.

Immediately after the war some commentators were predicting that if a case reached the Supreme Court, the justices would find enforcement of the restrictions unconstitutional.[34] By the time a case did reach the Court, the Cold War had erupted. At an NAACP lawyers' conference on January 26, 1947, Francis Dent predicted that given the current state of international relations, the Court "would be most loath to uphold and enforce restrictive covenants since it would be embarrassing to the American position in foreign policy in which we propose to be the leader of the democratic forces."[35]

In *Shelley v. Kraemer* (1948),[36] Chief Justice Vinson ruled for all six sitting justices that so long as the discriminatory intent of the covenants had to be enforced in state courts, then the states were sanctioning racial discrimination in violation of the Fourteenth Amendment. The justices did not rule the covenants themselves illegal since private discrimination remained constitutionally permissible, but it did make them unenforceable. In a companion case the Court also voided enforcement of restrictive covenants in the District of Columbia. Although the Fourteenth Amendment did not apply to the national government, the justices held that such agreements violated the 1866 Civil Rights Act and that it went against public policy to allow a federal court to enforce an agreement that was unenforceable in state courts.[37] Frankfurter entered a separate concurrence in the second case. The expert on jurisdiction preferred that the Court base its

---

33. *Buchanan v. Warley,* 245 U.S. 600 (1917).

34. D. O. McGovney, "Racial Residential Segregation by State Court Enforcement of Restrictive Agreements, Covenants or Conditions in Deeds is Unconstitutional," 33 *California Law Review* 5 (1945). McGovney sent a copy of this article to Frankfurter.

35. Minutes of lawyers' conference, January 26, 1947, Papers of the National Association for the Advancement of Colored People, Library of Congress.

36. 334 U.S. 1 (1948). Justices Reed, Jackson, and Rutledge did not participate in this case, presumably because each owned property covered by a restrictive covenant. Jackson to Irving Brant, February 9, 1948, Jackson Papers, Library of Congress.

37. *Hurd v. Hodge,* 334 U.S. 24 (1948). For a contemporary legal analysis of these cases, see Mark V. Tushnet, "*Shelley v. Kraemer* and Theories of Equality," 33 *New York Law School Review* 383 (1988); see also the older but still useful broader study by Clement Vose, *Caucasians Only: The Supreme Court, the NAACP, and the Restrictive Covenant Cases* (Berkeley: University of California Press, 1959).

decision on the traditional discretion allowed to equity courts because "equity is rooted in conscience. . . . In good conscience, it cannot be 'the exercise of sound judicial discretion' by a federal court to grant the relief here asked for when the authorization of such an injunction by the States of the Union violates the Constitution."[38] Privately, however, as Frankfurter explained to Vinson, the reliance on Fourteenth Amendment grounds would support the argument Black had made in *Adamson*, which Frankfurter rejected "both as scholarship and as law."[39]

The importance of the case lay not just in its immediate results or even in the fact that this was the strongest statement yet made by the Court against segregation. By defining state action to include enforcement of a contract by state courts, the decision greatly expanded the meaning of state action. In the future, the Warren Court would use the nexus of state action to strike down any form of segregation that had even a remote connection to state government.[40] The state action doctrine proved a potent tool against discrimination and put teeth into the Fourteenth Amendment's Equal Protection Clause.

Following *Shelley*, the Court began to hear more and more cases involving claims of racial segregation. Some cases involved restrictive covenants,[41] and some involved labor unions,[42] but everyone recognized that the most explosive issue would be segregation in public schools.

In 1948, a few months before *Shelley*, the Court heard and decided the case of Ada Lois Sipuel, a black woman who had been excluded from the University of Oklahoma Law School. Sipuel had compiled an excellent record at the State College for Negroes in Langston and then had applied to the University of Oklahoma Law School, the only one in the state. The president of the University of Oklahoma, George Lynn Cross, personally opposed racial segregation, and in fact a younger generation of Oklahomans also disapproved of Jim Crow. When Sipuel came to the Norman campus to deliver her application in person, a number of white students turned out to greet her and wished her well in her application. But state

---

38. 334 U.S. at 36.

39. Frankfurter to Vinson, April 27, 1948, Frankfurter Papers, Harvard Law School Library.

40. Using the state action doctrine, the Warren Court voided the exclusion of blacks from a private theater located in a public park (*Muir v. Louisiana Park Theatrical Assn.*, 347 U.S. 971 [1955]), from a private restaurant in a courthouse (*Derrington v. Plummer*, 353 U.S. 924 [1957]), and from a private restaurant in a municipally owned and operated parking garage (*Burton v. Wilmington Parking Authority*, 365 U.S. 17 [1961]).

41. *Barrows v. Jackson*, 346 U.S. 249 (1953).

42. *Brotherhood of Railway Trainmen v. Howard*, 343 U.S. 768 (1952).

law prohibited the university from accepting African-Americans; in fact, the legislature was so vehement in its opposition to racially integrated education that it enacted a variety of statutes calling for fines of one hundred to five hundred dollars a day against any institution that taught whites and blacks together; and any student—white or black—attending such a school could be fined five to twenty dollars a day.

Given this situation, both the university administration and Ada Sipuel knew what the response would be when the president met with her. She did not know, however, that he too hoped for a lawsuit to force the end of segregation at his school. At the meeting with her and an NAACP attorney, President Cross asked what she wanted. Sipuel said she wanted to go to law school. Cross responded that the law would not allow that but asked if he could do anything else for her. "Yes," her attorney responded; "give us a letter stating that the only reason Ada Sipuel cannot be admitted is because she is Negro." Cross smiled, knowing exactly what the NAACP wanted, and gladly drafted the letter.[43]

The NAACP immediately sued in state court for admission, knowing it would lose, but with Cross's letter as part of the factual record, it could then appeal to the Supreme Court on the basis of *Gaines*. After Oklahoma's highest court upheld the segregation statutes, the NAACP sought review in Washington. The Supreme Court granted certiorari and heard oral argument on the case in the first week of 1948. Only four days later, the justices handed down a *per curiam* opinion ordering Oklahoma to provide Ada Sipuel with a legal education "in conformity with the equal protection clause of the Fourteenth Amendment and provide it as soon as it does for applicants of any other group."[44] It sent the case back to the Oklahoma Supreme Court, which now had no choice but to order the university to admit Sipuel to the existing all-white law school or open a separate one for her or close the existing law school until such time as there was one for blacks.

The state board of regents angrily created a law school overnight, roping off a small section of the state capitol in Oklahoma City and assigning three teachers to attend to the instruction of Sipuel and "others similarly situated." Ada Sipuel would have nothing to do with this farce, and more than a thousand white students on the University of Oklahoma campus

43. Years later Cross and Ada Sipuel (by this time Ada Suipuel Fisher) became good friends, and in 1992 she was named a regent of the University of Oklahoma. For this information I am indebted to Professor David W. Levy of the University of Oklahoma, who is writing a history of that institution. After Sipuel's meeting with Cross, a number of white students took her out to lunch and urged her not to give up. See Levy, "Before the *Brown* Decision: The Integration Struggle at the University of Oklahoma," *Extensions* (Fall 1994): 10–14.

44. *Sipuel v. Oklahoma State Board of Regents*, 332 U.S. 631 (1948).

held a protest rally against the regents' decision. Addressing the rally, one law school professor decried the action as "a fake, a fraud, and . . . indecent." When the NAACP appealed back to the Supreme Court, a majority of the justices refused to consider whether the state had in fact established an equal facility. The chief justice worked hard to keep the brethren from going beyond what he termed "the only question before us," namely, "whether or not our mandate has been followed." Vinson declared it "clear that it has been followed."[45] In a 7–2 opinion, from which Murphy and Rutledge dissented, the Court held that the original *Sipuel* case had not presented the issue of whether the Equal Protection Clause prevented a state from establishing a separate law school for blacks.[46] To a friend Rutledge wrote, "I was not greatly surprised at the outcome. . . . It is not for me to criticize the action of my brethren, at any rate in any public way other than by speaking in dissent, but I can say to you in confidence that this is not the only time this term when I have felt great discouragement resulting from action taken by the Court."[47]

The NAACP could not claim any real victory in the *Sipuel* case, mainly because the Court still refused to face the central issue of whether separate education could be truly equal under the Constitution. The strategy that the organization had been relying on for more than a decade had been to force the southern states to pay so much to make black facilities equal to those of whites that in the end the states would finally agree to integration because of the costs involved. One of the NAACP expert witnesses in the state trial of Ada Sipuel's suit was Walter Gellhorn of Columbia University Law School. During a recess he spoke with Mac Q. Williamson, the attorney general of Oklahoma, who was defending the state's Jim Crow law. As Gellhorn recalled,

> I was saying to him how I thought that even if they were eventually able to persuade the Supreme Court that the facilities of the Negro school were equal, what was the state going to do when a Negro applied for a medical education—build him a whole medical school? He suddenly saw a flash of light, I guess, and struck his forehead with his palm as the revelation hit him. "Oh, my God," he said, "suppose one of them wanted to be a petroleum engineer! Why, we've got the biggest petro-

---

45. Vinson, Memorandum to the Conference, February 13, 1948, Jackson Papers, Library of Congress.

46. *Fisher v. Hurst*, 333 U.S. 147 (1948). Sipuel had recently married, so the case came under her married name, Ada Fisher. She continued to fight for admission and in the end was admitted to and graduated from the University of Oklahoma Law School.

47. Rutledge to Aubrey Williams, February 26, 1948, Rutledge Papers, Library of Congress.

leum-cracking laboratory in the country here." And I think the fire went out of his case after that.[48]

Perhaps some southerners like Williamson saw the economic problems of continued segregation as potentially ruinous, but as long as *Plessy* remained unchallenged, the NAACP saw no way to force the issue. Thurgood Marshall and his staff, while dropping hints in their legal briefs that separate could never be truly equal, had so far seen no indication that the justices had an inclination to overrule *Plessy*, much less even open up that avenue.

Then on June 5, 1950, the Court handed the NAACP three major victories. In addition to the *Henderson* decision, it once again slapped down the University of Oklahoma. Following the *Sipuel* decision, the University had grudgingly admitted sixty-eight-year-old George W. McLaurin to its graduate school, where he hoped to earn a doctorate in education. But McLaurin had to sit in the corridor outside the regular classroom, use a separate desk on the mezzanine of the library, and eat alone in a dingy alcove in the cafeteria and at a different time from when the white students ate. McLaurin, who had a master's degree and had long been a teacher in an all-black college, came before a special three-judge federal district court and declared that it was "quite strange and humiliating to be placed in that position." The district court nonetheless turned McLaurin down,[49] and Thurgood Marshall appealed the case directly to the Supreme Court.

When the Court accepted the appeal, university officials allowed McLaurin inside the classroom but surrounded his seat with a railing marked "Reserved for Colored." White students tore the sign down and protested until the university relented and permitted McLaurin to sit in an unmarked row set aside for him. They also let him onto the main floor of the library and let him eat at the same time as white students, but still in a separate place. In its brief to the Court, Oklahoma described these restrictions as merely nominal, and necessary for the university to obey the state's separate-but-equal laws. The state, however, portrayed a dark picture of the social turmoil that would result should McLaurin be allowed to intermingle freely with the white students.

The Court now had to begin facing up to the core issue of segregation. The state had not attempted to shuttle McLaurin off to a completely sepa-

---

48. Kluger, *Simple Justice,* 258–59.

49. *McLaurin v. Oklahoma State Regents for Higher Education,* 87 F. Supp. 528 (W.D. Ok. 1949).

rate school, as it had done Sipuel; McLaurin received the same education as white students in objective terms—the same courses, same buildings, same faculty, same state outlay of funds per pupil. But he had been forced to sit by himself, eat by himself, and study by himself; in short, he had been segregated. Did this in any way make his education inferior?

At the same time it heard the Oklahoma case, the Court also heard the NAACP argue the case of Herman Marion Sweatt, a black mailman who sought admission to the University of Texas Law School. Sweatt had first applied for admission in 1946, about the same time that Ada Sipuel tried to get into Oklahoma, and a trial court in Travis County gave the state six months to establish a law school at the all-black Prairie View University. Prairie View represented all that was wrong with segregated higher education; it had a ramshackle physical plant and gave college credit for broom making and other vocational skills. If the state did not establish a law school, then Sweatt would have to be admitted to the University of Texas in Austin.

The president of the University of Texas, Homer Rainey, also believed that segregation should end, and his remarks about providing better educational opportunities for blacks so displeased the trustees that they fired him and replaced him with an archsegregationist, Theophilus Schickel Painter. Texas fought the case at every step of the way, and when the original *Sipuel* decision came down, it even went so far as to appropriate three million dollars to create a new Texas State University for Negroes, of which a hundred thousand dollars would be earmarked for the establishment and maintenance of a law school. In the meantime the state abandoned the Prairie View travesty and, for the period until the new Texas State University for Negroes would be in operation, opened a law school in downtown Austin, just blocks away from the state capital and the University of Texas. The school consisted of three small rooms in a basement, three part-time faculty members who were first-year instructors across town at the regular law school, a library of ten thousand volumes, and access to the state law library in the capital. It would open on March 10, 1947, if Sweatt chose to attend. He did not. He went back to court.

The Court that heard the *McLaurin* and *Sweatt* cases had lost two of its most liberal members, Frank Murphy and Wiley Rutledge. They had been replaced by Tom Clark and Sherman Minton, neither of whose record gave civil libertarians much comfort. But Clark, in a memorandum to the brethren, said he believed that both cases had to be reversed. The restrictions applied to McLaurin appalled him and directly implicated the *Plessy* doctrine. While he was not willing at the time to overrule *Plessy*, he laid out a number of reasons why the precedent should not apply to graduate schools.[50]

The justices discussed the two cases at their conference on April 8, 1950. It is one sign of the changing attitude within the Court, and one may venture to say in the country as well, that in both cases they unanimously agreed to uphold the challenges of the black plaintiffs.[51] The Court did not go as far as Thurgood Marshall would have liked, but it opened the door at least a crack, large enough for the NAACP to take hope and move ahead. Moreover, in a move no one had anticipated, the Justice Department filed *amicus* briefs in both cases bluntly urging the Court to abandon *Plessy*. The justices were still not ready. In a memo to Vinson, Frankfurter urged that the Court "now not go a jot or tittle beyond the *Gaines* test. The shorter the opinion, the more there is an appearance of unexcitement and inevitability about it."[52]

Vinson did in fact draft narrow opinions in the two cases, and, as he had hoped, he managed to get a unanimous Court in both. He announced the two decisions together, along with the *Henderson* opinion. In the case of George McLaurin, Vinson made no bones about the Court's view that Oklahoma had treated him shamefully, and these "inequalities" (the Court chose not to use the word "segregation") had to be ended. Such indignities would, in fact, harm McLaurin's education. McLaurin, Vinson declared,

is attempting to obtain an advanced degree in education, to become, by definition, a leader and trainer of others. Those who will come under his guidance and influence must be directly affected by the education he receives. Their own education and development will necessarily suffer to the extent that his training is unequal to that of his classmates. State-imposed restrictions which produce such inequalities cannot be sustained.

As to the state's argument that lifting the restrictions would not make any difference in how other students treated McLaurin, Vinson responded:

There is a vast difference—a Constitutional difference—between restrictions imposed by the state which prohibit the intellectual commingling

---

50. Clark, Memorandum to the Conference, April [7,] 1950, Douglas Papers, Library of Congress.
51. Douglas, Conference notes of April 8, 1950, *ibid.*
52. Frankfurther to Vinson, May 19, 1950, Frankfurter Papers, Harvard Law School Library.

of students, and the refusal of individuals to commingle where the state presents no such bar. . . . The removal of the state restrictions will not necessarily abate individual and group predilections and choices. But at the very least, the state will not be depriving appellant of the opportunity to secure acceptance by his fellow students on his own merits.[53]

In the Texas case, the state had contended that it had in fact created an equal law school, and the fact that Sweatt chose not to go there did not mean that he had to be admitted to the University of Texas. But if nothing else, the justices knew what made a good law school, and they unanimously rejected the state's claim that its separate law school for blacks was equal to that at Austin. According to the chief justice,

The University of Texas Law School possesses to a far greater degree those qualities which are incapable of objective measurement but which make for greatness in a law school. Such qualities, to name but a few, include reputation of the faculty, experience of the administration, position and influence of the alumni, standing in the community, traditions and prestige. It is difficult to believe that one who had a free choice between these law schools would consider the question close.[54]

The Court ordered Sweatt admitted to the University of Texas Law School—the first time it had ever ordered a black student admitted to a previously all-white institution.

Some southern states promptly responded to the *Sweatt* decision. For example, after *Sipuel,* South Carolina had established a black law school at South Carolina State College, but after *McLaurin* and *Sweatt,* the state closed down the State College law school and gradually began to accept blacks into the previously all-white University of South Carolina Law School.

Although the NAACP and the Justice Department had invited the Court to reexamine the *Plessy* doctrine, the justices had declined. But in detailing how the inequalities afflicting George McLaurin detracted from the quality of his education and how the separate law school in Texas lacked the intangible aspects of a great law school, the opinions in the two cases did in fact indicate that the Court, willingly or not, now stood ready to reconsider the separate-but-equal doctrine. For Thurgood Marshall, the Texas opinion was "replete with road markings telling us where to go

53. *McLaurin v. Oklahoma State Regents,* 339 U.S. 637, 549 (1950).
54. *Sweatt v. Painter,* 339 U.S. 626, 634 (1950).

next."[55] The NAACP would now attack the *Plessy* doctrine frontally by massing overwhelming evidence to show that separate education could never be truly equal.

Some members of the Court had anticipated that a direct attack against the separate-but-equal doctrine would soon be on their doorstep. Seventeen southern and border states, as well as the nation's capital, legally required racial segregation in public schools; another four states permitted it. The attack on segregation per se and not just on the lack of equal facilities had been the goal of the NAACP for years, but in deciding to take on these cases Thurgood Marshall and his legal team knew they would face formidable obstacles. On June 7, 1952, the Court announced that it would hear arguments the following December in cases challenging the school segregation laws of Delaware, Virginia, South Carolina, and Kansas as well as the District of Columbia. The Court consolidated the cases with the Kansas appeal as the lead case so that, according to Justice Clark, "the whole question would not smack of being a purely Southern one."

In the same term that the brethren wrestled with the school cases they also heard another challenge to the South's white primary system. For more than fifty years the Jaybird Democratic Association of Fort Bend County, Texas, just southwest of Houston, had been holding a May primary separate from the official one run by the county the following month. The criteria for voting in the Jaybird election were almost identical to those of the county except that blacks could not participate (as they did in the county primary, thanks to *Smith v. Allwright*), and in court the Jaybird officials acknowledged that their intent had been to exclude blacks. Whoever won the Jaybird primary always won in the county primary and in the general election. The Jaybirds argued that they ran a private canvass without money from or regulation by the state, and therefore their exclusion of blacks did not qualify as state action.

Writing for the Court in *Terry v. Adams*, however, Justice Black saw the Jaybird primary as a subterfuge, one tolerated by the state to defeat the purpose of the Fifteenth Amendment. As he explained, "The only election that has counted in this Texas county for more than fifty years has been that held by the Jaybirds. . . . [It] has become an integral part, indeed the only effective part, of the elective process that determines who shall rule and govern in the county."[56] Only Harold Minton accepted the Jaybird's

---

55. Tushnet, *NAACP's Strategy*, 135.

56. 345 U.S. 461, 469 (1953). Frankfurther entered a concurring opinion at 470, and Clark, joined by Vinson, Reed, and Jackson, concurred at 477. See also Frankfurter to Burton, March 17 and 18, 1953, Frankfurter Papers, Harvard Law School Library. For a study of the primary cases, see Darlene Clark Hine, *Black Victory: The Rise and Fall of the White Primary in Texas* (Millwood, N.Y. KTO Press, 1979).

claim of being a private group, and he noted in his dissent that the record "will be searched in vain for one iota of state action sufficient to support an anemic inference" that the official government had been involved in the plan.[57]

The major civil rights issue that term remained the school cases. The justices had assigned an unusual three days to hear oral arguments—December 9, 10, and 11—and then met for the first time in conference to discuss the matter on December 13. Not surprisingly, they could not reach agreement, and there has been some disagreement over exactly who on the Court was ready to strike down *Plessy*. For a number of years, scholars followed the version put forward in what is undoubtedly the classic study of the case, Richard Kluger's *Simple Justice*.[58] By this account, the justices stood deeply divided after the initial arguments. Frankfurter later wrote to Reed that he had no doubt that if the segregation cases had been decided earlier, there would have been at least four dissents—by Vinson, Reed, Jackson, and Clark—and multiple majority opinions. Law clerks at the time believed that a majority of the justices would not have voted to overrule *Plessy*, and John W. Davis, who argued on behalf of South Carolina, commented after the oral argument, "I think we've got it won, five-to-four—or maybe six-to-three."[59]

By this accounting, Black and Douglas had been prepared to overturn segregation from the start and had the support of Burton and Minton. Frankfurter and Jackson, although personally opposed to segregation, had reservations about the Court's power in this area as well as how such a reversal of *Plessy* would be received in the South, and Frankfurter in particular urged caution and delay. Vinson and Reed, both from Kentucky, saw nothing wrong with segregation so long as the southern states provided equal facilities, and Tom Clark leaned in their direction.

---

57. 345 U.S. at 484, 485–86. Minton's dissent may well be ascribed to his longtime activism in the Democratic Party; Frankfurter once characterized him as "an almost pathological Democrat." Minton otherwise proved to be a staunch advocate of civil rights, and he wrote the Court's opinion in *Barrows v. Jackson*, 346 U.S. 249 (1953), which expanded the definition of state action in *Shelley* to prevent white signatories to restrictive covenants from suing for damages against other signers who sold their property to blacks. In that case only Chief Justice Vinson dissented. For an analysis of how the various state action cases of the Vinson era meshed, see Thomas P. Lewis, "The Meaning of State Action," 60 *Columbia Law Review* 1083 (1960).

58. This account is also followed in Bernard Schwartz's admirable and admiring study of the Warren Court, *Super Chief: Earl Warren and His Supreme Court—A Judicial Biography* (New York: New York University Press, 1983), and to a larger extent in Howard Ball and Phillip J. Cooper, *Of Power and Right: Hugo Black, William O. Douglas, and America's Constitutional Revolution* (New York: Oxford University Press, 1992).

59. Schwartz, *Super Chief*, 72; Kluger, *Simple Justice*, 614, 581.

Much of this account relies on notes and statements made after the Court finally decided the segregation cases in May 1954. In a memorandum to the files written on the day Earl Warren announced the *Brown* decision, William O. Douglas declared that

> in the original conference there were only four who voted that segregation in the public schools was unconstitutional. Those four were Black, Burton, Minton and myself. Vinson was of the opinion that the *Plessy* case was right and that segregation was constitutional. Reed followed the view of Vinson and Clark was inclined that way. In the 1952 conference Frankfurter and Jackson viewed the problem with great alarm and thought that the Court should not decide the question if it was possible to avoid it. Both of them expressed the view that segregation in the public schools was probably constitutional. Frankfurter drew a distinction between segregation in the public schools in the States. He thought that segregation in the public schools of the District of Columbia violated due process but he thought that history was against the claim of unconstitutionality as applied to the public schools of the States.[60]

The problem is that Douglas's memo is not completely reliable, given the bad blood between himself and Frankfurter, and he wrote these memos to the file with a distinct eye to making sure that historians would appreciate his view of what happened.[61] At the same time, Frankfurter also left a considerable paper trail, and he told many people that he had delayed the decision in *Brown* to help the Court reach the right judgment.[62]

Recent scholarship, as well as common sense, tells us that the supposed divisions on the bench in 1952 could not have been that concrete since, with the exception of one person, the Court that handed down the unanimous decision in *Brown* in 1954 was the same Court that first heard it in 1952. In an exhaustive survey of manuscript records that had been unavailable to earlier scholars, Mark Tushnet and Katya Lezin have suggested that there was less division on the Court than had been supposed and that while Frankfurter supplied a format on which the Warren Court could agree, the

---

60. Dougal, *Memorandum for the File*, 17 May 1954, Douglas Papers, Library of Congress.

61. See, for example, a similar memorandum to the file, 8 October 1958, detailing Frankfurter's obstructionism in the Little Rock case (*Cooper v. Aaron*, 358 U.S. 1 [1958], *ibid.*

62. See in particular Philip Elman, "The Solicitors General's Office, Justice Frankfurter and Civil Rights Litigation 1946–1960: An Oral History," 100 *Harvard Law Review* 817 (1987). Elman, a former clerk to Frankfurter, was then in the solicitor general's office, spoke with Frankfurter on a regular basis, and has supported the notion that it was Frankfurter who masterminded the strategy that eventually led to an unanimous decision.

key person in shaping the Warren Court's mind may well have been Justice Jackson.[63]

In the last year of the Vinson Court, the segregation cases worried all of the justices. The Court, in granting review, could no longer avoid the question of whether segregation, even in equal facilities, violated the Constitution; they would have to either overrule *Plessy* or reaffirm it. Frankfurter's caution on segregation has occasionally been misinterpreted as hostility to civil rights or support for the separate-but-equal doctrine. In the late 1940s Frankfurter began a file on school segregation for his personal use, and he understood how sensitive and volatile a departure from the separate-but-equal principle would be. This added to his already cautious approach to decision making, and he kept warning his colleagues in the pre-*Brown* cases to write as narrowly as possible. Instead of charging up to the central question—and, to Frankfurter, the inescapable question—of whether segregation violated the Constitution, he preferred a more conservative approach, taking cases as they came and deciding them on the narrowest possible grounds. The Court did not have to "go out and meet problems," he told his colleagues.[64]

But Frankfurter's commitment to civil rights should not be doubted. He had been an early supporter of the NAACP, and in every case involving civil rights for African Americans that came before the Court in his twenty-three-year tenure, he voted to support the claims of black Americans. It was Frankfurter who hired the first black clerk on the high court, and as he told Paul Freund, "I don't care what color a man has, any more than I care what religion he professes or doesn't."[65] William Coleman, who broke the color barrier in clerking for Frankfurter in the October 1948 Term, always considered Frankfurter a champion of civil rights, but one who felt constrained by the limits of judicial restraint.[66]

Frankfurter and Robert Jackson, the Court's two leading advocates of judicial restraints, did not know whether the Court could reach out and

---

63. Tushnet and Katya Lezin, "What Really Happened in Brown v. Board of Education," 91 *Columbia Law Review* 1867 (1991); see also Dennis J. Hutchinson, "Unanimity and Desegregation: Decision making in the Supreme Court, 1948–1958," 68 *Georgetown Law Journal* 1 (1979).

64. James F. Simon, *The Antagonists: Hugo Black, Felix Frankfurter and Civil Liberties Modern America* (New York: Simon & Schuster, 1989), 216–17.

65. Frankfurter to Paul Freund, 18 December 1947, Frankfurter Papers, Harvard Law School Library. Henry Hart chose Frankfurter's clerks, with advice from Freund; and just as Brandeis and Holmes had given him full power of selection, so Frankfurter gave a similar authority to Hart.

66. William T. Coleman, Jr., "Mr. Justice Frankfurter: Civil Libertarian as Lawyer and as Justice: Extent to which Judicial Responsibilities Affected His Pre-Court Convictions," in Ronald D. Rotunda, ed., *Six Justices on Civil Rights* (New York: Oceana, 1983), 85–105.

summarily overturn a half-century of precedent to invalidate segregation. Frankfurter hoped that history might shed some light on what the framers of the Fourteenth Amendment had intended, and he set his law clerk, Alexander Bickel, to work researching that topic. Bickel's labors yielded a lengthy memorandum that, at best, indicated an ambiguity on the part of those who drafted and then voted to ratify the amendment. While it certainly did not provide the support Frankfurter wanted, to his credit he circulated the memorandum so that his colleagues, whatever their views, might be able to consult it.[67]

Frankfurter correctly understood that if the Court decided to reverse *Plessy*, it could not do so by a 5–4 or even a 6–3 vote; it would have to be unanimous. According to Bickel, the Justice worried that a decision striking down segregation would be disobeyed, "which would be the beginning rather than the end of a controversy."[68] So with the exception of Douglas and Black, all the other justices had good reason to want the cases delayed. Some merely wanted to avoid a hard decision; for Frankfurter procrastination might be the only way eventually to bring the Court around to a position acceptable to all of its members. During that spring of 1953, Frankfurter described himself as a *Kochleffel*, a cooking spoon, stirring things up and keeping them simmering until the right time would come for the Court to act.[69]

As the term came to an end, Frankfurter circulated a series of questions that he suggested should be addressed by counsel when they reargued the case.[70] For once the brethren agreed with him, and at the last conference of the term, on May 29, 1953, the Court set down the segregation cases for reargument the following fall. The Court asked all sides to address the issues of (1) congressional intent in the drafting of the Civil War amendments; (2) what the framers of these amendments understood regarding segregation in public schools; (3) whether federal courts could abolish public school segregation; and (4) what kinds of remedies the Court should adopt if it found *Plessy* inconsistent with the Fourteenth Amendment.[71]

---

67. The piece was so good that Bickel, with Frankfurter's blessing and encouragement, published it in slightly modified form as "The Original Understanding and the Segregation Decision," 69 *Harvard Law Review* 1 (1995).

68. Leonard Baker, *Brandeis and Frankfurter: A Dual Biography* (New York: Harper & Row, 1984), 479.

69. Elman, "The Solicitor General's Office," 832.

70. The justices, over Hugo Black's objection, had also invited the attorney general to argue the government's *amicus* position before the Court. See Black, *Memorandum to the Conference*, 13 June 1953, Black Papers, Library of Congress.

71. Frankfurter, Memoranda to the Conference, May 27, and June 4, 1953, and Frankfurter to Vinson, June 8, 1953, Frankfurter Papers, Harvard Law School Library.

Frankfurter's demand for caution and delay found a ready response with the chief justice. But as recent scholarship has shown, Vinson, while he may have been uncomfortable at the idea of directly overruling *Plessy*, had nonetheless been moving steadily in that direction. The 1950 trilogy of civil rights cases put a "hydraulic pressure" on all the justices, but especially on those most wary of a broad-based challenge to segregation.[72] It would appear that the chief justice's real concerns lay primarily in matters of timing and the scope of the remedy.[73] Had he overcome these considerations earlier, it might well have been, as Philip Kurland has suggested, that Vinson and not his successor could have written the unanimous opinion in *Brown*.[74]

Then on September 8, 1953, Fred Vinson died of a heart attack in his Washington hotel apartment at the age of sixty-three. All the members of the Court came to his funeral in Louisa, Kentucky, and at the graveside at least one of them quietly rejoiced in his passing. Felix Frankfurter wrongly viewed Vinson, despite his opinions in *Sipuel, Shelley,* and *Sweatt,* as having been the chief obstacle to the Court's reaching a workable and judicially defensible settlement of the segregation cases. With the five consolidated cases due for reargument that fall, Frankfurter viewed Vinson's death as almost providential. "This is the first indication I have ever had," he somewhat maliciously told a former clerk, "that there is a God."[75] Three weeks later, Dwight Eisenhower named Earl Warren chief justice of the United States, and a new era in American constitutional history began.

That new era would not have been possible without the decisions made during the time Harlan Fiske Stone and Fred Vinson served as chief justices of the United States. It is not that the Court in these years clearly set out on a new jurisprudential path but rather that the justices began to accommodate themselves to a new agenda that looked primarily at civil rights and liberties rather than at property rights. The first steps down that path had been taken well before 1941, in fact even before the constitutional crisis of 1937. The journey had begun in the 1920s when Louis Brandeis had suggested that the Fourteenth Amendment's Due Process Clause included protection of individual liberties as well as property, and it had begun to accelerate in the 1930s as the Court adopted the process of incorporation. The crisis of 1937 put an end to the so-called Old Court with its preoccupation with protecting property against the alleged depredations

72. Hutchinson, "Unanimity and Desegregation," 87.
73. Tushnet and Lezin, "What Really Happened," 1902–4.
74. Philip Kurland, "Earl Warren, the 'Warren Court,' and the Warren Myth," 67 *Michigan Law Review* 353, 356 (1968).
75. Kluger, *Simple Justice,* 656.

of the state. As we have seen, the constitutionality of economic regulation played practically no role in the deliberations of the Stone and Vinson Courts.

The great steps taken to protect civil rights and liberties in the Warren and Burger Courts would not have been possible without the debates and explorations of their predecessors. While the conflict between Felix Frankfurter and Hugo Black did much to define the constitutional parameters of that debate, one should not lose sight of the critical facts that both men believed in judicial restraint, both believed the government had the power to regulate the economy, and above all, both believed that the Supreme Court had the obligation to protect the rights of individuals. Their differences helped their colleagues and the country determine how far the judiciary should go in this quest, but they and their brethren on the Court during these years believed that the Court could not avoid this responsibility. Looking back, we can now see the Stone and Vinson era, despite the division and discord, for what it was, a period of transition, one that would have profound effects on the nation and on the Court in years to come.

# Appendix

# MEMBERS OF THE SUPREME COURT, 1941–1953, AND DATES OF SERVICE

## (Arranged in Order of Appointment)

| | |
|---|---|
| Owen Josephus Roberts | Confirmed 20 May 1930<br>Retired 31 July 1945 |
| Harlan Fiske Stone | Confirmed as justice 2 February 1925;<br>confirmed as chief justice<br>27 June 1941<br>Died 22 April 1946 |
| Hugo LaFayette Black | Confirmed 17 August 1937<br>Retired 17 September 1971 |
| Stanley Forman Reed | Confirmed 25 January 1938<br>Retired 25 February 1957 |
| Felix Frankfurter | Confirmed 17 January 1939<br>Retired 28 August 1962 |
| William O. Douglas | Confirmed 4 April 1939<br>Retired 12 November 1975 |
| Francis (Frank) William Murphy | Confirmed 16 January 1940<br>Died 19 July 1949 |
| James Francis Byrnes | Confirmed 12 June 1941<br>Resigned 3 October 1942 |
| Robert Houghwout Jackson | Confirmed 7 July 1941<br>Died 9 October 1954 |
| Wiley Blount Rutledge | Confirmed 8 February 1943<br>Died 10 September 1949 |
| Harold Hitz Burton | Confirmed 19 September 1945<br>Retired 13 October 1958 |
| Frederick Moore Vinson | Confirmed 20 June 1946<br>Died 8 September 1953 |

| Tom Campbell Clark | Confirmed 18 August 1949 |
| | Retired 12 June 1967 |
| Sherman Minton | Confirmed 4 October 1949 |
| | Retired 15 October 1956 |

# BIBLIOGRAPHY

## MANUSCRIPTS AND MEMOIRS

Hugo LaFayette Black Papers, Library of Congress, Washington, D.C.

Leonard Boudin Memoirs, Columbia University Oral History Collection, Columbia University, New York, N.Y.

Harold Hitz Burton Papers, Library of Congress, Washington, D.C.

William O. Douglas Papers, Library of Congress, Washington, D.C.

Thomas Emerson Memoirs, Columbia Oral History Collection, Columbia University, New York, N.Y.

Felix Frankfurter Memoirs, Columbia Oral History Collection, Columbia University, New York, N.Y.

Felix Frankfurter Papers, Harvard Law School Library, Cambridge, Mass.

Felix Frankfurter Papers, Library of Congress, Washington, D.C.

Robert Houghwout Jackson Memoirs, Columbia Oral History Collection, Columbia University, New York, N.Y.

Robert Houghwout Jackson Papers, Library of Congress, Washington, D.C.

Thomas Reed Powell Papers, Harvard Law School Library, Cambridge, Mass.

Stanley Forman Reed Memoirs, Columbia Oral History Collection, Columbia University, New York, N.Y.

Wiley Blount Rutledge Papers, Library of Congress, Washington, D.C.

Harlan Fiske Stone Papers, Library of Congress, Washington, D.C.

## BOOKS

Allen, Robert S., and William V. Shannon. *The Truman Merry-Go-Round* (New York: Vanguard, 1950).

American Bar Association. *Model Code of Professional Responsibility and Code of Judicial Conduct* (Chicago: ABA, 1980).

Baker, Leonard. *Brandeis and Frankfurter: A Dual Biography* (New York: Harper & Row, 1984).

Ball, Howard, and Phillip J. Cooper. *Of Power and Right: Hugo Black, William O. Douglas, and America's Constitutional Revolution* (New York: Oxford University Press, 1992).

Barnes, Catherine A. *Journey from Jim Crow: The Desegregation of Southern Transit* (New York: Columbia University Press, 1983).

Belknap, Michal R. *Cold War Political Justice: The Smith Act, the Communist Party, and American Civil Liberties* (Westport, Conn.: Greenwood, 1977).

Berry, Mary Frances. *Stability, Security and Continuity: Mr. Justice Burton and Decision-Making in the Supreme Court (1945–1958)* (Westport, Conn.: Greenwood, 1978).

Beth, Loren P. *The Development of the American Constitution, 1877–1917* (New York: Harper & Row, 1971).

Biddle, Francis. *In Brief Authority* (Garden City, N.Y.. Doubleday, 1962).

Black, Hugo L. *A Constitutional Faith* (New York: Knopf, 1968).

Blackman, John L., Jr. *Presidential Seizure in Labor Disputes* (Cambridge: Harvard University Press, 1967).

Bosch, William J. *Judgment on Nuremberg: American Attitudes Toward the Major War-Crime Trials* (Chapel Hill: University of North Carolina Press, 1970).

Burt, Robert A. *Two Jewish Justices: Outcasts in the Promised Land* (Berkeley: University of California Press, 1988).

Byrnes, James. *All in One Lifetime* (New York: Harper, 1958).

Cahn, Edmond, ed. *Supreme Court and Supreme Law* (Bloomington: Indiana University Press, 1954).

Carr, Robert K. *Federal Protection of Civil Liberties* (Ithaca: Cornell University Press, 1947).

Caute, David. *The Great Fear: The Anti-Communist Purges Under Truman and Eisenhower* (New York: Simon & Schuster, 1978).

Cooley, Thomas M. *A Treatise on Constitutional Limitations . . .* (Boston: Little, Brown, 1868).

Cortner, Richard C. *The Apportionment Cases* (New York: Norton, 1970).

———. *The Supreme Court and the Second Bill of Rights: The Fourteenth Amendment and the Nationalization of Civil Liberties* (Madison: University of Wisconsin Press, 1981).

Corwin, Edward S. *Total War and the Constitution* (New York: Knopf, 1947).

Crosskey, William W. *Politics and the Constitution in the History of the United States* (Chicago: University of Chicago Press, 1953).

Currie, David P. *The Constitution in the Supreme Court: The Second Century, 1888–1986* (Chicago: University of Chicago Press, 1990).

Curtis, Michael Kent. *No State Shall Abridge: The Fourteenth Amendment and the Bill of Rights* (Durham: Duke University Press, 1986).

Donovan, Robert J. *The Tumultuous Years* (New York: Norton, 1982).

Douglas, William O. *The Court Years: 1939–1975* (New York: Random House, 1980).

———. *Go East, Young Man: The Early Years* (New York: Random House, 1974).

———. *Of Men and Mountains* (New York: Harper, 1950).

Dubofsky, Melvyn, and Warren Van Tine. *John L. Lewis: A Biography.* Abridged ed. (Urbana: University of Illinois Press, 1986).

Dulles, Foster Rhea, and Melvyn Dubofsky. *Labor in America: A History.* 4th ed. (Arlington Heights, Ill.: Harlan Davidson, 1984).

Dunne, Gerald T. *Hugo Black and the Judicial Revolution* (New York: Simon & Schuster, 1977).

Fassett, John D. *New Deal Justice: The Life of Stanley Reed of Kentucky* (New York: Vantage, 1994).

Fine, Sidney. *Frank Murphy: The Washington Years* (Ann Arbor: University of Michigan Press, 1984).

Forbath, William E. *Law and the Shaping of the American Labor Movement* (Cambridge: Harvard University Press, 1991).

Frankfurter, Felix, and Nathaniel Greene. *The Labor Injunction* (New York: Macmillan, 1930).

Freedman, Max, ed. *Roosevelt and Frankfurter: Their Correspondence, 1928–1945* (Boston: Atlantic Little, Brown, 1967).

Freyer, Tony. *Harmony & Dissonance: The Swift and Erie Cases in American Federalism* (New York: New York University Press, 1981).

———. *Justice Hugo Black and Modern America* (University: University of Alabama Press, 1990).

Friedman, Leon, and Fred L. Israel, eds. *The Justices of the Supreme Court, 1789–1969: Their Lives and Opinions.* 4 vols. (New York: Chelsea House, 1969).

Garraty, John A., ed. *Quarrels That Have Shaped the Constitution* (New York: Harper & Row, 1964).

Gerhart, Eugene. *America's Advocate: Robert H. Jackson* (Indianapolis: Bobbs-Merrill, 1958).

Goings, Kenneth W. *"The NAACP Comes of Age": The Defeat of Judge John J. Parker* (Bloomington: Indiana University Press, 1990).

Gosnell, Harold F. *Truman's Crises: A Political Biography of Harry S. Truman* (Westport, Conn.: Greenwood, 1980).

Graham, Fred. *The Self-Inflicted Wound* (New York: Macmillan, 1970).

Gunther, Gerald. *Learned Hand: The Man and the Judge* (New York: Knopf, 1994).

Harper, Fowler V. *Justice Rutledge and the Bright Constellation* (Indianapolis: Bobbs-Merrill, 1965).

Hawthorne, Daniel. *Judge Medina: A Biography* (New York: Funk, 1952).

Herring, George C., Jr. *Aid to Russia, 1941–1946* (New York: Columbia University Press, 1973).

Hine, Darlene Clark. *Black Victory: The Rise and Fall of the White Primary in Texas* (Millwood, N.Y.: KTO, 1979).

Hirsch, H. N. *The Enigma of Felix Frankfurter* (New York: Basic Books, 1981).

Holmes, Oliver Wendell. *The Common Law* (Boston: Little, Brown, 1881).

Howard, J. Woodford, Jr. *Mr. Justice Murphy: A Political Biography* (Princeton: Princeton University Press, 1968).

Hurst, J. Willard. *The Law of Treason in the United States* (Westport, Conn.: Greenwood, 1971).

Ickes, Harold L. *The Secret Diaries of Harold L. Ickes.* 3 vols. (New York: Simon & Schuster, 1954).

Irons, Peter. *Justice at War* (New York: Oxford University Press, 1983).

Jackson, Robert H. *The Struggle for Judicial Supremacy* (New York: Knopf, 1941).

Jacobs, Clyde E. *Law Writers and the Courts: The Influence of Thomas M. Cooley, Christopher G. Tiedeman, and John F. Dillon upon American Constitutional Law* (Berkeley: University of California Press, 1954).

Johnson, John W., ed. *Historic U.S. Court Cases, 1690–1990: An Encyclopedia* (New York: Garland, 1992).

Kalman, Laura. *Legal Realism at Yale, 1927–1960* (Chapel Hill: University of North Carolina Press, 1986).

Kalven, Harry, Jr. *A Worthy Tradition: Freedom of Speech in America* (New York: Harper & Row, 1988).

Kluger, Richard. *Simple Justice: The History of Brown v. Board of Education and Black America's Struggle for Equality* (New York: Knopf, 1976).

Kurland, Philip. *Religion and the Law of Church and State and the Supreme Court* (Chicago: Aldine, 1962).

Kutler, Stanley I. *The American Inquisition: Justice and Injustice in the Cold War* (New York: Hill & Wang, 1982).

Lael, Richard. *The Yamashita Precedent* (Wilmington, Del.: Scholarly Resources, 1982).

Landynski, Jacob W. *Search and Seizure and the Supreme Court* (Baltimore: Johns Hopkins University Press, 1966).

Lash, Joseph, ed. *From the Diaries of Felix Frankfurter* (New York: Norton, 1975).

Leonard, Charles A. *A Search for a Judicial Philosophy: Mr. Justice Roberts and the Constitutional Revolution of 1937* (Port Washington, N.Y.: Kennikat, 1971)

Leuchtenburg, William E. *Franklin D. Roosevelt and the New Deal, 1932–1940* (New York: Harper & Row, 1963).

———. *The Supreme Court Reborn* (New York: Oxford University Press, 1995).

Levantrosser, William F., ed. *Harry S. Truman: The Man from Independence* (Westport, Conn.: Greenwood, 1986).

Levy, Leonard W. *The Establishment Clause: Religion and the First Amendment* (New York: Macmillan, 1986).

Lewis, Anthony. *Gideon's Trumpet* (New York: Random House, 1964).

Lichtenstein, Nelson. *Labor's War at Home: The CIO in World War Two* (Cambridge: Cambridge University Press, 1982).

Lofgren, Charles A. *The Plessy Case: A Legal-Historical Interpretation* (New York: Oxford University Press, 1987).

Lurie, Jonathan. *Arming Military Justice.* Vol. 1, *The Origins of the United States Court of Military Appeals, 1775–1950* (Princeton: Princeton University Press, 1992).

Magee, James J. *Mr. Justice Black: Absolutist on the Court* (Charlottesville: University of Virginia Press, 1980).

Manwaring, David. *Render Unto Caesar: The Flag Salute Controversy* (Chicago: University of Chicago Press, 1962).

Marcus, Maeva. *Truman and the Steel Seizure Case: The Limits of Presidential Power* (New York: Columbia University Press, 1977).

Mason, Alpheus T. *Harlan Fiske Stone: Pillar of the Law* (New York: Viking, 1956).

———. *Security Through Freedom: American Political Thought and Practice* (Ithaca: Cornell University Press, 1955).

McCloskey, Robert G. *The American Supreme Court* (Chicago: University of Chicago Press, 1960).

McClure, Arthur F. *The Truman Administration and the Problems of Postwar Labor, 1945–1948* (Rutherford, N.J.: Fairleigh Dickinson University Press, 1969).

McCollum, Vashti. *One Woman's Fight* (Garden City, N.Y.: Doubleday, 1951).

McCullough, David. *Truman* (New York: Simon & Schuster, 1992).

Mendelson, Wallace, ed. *Felix Frankfurter: A Tribute* (New York: Reynal, 1964).

———. *Justices Black and Frankfurter: Conflict in the Court* (Chicago: University of Chicago Press, 1961).

Miller, Merle. *Plain Speaking: An Oral History of Harry S. Truman* (New York: Berkeley, 1974).

Miller, Arthur S. *Death by Installments: The Ordeal of Willie Francis* (New York: Greenwood, 1988).

Miller, Loren. *The Petitioners: The Story of the Supreme Court of the United States and the Negro* (Cleveland: World, 1966).

Millis, Harry A., and Emily Clark Brown. *From the Wagner Act to Taft-Hartley: A Study of National Labor Policy and Labor Relations* (Chicago: University of Chicago Press, 1950).

Minear, Richard H. *Victor's Justice: The Tokyo War Crimes Trial* (Princeton: Princeton University Press, 1971).

Murphy, Bruce. *The Brandeis/Frankfurter Connection* (New York: Oxford University Press, 1982).

Murphy, Paul L. *The Constitution in Crisis Times, 1918–1969* (New York: Harper & Row, 1972).

Nelson, William E. *The Fourteenth Amendment: From Political Principle to Judicial Doctrine* (Cambridge: Harvard University Press, 1988).

Newman, Roger K. *Hugo Black: A Biography* (New York: Pantheon, 1994).

O'Brien, F. William. *Justice Reed and the First Amendment: The Religion Clauses* (Washington: Georgetown University Press, 1958).

Palmer, Jan. *The Vinson Court Era: The Supreme Court's Conference Votes: Data and Analysis* (New York: AMS Press, 1990).

Parrish, Michael. *Felix Frankfurter and His Times: The Reform Years* (New York: Free Press, 1982).

———. *Securities Regulation and the New Deal* (New Haven: Yale University Press, 1970).

Philips, Harlan, ed. *Felix Frankfurter Reminisces* (New York: Reynal, 1960).

Piccigallo, Philip R. *The Japanese on Trial: Allied War Crimes Operations in the East, 1945–1951* (Austin: University of Texas Press, 1979).

Post, Charles Gordon, Jr. *The Supreme Court and Political Questions* (Baltimore: Johns Hopkins University Press, 1969).

Power, Theodore. *The School Bus Law: A Case Study in Education, Religion, and Politics* (Middletown, Conn.: Wesleyan University Press, 1960).

Pritchett, C. Herman. *Civil Liberties and the Vinson Court* (Chicago: University of Chicago Press, 1954).

———. *The Roosevelt Court: A Study in Judicial Politics and Values, 1937–1947* (New York: Macmillan, 1948).

Reel, A. Frank. *The Case of General Yamashita* (Chicago: University of Chicago Press, 1949).

Rehnquist, William H. *The Supreme Court: How It Was, How It Is* (New York: William Morrow, 1987).

Riley, Glenda. *Divorce: An American Tradition* (New York: Oxford University Press, 1991).

Roberts, Owen J. *The Court and the Constitution* (Cambridge: Harvard University Press, 1951).

Rodell, Fred. *Nine Men* (New York: Random House, 1955).

Rotunda, Ronald D., ed. *Six Justices on Civil Rights* (New York: Oceana, 1983).

Rudko, Frances Howell. *Truman's Court: A Study in Judicial Restraint* (Westport, Conn.: Greenwood, 1988).

Schubert, Glendon. *Dispassionate Justice: A Synthesis of the Judicial Opinions of Robert H. Jackson* (Indianapolis: Bobbs-Merrill, 1969).

Schwartz, Bernard. *Super Chief: Earl Warren and His Supreme Court—A Judicial Biography* (New York: New York University Press, 1983).

Schwarz, Bernard, with Stephan Leshar. *Inside the Warren Court* (Garden City, N.Y.: Doubleday, 1983).

Semonche, John E. *Charting the Future: The Supreme Court Responds to a Changing Society, 1890–1920* (Westport, Conn.: Greenwood, 1978).

Silverstein, Mark. *Constitutional Faiths: Felix Frankfurter, Hugo Black, and the Process of Judicial Decision Making* (Ithaca: Cornell University Press, 1984).

Simon, James F. *The Antagonists: Hugo Black, Felix Frankfurter and Civil Liberties in Modern America* (New York: Simon & Schuster, 1989).

———. *Independent Journey: The Life of William O. Douglas* (New York: Harper & Row, 1980).

Smith, Page. *Democracy on Trial: The Japanese-American Evacuation and Relocation in World War II* (New York: Simon & Schuster, 1995).

Strum, Philippa. *Brandeis: Beyond Progressivism* (Lawrence: University Press of Kansas, 1993).

———. *The Supreme Court and "Political Questions": A Study in Judicial Evasion* (University: University of Alabama Press, 1974).

Swindler, William F. *Court and Constitution in the 20th Century: The New Legality, 1932–1968* (Kansas City: Bobbs-Merrill, 1970).

Taylor, Telford. *The Anatomy of the Nuremburg Trials: A Personal Memoir* (New York: Knopf, 1992).

Ten Broeck, Jacobus, Edward N. Barnhart, and Floyd W. Matson. *Prejudice, War and the Constitution* (Berkeley: University of California Press, 1954, 1968).

*To Secure These Rights: The Report of the President's Committee on Civil Rights* (Washington: Government Printing Office, 1947).

Tiedeman, Christopher G. *A Treatise on the Limitations of Police Power in the United States . . .* 2 vols. (St. Louis: F. H. Thomas, 1886).

Tomlins, Christopher L. *The State and the Unions: Labor Relations, Law, and the Organized Labor Movement in America, 1880–1960* (Cambridge: Cambridge University Press, 1985).

Truman, Harry S. *Memoirs.* 2 vols. (Garden City, N.Y.: Doubleday, 1955–56).

Tusa, Ann, and John Tusa. *The Nuremberg Trial* (New York: Atheneum, 1983).

Tushnet, Mark V. *Making Civil Rights Law: Thurgood Marshall and the Supreme Court, 1936–1961* (New York: Oxford University Press, 1994).

————. *The NAACP's Strategy Against Segregated Education, 1925–1950* (Chapel Hill: University of North Carolina Press, 1987).

U.S. Commission on Wartime Relocation. *Personal Justice Denied* (Washington: Government Printing Office, 1983).

Urofsky, Melvin I. *Felix Frankfurter: Judicial Restraint and Individual Liberties* (Boston: Twayne, 1991).

————, ed. *The Supreme Court Justices: A Biographical Dictionary* (New York: Garland, 1994).

Urofsky, Melvin I., and David W. Levy, eds. *"Half Brother, Half Son": The Letters of Louis D. Brandeis to Felix Frankfurter* (Norman: University of Oklahoma Press, 1991).

————, eds. *Letters of Louis D. Brandeis.* 5 vols. (Albany: State University of New York Press, 1971–78).

Vose, Clement. *Caucasians Only: The Supreme Court, the NAACP, and the Restrictive Covenant Cases* (Berkeley: University of California Press, 1959).

Wasby, Stephen L., ed. *"He Shall Not Pass This Way Again": The Legacy of Justice William O. Douglas* (Pittsburgh: University of Pittsburgh Press, 1990).

————, ed. *The Impact of the United States Supreme Court: Some Perspectives* (Chicago: Dorsey, 1970).

Westin, Alan F. *Privacy and Freedom* (New York: Atheneum, 1967).

White, G. Edward. *The American Judicial Tradition.* Expanded ed. (New York: Oxford University Press, 1988).

Woodward, C. Vann. *The Strange Career of Jim Crow.* 2d ed. (New York: Oxford University Press, 1966).

Yarbrough, Tinsley E. *Mr. Justice Black and His Critics* (Durham: Duke University Press, 1988).


## ARTICLES, BOOK CHAPTERS, AND OTHER SOURCES

Adams, Edward W. "State Control of Interstate Migration of Indigents." 40 *Michigan Law Review* 711 (1942).

Allen, Francis A. "Chief Justice Vinson and the Theory of Constitutional Government: A Tentative Appraisal." 49 *Northwestern University Law Review* 3 (1954).

————. "The Wolf Case: Search and Seizure, Federalism, and Civil Liberties." 45 *Illinois Law Review* 11 (1950).

Anthony, J. Garner. "Martial Law in Hawaii." 30 *California Law Review* 379 (1942).

————. "Recent Developments of Martial Law in the Pacific Area." 29 *Iowa Law Review* 481 (1944).

Arkes, Hadley. "Civility and the Restriction of Speech: Rediscovering the Defamation of Groups." 1974 *Supreme Court Review* 181.

Atkinson, David N. "American Constitutionalism Under Stress: Justice Burton's Response to National Security Issues." 9 *Houston Law Review* 271 (1971).

————. "From New Deal Liberal to Supreme Court Conservative." 1975 *Washington University Law Quarterly* 361.

————. "Justice Harold H. Burton and the Work of the Supreme Court." 27 *Cleveland State Law Review* 69 (1978).

Auerbach, Jerald S. "The LaFollette Committee: Labor and Civil Liberties in the New Deal." 51 *Journal of American History* 435 (1964).

Aynes, Richard L. "Charles Fairman, Felix Frankfurter, and the Fourteenth Amendment." 70 *Chicago-Kent Law Review* 1197 (1995).

Barber, Hollis W. "Religious Liberty v. The Police Power: Jehovah's Witnesses." 41 *American Political Science Review* 226 (1947).

Barnhard, William J. "Haddock Revised." 31 *Georgetown Law Journal* 210 (1943).

Bernstein, Cyrus. "The Saboteur Trial." 11 *George Washington Law Review* 131 (1943).

Bernstein, Nahum A. "The Fruit of the Poisonous Tree. . . ." 37 *Illinois Law Review* 99 (1942).

Beth, Loren P. "Group Libel and Free Speech." 39 *Minnesota Law Review* 167 (1955).

Bickel, Alexander. "Applied Policies and the Science of Law: Writings of the Harvard Period," in Wallace Mendelson, ed., *Felix Frankfurter: A Tribute* (New York: Reynal, 1967).

————. "The Original Understanding and the Segregation Decision." 69 *Harvard Law Review* 1 (1955).

Black, Hugo. "Mr. Justice Frankfurter." 78 *Harvard Law Review* 1521 (1965).

Borchard, Edwin. "Extraterritorial Confiscation." 36 *American Journal of International Law* 275 (1942).

Boudin, Louis B. " 'Seditious Doctrines' and the 'Clear and Present Danger' Rule." 38 *Virginia Law Review* 143, 315 (1952).

Brudney, Victor, and Richard F. Wolfson. "Mr. Justice Rutledge: Law Clerks' Reflections." 25 *Indiana Law Journal* 455 (1950).

Carr, Robert K. "Screws v. United States: The Georgia Brutality Case." 31 *Cornell Law Quarterly* 48 (1945).

Cohen, Julius. "The Screws Case—Federal Protection of Negro Rights." 46 *Columbia Law Review* 94 (1946).

Cohen, William. "Justice Douglas and the *Rosenberg* Case: Setting the Record Straight." 70 *Cornell Law Review* 211 (1985).

Coleman, William T., Jr. "Mr. Justice Frankfurter: Civil Libertarian as Lawyer and as Justice: Extent to Which Judicial Responsibilities Affected His Pre-Court Convictions," in Ronald D. Rotunda, ed., *Six Justices on Civil Rights* (New York: Oceana, 1983), 85–105.

Corwin, Edward S. "Out-Haddocking Haddock." 93 *University of Pennsylvania Law Review* 341 (1945).

————. "The Passing of Dual Federalism." 36 *Virginia Law Review* 1 (1950).

————. "The Supreme Court as National School Board." 23 *Thought* 665 (1948).

Cox, Archibald. "Strikes, Picketing and the Constitution." 4 *Vanderbilt Law Review* 574 (1951).

Cushman, Robert E. "The Case of the Nazi Saboteurs." 36 *American Political Science Review* 1082 (1942).

————. "The Texas 'White Primary' Case—Smith v. Allwright." 30 *Cornell Law Quarterly* 66 (1944).

Danzig, Richard. "Justice Frankfurter's Opinions in the Flag Salute Cases: Blending Logic and Psychologic in Constitutional Decisionmaking." 36 *Stanford Law Review* 675 (1984).

Dembitz, Nanette. "Racial Discrimination and the Military Judgment: The Supreme Court's Korematsu and Endo Decisions." 45 *Columbia Law Review* 175 (1945).

Divine, Robert A. "The Case of the Smuggled Bombers," in John A. Garraty, ed., *Quarrels That Have Shaped the Constitution* (New York: Harper & Row, 1964), 210–21.

Dodd, E. Merrick. "Picketing and Free Speech: A Dissent." 56 *Harvard Law Review* 513 (1943).

Donelson, Lewis R. III. "Federal Supremacy and the Davidowitz Case." 29 *Georgetown Law Journal* 755 (1941).

Dorin, Denis D. "Truman's 'Biggest Mistake': Tom Clark's Appointment to the Supreme Court," in William F. Levantrosser, ed., *Harry S. Truman: The Man from Independence* (Westport, Conn.: Greenwood, 1986), 323–55.

Douglas, William O. "The Bill of Rights and the Free Society: An Individual View." 13 *Buffalo Law Review* 1 (1963).

————. "The Black Silence of Fear." *New York Times Magazine* (13 January 1952), VI, 7ff.

Dowling, Noel T. "The Methods of Mr. Justice Stone in Constitutional Cases." 41 *Columbia Law Review* 1160 (1941).

Duke, Stephen B. "Justice Douglas and the Criminal Law," in Stephen L. Wasby, ed., *"He Shall Not Pass This Way Again": The Legacy of Justice William O. Douglas* (Pittsburgh: University of Pittsburgh Press, 1990), 133–48.

Elman, Philip. "The Solicitor General's Office, Justice Frankfurter and Civil Rights Litigation, 1946–1960: An Oral History." 100 *Harvard Law Review* 817 (1987).

John Hart Ely, "The Irrepressible Myth of Erie," 87 *Harvard Law Review* 693 (1974).

Emerson, Thomas. "Mr. Justice Douglas' Contribution to the Law: The First Amendment." 74 *Columbia Law Review* 354 (1974).

Fairman, Charles. "Does the Fourteenth Amendment Incorporate the Bill of Rights? The Original Understanding." 2 *Stanford Law Review* 5 (1949).

Fitzgerald, Mark J. "Justice Reed: A Study of a Center Judge" (Diss.: University of Chicago, 1950).

Fraenkel, Osmund K. "Peaceful Picketing — Constitutionally Protected?" 99 *University of Pennsylvania Law Review* 1 (1950).

————. "War, Civil Liberties and the Supreme Court, 1941 to 1946." 55 *Yale Law Journal* 715 (1946).

Frank, John P. "Ex Parte Milligan v. The Five Companies: Martial Law in Hawaii." 44 *Columbia Law Review* 639 (1944).

————. "Fred Vinson and the Chief Justiceship." 21 *University of Chicago Law Review* 212 (1954).

————. "Review and Basic Liberties," in Edmund Cahn, ed., *Supreme Court and Supreme Law* (Bloomington: Indiana University Press, 1954).

Glennon, Michael J. "Douglas the Internationalist: Separation of Powers and the Conduct of Foreign Relations," in Stephen L. Wasby, ed., *"He Shall Not Pass This Way Again": The Legacy of Justice William O. Douglas* (Pittsburgh: University of Pittsburgh Press, 1990), 261–78.

Gregory, Charles O. "Government by Injunction Again." 14 *University of Chicago Law Review* 363 (1947).

———. "Picketing and Coercion: A Defense." 39 *Virginia Law Review* 1053 (1953).

Hastie, William H. "Appraisal of Smith v. Allwright." 5 *Lawyers Guild Review* 65 (1945).

Heffernan, Robert Emmet. "Communism, Constitutionalism and the Principle of Contradiction." 32 *Georgetown Law Journal* 405 (1944).

Hutchinson, Dennis J. "The Black-Jackson Feud." 1988 *Supreme Court Review* 203.

———. "Felix Frankfurter and the Business of the Supreme Court, O.T. 1946—O.T. 1961." 1980 *Supreme Court Review* 143.

———. "Unanimity and Desegregation: Decisionmaking in the Supreme Court, 1948–1958." 68 *Georgetown Law Journal* 1 (1979).

Irons, Peter. "Fancy Dancing in the Marble Palace." 3 *Constitutional Commentary* 35 (1986).

Israel, Jerold. "Gideon v. Wainwright: The 'Art' of Overruling." 1963 *Supreme Court Review* 211.

Jackson, Robert H. "Full Faith and Credit—The Lawyer's Clause." 45 *Columbia Law Review* 1 (1945).

Jaffe, Louis L. "Mr. Justice Jackson." 68 *Harvard Law Review* 940 (1955).

Jessup, Philip. "The Litvinov Assignment and the Pink Case." 36 *American Journal of International Law* 282 (1942).

Jones, Edgar A., Jr. "Picketing and Coercion: A Jurisprudence of Epithets." 39 *Virginia Law Review* 1023 (1953).

Jones, John Paul. *"The Business of the Supreme Court* Revisited." 1995 *Journal of Supreme Court History* 136.

Kurland, Philip. "Earl Warren, the 'Warren Court,' and the Warren Myth." 67 *Michigan Law Review* 353 (1968).

Levinson, Sanford. "Skepticism, Democracy, and Judicial Restraint: An Essay on the Thought of Oliver Wendell Holmes and Felix Frankfurter" (Diss.: Harvard University, 1969).

Levy, David W. "Before the *Brown* Decision: The Integration Struggle at the University of Oklahoma." *Extensions* (Fall 1994), 10–14.

Lewis, Thomas P. "The Meaning of State Action." 60 *Columbia Law Review* 1083 (1960).

Marquardt, Ronald. "The Judicial Justice: Mr. Justice Burton and the Supreme Court" (Diss., University of Missouri, 1973).

McGovney, D. O. "Racial Residential Segregation by State Court Enforcement of Restrictive Agreements, Covenants or Conditions in Deeds is Unconstitutional." 33 *California Law Review* 5 (1945).

McManamon, Mary Brigid. "Felix Frankfurter: Architect of 'Our Federalism.' " 27 *Georgia Law Review* 697 (1993).

Mendelson, Wallace. "Clear and Present Danger—From Schenck to Dennis." 52 *Columbia Law Review* 52 (1952).

Mollan, Robert. "Smith Act Prosecutions: The Effect of the Dennis and Yates Decisions." 26 *University of Pittsburgh Law Review* 710 (1965).

Nathanson, Nathan. "The Communist Trial and the Clear-and-Present-Danger Test." 63 *Harvard Law Review* 1167 (1950).

Note. "Constitutionality of State Laws Providing Sterilization for Habitual Criminals." 51 *Yale Law Journal* 1380 (1942).

Note. "The Constitutionality of the Emergency Price Control Act (O.P.A.)." 18 *Temple University Law Quarterly* 518 (1944).

Note. "Federal Military Commission." 56 *Harvard Law Review* 631 (1943).

Note. "Labor Picketing and Commercial Speech: Free Enterprise Values in the Doctrine of Free Speech," 91 *Yale Law Journal* 938 (1982).

Note. "Peaceful Picketing and the First Amendment." 82 *Columbia Law Review* 1469 (1982).

Note. "The Released Time Cases Revisited: A Study of Group Decisionmaking by the Supreme Court." 83 *Yale Law Journal* 1202 (1974).

Parrish, Michael E. "Cold War Justice: The Supreme Court and the Rosenbergs." 82 *American Historical Review* 805 (1977).

———. "Justice Frankfurter and the Supreme Court," in Jennifer Lowe, ed., *The Jewish Justices of the Supreme Court Revisited: From Brandeis to Fortas,* "special issue of the *Journal of Supreme Court History* (1994), 61–80.

Pettit, William. "Justice Byrnes and the United States Supreme Court." 6 *South Carolina Law Quarterly* 423 (1954).

Petro, Slyvester. "The Supreme Court and the Steel Seizure." 3 *Labor Law Journal* 451 (1952).

Powe, Lucas A., Jr. "Evolution to Absolutism: Justice Douglas and the First Amendment." 74 *Columbia Law Review* 371 (1974).

———. "Justice Douglas, the First Amendment, and the Protection of Rights," in Stephen L. Wasby, ed., *"He Shall Not Pass This Way Again": The Legacy of Justice William O. Douglas* (Pittsburgh: University of Pittsburgh Press, 1990), 69–90.

Powell, Thomas Reed. "And Repent at Leisure, an Inquiry into the Unhappy Lot of Those Whom Nevada Hath Joined Together and North Carolina Hath Put Asunder." 58 *Harvard Law Review* 930 (1945).

———. "Insurance as Commerce in Constitution and Statute." 57 *Harvard Law Review* 937 (1944).

———. "Northwest Airlines v. Minnesota: State Taxation of Airplanes—Herein Also of Stamps and Sealing Wax and Railroad Cars." 57 *Harvard Law Review* 1097 (1944).

Powers, Francis. "Note: Freedom of Speech for Labor Organizers." 43 *Michigan Law Review* 1159 (1945).

Pritchett, C. Herman. "Dissent on the Supreme Court, 1943–44." 39 *American Political Science Review* 42 (1945).

Riesman, David. "Democracy and Defamation: Control of Group Libel." 42 *Columbia Law Review* 727 (1942).

Rockwell, Landon G. "Justice Rutledge on Civil Liberties." 59 *Yale Law Journal* 27 (1949).

Rostow, Eugene V. "The Japanese-American Cases—A Disaster." 54 *Yale Law Journal* 489 (1945).

Scheiber, Harry N., and Jane L. Scheiber. "Constitutional Liberty in World War II: Army Rule and Martial Law in Hawaii, 1941–1946." 3 *Western Legal History* 341 (1990).

Schilling, George T. "Saboteurs and the Jurisdiction of Military Commissions." 41 *Michigan Law Review* 481 (1942).

Schneider, Mark D. "Note: Peaceful Labor Picketing and the First Amendment," 82 *Columbia Law Review* 1469 (1982).

———. "Note: Labor Picketing and Commercial Speech: Free Enterprise Values in the Doctrine of Free Speech," 91 *Yale Law Journal* 938 (1982).

Sellers, Ashley, and Jesse E. Baskette, Jr. "Agricultural Marketing Agreement and Order Programs, 1933–1943." 33 *Georgetown Law Journal* 123 (1945).

Sprecher, Robert A. "Price Control in the Courts." 44 *Columbia Law Review* 34 (1944).

Stone, Harlan Fiske. "The Chief Justice." 27 *American Bar Association Journal* 407 (1941).

Symposium. "Constitutional Rights in Wartime." 29 *Iowa Law Review* 379 (1944).

Symposium. "Some Aspects of O.P.A. in the Courts." 12 *George Washington Law Review* 414 (1944).

Symposium. "South-Eastern Underwriters." 1944 *Insurance Law Journal* 387.

Tanenbaum, Joseph. "Picketing as Free Speech: The Growth of the New Law of Picketing from 1940 to 1952." 38 *Cornell Law Quarterly* 1 (1952).

Teller, Ludwig. "Picketing and Free Speech." 56 *Harvard Law Review* 180, 204 (1942).

Timahseff, N. S. "The Schneiderman Case: Its Political Aspects." 12 *Fordham Law Review* 209 (1943).

Tushnet, Mark V. "*Shelley v. Kraemer* and Theories of Equality." 33 *New York Law School Review* 383 (1988).

Tushnet, Mark V., and Katya Lezin. "What Really Happened in Brown v. Board of Education." 91 *Columbia Law Review* 1867 (1991).

Urofsky, Melvin I. "The Brandeis-Frankfurter Conversations." 1985 *Supreme Court Review* 299 *passim.*

———. "Conflict Among the Brethren: Felix Frankfurter, William O. Douglas, and the Clash of Personalities and Philosophies on the United States Supreme Court." 1988 *Duke Law Journal* 71.

———. "State Courts and Protective Legislation during the Progressive Era: A Re-evaluation." 72 *Journal of American History* 63 (1985).

———. "William O. Douglas as Common Law Judge." 41 *Duke Law Journal* 133 (1991).

Urofsky, Philip E. "The Douglas Diary, 1939–1940." 1995 *Journal of Supreme Court History* 78.

Waite, Edward F. "The Debt of Constitutional Law to Jehovah's Witnesses." 28 *Minnesota Law Review* 209 (1944).

Wallace, Harry L. "Mr. Justice Minton—Hoosier Justice on the Supreme Court."
      34 *Indiana Law Journal* 145 (1959).
White, G. Edward. "The Anti-Judge: William O. Douglas and the Ambiguities of
      Individuality." 74 *Virginia Law Review* 17 (1988).
————. "Felix Frankfurter, the Old Boy Network, and the New Deal: The Place-
      ment of Elite Lawyers in Public Service in the 1930s." 39 *Arkansas Law Review*
      631 (1986).
Young, Grover C. "The Legal Status of Wire Tapping Under the Federal Constitu-
      tion." 6 *University of Detroit Law Journal* 69 (1943).

# TABLE OF CASES

# INDEX